Diary of a Dark Horse

The 1980 Anderson Presidential Campaign

MARK BISNOW

With a Foreword by Tom Wicker

Southern Illinois University Press

Carbondale and Edwardsville

Library of Congress Cataloging in Publication Data

Bisnow, Mark, 1952–
  Diary of a dark horse.

  Includes index.
  1. Anderson, John Bayard, 1922–
2. Presidents—United States—Election —1980.
3. Bisnow, Mark, 1952–   I. Title.
E840.8.A52B57   1983   324.973'0926   83-329
ISBN 0-8093-1114-3

86 85 84 83   4 3 2 1

To Margot,

who was there, always

Contents

Illustrations   ix

Foreword by Tom Wicker   xi

Preface   xvii

Prologue   1

1 1978: Roots and Beginnings   5

2 January–June, 1979: Deciding to Run   34

3 June–December, 1979: A Campaign Is Launched   57

4 January–February, 1980: The Primaries Begin   98

5 March, 1980: Success, Frustration, Opportunity   139

6 April, 1980: From Republican to Independent   177

7 May–June, 1980: The Campaign Changes
   Character   207

8 July–August, 1980: Losing Ground   250

9 September–November, 1980: A Last Breath   287

Index   323

Illustrations

Bisnow and Anderson   23
Announcing for president   55
Herblock cartoon   76
Iowa debate   106
Herblock cartoon   109
Nashua debate   137
Herblock cartoon   140
Massachusetts primary night   149
Doonesbury cartoons   153
Anderson campaigning   245
Conrad cartoon   265
Kennedy-Anderson meeting   275
Lucey and Anderson   297
Anderson and Garth   304
Anderson and Reagan   305
Conrad cartoon   307
Last night   320

Foreword

By Tom Wicker

One of these days, the American people might well break from the mold of the two-party system, and elect the candidate of a new party, or an independent, as president of the United States. That hasn't happened since 1860, when the then-new Republican party (aided by a Democratic split and a four-candidate race) put Abraham Lincoln into the White House. Some think it never will happen again, given the extent to which Republicans and Democrats have established themselves almost as "authorized" parties.

But George Wallace's campaign in 1968 cleared the legal way for independent and third-party candidates to get on the ballot in all fifty states—albeit not easily. Twelve years later, John Anderson of Illinois, starting out as a Republican, became a challenging independent candidate with a substantial national campaign. Both Wallace and Anderson, though otherwise unalike, demonstrated that large bodies of American voters, when dissatisfied with the candidates and programs of the major parties, can and will vote for someone else. To a lesser extent, and with a less publicized independent effort, Eugene McCarthy demonstrated the same thing in 1976.

In Britain, which also had been firmly in the grip of a two-party system (the Liberals having been a minor party since the twenties), similar dissatisfactions with the Conservative and Labor parties gave recent birth to the Social Democratic party. The SDP in alliance with the Liberals quickly established itself as a real challenger for national power. British developments are obviously not a model for American, but the rise of the SDP does suggest that there's nothing sacred or ordained about a two-party system. Mark Bisnow's *Diary of a Dark Horse,* a fascinating interior view of the rise and fall of John Anderson's 1980 campaign, suggests that the Anderson campaign may have muffed an opportunity similar to that of the SDP.

In the light of Ronald Reagan's ultimate triumph, and all that's happened since, some may think the Anderson campaign a mere footnote to the presidential election of 1980. Bisnow's account is a reminder that, starting from absolute obscurity in national politics, Anderson ran well enough in Republican primaries to be briefly favored to win in his home state of Illinois; that as an independent, after his Republican prospects faded, he once stood as high as 25 percent in national polls (in a three-way match against Reagan and President Carter); and that midway in the campaign he was getting about as much vitally important media coverage as the major-party leaders.

Even though Anderson slipped badly in the heat of the Reagan-Carter campaign, he finished with 6 percent of the vote, enough to qualify him for federal subsidy if he should run again in 1984. Mark Bisnow argues persuasively that Anderson could and would have done better than that, had he stuck more nearly to his early position as a candidate putting forward innovative ideas and willing to accept defeat rather than tailor himself to the cynical "realities" of politics. Bisnow contends that Anderson's acceptance of the idea that he might win, together with the "professional" management that he then sought, ruined the spontaneity and distinction of his campaign—hence, ironically, whatever chance he might have had. Be that as it may, the evidence of this book is that in 1980 enough voters were alienated from two-party politics and offended by the unattractive major-party candidates (as they seemed in, say, September) to have made an independent candidacy a realistic prospect, even briefly.

But no one, this book also demonstrates, should have any illusions about the difficulties of independent or new-party politics. From the difficulty of getting on the ballot in numerous states to the rules of federal campaign subsidies, the system is heavily stacked in favor of the Democratic and Republican parties. Worse, the ingrained American political attitude is that these are the "major parties" and that anybody running on any other kind of ticket is automatically a "minor" candidate—hence a sure loser. From that controlling assumption, all sorts of crippling difficulties flow—low poll standing, lack of media attention, inadequate funding, exclusion from major-party events (debates, for example).

All that, of course, reenforces in a kind of vicious circle the public conviction that a "minor" candidate is a loser. And since no one likes to waste his vote, that perception is fatal. Bisnow accurately sees that the biggest difficulty for any non-major party candidate is to overcome the assumption that he or she, no matter how attractive and persuasive, is bound to lose. John Anderson, on the verge of that achievement in April and May, never quite made it and by September was on the way down.

Many historians and political analysts believe that was as it should have been—not just in Anderson's case, but in the case of any challenge to the two-party system. In their view, that system—two umbrella parties, each sheltering a range of opinion and both near the political center—gives American politics its essential stability and continuity. But it could also be argued that two-party politics enforces the status quo and works against needed political change in an era when almost everything else—the economy, social and family mores, technology, geopolitical relationships—is in flux. And the fact is, anyway, that since the 1950s stability and continuity have not been hallmarks of our politics. Only Richard Nixon has been elected to two presidential terms since Dwight Eisenhower; no president has served two full terms. In 1972 we elected a Republican, in 1976 a Democrat, in 1980 a Republican—none of which was without severe cost to coherent foreign and domestic policy; and the odds are reasonably good that in 1984 we'll switch parties again, at a similar price.

Throughout the seventies the public perception that government was making things worse, not better, was on the increase—climaxed, perhaps, by the enormous victory of Proposition 13 in California in 1978. By 1980, a mere half of the electorate voted in the presidential election and Ronald Reagan's "landslide" was effected by a little more than a quarter of the voting-age population. By 1983, signs of voters' growing disdain not only for politics and politicians but for the political system itself were everywhere. Serious talk was even heard of sweeping if ill-conceived Constitutional change—a single six-year term for the president, or even a shift to parliamentary government.

Independent and new-party candidacies like those of Wallace, McCarthy, and Anderson—not to mention Barry Commoner and the Progressives of 1980, or the radical Libertarians—did not cause such problems; it's the other way around. The perceived failures of two-party politics and the low quality of their nominees (in the summer of 1980, Carter and Reagan were the least popular pair of presidential candidates in modern times) inevitably spawned challengers. It's doubtful that this is a passing phenomenon. One strong reason is that non-major party candidates now have certain advantages over their counterparts in earlier years—mostly because of television politics. Television, first among other modern political forces, has tended to diminish party loyalties and identification—although not yet the controlling assumption that Republican and Democratic nominees are the "major" candidates.

But as more people regard themselves as something other than unswerving party loyalists, and as the Republicans and Democrats follow each other in governing failures, new parties and independents obviously have a better chance for acceptance. Television, moreover, can give such mavericks identification and exposure; with enough money and a suitable TV manner, their names can become household words even without a party label. (John Anderson, unfortunately, proved a little too "hot" on the cool medium of the home screen.) It's true that, like Anderson, political newcomers have a hard time attracting television coverage; but once discovered—again like him—the news producers may regard them as more "glamorous" and interesting than old, familiar faces. So here's a plausible—not necessarily a certain—scenario for some future presidential election:

The incumbent president—like Johnson, Ford, Carter, and now Reagan—is perceived to have been something between a disappointment and a flat failure. He promises more of the same and the "major-party" opponent is an old war-horse who seems to have nothing new to offer. The country is widely believed to be in a mess, with much evidence to support that view. Up stands Mr. Independent (it'll take a little longer, I fear, before it'll be Ms. Independent). Successful in some impressive field, attractive on television, well-funded, and with offbeat but striking ideas, he'll declare his disdain for the primaries and the nomination of either party, and his intention to be on the ballot in fifty states in the November election, to speak his mind even if it costs him the election, to rise above the old politics of wheel-and-deal, and to point the way out of the mess into which the selfish and intellectually bankrupt old parties have led the country. He sticks to that script and plays the part well. The media love the drama of it all and cover him fully. The presidential debates are three-cornered and he is adjudged the winner by a national jury. On election day he wins maybe 40 percent of the popular vote and a bare majority of the electoral college. Don't bet it can't happen.

That's not far, of course, from the script Mark Bisnow believes John Anderson could and should have followed in 1980. Whether Anderson might have won if he had is a question this book by one of his closest associates fully explores. And the Anderson experience is as good a guide as we have to the barriers some future candidate will encounter, when he, too, turns his back on the "major parties."

Preface

It is fashionable today to look back and say that John Anderson never had a chance. That is not what people thought in the spring of 1980. The level of discontent with Carter and Reagan was enormously high; at one point, a third of Americans indicated Anderson to be their first choice for president; his comings and goings were followed with the same intensity of interest as those of his rivals; pollsters agreed unanimously that his election as president was a genuine, if outside, possibility. Yet it turned out that Anderson attained virtually his highest point of popularity at the moment he declared as an independent, in late April of 1980. Thereafter, he declined steadily in the polls, at the rate of almost one percentage point every one and one-half weeks.

Some will say that the problems John Anderson faced were inherent in the running of an independent campaign: raising money and organizing; challenging the tradition of a two-party system; convincing voters that an independent could win. These were serious obstacles, to be sure, but at times Anderson showed signs of overcoming them. Some will contend it was all a matter of time, that if only the independent campaign had started out earlier, it would have done better. This argument has an appealing logic, and yet the reality is that the longer the independent campaign progressed, the worse it did. Finally, it will be said that Anderson's support was "soft," largely an embodiment of protest against Carter and Reagan, and that eventually it was bound to erode. Yet presidents regularly get elected on the basis of soft support; Carter and Reagan are themselves examples.

It is the burden of this book to suggest that the flaw which undid John Anderson's efforts in 1980 was not an inherent one at all, but, instead, a deliberate change in campaign style introduced by outside consultants hired to direct the independent phase of the campaign. John Anderson had won startling attention and support in the Republican primaries as the result of a public perception that there existed an "Anderson difference," an unconventional willingness to speak out with candor and specificity on important issues, even at personal political risk. Under strategies adopted by new campaign management, the edges of this distinction became blurred in the early months of the independent campaign. The press, which had once seemed so partial to Anderson, began to lose its sympathy. Slowly, but perceptibly, Anderson's public support faded throughout late spring and then the long summer; the publicity drawn away from Anderson by the Republican and Democratic conventions toward the end of this period sealed his decline. By the time the fall election season arrived, it did not seem to matter that the campaign was taking on again its original characteristics of spontaneity and outspokenness: Anderson's poll standings had dropped to the point where voters no longer considered him as having a chance to win. Neither presidential debates nor last-minute advertising efforts would be enough to restore his standing; as election day approached, it was inevitable that the campaign would fizzle out.

Of course there were other critical factors in the overall electoral equation of 1980: Carter's decline in popularity due to the Iranian hostage situation, his position on presidential debates, the state of the economy; Reagan's success at establishing himself as an alternative more palatable to mainstream voters; Anderson's own positions and personality, which certainly did not find favor with everyone. And so it is decidedly not my argument that, had the approach of the Anderson campaign only remained unchanged, John Anderson would necessarily have been elected president. It is my argument, however, that he would have had an honest chance. To a larger extent than has been recognized, the campaign's fate rested in its own hands.

The account of a campaign that follows is an entirely personal memoir; it is not intended to be a biography of John Anderson nor an encyclopedic history of his race for the presidency. Neither is it intended to concentrate only on his independent campaign; over half of the book is devoted to the remarkable two-year period during which Anderson pursued the Republican presidential nomination and climbed from his status as an asterisk in the polls to near triumph in several early primaries. Its purposes are meant to be broader: to tell the human story of an obscure political candidate who, against all odds, becomes an overnight national sensation, but whose efforts ultimately fall victim to their own success; to describe the haphazard, at times incredible, process by which one runs for president in the 1980s, the nuts and bolts of a dark horse candidacy, and the unusual approaches and techniques of the Anderson operation in particular; and, finally, to try to bare the inner workings of a presidential campaign in such a way that something can be learned by other dark horse candidates in the years ahead, and by voters who continue to seek politicians with a "difference." The failure of the Anderson campaign will only be compounded if future candidates, and future voters, misread the lessons of its experience.

I must acknowledge from the outset that the story told in these pages is far from objective; to the contrary, it reflects strong feelings which I am not easily able to hide. The independent phase of the campaign, as I observed it, departed drastically from many of the principles which defined the original Anderson campaign of the Republican primaries. Moreover, at the very height of Anderson's success, just as he became an independent, I myself was moved from a role as the candidate's press secretary, speechwriter, and principal advisor traveling constantly at his side to a much less central position working on issues back in the Washington office. These circumstances obviously colored my perceptions. I have tried to write with restraint and a sense of balance, and to keep my personal sensibilities from intruding, as best I can, on my more dispassionate perceptions. Campaigns stir great emotions, however, and I have no illusions that everyone will recognize my particular account as his own version of the truth. My only defense can be that what I have written represents my own experience.

A work like this cannot be done without the confidence and support of many people. A number of friends, who followed the 1980 campaign closely but who bring to bear the more judicious perspective of outside observers, were kind enough to read the entire manuscript and offer countless valuable suggestions: Dennis Farney of the *Wall Street Journal*, Robert E. Machol of Northwestern University, author Abigail McCarthy, Annette Miller of the "MacNeil-Lehrer Report," Norman Ornstein of the American Enterprise Institute, Bill Peterson of the *Washington Post*, John Stacks of *Time* magazine, and Evan Thomas also of *Time.* Of course they bear no responsibility for the failings that remain. I am indebted to Larry L. King and Eric F. Goldman, teachers at Princeton who first introduced me to the inside stories of Washington and the principles of political writing; both have encouraged me in the present project. Rick Meyer of the *Los Angeles Times* gave me early motivation to pursue it. Readers have been spared a manuscript originally almost twice its present size by the experienced judgment of the editorial and production staff at Southern Illinois University Press: Steve Smith, Gordon Lester-Massman, Kenney Withers, and John De-Bacher.

Thanks is not a strong enough word to John and Keke Anderson, who, literally and figuratively, allowed me the privilege of being a part of their family for several memorable years of my life. Though we disagreed strenuously at times about the course of the campaign in its later phases, I know no two more high-minded individuals. They are extraordinary people, and I hope it is enough to say that I stayed with John Anderson until the end because I thought he would make the best president.

Thanks to my friends, who put up with my antisocial proclivities during early 1981, when I was so often cloistered inside writing on nights and weekends; and to my daytime employers who did not seem to mind my sometimes bleary-eyed work. Thanks to the dedicated and idealistic Anderson campaign workers who helped to give the campaign its spark and purpose, and to those who, in sharing my bewilderment and disappointment about events late in the campaign, urged me to commit to paper some thoughts on what went wrong. Finally, it is hard to express what I owe my wife Margot, who has always given me the support that most mattered, when it mattered most.

Diary of a Dark Horse

Prologue

The scene at the shuttle terminal of La Guardia Airport in New York had grown increasingly familiar as the months of commuting along the corridor from Washington to New Hampshire wore on. It was January of 1980, and in the crowded waiting area, an obscure presidential candidate went easily unnoticed. We had arrived early that evening to catch the shuttle to Boston. We felt lucky to have made it at all. It had not been easy to find a cab in the darkened precincts of East End Avenue in Manhattan where we had left a reception just thirty-five minutes before. When a cab finally came by, we hailed it frantically. Five of us—John Anderson, myself, and three reporters—crammed into it. At the end of the ride, at last relieved of our cramped condition, we were only too glad to pool our money and leave the driver a generous tip.

We dragged our luggage out of the trunk and hauled it into the terminal. The day had already been a long one. Still ahead was a forty-five minute flight, then a drive of undetermined duration to an as-yet undisclosed location in southern New Hampshire where the next morning we would be awakened at sunrise to follow Anderson to a hand-shaking ritual at a factory gate. We were a small, and highly portable, campaign. That we did not possess more explicit information about our itinerary was due to the absence at this early stage of the squads of advancemen, schedulers, and other ubiquitous assistants whose purpose in life it is to supervise the care and feeding of a campaign traveling party. For the time being, we could content ourselves only with the hope that it would not be too long before we could stretch out and get some rest.

The reception from which we had just come had been an extraordinary event, and Anderson lost no time in finding a pay phone to call his wife and let her know all about it. He walked over toward a wall of telephones at one side of the waiting area, fumbled for change, thought a moment, and called me over. "Are you getting anything to eat?" he asked, casting a look in the direction of a modest snack bar across the way. "Yeah, I suppose so," came the answer. "Well, do you think you might get me a hot dog and a coke?" he asked. "I have the money right here," he said, opening his palm to prove it. "And you should get yourself something, too."

He resumed his call. The dimes dropped in, he told the operator the number he wanted the call billed to, and soon he was leaning back, removing his coat, and talking to his wife, Keke. Like a student who had just been awarded an A in a chemistry course he had barely expected to pass, he reported his news. His voice was filled with equal measures of pride and amazement. The reception had been expected to be a typical one for the campaign, attracting perhaps thirty or forty curious but uncommitted onlookers. Instead, some two hundred passionate enthusiasts had turned out, as if religious converts to a new cause, many of whom seemed to have learned the name John Anderson only days before. It was a stand-up affair, but, even so, the apartment in which it was held could accommodate the teeming masses only in two separate shifts. Those who arrived late had to line up in the hall outside and wait their turn. No one seemed to mind the congestion, the pushing, the smoke. It was an impressive scene which made those who came feel that in their very presence a new political phenomenon was being born.

Such a spectacle could not have been better timed for the campaign. Just by coincidence, we had accompanying us this evening the largest entourage of press assembled by the campaign to date: Dolley Langdon of *People Weekly* magazine, Stan Trettick, her photographer, and—we could barely conceal our pride—Sally Quinn of the *Washington Post*. As we stood around waiting to board the shuttle, we talked briefly about their recent experiences covering other campaigns. "Is this really all the press we're going to have with us?" they asked with only a slight look of amusement. They had taken a liking to our intimate little campaign, and were trying hard not to seem patronizing. But it was clear that the Anderson campaign did not quite measure up to their usual standards.

Our attitude toward having Sally Quinn with us was somewhat mixed. On the one hand, we took it as a heartwarming signal that the campaign had arrived, to have attracted the interest of Washington's premier social columnist. On the other hand, her reputation for reporting scurrilous detail in her profiles of public figures fairly made us quiver. At first, when she had called the campaign office inquiring about the possibility of traveling with the candidate, the schedulers hesitated, thinking we were destined only to become the next victim of Sally Quinn's poisoned pen. Nonsense, I said, John Anderson is different. She would like him. Besides, we needed the publicity, and we could not afford to be choosy. Longshot campaigns had to take risks. Above all, I had an optimistic premonition: Quinn's profile of Zbigniew Brzezinski had just recently been published, and it was being hailed around Washington as the hatchet job to end all hatchet jobs. Surely she would want to prove to the world that she was capable of positive pieces as well. We could play into her hands.

So while we were careful to conduct ourselves decorously in her presence, I knew there was no real reason for fear. Given the general assessment that our campaign, despite occasional flashes of style, was inevitably going nowhere, the temptation had often proved irresistible for reporters to suspend the criticism normally accorded front-runners, and to give us the journalistic equivalent of a pat on the back.

Anderson, in any case, was never one to feel much trepidation about how he would be covered. Long years as an elected official in the public limelight had convinced him that the press was often unpredictable, and that one could lose hours of sleep worrying about little things in the newspapers that would pass by and be forgotten forty-eight hours later. It never occurred to him to act like anything but himself in front of her. Sure enough, on the basis of covering us for two days on the road, and then conducting an extended personal interview back at the Anderson home the next weekend, she eventually wrote a warm and favorable piece.

Even so, Sally still proved capable of lapsing into her more accustomed vitriol. Since she liked Anderson so much, however, it had to be aimed not at her principal subject, but at his unsuspecting, and, I might add, perfectly defenseless aide. And so one Sunday, I made my debut in the much-read pages of the *Washington Post* Style section. There I was, placed prominently in her story and identified gratuitously by name, the subject of two embarrassing references: having failed to call a cab in advance of our leaving the East Side reception; and then once we had piled into the cab, having caused further delays by running back into the apartment building to rescue a forgotten briefcase.

I should have known it was coming. Given the big, professional campaigns she was used to, ours must have seemed like an Our Gang comedy. My heart sank. Would my inadvertent bumbling, advertised now in the neon lights of a Sally Quinn column, bring down scorn and ridicule on our well meaning, but fledgling, campaign? I was soon reassured. One by one, friends who had just read their Sunday paper at the breakfast table called me to say they had seen the story. Before I could volunteer my lame explanations, they hastened to console me: "Don't worry, Mark, it's not that bad a story. Besides, Sally Quinn always exaggerates."

But, no matter. There will always be a soft spot in my heart for Sally. She is the one who put the idea in my head to do this book. In her story about Anderson, she described our first exchange on the subject. We were still in the La Guardia terminal. Anderson was busy talking to his longtime colleague, Congressman Charles Rangel, who happened to be passing through. Sally turned her attention back to me:

> Meanwhile, Bisnow, the aide, was advised by the traveling press that he should begin to take notes now that the Anderson campaign looked like it was taking off because of the Iowa debate. "What should I write?" he asked, genuinely perplexed. Impressions, anecdotes, ideas, he was told. Encouraged, he went to the news stand to buy a notebook. Walking back to the group, he took out his pen and began to write, very earnestly, in the notebook: "Diary of a Dark Horse."

Ours was still very much a dark horse campaign. But it was at this moment that I felt, for the first time, a glimmer of hope that one day we might have a story worth telling. Thousands of miles and many emotions later, I am convinced that there are indeed some interested people out there who wonder what really happened.

1

1978: Roots and Beginnings

How does an otherwise innocent young man, only a few years out of college, get mixed up in a presidential campaign?

In my case, I came to know someone named John Anderson during visits to the unlikeliest of places: Lesotho, Africa, in November, 1976; and Bali, Indonesia, in April, 1977. We were there to attend international conferences on issues pertaining to Southern Africa and Southeast Asia, he in his role as an influential Republican congressman, and I in the lesser role of a Capitol Hill staffer, working at those times for other members of Congress.

The trip to Lesotho was taken with a delegation of ten congressmen. We all assembled one cold morning at Andrews Air Force Base on the outskirts of Washington. Staff people like myself had made their way before dawn to Capitol Hill, and from there boarded a bus to Andrews. By the time we arrived, the congressmen were already gathering in a lounge. They had been picked up individually at their homes and driven out to the base in special Air Force sedans. Several of them commented how nice it was to travel in style. They were planning to have a good time on this trip; some of them had brought spouses along, and, for good measure, there was even a father, a brother, and a daughter. Suddenly someone spotted John Anderson near the door: "Looks like we won't be junketing on this trip— Anderson's here."

It was a telling remark: John Anderson might have been one of those congressmen who enjoyed taking frequent trips overseas, but he carried with him a reputation for being serious-minded, strait-laced, and dedicated to business. On this trip, he was true to form.

It took three days and over seventeen hours of flying time to reach our destination, but Anderson sat stoically through most of it, his eyes glued to a voluminous black briefing book, breaking his discipline only rarely to chat with his wife, Keke, who had accompanied him. At last we arrived in Lesotho, a tiny independent black nation landlocked inside white-ruled South Africa. Its capital, Maseru, the site of our conference, was an impoverished little town which in November, owing to its location in the Southern Hemisphere, was dusty, hot, and inhospitable. For days we met in the colonial-style parliament building as speaker after speaker, representing a number of African countries as well as American groups, talked on.

One evening after a particularly long session, when most of the congressmen had long since departed for the hotel swimming pool, the presiding officer announced an addition to the agenda: for those who cared to stay longer, there would be an opportunity to hear from several young high school students who had just fled across the border from South Africa into Lesotho in the wake of recent rioting in Johannesburg's black township of Soweto. They were being sought by South African authorities on charges of complicity in instigating the disturbances, and this would be a chance for them to air their side of the story.

It might have seemed an interesting extracurricular event to attend, but clearly it went beyond the call of duty, and so all the remaining congressmen left. All the congressmen that is, save one: John Anderson. No doubt to the average American these high school students would have sounded like little urchins up to no good, but John Anderson was someone who wanted to hear them out. He listened to their grievances attentively, if occasionally with some skepticism. He asked hard questions, and thanked them when they finished. Nothing in particular ever came of the occasion, but the scene was a memorable one: here was the lone Republican in the entire congressional delegation, also the only one interested enough in an issue to forgo the good time he might have been having elsewhere.

Instances like this sometimes left people with the impression that Anderson was overly serious. When thrust into social situations, he could be among the most relaxed and entertaining of conversationalists, and in private settings he was warm, outgoing, and thoughtful. But in general, the side he showed publicly was a highly controlled and often intense one; he comported himself more like a scholar than like the stereotype of a glad-handing politician. And yet, a half-year later in Bali when I next saw him, I got my first clear glimpse of his wry and sardonic side, which, though too rarely displayed, more than redeemed his usual sobriety. This conference, too, went on for several days; it culminated one night as all the participants gathered to drink and dance in the hotel ballroom. The band was playing a brassy tune, the lights were dimmed, the guests were making merry. Suddenly the lights came on and the music stopped. In an inexplicably bad display of timing, the chairman of the conference marched up to a microphone on stage and said, "Okay, we are going to have some of the participants come up now and summarize the results of the conference." Nearby, Ghazali bin Shafie, the home minister of Malaysia, shouted: "This is crazy! Turn the music back on!" The speaker was oblivious. "Congressman Anderson, our good friend from America, please come forward and present the first summary."

Anderson reluctantly walked up to the stage with the most sheepish expression on his face. He had been asked to prepare some notes for a presentation, but never imagined he would be expected to deliver them in these circumstances. He quickly sized up the situation, as he took the microphone: "My friends," he said, "I have decided that on this great and historic occasion, when there is nothing all of us would rather do than listen to my sober and eloquent summary of the great problems of Southeast Asia, there really is only one thing I can do which is appropriate." And at that point, with an exaggerated sweep of his hands, he ripped apart the pieces of paper on which his notes were written, tossed them off the stage, bowed gracefully, and returned to his seat. The audience roared its approval, and the music began again.

Time passed, and I saw little of Anderson except an occasional glimpse of him asking animated questions of witnesses at committee hearings, or rising to deliver an impassioned speech on the floor of the House. It was not until March of 1978 that I heard he might be giving thought to a race for the White House. A column by David Broder appeared one Sunday in the *Washington Post*, prophesying the shape of the 1980 campaign, far off in the future though it was. Looking at the Republican race, Broder catalogued the possibilities exhaustively: Baker, Reagan, Dole, Connally, Bush, Milliken, Ray, Thompson, perhaps Lowell Weicker or even Richard Schweiker.

"That almost completes the list," Broder wrote, "unless you want to include Rep. John B. Anderson of Illinois." As if such an improbable entry begged justification, Broder hastened to explain: "Inspired by the 1976 example of his friend, Rep. Morris Udall, Anderson is eager to prove that on the Republican side, too, the House is the best breeding ground of that precious political type, the gracious guy who can lose with class."

From the onset, evidently, the prognosis for John Anderson's candidacy was something less than optimistic. And yet considering that a majority of Americans were to remain unaware of his very existence until primary night in Massachusetts and Vermont a full two years later, it probably represented no small accomplishment even to be acknowledged in a footnote at this early date.

I decided I wanted to work for John Anderson. I knew it was somewhat dubious, in the nature of things, that he would really end up running for president, but if he did, it seemed to me, it held the prospect to be a once-in-a-lifetime adventure. He may have been obscure nationally, but in Washington he was relatively well known and held in uncommonly high esteem. He took an active role in most major policy debates in the Congress, and his eloquence was often credited with influencing the course of legislation. He was not known particularly for his mechanical aptitude in shepherding actual pieces of legislation through the arcane committee process, although, as a strategically placed Republican on the House Rules Committee, he could on occasion prove an effective infighter in defending his party's procedural prerogatives. Those who later researched the record were surprised to discover how few bills bore his name as principal author and sponsor. His reputation in Washington had grown largely out of a willingness to take positions which ran against the grain of his party, or which, in some other way, required more courage than customarily displayed in the political world; and, coupled with that, a rare oratorical ability in defending his stand. He was reminiscent of the college professor who has not taken the trouble to publish very regularly, but who everyone knows anyway to be the best teacher of the lot.

And so it was that where John Anderson stood on a bill mattered a great deal to many people; and that when he rose to speak about something in the House of Representatives, he had the power to still an otherwise raucous chamber, so intent were colleagues on both sides of the aisle to hear what he had to say. It seemed clear to me that if John Anderson did in fact mount a campaign, it would be a distinctive and worthy one which, more than others, would stick to the issues and elevate the tone of the 1980 presidential race.

So one day in May, 1978, I wrote Congressman Anderson about my interest in working for him. It seemed to me he might be expanding his staff in anticipation of a campaign, and that this could be an opportune time to make contact. I expected only a form letter in reply; instead, I got a call. "This is John," the voice at the other end announced, neglecting, as usual, to add a last name. "It was good to hear from you again. Think you can sneak away from work and meet me in the House Dining Room? I might even buy you a Tab."

The House Dining Room is located on the first floor of the Capitol Building, a flight down from the House chamber, and across the street from the several auxiliary office buildings where Congressmen and their staffs maintain individual suites of offices. Unlike many other Congressmen, who spend whatever time they can back in their offices attending to constituent matters or simply enjoying a private place to read or make phone calls, Anderson could more often be found at the Capitol itself. Here he would spend much of his time listening to the ongoing speeches in the House chamber, though it was usually empty of most of his colleagues, except when the bells rang several times a day and they would all flood in for a few minutes to cast a vote. When Anderson himself was not there, he could usually be found in the hearing room of the House Rules Committee, a committee whose power was evident from the fact that its offices were located in the prime real estate of the Capitol Building, rather than in one of the office buildings, like other committees. It became Anderson's habit to take his lunch in the convenient House Dining Room, usually a meal along the lines of a cheeseburger or cottage cheese salad, and then in the afternoon to treat himself to a dietetic soft drink. Sometimes he ate in solitude, sometimes he used the opportunity to conduct business. I was to meet him in the House Dining Room countless times in the next couple of years.

I arrived early for our rendezvous. He came a little late, fumbling with his wallet as he attempted to replace the plastic card he had just used to cast an electronic vote on the House floor. The tuxedoed older black gentleman who had acted for years as maître d' greeted Anderson knowingly and promptly ushered us to a table. The table was nudged up against a window along the wall, and quite private. It did not matter: it was the afternoon, and few others were around. Anderson asked me how I had been, how I was enjoying my work. He cleared his throat a couple of times self-consciously; he never seemed comfortable discussing personnel matters.

"Well, you know," he said, "I'm thinking of dipping my toe into presidential waters." He was lucky: he was talking to one of the few people in the Western Hemisphere immersed enough in political trivia to know at that moment that he was, in fact, thinking of such a thing. And so I nodded gamely. "If I do this thing," he continued, "I'll be on the road a lot, I'll be making speeches, meeting people, raising money. It's an intimidating thing to contemplate. I have no idea if it'll go anywhere, but I think I want to try."

Given the adverse circumstances he was sure to confront, Anderson's attitude seemed inspired. If he were willing to try, why then, for my small part, so was I. We agreed that I would join him as his speechwriter and energy and foreign policy specialist. In the ensuing months, I would become his press secretary and traveling aide as well. I started working for him on July 1, 1978, but for the month or so beforehand, he called me frequently at my senate job to request assistance on other projects. I soon learned that if either the congressman or his wife had anything on their minds, they would not confine their communications to regular office hours; working for John Anderson meant being on call nights and weekends. But that was fine with me: there is no greater employee satisfaction than working for someone you respect, and feeling that what you do is useful to him and appreciated.

Pretty soon, in part because other staff members in the Anderson office were preoccupied at their regular assignments, I became informally designated as the person Anderson would turn to when he wanted to discuss politics. For a while I thought it odd that he would allow himself to rely on advice from someone like myself who lacked evident political experience, let alone detailed knowledge and insight about something as awesome as a presidential campaign. But later I realized that this was precisely my virtue in Anderson's eyes: I was not a jaded professional who would scoff at his ambitions, work for him only out of mercenary motivations, or try to constrain his behavior to conventional molds.

Anderson had a relatively small congressional staff; he was, in fact, one of the few congressmen who regularly returned unused staff salaries to the Treasury. Some took this to be a statement of fiscal conservatism, others supposed it was intended merely to leave a good impression with tax-paying constituents. But the real explanation was simply that Anderson had an aversion to big staffs; he felt he had been around long enough, and was sufficiently well-versed in the issues, that he did not need extra bodies surrounding him which would just get in the way. Something else that spoke volumes about Anderson was the physically unspectacular office he maintained. He had accumulated enough seniority to be eligible for, had he wanted it, a much larger and grander suite in the marble landmark of Washington known as the Rayburn House Office Building, where most veteran congressmen request to be housed. But Anderson was always unpretentious in his material surroundings, and he knew he would not be spending much time in his office anyway. So he applied his seniority toward getting a smaller office which, however, boasted the best location available on the House side of the Capitol—namely, the one office closest to the Capitol Building itself, from which it was possible to slip out a side door, walk right across Independence Avenue, and make it onto the House floor for a vote in less than two minutes. That summed up Anderson's priorities: He would rather have made his votes than have rattled around in a gilded room with fifteen-foot ceilings.

Within a several-room suite of offices, Anderson's personal sanctum was unusually modest. It was outfitted with all the standard-issue furniture that decorated many a congressional office: a nondescript and slightly worn navy-blue leather couch; green curtains behind the desk that looked as if they belonged in a mortuary, and which were often drawn so as to obscure the one redeeming aspect of the office: a dramatic view of the Capitol dome; a pair of arm-chairs to match the couch; and a big wooden desk that always seemed to be spilling over with papers, on one side of which sat something loosely considered to be the In box, and on the other side of which sat the supposed Out box, though they were often confused one for the other. On the table behind the desk sat a motley row of books which had probably taken refuge there for lack of storage space elsewhere; and alongside of them, or sometimes perched precariously on top, various snapshots of the congressman's family, preserved for posterity in what looked to be frames that had been purchased at a local dime store. The walls were lined with pictures, most of them quite dated, as though the decor had not been changed in years. To round out the office ambience, there was, finally, an enormous portrait of Jesus, peering down at Anderson's desk, which somehow seemed a little out of place, resting as it was above a TV set which was usually blaring half the day with closed-circuit proceedings from the floor of the House.

To some members of Congress, concerned with the trappings of power, such a disheveled office would have been an embarrassment to the status they sought. But John Anderson clearly considered it inconsequential, and it was this insouciance about the mundane which was part of his charm. He was determined to concentrate his energies on things that mattered. He rose early in the morning, often skipped breakfast, scoured the *Washington Post*, flipped on the TV to the morning news shows, and looked forward to arriving in his office where the *New York Times* and the *Wall Street Journal* would be waiting on his desk. His life seemed to revolve around keeping abreast of the news. He would leave his modest, split-level suburban home in Bethesda, Maryland, at about 8:00 or 8:30 in the morning, and cruise down Massachusetts Avenue and Rock Creek Parkway in a big old Buick convertible, which was usually low on gas and made noises as though it were continually heaving its last breath of life. On occasions when the car was recalcitrant and refused to leave the driveway, Anderson was known to walk a few blocks and catch the bus into town.

It would later strike me as odd that, once Anderson had acquired celebrity in the primaries, his campaign staff back in Washington assumed he would expect lavish suites in the best hotels and would want to take his meals in expensive restaurants. He could not have wished it less. Left to his own druthers, he would have preferred a twin bed at the Holiday Inn, and a cheeseburger from room service. He would resent the spendthrift ways his campaign was imposing on him, and yet relent when his staff protested that it was all necessary for a professional image. But the trappings of a big-time campaign never quite seemed appropriate to someone of such simple tastes.

Once an interviewer asked him what extravagances he permitted himself. He thought long and hard. No, he said, he did not spend his money on homes, or clothes, or cars, or travel, or food, or opera, or just about anything but the barest essentials. Indeed, he would sometimes look forward to campaigning in Boston so he could detour to Filene's bargain basement when there was a need to replenish his wardrobe; of course, when his picture began appearing on front pages, his wife beat a hasty path to the more elegant Georgetown University Shop in Washington, to order him some new clothes. But on his own, he would never have indulged such expenses. The interviewer was disappointed: imagine, a politician without extravagances. What a dreary story that would make. Anderson felt obliged to satisfy her question: It would have been an historic first were he to have found himself at a loss for words in an interview. He thought a couple minutes more. "I know!" he exclaimed. "My metaphors—that's my extravagance!" Everyone around who was familiar with the Anderson oratorical style nodded knowingly.

Anderson was intellectual, rather than political; studious, rather than gregarious; he could sit for long stretches at his office desk reading his newspapers and correspondence; he did not feel a need to reach for the phone, or to walk around asking people how they had spent their weekends. He had a marvelous ability to ignore distractions, and hardly noticed, for example, if his staff walked through his office while he was reading because they found it a shortcut route to the Xerox machine. He had an open-door policy, and rarely minded if someone walked in unannounced and interrupted what he was doing. He would look up and ask what was on their mind. He could be extraordinarily considerate, and be made to feel embarrassed if someone else had to carry his suitbag or went out of their way to pick up his laundry or drive him home. On the other hand, he could be icy cool to people with whom he felt a tension; he hated making small talk; and he never went to much trouble to establish or to maintain social friendships. He and his wife rarely went to parties, as many invitations as they received; on beautiful, sunny weekends, they could often be found spending their time indoors reading. Even when he seemed to be letting his hair down, one sensed a formality about Anderson. He often seemed to be performing; his sentences always remained long and complex; he almost never swore; and sometimes he seemed to be talking more for his own benefit than for that of his listener. With few exceptions, his staff always called him Mr. Anderson, and those exceptions, ironically, were people who did not know him well and, coincidentally or not, soon fell out of his favor.

Such a style reflected not the arrogance it was sometimes taken for, but a shyness. Anderson kept his distance from most people, in public and in private. He could be disarmingly candid, and frequently gave his more squeamish campaign handlers a scare in the way he casually treated what they thought were terribly sensitive political matters. But not even to those in whom he chose to confide would he tell everything. He liked to use people as sounding boards, but different people for different purposes. Anderson's administrative style could have been compared to that of Franklin Roosevelt. Like FDR, Anderson would give the same assignment to several people, not telling them he was doing so. He would maintain individual channels to each of them and, perhaps deliberately, encourage a competition for his ear. Management experts might call such a style "functional chaos." Its utility was that it ensured Anderson's exposure to a variety of opinion, rather than just the one that funneled up through the staff hierarchy. Others would have looked at Anderson's office and reached a different conclusion: that administrative detail, far from being his forte, was something he disdained, felt uncomfortable with, and simply tried at all costs to avoid. Indeed, he said as much when he frequently voiced criticism of Jimmy Carter's "nuclear engineer mentality," and philosophized that the nation would be better governed by a Churchillian leader who focused his attention on the big picture.

And that is why John Anderson, in part, was motivated to run for president. He felt, and frequently said, that after almost two decades front and center studying and debating national issues, he understood them, appreciated their interconnections, and had some strong and informed ideas on what to do about them. He resented Carter's seeming ignorance of the details and subtleties of many national issues, as if he had been born yesterday; his naïve conception of the workings of Congress; and his use of the office of president for on-the-job training. Why had fate seen fit to elevate a novice like Jimmy Carter to the highest office in the land, he wondered, while continuing to consign an accomplished public servant like himself to the unheralded minor leagues of the House of Representatives? All of the Republican candidates being talked up for the 1980 presidential race fell short as well. A couple of them might have had his experience, but surely none had his ability to articulate issues and inspire people to do something about them.

Coupled with a self-confidence that he could fill the shoes of a president was Anderson's growing frustration with his role in the Congress. He felt the job had become stale and that it was time to move on. He did not relish the prospect of fighting every two years for re-election, nor of continuing to labor away in Congress with only occasional national influence and recognition. Anderson had climbed the leadership ladder in the House of Representatives as far as he would probably be allowed to go. He was chairman of the House Republican Conference, the third-ranking leadership position among House Republicans, after the minority leader and the minority whip. But he had grown more moderate over time in the Congress, and conservatives both in his district and on Capitol Hill were training their guns on him. Ever since 1968, when he had cast a deciding vote in the Rules Committee in favor of historic open-housing legislation, he had been acquiring a reputation among many of his Republican peers as a maverick on certain issues such as civil rights, foreign aid, and later the Equal Rights Amendment and freedom of choice on abortion. His positions were looked upon, at least by staunch conservatives, as outright apostasies. Anderson resented this attitude as small-minded and ungrateful: over the years, he had been an outspoken and influential advocate of basic

Republican positions on economic, energy, defense, and other issues which he considered to be more important in defining the creed of his party.

In the spring of 1978, Anderson faced bruising primary opposition from a fanatical right-wing preacher in his district, Don Lyon. Anderson weathered the challenge, but it came a bit too close for comfort. National conservative groups, hoping to make Anderson a test case of their strength, poured in enough outside money that Lyon's total spending exceeded $240,000, an enormous amount by historic standards for an election in Rockford, Illinois. Anderson himself was forced to spend $150,000 in self-defense against Lyon's spirited, and frequently irresponsible, attacks. In the course of the campaign, some pent-up resentments against Anderson in his district boiled to the surface. It was the classic case of a constituency feeling that the hometown boy they had proudly sent off to Washington years before had grown too big for his britches. While some were no doubt proud that he had risen to a position of congressional leadership, and made a name for himself, others felt that Anderson had become so consumed in national issues that he had lost touch with his roots, and had become unresponsive to the temperament of his district.

Surely there was some truth in this. Given his many official duties in the House, Anderson was left with little time to do some of the mending of local fences that congressmen need to do to keep their seats secure. He also had less and less inclination. He himself felt a growing estrangement from Rockford; he would rather have spent his time attending a luncheon meeting with a Cabinet member than sitting at his desk making courtesy calls to local bank presidents. Some of his constituents' local concerns seemed pretty parochial now, and it was demeaning to have to stand up and defend them in the Congress. Anderson had gradually earned a reputation as someone who could be counted on to rise above seeming self-interest and to take the long and broad view on issues of public policy. He did not seem to mind the reputation; his critics accused him of positively courting it. Clearly he had a growing fondness for the opportunity to play a role upon the national stage.

It is interesting that Anderson did endeavor during the 1978 congressional primary to prove his credentials as a Republican. He specially requested Gerald Ford, Henry Kissinger, and Congressman

Jack Kemp to come out and campaign in his behalf. Later he was to admit that he had remained a supporter of the Kemp-Roth tax bill longer than he would have otherwise in deference to the favor Kemp had done him in visiting his district. Once, in late 1979, Anderson was quoted in a newspaper article referring to what he called the "idolatrous worship" that had been displayed toward the Kissinger era. Though the remark was buried deep in an article, Kissinger fired back a reply which we received in the office the next day. It was curt and read something like: "Dear John, You did not seem to mind the 'idolatry' when you asked me to come out and campaign for you in 1978. Yours, Henry."

But if Anderson succumbed to the natural temptation during his 1978 primary to accentuate the positive, he cannot be accused of having hidden his basic colors. To the contrary, he remained his outspoken self. He talked proudly of his progressive views on social issues, and simply tried to offset some of the hostility this engendered in Republicans by hastening to note his unimpeached record of fiscal conservatism. He called Lyon a "yahoo" and a "know-nothing," and made clear his feeling that the Republican party would drive itself out of existence if it allowed itself to swerve so far to the right. Anderson passionately defended his right to be a moderate Republican, and he took the fight to heart. Some time after the primary election, he was asked whether he intended to make up with the conservatives. "Now that they've sunk their axes in my back?" he said. "After they've publicly excoriated me? No, I don't plan any rapprochement with them."

Neither did they plan any rapprochement with him. No sooner had he been reelected and returned to Washington than he was challenged once again for his job as chairman of the House Republican Conference. He had first been elected to the post in 1969, and reelected every two years since. But the last few elections, he had faced bitter contests with candidates put up by the right wing. This match would be no exception. Anderson won by a handy margin, but, as usual, he had to endure in the process the indignity of having a large number of his colleagues impugn his fitness as a Republican spokesman and vote to unseat him. Gene Snyder of Kentucky, for example, while acknowledging that Anderson was bright and articulate, echoed the sentiments of many when he said, with some exaggeration, "I only wish he were on our side over fifty percent of the time." And Barber Conable, a respected moderate Republican from upstate New York who had actually made a seconding speech in favor of Anderson's reelection to the prestigious post, was forced to admit, "Members are almost embarrassed by the fervor John brings to some of his causes."

In such an uncongenial environment, it was not surprising that Anderson looked to a possible presidential race as the outlet for his frustrated talents. Most of the summer of 1978 he kept a low profile on his thinking, mentioning his ambition only in the most tentative and casual fashion. Only rarely was it reported in the newspapers, and even then, it was relegated to space-filler status. For the time being, Anderson concentrated on sounding out friends back in Rockford who could provide some of the preliminary seed money a campaign would require. By the end of 1978, $150,000 had been collected, though it was not until early 1979 that our first full-time campaign worker was hired, and not until the middle of that same year that we began contemplating establishment of a formal campaign office. As of the summer of 1978, what campaign apparatus there was consisted of an informal kitchen cabinet which included an attorney, a CPA, and others back in Rockford who were starting to think about finances; Paul Henry, a former Anderson staff member who was now teaching political science at a small college in Michigan and turning out for Anderson an occasional strategy memo; Mike MacLeod, executive director of the House Republican Conference, who offered advice from his perspective as a former staff official of the liberal Republican Ripon Society; myself, whose job it was, in part, to produce speeches that would begin to lay a philosophical premise for the Anderson candidacy, and who, in addition, had been taken under Anderson's wing as something of a confidant; and, not least, Anderson's wife, who, in her uninhibited manner, opposed any brooding about a decision, generally voicing the opinion that the water was fine and that her husband should go right ahead and plunge in.

Anderson himself was busy during the summer of 1978 performing his role as a congressman, rather than a presidential campaigner; it would not be until the new year that he began to absent himself from Washington for long periods of campaigning in the field. But he did try to use his congressional opportunities to advantage: he spoke out in favor of the ERA extension when it came to the House floor; he actively defended large new loan guarantees to New York City, saying it would be a humiliation if our premier American city were permitted to go bankrupt; he joined Father Drinan, the liberal Democratic congressman from Boston, in welcoming the wife of Anatoly Scharansky, the Soviet dissident, to Capitol Hill. But it would be a long time before John Anderson reached the point that he was taken seriously when he admitted an interest in being president.

One night we attended a reception for a correspondent departing the Washington office of the *Wall Street Journal*. Anderson made the rounds, trading friendly banter with a number of reporters he knew. But by and large, most people still did not recognize him. On the way back to the car, we stopped on the sidewalk to wait for a red light. A shiny new sedan paused in front of us. From the passenger side, somebody yelled out, "Hi, John." We looked in. "Well, Mr. President," Anderson replied. It was Senator Edward Kennedy, perhaps headed to the same party, and Anderson's remark was meant to tease him about the high poll standings he was then enjoying. The light changed, and Kennedy's car pulled away. "Bet he won't have any trouble being recognized," Anderson said, longingly.

Anderson was attending receptions frequently in an effort to get his name better known, and his prospects as a presidential candidate talked up. He would not normally have availed himself of the cocktail party circuit, and required some prodding. I would check regularly with his efficient personal secretary, June Foster, to see what invitations he had available to him, and if anything sounded halfway promising, I would urge him to go. As an incentive, I promised to accompany him and help fend off people who would come up to browbeat him about one piece of legislation or another. Our purpose at these affairs was clear: to shake as many hands as possible, conduct as few conversations as we had to, and then leave quickly. It always served to make a premature departure less embarrassing if everyone saw an aide conspicuously tugging at the candidate's side, as if to imply the candidate were important enough to be due momentarily at another engagement. And so we spent many an hour together buzzing in and out of carbon-copy receptions, hoping that in some small way this would contribute to the groundwork that we knew needed to be laid for a possible presidential candidacy. The next day it was my practice to bombard anyone we had met with follow-up letters to reinforce what we hoped was a positive disposition toward our candidate. How significant this all was is not obvious, but at least it gave us the satisfaction that we were doing something tangible with our time to further his prospects.

On August 2, 1978, we got a first flavor of what it might be like if and when Anderson formally began to run for president. It was on that date that the first entrant in the presidential race, conservative Congressman Phil Crane, also of Illinois, officially announced his intention to seek the Republican nomination. His announcement was held in one of the smaller meeting rooms in the Capitol, but clearly that was the trick of a clever advanceman, meant to give the occasion an aura of importance, what with the excitement of a couple of hundred people elbowing in, and the appearance of a standing-room-only crowd.

Anderson, of course, could not attend the event personally, for that was not the proper etiquette, but he was understandably interested to know what it was like, what questions were asked, whether his name had come up. He designated me to attend as his spy, and so I did, dutifully taking notes. Afterwards, I went straight to the Republican cloakroom of the House chamber to share them. We sat on a ledge in the corridor outside, Anderson listening closely to a recitation of the questions and answers as though one day soon he might be put through the same exercise.

The announcement and ensuing news conference had been interesting. Crane had said he would enter all thirty-six primaries; that he was not a stalking horse for Ronald Reagan; that he was declaring this early to give himself a better chance to catch up on name identification; that he expected to need several million dollars to finance his campaign. Here, Anderson stopped me: "Several million dollars?" he repeated. I nodded. "Well," Anderson ruminated, "I suppose it does take that much money." At this early date, we had not given a great deal of thought as to how much we would have to raise for our own efforts; we usually brushed aside the thought as though perhaps it would all be a simple matter to collect whatever we needed, once we got our campaign apparatus in place. Of course it proved not to be.

Next we discussed what Anderson should say were he interviewed about the Crane announcement. We agreed on a number of things: that the fact people were choosing to declare this early— the earliest date ever—reflected a growing assumption that Carter was a one-termer; and that Carter himself, in dethroning Gerald Ford, had established the precedent that incumbents were eminently vulnerable. Anderson wanted also to use the Crane announcement as an opportunity to argue the proposition he was most fond of using to explain his own interest in running: that the Republican party should be concerned about electability first and foremost, not ideological purity, and that it would have to field an Anderson in 1980, rather than a Crane, if it intended to be competitive with the Democratic nominee in winning votes. Indeed, Anderson had been quoted frequently in his local papers as saying that the right wing of the party simply could not nominate an electable candidate. And now he would say that he hoped Phil Crane was not suffering under the illusion that the United States was just Mount Prospect, Illinois—Crane's conservative hometown—writ large.

Anderson certainly had statistics on his side: registered Republicans constituted barely 20 percent of the national electorate, and a successful nominee of the party would indeed have to be endowed with the ability to reach out and attract the votes of Democrats and Independents, and perhaps even of some who did not usually vote. Anderson used to cite his own success as a Rockford congressman in winning reelection with the help of a large number of Democratic crossovers, and in receiving occasional public support from labor leaders and elected Democratic officials. To Anderson, Phil Crane typified those who had their heads buried in the sands of conservative Republicanism and did not understand electoral realities, and who, to aggravate matters, exhibited a self-righteousness and an unnecessary intolerance toward the beliefs of others. Keke was a little less subtle on the subject: At a later point in the campaign, she was quoted as saying about some of the other Republican candidates: "Connally's a crook, Reagan's a nut, and Crane's a fascist." Subsequently she retracted her remarks about Reagan, but refused to budge in the way she had labeled the others. Her husband may have shrugged his shoulders in mock embarrassment, but he never seemed at pains to disassociate himself from his wife's observations, which may not have been very far from his own.

For a long time, when I mentioned to people that I was working for a Republican congressman from Illinois who was thinking about running for president, they frequently assumed that I was referring to Phil Crane and, having read about his ultraconservatism, looked at me askance for a moment until I explained to them that there was someone else in the race from Illinois. The first and only spurt of publicity obscure presidential contenders can expect until they begin to triumph in the primaries is on the day they announce, and Anderson was not to do so until June of 1979, a full ten months after Crane. And so he would have to be content for some time living in the shadow of a junior colleague.

Frequently we encountered a defeatist notion that members of the House of Representatives, in recent times anyway, were not well suited to running for president. According to the argument, they simply did not have the political base, the resources, the visibility, or the stature enjoyed by senators and governors. We knew there was truth in this, but Anderson frequently pointed to the example of Congressman Morris Udall who had done quite well in 1976. I acknowledged that this was a good omen, but then noted some other examples of recent House members who had run for president: Wilbur Mills, John Ashbrook, and Shirley Chisholm. This was not a pantheon of successful presidential candidates. Udall, in a sense, seemed the exception that proved the rule. But he had had something that the others lacked: he had positioned himself as the heir to the mantle of McGovern liberalism. As a result, he had a ready-made constituency and found a flock of student workers all set to help him get out of the starting gate.

It was also easy to think of a number of senators and governors who had not fared spectacularly well in the previous presidential election, such as former Governor Milton Shapp of Pennsylvania and Senator Lloyd Bentsen of Texas. Anderson many times said to me, "Well, all I know is I just don't want to end up like Fred Harris, riding around in a trailer." This was a reference to the ex-senator from Oklahoma, who had faded quickly in his 1976 presidential

Mark Bisnow and John Anderson in 1978. Early days on the campaign trail were not far from home. (House of Representatives photo)

campaign effort. I tried to reassure Anderson. I told him that it could be worse, that he could end up like the former mayor of Los Angeles, Sam Yorty, when he dabbled once in presidential primaries: riding around in something called a "Yortymobile."

Furthermore, I argued, almost everyone who ran for president ultimately enhanced his stature. Even Robert Byrd, the senator from West Virginia, had talked about running in 1976, reportedly as a stratagem to boost his reputation mainly for purposes of election to the post of Senate majority leader. If Anderson did not end up doing well in the primaries, or did not even last until New Hampshire, he would still have moved up a notch in the estimation of his peers for having achieved a small degree of fame. Moreover, in the event of failure, the likely interpretation would be that he was too liberal for his party, or not sufficiently well-known or well-financed, rather than that he was not a worthy contender.

Fortified in the ambition to continue exploring, Anderson spoke to virtually every group which would have him. Over the months, he appeared before what seemed like a million and one Rotary Clubs and Chambers of Commerce, not to mention other groups, from the Illinois Radio Relay League to the Chase Manhattan Bank Board of Directors. After his speeches, I would call the sponsor and try to obtain a list of those who had been in attendance. They would then receive form letters signed by Anderson, expressing his pleasure at having had the chance to address their particular group. We used the opportunity to mention again that he was thinking about the presidential race, and to invite them to write us with their reactions or advice. We were simply too bashful at this point to say anything more, such as explicitly requesting contributions, or other forms of concrete campaign assistance. It would be a long time before we got up the nerve; how could we ask people to help when we were not sure Anderson was even running, and when, in all likelihood, such a request might only cause people to laugh and think the less of us for it? People just did not take us seriously yet. Moreover, time and again we would learn that most people were not willing to focus on a presidential race until roughly the time the primaries actually began. At this point, they were a year-and-a-half away.

One of our biggest catches during the exploratory phase came in late August, 1978, when Anderson received an invitation to appear before a plenary session of the National Governors' Conference in Boston to give a speech on deregulation, a topic it must have been supposed would befit a nice Republican congressman from the Midwest. The trip constituted our first real campaign foray into the big time, and the first one taken outside Illinois or Washington at a point when it was becoming known to political cognoscenti that Anderson was mulling over a presidential race—even if observers were perhaps inclined to think that such a campaign would never actually materialize.

On our first night in Boston, I joined Anderson and his son (who was attending college in the area) for dinner. We went to a

California-style restaurant near our hotel: surrounding us at our table seemed to be equal numbers of students and hanging plants. Everyone ordered cheeseburgers. Anderson's son turned to him and said: "Dad, are you really going to go through with this? None of my friends at school think you have a chance." His father, used to such expressions of skepticism, even from his own family, said with some irritation: "Well, of course the whole point is to see whether there's any support before I announce. Maybe there won't be any support, I don't know." His son shrugged in resignation, apparently contenting himself with the hope that his father would remember his children's concerns and spare them any possible embarrassment.

The next morning, Anderson proceeded into the hotel ballroom where he was to give his speech. The crowd was large, and the meeting already in session. We stood in the back for a few moments listening, then took seats in the audience. Ted Kennedy, as it happened, was in the middle of a presentation on the subject of national health care policy, a well-known specialty of his. Immediately the difference in clout between Kennedy and Anderson was clear to us: Kennedy had been allowed to choose a topic to his liking; we had been thankful enough for an invitation to speak and therefore had allowed the Governors' Conference to choose our topic for us. We consoled ourselves: beggars couldn't be choosers. But time and again we learned that presidential races, like life, are unfair.

As we watched, Kennedy was busy pointing to charts and diagrams, and giving his usual impassioned plea for a national health insurance program. We were delighted to see all the lights and cameras in the room. Although we knew our speech would be overshadowed by Kennedy's, we thought at least we would get a little more coverage than we would have otherwise, because his presence had caused so many reporters to converge on the room, and they would surely stay to hear us too. We were naïve. On the conclusion of his speech, Kennedy left the hall, apparently to hold a press conference. With that, three-fourths of the reporters rose as one and followed Kennedy out, and the noise of the cameramen packing their equipment practically drowned out the first part of Anderson's speech.

It may have been just as well; Anderson was not in his top form. He was probably nervous because of the importance of his audience;

he wanted very much to show some of the prominent governors in attendance—Jerry Brown and Pete DuPont and Jay Rockefeller and Dixy Lee Ray and the rest—that he was as much presidential timber as the speaker they had just heard.

I had worked hard on the speech Anderson was to deliver. Unfortunately, as was so often the case with his delivery, he would read a couple of sentences, look up and orate extemporaneously, then look back down and make an awkward and roundabout transition to the next sentence that caught his eye. Sometimes he would glance at a whole paragraph and try to phrase it in his own words. This only made him verbose. Trying to express someone else's thoughts was not as efficient as expressing his own. Anderson felt such a pride in his own speaking ability that he did not want anyone to think he was reading from a staff-prepared text. Even when he acquiesced in reading parts of a text, he would sometimes pretend to be shuffling papers at the lectern as if he were consulting just a few skimpy notes, rather than reading. I used to tell him that he was often at his best when he was completely extemporaneous, almost as good when he was reading faithfully from a text, but absolutely worst of all when he tried to do both at the same time. And yet this latter practice was the one he persisted in.

On this occasion, as I often did during some of Anderson's more rambling speeches, I fidgeted, wishing he would just swallow his pride and read the speech as it was written. It was not that I had a proprietary interest in my own prose; I am sure he could have written a better speech if he had had the time. But he had not, and, as a result, his speech had a stream-of-consciousness style to it, wandering all over the map and lacking in the crispness that makes audiences responsive. Almost everybody who listened to him long enough reached the same conclusion, and wondered why he had such a blind spot to this failing. He used to reply, when we discussed it, that he simply felt the only way to fire up an audience was to speak extemporaneously. But that failed to explain why he always insisted on having a freshly prepared text for each occasion, and why so many of these "semi-extemporaneous" speeches left people yawning. It also failed to explain why people like Ronald Reagan and Ted Kennedy were able to fire up audiences reading from texts prepared by others.

I used to chide Anderson about how he would have delivered the Gettysburg Address, if Lincoln's text had been placed in front of him.

> About seventy or eighty years ago, which is to say, about four score—and yet who knows, with the new math—our fathers—and I should hasten to say our mothers, too, because I am, and have always been, a strong supporter of the ERA, which as you know refers to the Equal Rights Amendment, and I have fought for the extension of that Amendment in the Congress, very hard, I might add; our fathers—and among them, I include my own 95-year-old father, who came to the shores of this great nation from his native Sweden, yearning for the new life America promised; our fathers brought forth upon this continent, from east to west, and north to south, and let us not forget the Midwest, from which I myself hail, a new country, a new entity, a new nation, conceived in liberty, or, as the French would say, *liberté, egalité, fraternité,* although actually the Framers of the Constitution, surely, looked as much to English sources, such as Edmund Burke, as to the French *philosophes* . . . but I digress . . .

Around noontime, we left the hotel for a meeting at the downtown Harvard Club. The meeting had been arranged through the good offices of Polly Logan, the GOP state committeewoman in Massachusetts. Polly was a human whirlwind of activity whose purpose in life seemed to be to provide hospitality to aspiring presidential candidates. She lavished it on us, and since no one else was paying much attention to us at the time, we were enormously grateful. The object of the Harvard Club meeting was to allow Anderson to acquaint some important party people with his plans, and, of course, for them to have a chance to look him over. He explained to them that he had met with a small group of his Rockford financial backers just ten days before, and that he had been assured the money was available (he was estimating about $50,000 to $100,000 at this time) to undertake a serious presidential exploratory effort.

That evening, Polly also invited us to a hospitality suite in the Sheraton Boston, where she was hosting a reception for Massachusetts dignitaries. People mingled for a while, then she called the crowded room to order. John Volpe, the former Massachusetts governor and secretary of transportation under Nixon, spoke first. He made kind references to a number of people in the room, including Anderson. We were immensely gratified that someone of Volpe's stature would make such favorable comments and publicly attribute a seriousness to the Anderson campaign. Anderson himself was then introduced, and he spoke a few moments. He explained his exploratory intentions in only the most cursory fashion, and yet it was probably farther than he had ever gone before with an important group. Slowly we were beginning to take ourselves seriously.

Perhaps the most important event of the trip to Boston, however, was a lunch Anderson had the next day with David Broder, the *Washington Post* political columnist. As Anderson and I were walking around in the lobby of the Sheraton that morning, I remarked to him that somehow it did not seem we had taken advantage of the fact that the place was swarming with national reporters. "Most people still have no idea you're thinking of running," I said. "If you're going to explore, you need to get people's reactions. You need to send up trial balloons." Anderson was cautious. "Well, I don't know whether you just go up to reporters and start spilling out all your plans. You don't want to look overeager, you know." "True," I said, "but it's better than not having anybody notice you." He agreed reluctantly. "So what should we do?" he asked. "You stay here," I said. "You know David Broder. I'll go into the press room, and ask him if he'd like to join you for lunch. Tell him what you're thinking. Maybe he'll make a story out of it, and get the ball rolling."

The lunch took place, and the next day, Wednesday, August 30, 1978, a major article appeared under Broder's byline on the second page of the *Washington Post*. It was topped by a bold headline: "ANDERSON OF ILLINOIS ENTERING 1980 RACE." The headline overstated the case a little. Anderson was not definitely entering the race. As he would say often, the testing of the waters that he was engaging in during this period was much more of a genuine exercise than it was for other candidates, many of whom were only going through a ritual which would lead to the foregone conclusion of a declaration of candidacy. In Anderson's case, it was not to be clear until mere weeks before his announcement that he would really go through with it. Up until then, there would always remain a large question mark as to whether the potential financial and political support existed nationally for someone of his moderate stripe and modest name recognition.

Several weeks later, Anderson was invited to appear on the TV show "Issues and Answers," sharing the program with Senator Charles Percy of Illinois. Anderson had appeared on these Sunday news programs a number of times over the years, but he had always been invited in his capacity as a Republican leader in the House. This time, since it came in the wake of the Broder story and some ensuing talk around Washington of Anderson's plans, we assumed that he would be treated as a bona fide presidential contender, and questioned along appropriate lines. I met Anderson at his home Sunday morning, to talk over with him what the questions might be, to bounce off each other some possible answers, and, finally, to drive him to the television station downtown at the appointed hour.

This was to become a tradition the many times that he appeared on Sunday morning news shows in the following two years. I would arrive about 9:30 A.M., by which time Anderson had already perused three morning papers. Keke would show me into the little corner study off the kitchen, where he would be sitting back on the couch, perhaps sipping coffee, and reading the morning editorials a little more closely. When I walked in, he would be anxious to share with me particular thoughts that were going through his mind about some of the things he had been reading. Keke was always very hospitable, and would immediately offer me a cup of coffee from their old percolator-style coffee pot, the glass top of which had long ago been broken and replaced in makeshift fashion with a small juice glass. Sporadically, she would join the conversation, interjecting animated views as to what he should say if he were asked this question or that. Anderson always seemed to do best when his preparation consisted of having been left alone with his newspapers and perhaps one or two people to chat with. Strangers who ran his campaign in later days found this difficult to understand. Their disposition would be to surround him with countless aides and advisors who would try to prime him intensively. These advisors each typically insisted that it was critical he make a particular point that they had devised, and the combination of all this disparate advice being aimed at him from so many different directions succeeded only in cluttering his mind and increasing his tension.

On this day, as we arrived at the studio about 11:30, one of the show's interviewers came in and told us to expect, toward the end of the broadcast, a question about Anderson's presidential intentions. This disappointed us, that something we felt so important could be relegated to secondary status; but we readily recognized that something was better than nothing. The Camp David summit of Carter, Sadat, and Begin was still in progress, and questions about this, as well as about the Kemp-Roth tax cut, dominated the interview. As it turned out, the questioning never even got around to the matter of Anderson's presidential candidacy; his role as a congressional spokesman was still considered more credible and newsworthy.

Months later, Anderson went over to Percy's office to discuss the presidential race. Percy made no secret of his vast admiration for Anderson. He encouraged Anderson in his exploratory efforts, though demurred in offering him a formal blessing or commitment of support. That would have to depend on who else would enter the race, and on how viable Anderson could demonstrate his candidacy to be. But in token of his interest in helping Anderson get an effort off the ground, Percy had an idea. He went to the closet in his senatorial office, rummaged through it a bit, and finally pulled out several large notebooks that contained the blueprint for a presidential race of his own that he had contemplated several years before. His consulting firm of Bailey and Deardourff, at a substantial cost to Percy, had compiled hundreds of pages of almost day-by-day recommendations on how to pull together a presidential campaign.

Anderson was touched by Percy's thoughtfulness in providing him this information. The two of us carried the notebooks awkwardly down the halls of the Dirksen Senate Office Building, onto the subway to the Capitol, through the Capitol basement, and finally through a tunnel back to our congressional office, thinking we were carrying valuable secrets. We set the notebooks down on the congressman's desk and started thumbing through. They were impressive in their sheer bulk and infinite detail. We had not begun thinking in such elaborate terms. We had to wonder: Would we ever be able to compete with the Percys, the Connallys, the Kennedys, and the others, who would always have greater resources and more professional assistance? The information the notebooks contained was quite dated, and in and of itself not useful, but it did help give us a better idea than we had had before of the financial, logistical, and political complexities involved in launching a national campaign.

As we were to learn and relearn many times, one of the fundamental requirements for being judged a serious candidate was to have electoral credibility. No matter how many flattering columns were written about Anderson, we would have traded them all for one column that said he actually had a chance to win. One day in October of 1978, we invited George Will, the articulate conservative columnist, to drop by for a chat. The point would be to allow him to size Anderson up, on the hunch that if he liked him, as we thought he would, he might give us some favorable publicity. Anderson met him early one morning, and the two of them went down to the Longworth House Office Building cafeteria for breakfast. They had a good talk. For a few days, we held our breath: What would Will write? The answer arrived shortly. On October 19, Will's column on Anderson appeared in the *Post*. It was, in a sense, flattering and poignant, but, in the end, it was devastating. Will wrote, in his inimitable way: "Although Anderson's wavy hair is as white as cotton, he is too young and vigorous to desire a future spent absorbing defeats as a member of the permanent Republican minority. So he may court a grander, more invigorating, form of defeat. He may seek the 1980 Republican Presidential nomination." Will went on: "If Anderson runs, he probably will lose, quickly. But that could be more appealing than a future as a Republican Congressman enduring routine [legislative] losses in the House."

And so the column set a tone that was to stick with us throughout much of the campaign, and perhaps never completely go away: that Anderson's motivation in running was not really to be president, but simply to have a last hurrah before leaving the House of Representatives, from which he probably would have retired in the near future in any case; and that he was determined to leave with a bang, rather than a whimper. Such characterizations, true or not, certainly did nothing to lift the spirits of our exploratory effort, but they did give us important early practice in learning to cope with the sometimes rude judgments of public opinion.

It was not only columnists who doubted our chances. About this same time, Anderson, Keke, and I took a trip to the Midwest so Anderson could campaign for other congressional candidates. One of them was Jim Leach, a young, moderate Republican congressman whom Anderson liked very much and wanted to help. The drive was a long one from a previous stop in Springfield, Illinois, along superhighways stretching through farmland to Leach's district in Davenport, Iowa. At first the Andersons took turns napping in the car while I drove. But after a while, they had both grown restless, sat up, and we became engaged in a lively, and at times heated, conversation about the course of the exploratory effort. Anderson was overcome with reservations about whether it was realistic to run. Keke thought he should go full-speed ahead. I felt he should continue to explore as far as his money and energy would take him, then assess the situation again. There would always be time to reverse course, and there seemed no great urgency to making any definite decision now. Anderson seemed to agree.

At last we arrived in Davenport. We stopped at a gas station so that Anderson could change into a fresh shirt. The reception was held at the home of Congressman Leach's parents, a large and impressive residence situated on the scenic banks of a river. At one point, Anderson gave an interview to a local TV crew; as usual, the questions pertained more to the candidate he had come out to campaign for than to his own presidential aspirations. When the reception ended, Leach invited us over to a carriage house on the property, where he and his wife maintained their own home. His wife had prepared a light supper, thinking we might still be hungry. We weren't particularly, but felt we should oblige her hospitality. As we were conversing over the meal, Leach said bluntly, "Well, John, I think you're terrific, but you know you don't have a chance to be president. I hope you're considering a strategy for vice-president." Anderson let the comment go unchallenged. But afterward I said to him, "That's kind of sad, even Jim Leach doesn't think you have a chance." Anderson said, "Well, maybe I don't. I don't know, *I just don't know.*"

Many was the time during trying moments of the campaign that we consoled ourselves with the thought that this might just be a crazy election year (as other election years had been) and that Anderson might just roller-coaster his way in some unexpected fashion to the Republican nomination. There were also discouraging moments, however, such as one we experienced in late 1978. Someone brought us word of a contest a local supermarket chain was conducting in Los Angeles. Apparently, grocery shoppers were earning the chance to win a free can of coffee if they could correctly identify the state that a congressman named John B. Anderson came from. As Anderson himself said, after hearing of the contest, "Well, I don't expect there's going to be a run on the world coffee supply."

And so, as the year 1978 closed, a paradox was already developing in the way our campaign and our candidate were being treated. On the one hand, veteran Washington reporters and politicians who knew him were gradually reaching the judgment that John Anderson was among the rare voices of reason and eloquence in the campaign, and perhaps even the candidate best qualified to be president. James Gannon of the *Des Moines Register* was not untypical when he wrote one Sunday in December that Anderson was "a silver-haired orator with a golden tongue, a 17-jewel mind, and a brass backbone," and that he was "a man of charm, grace, and intellect, whose Achilles heel is a passionate attachment to issues and a willingness to argue his viewpoint when it would be shrewder to shut up."

On the other hand, until the Anderson campaign began to put some bricks in place, and showed in some way that it had the ability to raise money and organize and attract a constituency, it would be written off as a lark. As the new year approached, our task was cut out for us: to begin to establish credibility not just as a campaign that should win, but as one that *could* win. That did not seem to us to be the essence of what choosing a president ought to be about, but, then, our whole campaign would be an exercise in facing unpleasant realities.

2

January–June, 1979: Deciding to Run

The evening of January 23, 1979, was a cold one in Washington, but John Anderson was required to be at the Capitol to hear Jimmy Carter deliver his annual State of the Union address. Anderson sat patiently with his colleagues on the floor of the House chamber, but afterward hurried to the press galleries upstairs to offer instant commentary on the speech. It had become a custom to do this after an important news event in the Capitol, although Anderson often had to be prodded to do so. He felt self-conscious presenting himself to reporters, as if he were a political ambulance-chaser looking for publicity. Of course, that was precisely the intention. A "reaction story" was the type of press attention most readily available to obscure presidential candidates. By trial and error, one learned to anticipate when the national press would be looking for quick comments from congressmen, and what types of short and punchy statements were most likely to be used in their stories. Anderson tried his best at these moments to affect a look of personal disinterest, as if he were merely doing his public duty to respond to the false and pernicious statements which had issued from the other party, but of course he was not unhappy to have attention paid to his comments.

The galleries were crowded and chaotic following the president's speech. Reporters were rushing to their typewriters to pound out their stories, and then to phones to file them. First we proceeded to the "print gallery" where reporters for newspapers and magazines normally congregated. The presence of Anderson at a table in the middle of the room symbolized his willingness to be questioned. This caused interested parties to converge on the area and to begin very informally eliciting Anderson's basic reaction to the speech: "What did you think of it?" "Do you think the president will really be able to get his program through the Congress?" "What would the Republicans have done differently?" Anderson was free to elaborate. Having anticipated such an opportunity, he had taken notes during the speech and was ready to comment. The president's "new foundations" speech—as it came to be dubbed, owing to the theme the president had conspicuously tried to sound—had been a disappointment, he said. Given that the president had described the state of the union in such rosy terms—he had said the economy was in good health, and our defense posture strong—it simply did not follow, Anderson argued, that it was necessary to create those new foundations. Why not have the administration apply its energies instead, he asked, to repairing some of the old foundations it had allowed to deteriorate: fiscal responsibility, consistency in foreign policy, confidence in government? The reporters scribbled furiously.

After this five-minute ritual ended, we walked across a hall and into the adjacent "radio-TV gallery" where, by tradition, self-appointed spokesmen or congressional leaders waited their turn in a small line outside an interview room. One by one they would be ushered in for a few minutes apiece and given the chance to make a statement or answer questions before a gaggle of cameras. They would sit at a formal desk, situated in front of a fake backdrop of bookshelves, as though they were speaking from the stately environs of their congressional offices. A dozen microphones would be clustered in front of them, lending the further impression that the interview subject was someone of estimable importance. When it came Anderson's turn, the reporters seemed more attentive than usual; they knew from experience that he might well turn a nice phrase which they would want to record.

We were never sure how much these various efforts paid off: how many comments actually made it out over the airwaves, or which ever saw the light of day in newspapers. But we knew at least a few of them did, because we heard them or saw them ourselves. In essence, our motivation was simply that it was an easy thing to do with a potentially large return. We needed publicity, and this was the best kind of all: free. Besides, it was another piece of concrete evidence to journalists that John Anderson was alive and kicking. It kept his name in circulation, and gave the impression he was an active, if undeclared, candidate. In the event a comment of his made it onto one of the national wires, his name could appear in hundreds of smaller papers coast-to-coast. If his name made it into the pages of one of the Washington papers, it would be seen by members of the huge Washington-based press corps, and in due course it might seep into their subconscious that John Anderson was that much weightier a persona. We were at this point a campaign without money and without organization; every bit of unpaid media recognition would help, and we would try as we could to get it.

Of course, we soon learned that getting Anderson's name into the newspaper was not necessarily tantamount to making it a household word. For the time being, mention of him was at best buried deep in the inside pages. This did not exactly send shock waves out across the country. It never ceased to amaze us how many people simply did not read a newspaper on a regular basis; and of those who did, how few read beyond the sports section, the comics, or the classified ads. Moreover, among the handful of good citizens who dutifully read lengthy news articles, a quotation from John Anderson seemed to register only if they already knew his name. Repeatedly I encountered people who no doubt considered themselves well informed, and yet, despite frequent brief mention of Anderson's candidacy in the newspapers, remained oblivious of it until I apprised them. Invariably, they would say, "He must not be campaigning very hard: I've never heard of him."

These same people were also quite generous in offering their opinions as to how we could achieve fame. "Come up with a new idea," they would say. Rarely did they have a specific one to propose. As for their other suggestions ("Make a strong statement against the MX missle"—"Give a hard-hitting speech against Carter's economic policies"), they seemed unaware that Anderson had been doing exactly that until he was blue in the face, to no avail. Painfully, we learned that it was not what one said, as much as who said it, which warranted press coverage. Someone well known could say something unoriginal, and Anderson could say something novel, and he would be no match in competing for attention. A Catch-22 was in operation: politicians are not really covered until they become famous, but they do not become famous until they are covered. That this could come as a revelation betrayed our inexperience in the workings of the press. But it had simply never occurred to us that box-office drawing power would be as predominant a consideration in choosing which presidential candidate to star in a news story as it is in deciding which Hollywood actress to cast in a movie.

Often we contrasted our lot with that of Jerry Brown, the young governor of California. Anderson admired many of Brown's attitudes: the premium he attached to new and creative approaches to problems; his questioning of traditional assumptions; a belief in long-range planning. Anderson had sounded many of these same themes himself. He and Brown also seemed to have an affinity insofar as they displayed an uncommon philosophical bent toward politics and conducted an intellectual style of campaigning. Why, then, Anderson wondered, was Brown the object of so much more public interest—will he run, won't he run, will he run—and Anderson relegated to such obscurity? Arguably, it was Anderson who deserved the attention: he was more articulate, more experienced, more knowledgeable and sophisticated about national issues. After all these years of dedicated and distinguished public service, why did the system seem to delight in allowing Anderson to be upstaged by a sassy young upstart?

Perhaps it was simply the fact that Brown was a governor, and governors outclass congressmen, just as a full house in poker beats three-of-a-kind. Indeed, Brown was no less than governor of the nation's most populous state, and Anderson represented only a small-potato congressional district in northern Illinois. Perhaps it was that Brown, by virtue of his Zen Buddhist philosophizing, had captured the imagination of the press, which always seemed to be hot after a new angle, while Anderson, the midwesterner, cast a dull aura of being staid and traditional; Brown may have been what reporters considered simply a "sexier" subject to cover. And of course it may have had something to do with Brown's having had a demonstrated presidential appeal during the several primaries he entered in late 1976 against Jimmy Carter. Whatever the case, Anderson sometimes had to wonder why it was he just did not seem to stack up in the eyes of the press. Was there something inadequate about himself he had not realized? Was he perhaps just an over-the-hill egocentric congressman playing out of his league?

More than once, I tried to reassure Anderson on this point: I explained what some of the motivations of the press must be; informed him that his staff shared his frustration; reminded him that Jimmy Carter and Walter Mondale and others before him had all suffered the identical experience; and finally consoled him with the thought that if we just showed patience, worked hard, and were clever in some of the things we did and said, perhaps our turn would come. He would listen patiently to my lame explanations and then say, with a sign of resignation, "I suppose so, I suppose so." The name John Anderson, we recognized, was never going to become known to the masses until it was announced in large headlines or by Walter Cronkite. Perhaps we would never make such a breakthrough unless we did well in the primaries, another year off. But in the meantime, we would keep up our efforts to make even cameo appearances in the press, in the hope that at least we might be reaching a few opinion makers who, in some way or other, would be able to help us along the way.

A good performance in the primaries, we knew, would require a strong effort in the field. Anderson would have to become known locally in states such as New Hampshire and Massachusetts, where the early contests would be held that had the power to make or break a campaign. To some extent, the fame he earned in Washington could precede him. But sooner or later, Anderson would have to begin spending a great deal of time in these other places. He would have to attend coffee klatches with local party people and try to win their stamp of approval; speak to local garden clubs and hope that in a small community his name might travel by word-of-mouth; call scores of strangers whose names would be suggested to him as potential local organizers; and stop in to visit every newspaper which could spare a reporter to interview him.

In late 1978, Anderson had made his first two trips to New Hampshire. He was lucky to have a former administrative assistant practicing law in Concord, who was able to arrange speaking engagements at local churches and the like, as well as get-acquainted meetings with moderate Republican party activists. One thing led to another, and soon a number of people in New Hampshire had been identified as prospective Anderson supporters and organizers. Of course, it was only a small fraction of what earlier birds, such as Crane and Bush, had been able to attract; moreover, we had as yet no campaign machinery to catalogue and follow up these initial contacts. Everything very much depended on Anderson himself making personal visits to New Hampshire and continuing to stoke the few fires he had lit.

Unfortunately, after another visit in late January for some further meetings in Concord, Anderson did not return again to New Hampshire until late April. George Bush's organizers, in particular, moved into the vacuum, and often in later months people would tell us that while they had been impressed by Anderson originally, and had been inclined to support him, subsequently they threw their support to other candidates because they were not sure he was really running. A lot of people in New Hampshire seemed to enjoy getting started early in helping a candidate, and there were only so many shows in town.

Anderson had stayed away from the state during those months pretty much for reasons of inertia. He had not reached the point where he was sufficiently sure about running to feel comfortable absenting himself from his accustomed role in Congress. He was used to being an active participant in committee and floor activities, and he knew his colleagues valued both his votes and his debating skills. Then, too, he was concerned about the resentment that might be aroused among his constituents in Rockford were he seen to be neglecting his congressional duties, especially if it were only for the sake of what many of them seemed to feel was the most fanciful presidential quest. Furthermore, it was never clear to Anderson why such early visits to New Hampshire were essential. Like other obscure candidates before him, he would sometimes arrive at a meeting hall to find a crowd of only four or five people waiting to hear him. And for every person who might be eager to start helping him, he had run into others who seemed to express the attitude, "Can't you leave us in peace and come back next year?"

In the meantime, more and more voices were urging Anderson to give some thought to entering the race in Illinois for the Senate seat held by Adlai Stevenson III. Stevenson was rumored to be thinking about retirement. Anderson mulled it over quite a lot—in fact, much more than he would generally admit—but in the end did not feel motivated to go to all the trouble that would be required with only the prospect of a Senate seat at the end of the rainbow. After all, even if he won, he would arrive in Washington in January of 1981 as a junior member of what presumably would still be the minority party (no one then could predict the Republican landslide of 1980), and this in a chamber where seniority and committee chairmanships counted for so much. It would be anticlimactic for someone who had already served in a House leadership position many years.

Of course, he might be looked on as something of an elder states-man rather than an average freshman face; the Senate might be a congenial place for someone who enjoyed orating; and even fresh-man senators had, in a sense, more power, prerogative, and influ-ence over legislation than did many senior congressmen. But a Sen-ate race would not necessarily be easy. Illinois was a huge state. Anderson would have to raise millions of dollars; he would have to campaign in unfamiliar downstate terrain. He might face tough competition from the state attorney general and the secretary of state, both popular vote-getters. And running for senator would be far different from being a senator. Anderson would have to talk about state issues, in which he had little interest or knowledge, rather than national issues. The last subject on which he would want to make speeches all summer was that of farm prices.

Ironically, running for president was, in a way, much more man-ageable an enterprise: a small-time candidate could concentrate his energies almost exclusively in New Hampshire for the time being, a state that constituted only two congressional districts, compared to the two dozen in Illinois. And a campaign addressed to national issues was simply more suited to the background and interests of someone whose political experience had been confined for twenty years to the United States Congress.

But even after Anderson had ruled out a Senate race, he continued for a long while to harbor real doubts about the difficulties of run-ning for national office as well. I did nothing at first to discourage these doubts. Presidential campaigns are exercises of such ridiculous audacity that it seemed to me a healthy sign that he had such doubts; something was needed to help him keep his perspective. At one point, I wrote him a memorandum about his impending decision. "Maybe Woody Hayes and Jimmy Carter are used to winning, but that sort of single-mindedness can make you less than human, and can also make you vulnerable to awful frustration if you don't reach your goal. It would be too high a price to pay if you found yourself losing your sense of humor, your time for reflection, or your self-respect in the event you did not make the grade you set for yourself."

This was still early 1979, and my recommendation was that Anderson postpone a decision until the spring; I knew that if he felt he had to decide any earlier than that, he would probably decide not to run. Clearly the national political situation would take a long time to clarify, and it would benefit him to gather as much data as possible before making an irrevocable decision. Over time, he would be able to judge how well he was doing by what was being written about him, what his colleagues were saying, what speaking invitations and contributions he was receiving, and how voters responded to him when he walked the streets of the New England primary states.

We knew the national political situation was ultimately unpredictable. Certainly nothing could be foreseen with any confidence a full year ahead of the first primaries. Observers were fond of noting that early front-runners had a way of peaking too soon, of losing face when they did not do as well as had been expected, of stumbling because they were being scrutinized so closely. An ample history of this was evident in looking back at the once-ballyhooed presidential campaigns of Ed Muskie, Scoop Jackson, George Romney, and Nelson Rockefeller. If the Reagan campaign were to fall by the wayside at some point, surely it would be a new ball game. Although conservatives would continue to exercise great influence in the GOP nominating process, the field in the early primaries might be so crowded and contentious that conditions would be ripe for the emergence of an articulate, forceful moderate. Perhaps the other candidates would be bunched up on the right wing of the spectrum, and Anderson could prevail by consolidating support from voters in the middle. And if the Democratic party were in turmoil as a result of a strong challenge to Carter by the forces of Ted Kennedy, maybe the vanquished in such a fight would consider, at least in open primary states, voting for a palatable Republican just to register a protest.

But idle speculation about future political circumstances was not enough to launch a formal political campaign. The time had come to bring on board the professional expertise capable of tackling the daunting organizational tasks before us. The hunt began for a campaign staff. Some felt that the most immediate priority was to hire a paid organizer or two in New Hampshire, to prevent the other candidates from stealing too great a march on us. Others seemed convinced, in more traditional fashion, that the first priority should be to acquire a full-fledged, Washington-based campaign manager whom we could point to and call our own. It was an understandable feeling, but the result of paying the large salary that was necessary to attract such a person was to leave us for several months with no money to employ the field organizers who were becoming so urgently needed. In February, 1979, as Anderson became increasingly anxious to demonstrate, as he said, that "bricks were being put in place," he decided to hire a campaign manager, selecting someone who had come to his attention named Jim Nowlan, an experienced political hand who had just finished a stint as campaign manager in the 1978 reelection effort of Senator Percy.

Percy had been reelected by a much narrower margin than expected, and when people learned that someone with such a track record was managing our campaign, they wondered about the caliber of the person Anderson had selected. We saw it from a different perspective; it seemed to us quite impressive that someone important enough to have run a major statewide campaign would agree to run ours. Nowlan was in his late thirties, had himself run for lieutenant governor in Illinois several years before and not done too badly, and otherwise had a background in college teaching. He dressed conservatively, wore owlish glasses, and was well mannered to a fault. He lacked a certain dynamism often associated with campaign managers, but, on the other hand, his lawyerly approach to problems inspired Anderson's confidence that he would begin to get a handle on the campaign. By the end of February, he had helped to establish some basic structure and goals for a campaign organization. Although our campaign coffers had accumulated only $100,000 by March 31, he set a year-end target of $1 million for our fund-raising efforts. This turned out to have been grossly over-optimistic; by the end of 1979, we had raised only $457,000, and even that with great pain. Nowlan had tried to get the ball rolling by hiring an Illinois-based firm to undertake a limited direct-mail effort. Later, when that proved unsuccessful, he brought on an in-house finance director, a youngster fresh out of college, who seemed so overwhelmed at the challenge before him that the thought of what to do next was practically immobilizing. As critical as fund-raising was, it was getting off to the most inauspicious start, and would lag chronically until early 1980.

During these early months, Nowlan also established an advisory group based in Rockford, which included local attorneys and accountants to help perform the campaign's mechanical chores, as well as some relatively more prominent names, designed to lend the campaign effort credibility. The most prominent of these was that of former Governor Richard Ogilvie, who many times went out of his way to make generous public comments about Anderson. One hypothesis was that Ogilvie regretted having decided against the appointment of Anderson to fill the unexpired term of the late Senator Everett Dirksen in 1969, as some had urged, and wanted in a small way to compensate for his mistake. Anderson was grateful for Ogilvie's help at a time when he was frequently challenged to identify important Republicans who supported his candidacy. Unfortunately, the value of Ogilvie's support was discounted somewhat insofar as, whenever pressed, he was forced to admit that signing up as an "advisor" was not in fact tantamount to giving Anderson his outright endorsement. We felt indebted to have such support in any form and hesitated to quibble with distinctions.

Meantime, a schedule was drawn up for Anderson which would take him through twenty states in three months. In the back room of the congressional office one weekend, a large makeshift calendar was posted on the wall. All the days of the year were blocked out, and notations were made as to which speaking engagements Anderson had accepted. Everyone who looked at the calendar came away with the same impression: there simply were not that many days in a year. We did not have much time to make a campaign, if we were really going to do it.

Several part-time employees were hired in March, including a secretary, a scheduler, and someone to accompany Anderson on occasional trips. These were the first tangible signs of organization. An idea which had mainly been in the artist's conception stage all this time was finally taking shape along a veritable assembly line. Compared to the scale of Phil Crane's fund-raising efforts, or George Bush's lists of county chairmen, our budding campaign paled into insignificance. But what we had was something, and it was much more than we had had before.

As we took stock of our limited resources, an obvious political strategy suggested itself: simply to do better than expected in the early primaries. We had observed enough campaigns to know that the media often focused attention not on how many votes a candidate received as much as on how those vote totals compared to what had been predicted. If one did better than expected, one was thought to possess "momentum." If one did worse, one's star was assumed to be fading. No one disputed the logic of our simple objective. It was a logic born of necessity, since we had only enough finances and organization to target a very select group of primaries. These were defined to be the earliest ones: those in New Hampshire, Massachusetts, Illinois, and Wisconsin. If we did well, we would parlay our victories from there. (Later, in December, 1979, and January, 1980, we were to become so strapped for money, and our candidate so short of time, that we would feel even this group of four primary states to be spreading our efforts thin. At that point, Anderson would order further scheduled visits to the Midwest scrubbed, and would begin spending almost full time in New Hampshire, with an occasional side trip into Massachusetts.)

By mid-spring, Nowlan had compiled the information he wanted, tried to test Anderson's financial and political potential in the hinterlands, and observed the candidate's mode of operation. He had always promised Anderson that he would offer him uninhibited advice, and so the time came to issue a bottom-line recommendation as to a course of action: he told Anderson he did not think he had a chance at the presidential race—the money was not there, the conservatism of the party was not congenial, the candidate lacked drive—and that he should consider instead the Senate race, or even something else, such as a college presidency. Anderson did not take the suggestion well, and the more Nowlan argued it, the more Anderson bristled. "I didn't hire him to tell me I can't do it," Anderson would say. "I can. I know I can, if I want. It's my decision, not his." Anderson had not yet made a decision about running, but he did not like the idea of someone saying that he did not have what it took.

Yet Nowlan, a veteran political campaigner himself, strongly felt that Anderson lacked what Nowlan called a "sixth gland," by which he meant such a burning desire to be president that he would put up with the superficialities, the indignities, the grueling and dehumanizing exercises required of successful presidential candidates. Walter Mondale, citing the reason he had dropped out of his early presidential exploratory activities in 1975, had said he could not stand to sleep in so many Holiday Inns; Nowlan could see Anderson saying that he simply could not stand shaking so many hands. Before each trip, Anderson would be handed a stack of index cards, on which were listed the names of VIPs that the campaign staff wanted him to call for either money or other strategic political purposes. Rather than rushing to the nearest phone booth when he found himself idling at airports between planes, Anderson would leave the index cards untouched in his briefcase.

Anderson would at times acknowledge his aversion to traditional forms of campaigning. He would even allow as to how he did not particularly care to be president if that was what it took. But in the next breath he would say he refused to believe that one really had to do those things, or ought to have to do those things, to win. Why should campaigning require skills so totally removed from those which would be important in the job itself? What kind of test was that? Anderson did not feel a presidential election was a contest to be won by ordeal. To the contrary, he felt one should qualify for the job on the basis of such things as experience, ideas, and sense of purpose. That is why he considered the demands of a campaign so incongruous to its purpose of electing a national leader. That he wanted passionately to *be* president in no way implied he was desperate to *run*. This ambivalence was sometimes difficult to hide.

One evening in early May, as Anderson was driving me home from work, he asked whether I wanted to go out to eat. Often we stopped somewhere for a quick bite, but tonight he wanted to have a more lingering dinner. I suspected he had something particular to talk about. We drove up Wisconsin Avenue in Northwest Washington to a restaurant called the Zebra Room. A dingy little bar that specialized in serving barely edible pizza and cheap beer, this had long been a favorite haunt of the unpretentious Anderson family. We found a booth and sat down. Only a few people were scattered elsewhere in the room.

Anderson was glum. Soon it became clear why: he was having second thoughts again about running. And why not? It was one of the most important decisions of his life. "I don't know," he said, "people keep saying it's foolhardy. Maybe I should go for the Senate. Maybe it's not too late." It was hard for me to tell whether these thoughts were really under serious consideration, or whether he was fishing for reassurance. Just in case, I took it upon myself to supply it. "Well, you could do something else, sure," I said. "Maybe you should. But announcing now isn't irreversible. Declare, see how it goes. Buy some time. Maybe you'll be able to raise more money when people see you're a definite candidate. Maybe things will go better. If they don't you can drop out. But if you don't try, you'll always be kicking youself, wondering what might have been."

Anderson had announced his intention not to seek another term in the House of Representatives. One of the reasons he had given publicly was that his presidential candidacy would not seem credible if people saw him also trying to cling to his House seat. I sensed that perhaps he was rethinking his situation. "Was it a mistake to say you won't run for the House again?" I asked. "Oh, no," he said. "I want to get out of there. It's time to do something different." We finished our conversation, and, as usual, Anderson was less skeptical. He had just wanted to talk things out. Once he actually declared his candidacy, he would commit himself totally and leave all doubts behind. But until then, he wanted to be sure he had considered every angle. No one else knew about our conversation, and I would not tell anyone. People would not understand. Days later, Anderson informed his staff he had made the definite decision to run. A formal announcement was set for June 8 in Washington, and preparations began.

In the interim, I made a point of attending other announcements in Washington of presidential candidacies. On May 1, it was George Bush's turn. His took place in the grand ballroom of the National Press Club in Washington. The room was filled with reporters, cameras, onlookers, and supporters who clapped strenuously at each statement that sounded even remotely as if it were meant for applause. I knew the scene at Anderson's announcement would be less boisterous: we would not have enough supporters to fill a room half this size. Bush introduced his mother, whom he reminded the press had been a regular visitor to Washington from the days when his father was a senator from Connecticut; he introduced Barber Conable, the respected moderate Republican congressman from New York, whom Anderson had considered a friend, but who it was now announced would be chairing the Bush-for-President national steering committee; and Bush's staff passed out a long and impressive roster of prominent supporters, listed state-by-state. All of this was almost too much to take. How could we be expected to compete with a candidate who seemed as if he could practically *inherit* the nomination?

But George Bush's announcement was made to seem almost pedestrian in comparison with that of former Texas Governor John Connally, held a short time later. It, too, took place in the National Press Club ballroom, but instead of an audience seated randomly in long rows of folding chairs, Connally's guests were seated at big tables and treated to a formal luncheon. The atmosphere reeked of wealth and power, and no expense seemed to have been spared to make the occasion look suitably presidential. Seated at Connally's head table were various movers and shakers who bore living witness to Connally's reputation as a man who might find the job of being president a step down from his normal niche in life. In answer to a question, at one point, he referred to the $14 million spending limit, which would apply to his campaign if he accepted federal matching funds, as a "constraint." Once again I experienced the sinking feeling that perhaps the Anderson campaign was not competing in its appropriate league.

It was not that we avoided cultivating the rich and powerful ourselves, knowing their potential utility to a struggling campaign. Once, out in San Francisco, we had managed to convene a breakfast meeting with fifteen or so of the city's top businessmen. The group which assembled could not have been more impressive: it included the presidents of Bank of America and Crown Zellerbach, the chairmen of Standard Oil of California and the Southern Pacific Railroad, and others of similar prominence. Anderson rose to the occasion and gave an extemporaneous tour-de-force talk on economics that seemed to combine the knowledge of a college professor and the flair of a Billy Graham. The businessmen left wondering why they had not heard about this candidate long before. When we returned to Washington, routine thank you notes were sent out. The idea was that after an initial softening-up, a second batch of letters, soliciting contributions, would follow. We were still bashful about asking for money too directly—thinking naïvely that if people liked what they heard, they would take the initiative themselves of contributing—and much time passed while we contemplated the right approach. Anderson became impatient, and one day, to make up for lost time, tried to reach some of the businessmen by phone. It was an accomplishment to get past their secretaries. The ones we reached indicated they had by this time committed themselves to other candidates. They left the clear impression that, while they had admired what they saw of Anderson, they were entrepreneurial enough to want to bet on winning, not losing, horses.

If businessmen withheld support for practical reasons, students never proved to be quite so squeamish. They did not seem particularly concerned with a candidates's standings, and may even have had a positive admiration for the pluck of the underdog. Anderson's politics were well suited to the disposition of a new career-oriented college generation: still progressive on social and international issues, but increasingly conservative on economic matters. Students were no longer Ted Kennedy's or George McGovern's for the asking; they wanted hard-headed solutions for the inflation that was raising their tuition, and for the stagnating economic growth that threatened to tighten the job market they would have to face at graduation. A year before the primaries, when Anderson would acquire folk hero status on campus, it became apparent that he had an unusual rapport with young people and that there existed real possibilities to enlist them as supporters.

On a swing through New York City in April, we stopped at Columbia University so Anderson could give a short talk at the student union. About forty or fifty itinerant-looking students filtered in, outfitted in blue jeans and backpacks. It was a lazy afternoon, and out through the big picture windows in the lounge we could see many times that number of students playing frisbee on the lawn. How would we ever be able to reach them?

As usual, Anderson tried to be as specific as possible in his remarks, which were addressed today to the proposition that economic aid to foreign countries was generally to be preferred to military aid. He urged a major new package of economic assistance for Uganda, which had just been liberated from the brutal rule of Idi Amin and urgently needed help in getting back on its feet; for Somalia, a country of considerable strategic importance for the United States, situated as it was on the Red Sea and Indian Ocean; and for Turkey, a NATO allay wrestling with terrible inflation and unemployment. The subject Anderson had chosen, characteristically, was a sober one, but it succeeded in its purpose of impressing the audience that the candidate before them was unusually knowledgeable, serious-minded, and willing to put forward his own specific ideas on an issue. As was often the case, however, it was not until the time came to take questions that the session livened up. Someone asked Anderson about gay rights. He replied that he was opposed to discrimination in any form. This seemed to signal the students immediately that, despite his white hair and Republican leadership position, this fellow Anderson was not too out-of-touch after all. Someone asked how it felt to spend his time running for president. He said it was tedious, and that at times he lost patience with the frivolity of it, but that in the end he hoped it would be worthwhile. He continued on in this vein, giving straightforward and thoughtful answers, and by the time he left, the audience had been charmed. I realized then, for the first time, that he had a potential, which most politicians did not, of earning the affections of students. How dramatic a potential, I did not yet imagine.

A similar situation occurred one month later when we paid a visit to the campus at the University of California at Santa Barbara. Anderson had been invited to deliver a lecture before a large undergraduate class in political science. The turnout was impressive, especially considering the close proximity of some of the finest beaches in California and the normal distractions of a Friday afternoon. Either the teacher had required attendance, or students found it more intriguing than adults usually did to see an obscure congressman who claimed he was running for president. Perhaps they had the premonition that they were witnessing another Jimmy Carter who might one day actually attain his preposterous goal.

Anderson was at his absolute best that day, wonderfully humorous and animated, his chemistry with the students perfect. Afterward, he got a huge ovation. It was announced that anyone interested in helping the campaign or learning more about the congressman could accompany him to the faculty lounge, where he would be attending a small coffee with professors. A large part of the class flocked after him, and when he arrived at the faculty lounge, the students sprawled at his feet, peppering him with wide-eyed questions. While I was standing at the door, someone handed me a recent article from the *Christian Science Monitor*, which quoted Senator Jacob Javits of New York as having said that he was personally leaning toward John Anderson in his own choice for president, but that Anderson had not yet made enough of a "splash" to warrant his active support. I thought to myself: If only Javits could see this splash.

In late May, as the day of the formal announcement of his candidacy approached, Anderson was faced with the need to find a new campaign manager. Nowlan did not care to commit himself further to what he had concluded was a hopeless exercise; and Anderson, for his own part, did not care to have someone who possessed a defeatist attitude running his campaign. Just about that time an old acquaintance of Anderson's from the Foreign Service, then serving as the United States ambassador to the African nation of Chad, happened to be back on home leave in the States, and stopped by Anderson's office to renew acquaintances. He mentioned that he was thinking of leaving the Foreign Service, and Chad in particular, which at that moment was erupting into civil war. Anderson asked him whether he might like to try his hand at running a presidential campaign, and thus did Bill Bradford arrive on the scene.

In retrospect, it appears to have been an odd choice for a campaign manager, but it did not seem so odd at the time. True, Bradford had served abroad for most of the previous thirty years; he would have been the first to acknowledge his lack of political experience. But he was older and more mature than the rest of the Anderson staff, and the flecks of gray in his hair helped to counteract the image we otherwise seemed in danger of acquiring, that our campaign was being run by kids. Moreover, he had a reputation at the State Department for having excellent organizational skills, something the campaign at this juncture found in short supply. Finally, Anderson realized it would be necessary, in announcing Nowlan's departure, to name a replacement. If it were someone of such stature as a United States ambassador, it would look like a more natural transition. Anderson could say that Nowlan had been hired strictly for the exploratory phase of the campaign, and that Bradford was more suited to handle a full-blown campaign operation.

In preparation for the announcement in June, we took the initiative to begin scheduling an intensive series of media interviews with Anderson. Much of the Washington press corps already knew a good deal about Anderson and seemed to admire him. But most had met him only casually over the years, and there was no question that coming over to his office for in-depth conversations gave them a new perspective on the man and, in general, strongly reinforced whatever favorable opinions they already entertained. It also induced them to write stories and columns about him. For our scheme was based on a supposition about journalistic psychology: What reporter likes to spend an hour taking notes in an interview, and then not put them to use? This seemed particularly true of people who wrote columns, and had to turn out several a week; they were constantly in search of material.

Anderson was so scintillating in private conversation that almost any journalist who interviewed him in his office, over lunch, or in some other intimate environment came away greatly impressed. They tended to consider it unfair that he was being neglected. To the extent these journalists did not think Anderson had much of a chance, they were tempted to compensate by writing generous commentaries about his personal characteristics. Our hope was that at some point the public would wonder, "Why isn't such a great person taken more seriously?"—and then maybe they *would* proceed to take him more seriously.

In the months preceding Anderson's announcement, several columnists had stopped by, and it is revealing what they wrote. Marquis Childs of the *St. Louis Post-Dispatch*, after interviewing Anderson, fairly gushed about him in a column, describing him, in the ultimate encomium, as "Lincolnesque." But then he concluded by remarking, "It is a refreshing performance that deserves more reward than it is likely to get." Similarly, Steve Chapman of the *New Republic* interviewed Anderson and not surprisingly produced a long and flattering piece. But the last line was the zinger: "The GOP could do a lot worse than to nominate John Anderson for President, and it probably will." For a long while, this would be almost the formula treatment Anderson received at the hands of the national press: great guy, no chance. In time, ironically, it would be helpful.

In the week before the announcement, journalists engaged Anderson's attention almost constantly. It was a useful experience, not only because it heightened the interest in his impending campaign, but because it helped Anderson himself in fleshing out his thoughts about running and in rehearsing before others both his political philosophy and strategy. He had breakfast with columnist Joe Kraft at the Georgetown Inn, lunch at Tiberio with several reporters from the *New York Times'* Washington bureau, cocktails one evening over at *Newsweek* with members of its Washington staff, and cocktails another night with columnist Clayton Fritchey at the latter's home. Hugh Sidey of *Time* magazine interviewed him, as did Marty Nolan of the *Boston Globe*, Jack Nelson of the *Los Angeles Times*, and Tom Foley of *U.S. News and World Report*. He spent considerable time with columnists in particular: James Reston, Tom Wicker, Colman McCarthy, Carl Rowan, Charles Bartlett, Elizabeth Drew, Nick Thimmesch, Meg Greenfield, William Raspberry, and Jim Wieghart.

We also made efforts to put Anderson in touch with scholars and academic figures. He had expressed the frustration, in contemplating what sort of announcement speech he would make, that there did not seem to be anything under the sun he could say which would be at once new and bold, and grab the intellectual interest of the public. He carried around in his briefcase a tattered column he had clipped weeks before from the *Washington Post* entitled "The Cupboard of Ideas is Bare." Its title summed up to him what was wrong with the world, and what he wanted his candidacy above all to address. Anderson had frequently met over the months with experts in fields that he found of particular interest. Mike Evans, then president of Chase Econometrics, came by to provide economic forecasts and analysis; Rudolph Penner of the American Enterprise Institute to discuss strategies for regulatory reform; Jan Lodal, a former National Security Council staff member, to argue the merits of the SALT II agreement; William Hyland, a close associate of Henry Kissinger's, to give a perspective on the Soviet invasion of Afghanistan. Anderson profited greatly from these sessions and those he had with many others. There was a bit of the frustrated scholar in him, and he felt strongly that a presidential candidate, far from having to sacrifice time for reflection in the interests of campaigning, ought to go out of his way to think about what he was doing.

Still, Anderson wondered what he could say on this important occasion that would be distinctive from what other candidates typically said. In exasperation, we drew up a list of scholars of the presidency and latter-day philosophers whom he could reach by phone and ask, "If you were in my shoes, and had the opportunity to set the agenda for a national campaign, what issues, what themes, would you articulate?" One of the first people we tried was Daniel Bell, the Harvard sociologist, who told me he did not wish to talk to Anderson, because a short phone call could not do justice to ideas. "It lends itself to sloganeering," he said. Others were more receptive. Anderson talked with quite a number, including Seymour Martin Lipset, Malcolm Moos, James MacGregor Burns, Nelson Polsby, and Aaron Wildavsky. Each had one or two different ideas for issues, but there seemed almost a consensus that the most important contribution a candidate could make would be to wake up the public to some of the crises the country was facing—the energy shortage, a chronic condition of inflation, the unresponsiveness of government—and to try to convey an urgency about dealing with them. Anderson took these admonitions to heart as he set about drafting his remarks.

June 8, 1979, arrived and Anderson's family gathered in his congressional office, each member dressed in his or her Sunday best, and all nervous as though they were novice actors about to make a debut on stage. At about 9:30 A.M. we proceeded over to the Capitol. The announcement was to be made in the chandeliered Rayburn

Room across the corridor from the House chamber. It was a relatively small room, normally used by congressmen for greeting guests and conducting business when they wanted to remain close to activity on the House floor. This morning, the tables in the room had been removed, and about a hundred chairs had been put in their place to accommodate the press and special guests. Behind this section, platforms had been constructed for the use of the several television crews which were covering the event. Crowded around the rim of the room were staff and onlookers. The room was a perfect one: elegantly appointed, befitting a presidential announcement, and small enough so that we could easily fill it and even create an aura of excitement.

As he entered the room, Anderson was applauded loudly by the partisan crowd. He strode up to the podium, which was photogenically situated beneath a massive portrait of George Washington, and introduced his family. Then he began his speech. Most of it he had labored over for the previous week, but the opening passage he had penned on an inspiration only the night before.

> What impels a man or woman to seek the highest office in the land—the Presidency of the United States? I can only offer you, in a personal testament, my own reasons. I am a second generation American, born of an immigrant father who came here at the turn of the century, echoing the thoughts of Goethe: "America, thou hast it far better than the Old World." For some two decades, I have served in the Congress, during some of the most turbulent events in the history of our Republic. I have watched five Presidents and ten Congresses grapple with the issues that have tested the very fabric of our democratic society, woven as it is from the diverse strands of many nationalities, cultures, and beliefs.

Anderson's deep and forceful voice gave his words an added eloquence. He went on to state what he believed to be his campaign's *raison d'etre.*

> Only a little more than half of our eligible voters participated in the last Presidential election, saying, in effect, that they did not believe that their vote could really make a difference . . . I seek the Presidency out of a profound sense of obligation to demonstrate . . . that we are still the last best hope of mankind. And that government does exist to serve the needs of all those who make up the mosaic of a country founded on the premise that all men were born to be free.

John Anderson announcing for president in the Rayburn Room across the corridor from the House chamber in the Capitol, June 8, 1979. (Wide World Photos)

He went on, in somewhat more academic fashion, to decry what he called the lack of a "public philosophy," and to castigate the Carter administration for the way it had "temporized and vacillated while problems have multiplied." Anderson concluded with the lofty rhetoric for which he had been searching.

> Others may boast of superior organization or financial resources. Still others speak in glittering generalities of their talents for leadership. I want to arouse an appeal to the conscience and reason of America, to speak of the America yet to be. . . . There must be a new hope that we can reclaim the promise that has always been ours, but that in recent years has been layered over with cynicism and despair. Let us

recreate in ourselves the hope that with God's help and our endeavor, we will all be present at a new creation.

The crowd paused a moment at the solemnity of the words, then it cheered. Anderson kissed his wife. The crowd cheered again. The press asked its questions. Soon, someone announced it was time for the press conference to end, because Anderson had a plane to catch. With that, he and his family, his staff, and a number of press people boarded a rented bus parked at the steps outside the Capitol. The bus drove off to National Airport, where the party would take a commercial flight out to Chicago, then Rockford, where a similar announcement ceremony, as well as a large local fund-raiser, were to be held. The Anderson campaign was at last official.

3

June–December, 1979: A Campaign is Launched

The reaction to John Anderson's announcement for president fell short of seismic dimensions. James Wechsler of the *New York Post*, though himself an avowed Anderson admirer, was typical in the way he greeted the newborn candidacy. "By all the prevailing standards of political realism," he wrote, "Congressman Anderson's decision to seek the Republican nomination invites dismissal as a quaint, quixotic venture. Certainly his emergence as even a serious contender," Wechsler went on, "would be the most remarkable revolution in Republican ranks since Wendell Wilkie came out of obscurity to become the GOP standard-bearer nearly four decades ago." Adam Clymer of the *New York Times* was no more charitable. He expressed what he seemed to regard as the supreme measure of disparagement when he said that John Anderson stood even less of a chance of capturing the Republican nomination than did his fellow candidate Bob Dole. Lest there be any doubt as to his meaning, he went on to translate this as signifying "probably not much."

The reality was plain: nobody would be particularly interested in what John Anderson had to say until they first thought he had a chance. When he walked into the room where his presidential announcement was made, he must have been gratified to see the standing-room-only crowd that greeted him, as though the public did indeed accord him recognition. He did not know how we had managed to fill the room. Sensing the potential for an embarrassing turnout, we had posted announcements everywhere in sight. Apparently a large number of suggestible young college students (many of whom work for the summer in congressional offices) were enticed to attend out of sheer curiosity. Most of the other people in the room that day were reporters and cameramen who had come mainly out of a feeling of public-service obligation on the part of their assignment editors.

Throughout the early stages of the campaign, we faced this continual challenge of how to create public interest in an unknown candidate. Days after his announcement, for example, Anderson paid another visit to New Hampshire. He walked down the various main streets he found, spoke at a senior citizens home, and had small private meetings with potential supporters. Such conventional activities accounted for the generally unheralded nature of Anderson's early campaign swings. What finally brought out the cameras on this trip was an inspiration someone had to position Anderson at the pump of a gas station in Concord, and let him work for an hour or so waiting on the cars that drove up. It was perfect local color for the media. Anderson rolled up his oxford-cloth shirt sleeves, accepted the risk of staining his gray flannel pants, and made a generally heroic effort to live down his reputation for being somewhat less than mechanically inclined. He also shook off his usual public stiffness, and quickly got into the swing of things. "Remember the name," he called after one man in a pickup truck whose tank he had just filled. "I may be the only one of the candidates to put gas in your truck."

In those early days, virtually anyone who asked to interview or photograph Anderson would be permitted to do so. One day a young woman showed up at the office with a camera slung over her shoulder and made a request to take pictures. I asked who she was taking pictures for. "*Time* and *Newsweek*," she replied. My eyes bulged, and for the next several hours I imposed on Anderson to accommodate her every photographic whim. That afternoon, it happened, we were having lunch with Meg Greenfield, editorial page editor of the *Post*. The photographer hovered obtrusively around our table; she seemed awkward, as if she were almost new to her profession. "Who *is* that?" Greenfield whispered, annoyed. "That," I replied proudly, "is a photographer for *Time* and *Newsweek*." Greenfield looked at me quizzically. "I don't think someone would be taking pictures for both," she said. "Oh, you're wrong," I corrected her. Greenfield shook her head again. "You should check it out," she said. I did so. In my naïveté, I had jumped to conclusions. What the young woman had meant in saying that she was taking pictures for the magazines was simply that she was planning to submit pictures to them in the hope that they would be published. She had no contract, no assignment, no relationship whatsoever with *Time* or *Newsweek*. In fact, she was a novice photographer who was still learning how to take pictures. None of her photographs of Anderson ever appeared in print. My on-the-job training continued.

Of course we could not depend on such limited "photo opportunities" to achieve for Anderson the massive publicity he needed to become an established candidate. Somehow we had to acquaint the press in a more thoroughgoing way with his qualifications and what he stood for, and convince them that he was, quite simply, as we ourselves knew, the best candidate. We would have to rely on the press to spread the word. What else could we do? Plainly, we did not have the organization, the fame, the political connections, or the money to compete on a par in these areas with the other candidates. In our constrained circumstances, necessity would be the mother of invention: we would take advantage of the one asset we did have, namely, an articulate and intelligent candidate who inspired enthusiasm and dedication among his supporters. To the extent that John Anderson was to become a "media candidate," it was not because the press conspired, for some mysterious reason, to build him and promote him, as Jimmy Carter later implied when he charged Anderson as having been a "creation of the press." Rather, it was that the press became widely exposed to him, came away genuinely impressed, and reported its honest impressions. There was no trick to this except to make John Anderson as accessible as possible, and then to rely on him to be his own best advocate.

No stone would go unturned in our quest to present Anderson to the media. Whenever we scheduled visits for him to new terrain outside Washington, for example, advisories would be sent to local radio stations and newspapers, alerting them to his impending arrival. Attached would be a packet of flattering press clippings, to create the impression that Anderson was a hot property to whom others in the press were already giving close attention. Even so, the

same telephone conversation could be heard over and over again during the next several days coming from my desk: "Yes, Anderson, A-n-d-e-r-s-o-n. Yes, he's running for president. Yes, of the United States. No, he's a Republican. He's been a congressman for 20 years. Yes, 20 years. No, I don't know why you haven't heard of him." And then, after a pause, "He has *already* announced." Such people were generally impressed to learn Anderson's biographical details and credentials, and, if they were not covering a local three-alarm fire, would consider a nominal interview with him worthwhile.

But it was on national news opportunities that our limited press operation focused its efforts. For despite all the disclaimers of the Washington press corps, it was my personal observation that there did indeed exist something akin to a small and inbred network of opinion-makers on a Washington-New York axis to whom newspaper and other media people elsewhere turned for their editorial cues. Many of the national political stories that appear in local papers across the country are filed from Washington, and the reporters who write them, like many other Washingtonians, wake up in the morning to read the *Washington Post* over coffee, find a copy of the *New York Times* waiting on their desk when they arrive at the office, and (before it folded in 1981) bought a copy of the afternoon *Washington Star* at the newspaper stand in the subway station on their way home. If favorable things start appearing about someone in the editorials and columns of leading papers available in Washington, chances are the sentiments will eventually trickle down to some of the local papers elsewhere in the country, and then to the wider public who will count so much when it comes to the elections in the primary states.

During the latter half of 1979, we solicited every well-known newspaper, magazine, and TV show that came to mind, suggesting a piece on Anderson. (Admittedly, we hesitated sending letters to a few publications, such as *Playboy, Rolling Stone,* and *National Enquirer,* with which we felt our straight-and-narrow candidate might not wish to be associated. Some of the more traditional-minded campaign staff reacted in horror that we could do anything so risky, but finally, after consultation with the Andersons, it was decided that our position as beggars did not warrant our being choosers.) Typical was a letter we sent to Public Broadcasting's TV show

"Bill Moyers' Journal," in which we suggested that "it would be a fascinating story to relate how a man, his family, and his friends go about the task of waging such an ambitious and uphill battle as their 1980 campaign represents, and yet how through it all they are sustained by a faith in their candidate and their cause." As a result of this letter, Bill Moyers himself became personally interested in doing precisely this: a profile on Anderson which would accent the human interest aspects of a long-shot bid for the presidency. And so such a show was arranged, filmed several months later in Vermont, and shown on nationwide TV in late February, about the time of the all-important first primaries. More than a few of our early supporters subsequently mentioned to us having seen it, and having been favorably affected by its poignant portrayal of John Anderson in his human dimension. Appearances on William Buckley's "Firing Line," CBS' "Sixty Minutes," and ABC's "20-20," as well as stories in the *New York Times Magazine, People* magazine, and the *Washington Post* Style section, and even a profile of Keke Anderson in *Us* magazine were induced by similar prodding. Our approach to the press at times was almost shameless in its forwardness and fervor, but we were not about to stand on formalities with so much potentially at stake.

The Sunday news shows on the TV networks were harder to crack. Usually our inquiries were bucked to people called associate producers who, in our limited experience, seemed to be functionaries in the news departments who specialized in fending off people like ourselves, placating us with perpetual claims that we were "under consideration," or that we would be scheduled "just as soon as possible." "Face the Nation" proved particularly intractable. The associate producer in this case had, back in 1978, asked Anderson to serve as an alternate guest in case Prime Minister Begin of Israel was unable to do the show as scheduled; his interview was being broadcast from Jerusalem, and there were questions until the last moment as to whether Knesset business or technical problems in the transmission might prevent the interview from materializing. Anderson agreed to cancel his schedule for the weekend, and to stay at home by the phone in case the show needed him to fill in. As it turned out, Begin went on the air without a hitch. But for his trouble, the associate producer had agreed in principle to give Anderson a show to himself in the near future. Months went by, and despite reminders, the associate producer displayed no obvious interest in observing the terms of the agreement. Anderson was simply not a newsworthy enough figure to enjoy leverage with a show concerned about competitive ratings. The stalemate ended only after the appearance by George Bush on two separate editions of "Face the Nation." The unfairness of Bush being given two such exposures before Anderson had even had one so galled us that Anderson agreed to call the president of CBS News directly to make our case. The top brass proved to be more flexible than their subordinates, and Anderson soon got his long-awaited invitation.

One of our most effective approaches to the press was to schedule meetings with the editorial boards (i.e., editors) of major Washington-based news organizations. Some were the national bureaus of newspaper chains: Knight-Ridder, Scripps-Howard, Hearst, Newhouse; some were the Washington bureaus of large papers around the country: the *Los Angeles Times*, the *Philadelphia Bulletin*, the *St. Louis Post-Dispatch*; and some were offices of the wire services: United Press International, the Associated Press. Editors and reporters based in Washington were generally more familiar with Anderson than were members of the press in other cities, and for that reason were more interested in hearing from him. Moreover, they were not generally accustomed to having candidates pay them such visits, and seemed both flattered by the attention and pleased to have an opportunity for an exclusive interview that might happen to stumble upon something of news value. Not only were they likely to run a story, having invested the time in an interview, but those reporters who would be writing about the presidential campaign for another year or more to come were caused by this new acquaintance with Anderson to begin watching a little more for his name than they might have otherwise, and to become a little more sympathetic with his progress.

On several occasions, we also made day trips to New York to argue our case with news editors and executives based there: breakfasts at NBC, lunches at the *New York Times*, meetings with editors at the *New York Daily News*, *Fortune*, *Business Week*, and others. Like their Washington counterparts, journalists in New York would also help to preside over Anderson's success or failure in the campaign. It would be through their eyes and through their interpretations that what Anderson said and did would be projected to a wider public audience. They would be judging his news value and deciding his news coverage throughout the rest of the campaign. After spending time with Anderson, almost everyone seemed promptly persuaded that he had the qualifications to be president. The persistent issue in interviews, however, was how he would be able to fashion a strategy for winning. Anderson tired of having to convince doubting audiences that his candidacy was "viable," "credible," and other standard political adjectives on which his inquisitors fastened. We became particularly frustrated with the tendency of journalists to dismiss a candidate's chances because he was not well known. Could not a name-identification problem be solved overnight, if the right circumstances developed, as was the case with Jimmy Carter? And, on the other hand, was a famous name—Scoop Jackson, John Connally, Teddy Kennedy—really a guarantee of success? Running for president often seemed just an endless repetition of the same answers to the same questions. It was a tedious business, and hardly what Anderson had bargained for when he originally contemplated what he hoped he could make an exhilarating intellectual exercise.

Nonetheless, Anderson did his best to construct a plausible argument for why the Republican party would ultimately offer him its presidential nomination. The purity of a candidate's views, he felt, would not be overriding in the calculations of convention delegates in the coming year, and his label as a moderate, far from being an obstacle, as many said, would prove an asset. "Scratch them a little bit," he told an interviewer, referring to party activists, "and down underneath you will find that, more than ideology, they want a winner. They want somebody who can go out there and peel away Carter's majority—blacks, blue collar workers, independents, young people." Anderson felt that, with the possible exception of Howard Baker, he was really the only one who possessed that drawing power. It seemed to him that the term "moderate" was being too loosely applied to some of his rivals for the nomination. He often said that the center of gravity in the Republican party had shifted in 1976 when Gerald Ford, whom Anderson always felt had shown an impeccable conservatism in the Congress, was suddenly labeled a moderate, only because of the contrast in his positions with those of Ronald Reagan. On a television interview show during the summer, Anderson said:

> If you look at the statistics, you will find only about two out of every ten people who vote are formally identified with the Republican party. All too often we have been a party simply talking to ourselves, and I believe that part of my task during this coming campaign for the nomination is to persuade my fellow Republicans that we simply have to reach out, and to bring into this party people who have never seen the Republican party as the vehicle for progress in this country.

It was an admirable philosophy, although it may not have been particularly realistic given the continued dominance of the right in the GOP nominating process. Indeed, Anderson was frequently asked why he thought he would be able to perform the singular feat of swinging the GOP back in a moderate direction, when even someone with the name and resources of Nelson Rockefeller had failed to do so time and again. Anderson would reply that the circumstances were quite different: that people in retrospect had seen the futility of nominating someone so conservative as a Goldwater (who had prevailed over Rockefeller in the 1964 nomination battle); that there had been far fewer open primaries in those days, where rank-and-file Republicans, rather than party bosses, could express their preferences; that Rockefeller's name had been a hindrance, rather than a help, in drawing support in many parts of the country. Anderson did not, at least as yet, bear such a stigma of cosmopolitan liberalism. To the contrary, he would point out, he was a solid Republican where it counted, on economic and pocketbook issues which he believed would be of paramount concern to primary voters. "I feel very comfortable with the views you would hear from the other [GOP] candidates on economic issues," he said flatly.

But Anderson continued to attract attention not for his conservative economic views, but for his more liberal inclinations in other areas. One such issue, for example, was court-ordered busing. In August, a constitutional amendment came to the floor of the House for debate, one that created enormous controversy because it sought to place into the Constitution an explicit proscription against busing for purposes of racial desegregation. Anderson had never been a strong proponent of busing, but he did feel that it was not appropriate for the Congress to intrude into the province of the Supreme

Court in deciding what methods were available to secure rights protected in the Constitution. Anderson requested five minutes to speak on the subject, just before the motion came to a vote. At the appointed time, he rose and gave his most impassioned extemporaneous oratory, concluding, "This is the wrong time, this is the wrong place, this is the wrong way to tamper with the Constitution of the United States." Anderson sat down to an extraordinarily rare standing ovation from colleagues on both sides of the aisle. Afterward, such black congressional leaders as Parren Mitchell of Baltimore and Ron Dellums of Berkeley came up to him to say he was a hero in their books, and that he was one person they would feel comfortable with in the White House.

Still another event in late summer helped to seal Anderson's growing reputation as a proud liberal among Republicans. A number of GOP presidential candidates gathered one Saturday in Rosemont, Illinois, outside Chicago, to make the case before a large group of Republicans from the state as to why they deserved to be their party's standard-bearer in 1980. While the other candidates chose conventional themes of how they wanted to cut budgets, slash bureaucracies, and practically eliminate taxes, Anderson chose the occasion to depart from similar prepared remarks and instead speak emotionally about the obligation he said Republicans had to show more compassion for the neglected and the underprivileged. "There are too many people," Anderson intoned, "for whom the sunshine today does not spell prosperity, but spells the pitiless glare of prolonged and sustained unemployment. . . . There is nothing so corrosive and debilitating as the bleak, hollow-eyed, hopeless stare of the man or woman out of a job."

Anderson sat down to tepid applause; some in the audience were reported afterward to be hostile. Many found it inexplicable that he would come before them to request their support only to hit them over the head with such an unpleasant, untraditional, and unpopular message. But Anderson felt that the Republican party, in its rush to attract the votes of disenchanted Middle America, was leaving behind whole segments of Americans who were already getting short shrift at the hands of the Carter administration. He thought it unfair, and unfounded, for the Democrats to assert a monopoly on compassion. At the least, Anderson wanted it to be known that there was one GOP candidate who thought the plight of the poor and the unemployed important enough to talk about. Ironically, the speaker who was most warmly applauded at the event was Ben Fernandez, a millionaire Los Angeles businessman who billed himself as the first Hispanic to run for the Republican presidential nomination. He did not choose to talk about the poor; quite the reverse, what he delivered was his usual conservative stump speech in which he recounted his Horatio Alger ascent from having been "born in a boxcar" to the point where he had earned all the material rewards America confers upon those who succeed. Clearly, Anderson's very different homily was out of sync with the atmosphere of this Republican convocation.

Of course, one of the reasons that tempted Anderson to highlight some of his unusual positions was the hope that he might thereby exercise an appeal to the 20 or 30 percent of New Hampshire Republicans, and probably more in Massachusetts, whom we calculated to fall into a liberal or moderate category. Pete McCloskey, the California congressman, had managed to win 20 percent of New Hampshire's Republican vote in 1972, when he had mounted an antiwar challenge to Nixon; and even in 1964, Henry Cabot Lodge, then perceived as a moderate alternative to Barry Goldwater, was able to capture the New Hampshire primary on the strength of a write-in vote. Anderson was convinced that there really was not much middle ground between himself and the conservatives. George Bush may have been perceived as a moderate because of his clean-cut Ivy League image, but Anderson argued that if pressed on the issues his true conservatism would be smoked out and show him to be, as Anderson put it, only a "Ronald Reagan in a Brooks Brothers suit."

At this point, many began to wonder whether Anderson's unwillingness to echo the conservative line of his peers betrayed a lack of real commitment to seeking and winning the presidency; some suspected that he was using his candidacy as a soapbox on which to make moral pronouncements, and never seriously entertained hopes of succeeding. There may have been an element of truth in this, but in larger measure, there was another explanation: Anderson felt strongly that while the object was assuredly to win, it was not to win at *any* price. He would say what he genuinely felt, and hope that it proved popular. If not, the compromise involved in getting elected would not be worth the price. Anderson grew fond of quoting Adlai Stevenson to the effect that a candidate should pursue the presidency in such a way that by the time he won he still deserved it.

But many insisted on reading more cynical designs into Anderson's behavior. Sometimes he would be accused of secretly wanting to be vice-president, and of pretending a liberalism that would encourage his selection as someone to balance a ticket. Once a reporter asked him point blank about it, and he replied bluntly: "I can turn on my steeliest look," he said, "and gaze deeply into your eyes—and tell you *No.*" He explained why. "I see the desirability of painting on a larger canvas." As if his answer still lacked credibility, he added:

> Just this morning, as I was driving into work, Fritz Mondale came roaring down the parkway just ahead of me in a big, black Lincoln, with four vehicles in the motorcade—here, in the middle of the energy crisis—and I said, "Who in God's name would want to shoot the vice president anyway? We haven't even heard from him in weeks." To me, it was an unnecessary set of precautions. I can't think of an office that holds less allure for me than the vice presidency.

That seemed to settle the subject. Anderson was interested in being president, period. And yet if he were really intent on constructing a winning strategy for the Republican nomination, it would not do to thumb his nose at many of the traditional attitudes of his party. To the contrary, while he certainly should be encouraged to express his convictions, he would need at the same time to emphasize some of the orthodox GOP positions he supported to make it clear that his feet remained planted firmly in the party. Anderson rejected the notion that he was painting himself a liberal—he thought he was expressing only "moderate," commonsense positions—and found equally unpalatable the notion that he should kowtow to the icons of orthodoxy in the party. He continually asserted his belief that the activists who attended party events such as the one in Rosemont were more conservative than the average Republican who would turn out at the polls during the primaries. From the beginning, Anderson said explicitly that he wanted to mount an appeal in large part to independent-minded voters, that he wanted to attract them because his positions made sense, not because they conformed to rigid ideological preconceptions.

It was this philosophy that gave birth to what later came to be labeled as Anderson's "campaign of ideas." Anderson had articulated its premise that spring when he spoke at a Wisconsin state Republican convention in Madison. "I don't care what you call me. You can call me a conservative. You can call me a liberal. You can call me a moderate. But don't call me a man who doesn't have ideas—because ideas are what are going to serve this party and the needs of the American people." We often quoted this particular statement of Anderson's and, over time, it became the virtual motto of the campaign.

It was inspirational rhetoric, and yet it was never completely clear to most people what Anderson had meant by it. Usually it was taken to mean that the campaign would be distinguished by a host of specific, concrete, bold, and imaginative policy proposals. Yet in practice, not only was the campaign unable to produce the abundance of such ideas which some seemed to expect, but that is not what Anderson, at least originally, had in mind. Rather, what he wanted to convey was simply the importance he attached to a president's having an intellectual interest in issues, and an open mind as to what approaches and policies on these issues ought to be pursued. The point was that a Republican ought to be willing to consider what might nominally be thought a Democratic idea on how to fight inflation, for example, rather than holding himself a prisoner of strict ideology. Of course, most candidates proudly asserted an interest in "issues"; the difference was that Anderson used every opportunity actually to talk about them.

Probably the one discrete "idea" that propelled Anderson the farthest was what became popularly known as his proposal for a fifty-cent tax on gasoline. (Later, it was renamed the 50-50 Plan, in a vain effort to call attention to the fact that the fifty-cent tax was only half of the plan; the other, and much more attractive, half was that the revenues raised from the tax would be immediately returned to American workers by way of a 50 percent reduction in Social Security payroll taxes.) The genesis of the proposal was an interesting one and hardly bore the illustrious origins of something one expected to win national attention.

The week before sequestering himself at Camp David during a bizarre two-week period in July of 1979, Jimmy Carter had been attending a seven-nation summit in Japan, and had been rumored to be planning a major energy speech on his return. Anderson, ascetic and obsessive intellectual that he sometimes could be, felt it necessary to put himself through the exercise of preparing the energy message that he would have given were he in the president's shoes. And so one Saturday morning, when other candidates would have been enjoying a relaxing weekend, Anderson busied himself at home in Bethesda drafting his own mock-presidential speech. He had written it in longhand, and phoned me early Sunday morning to ask whether I would come in to the office with him, check it over, and type it up. Coming from my boss, it was an offer I could not refuse. He said he would come by my apartment building and pick me up, and so I waited outside, looking for the sight of his familiar old Buick creeping down Connecticut Avenue at the snail's pace he usually drove. As many times as he had been to my apartment to drop me off or pick me up, he was apparently lost in thought, for as I stood there on the sidewalk, his car appeared around a curve in the road, and drove right on past me in halting fashion, as if he could not quite remember where he was supposed to be stopping. Anderson was one of the most retentive and alert people when it came to things that mattered deeply to him, such as national issues, but had the distinctive flavor of an absent-minded professor when it came to more mundane aspects of the world around him, such as navigating an automobile. I raced after the car, flagged it down, hopped in, and we drove the rest of the way less eventfully.

The energy statement Anderson had prepared charged that, as a result of the inability of the nation's leaders to address the energy crisis effectively, Americans were at the point of losing confidence in their institutions and even in themselves; it was not clear to them where they were headed as a nation. Despite much eloquent philosophy, however, the statement for the most part was conventional in its recommendations (the establishment of standby rationing authority for gasoline, an energy mobilization board designed to cut through red tape in approving energy projects, a steep windfall profits tax on decontrolled oil), with one large exception.

In the middle of the list of recommendations, Anderson had written, somewhat matter-of-factly, that to discourage unnecessary oil consumption, and to help meet the goal of reduced imports to which the United States had recently pledged itself, there should be established a "gasoline emergency excise tax" at the pump. Anderson stated this recommendation without elaboration, except to add, "I would suggest twenty-five cents a gallon."

Anderson's inclination toward such a dramatic gas tax was not the product, as one might have imagined, of long staff study or intensive consultation with experts. It just happened to be something he had seen recommended occasionally in various academic and editorial quarters, and felt offhand might be the sort of bold policy necessary to address America's parlous state of oil consumption. And yet, as I looked at the particular figure Anderson had suggested—twenty-five cents—it did not seem arresting enough. European taxes were enormously higher, and America was constantly being scorned abroad for persisting in its profligate ways, and, in particular, for its inability to ween itself away from an over-dependence on the automobile. My own instinct was that a tax, to be effective in changing deeply ingrained driving habits, would have to be at least fifty cents.

I was in the middle of typing Anderson's draft, and hated to put one thing in if I would have to go back and change it later. I wanted to check with Anderson, but he had left the office for an hour or so to take a swim at the congressional gym. I decided to go ahead and write in fifty cents, and simply try to convince Anderson of the merit of my editorial judgment when he came back. When he returned, I told him about it. He was skeptical at first. "Fifty cents?" he said. "That's a lot of money. Don't you think a quarter's enough?" "Well, obviously we ought to check with the experts to see what's really necessary to get conservation," I said, "but as a consumer I can tell you that fifty cents would pack a lot more punch than a quarter." Anderson mulled it over and said, "Okay, keep it in."

Anderson studied the final typed version, gave it his approval, and suggested that it be Xeroxed promptly and distributed to the press. His thought was that this would allow reporters to compare Carter's pending proposals with his own. I made copies and sent them around widely. Of course, most recipients ignored the statement; no one could have cared particularly what a seventh-ranked Republican presidential candidate thought about a national energy program at a time when there was so much to write about as to what the president himself was thinking on the subject. A few Illinois papers did pick up the statement, but abbreviated their reporting so as to make it a virtual one-paragraph story. In the main, however, the bold Anderson proposal for a fifty-cent gas tax went unnoticed and unreported.

This may seem in retrospect a frivolous origin for such a weighty idea, but Anderson was well enough versed in energy issues, and in what newspapers and experts were saying, that in a sense it was as informed and intelligent a decision on policy as candidates usually make, even when they have the benefit of large research staffs and armies of advisors. Anderson did so much of his own reading and thinking that, compared to more typical candidates, he did not require as much whispering of advice in his ear. Indeed, unencumbered by staff, the Anderson campaign may have been at times more creative and productive in those early days than it would be later. Once extra researchers, writers, and advisors were acquired, no idea could ever have been launched without first having been thoroughly labored over in the drafting stage. In consequence, delays of weeks and even months would occur, and in the end, so many people were involved in the decision-making that agreement often could not be reached on anything but the lowest common denominator of opinion.

Throughout the rest of 1979, our gas tax proposal continued to evolve. The more we discussed it, the more we recognized two serious shortcomings: first, it would have had a substantial inflationary impact, insofar as it drove up energy costs; and, second, the Congress would be extremely unlikely to pass it. Keke and some of the campaign staff were concerned that we had put forward a proposal too severe and, by conventional standards, impolitic; their intuition told them that a presidential candidate should not be in the business of scaring people, but rather should make it a point to reassure them that their material lives would improve with his election. Indeed, whenever Anderson was to talk of "sacrifice" during the campaign, his wife would give him a friendly nudge and say,

"Let's talk about 'cooperation,' dear." We were all in agreement, however: somehow the gas tax had to be made more salable. People would not accept it only on the strength of arguments that it was necessary to avert a worsening energy crisis; the "energy crisis" was a largely intangible phenomenon to most people, and something many of them considered exaggerated or even contrived.

One day in July, a letter to the editor appeared in the *New York Times* from a woman identified as an energy specialist at the Massachusetts Institute of Technology. In her letter, she made the suggestion—which the *Times* discussed sympathetically in an editorial a few days later—that a hefty gas tax could be combined with an arrangement to repeal state sales taxes, so that the tax burden for the average person would not be increased, but only redistributed. The value of the gas tax would remain: gasoline, a scarce commodity, would have a higher price relative to other goods, and people would use their money to buy less of it and more of other things. True, she said, a gasoline tax might hit poor people proportionately more than others, but that was no comparative disadvantage from the current situation, since a sales tax was at least equally regressive. I showed the article to Anderson, and he was intrigued.

On August 4, we issued a press release saying that Anderson was proposing urgent consideration of the idea, though not necessarily endorsing it. By this time, Bob Walker, our capable staff economist, had been brought in to study some of the intricacies further. After preliminary research, he came back with a different recommendation: that we combine the gasoline tax not with a reduction in state sales taxes—which not all states had, and which could be reduced only through action at the state government level—but with a reduction in Social Security taxes. These latter taxes could be altered by act of Congress. Moreover, they were scheduled to rise in the next two years to a level representing a burden on workers which ought, on its own merits, to be reduced. Arguably, these taxes also had an inflationary impact: to the extent employers paid a share of them, they incurred higher labor costs which had to be reflected in the price of products.

Bob did computations, consulted with experts, and finally an Op-Ed piece in Anderson's name was submitted to the *Times* in late August. We called the editorial page editors to be sure they recognized the importance Anderson attached to this "bold new idea," and shortly thereafter the column was published. We had no say, of course, in the title the column was given, and unfortunately, though naturally enough, it turned out to be headed, "FOR A FIFTY CENT TAX ON GASOLINE." Our efforts to create a clever package proposal that included a major tax reduction had been foiled by the instinct of journalists to compress complicated subject material into neat and convenient shorthand. One could be sure that infinitely more people saw the headline than read the article, and that such a dramatic headline would stick in their minds. Hereafter, they would always associate Anderson with the proposal for a new tax.

It was an ever-present challenge throughout the campaign to explain Anderson's proposal in its more complex dimensions. To this end, the campaign issued an extensive fact sheet that described all its provisions—there were many of them—and explained carefully how it would avoid hurting special classes of citizens about whom there would be obvious concern. Senior citizens, for example, might have imagined that the proposal would work against them, because they would be charged a higher price for gasoline like everyone, and yet would not be in a position to benefit from a reduction in social security taxes, which they did not pay. This was a logical concern, but it was easily answered: under the Anderson 50-50 Plan, enough revenues would be raised by a gas tax to provide an across-the-board increase in social security benefits, sufficient to offset the higher price of gasoline, given the average driving requirements of the elderly. For taxi drivers, truckers, traveling salesmen, farmers, and others who depended on cars for their livelihoods, the 50-50 Plan also included the provision of a tax credit for the business use of motor fuel.

It was an excruciating exercise in frustration, we soon learned, to try to propose an idea about which no one ever seemed to hear all the details or all the reasoning. When the proposal became better known, Anderson would often be confronted at speeches by angry questioners: "Why do you want to hurt the poor and the middle-class by charging us half a buck more for gasoline?" After Anderson finished a lengthy explanation of the proposal, the audience would leave with at least an open mind on the subject, and sometimes initial doubters would even undergo a conversion. The fact is, under the proposal, the average worker would actually have been no worse off if he continued to drive the same as before; and he might actually have been better off, to the extent that he cut down on frivolous driving, car pooled, took a bus, purchased a more fuel-efficient automobile, or moved closer to work. All the experts agreed it was really quite a marvelous idea. Somehow this had to be communicated to the public.

To cultivate editorial opinion on the subject, which one hoped might one day reach a wider audience, fact sheets were sent to over 250 editorial writers, plus individual letters in Anderson's name to many of the major columnists who would contribute to setting the tone of opinion on the subject. Encomiums gradually began to flood in. The difference between the reaction of columnists, economists, and informed people generally, on the one hand, and that of the average citizen, on the other, was extraordinary. The former seemed to appreciate the basic rationale: that somehow America had to end its terrible dependence on costly and uncertain supplies of foreign oil, and that we might as well do it by taxing ourselves as by allowing foreign potentates to tax us and take our money. If we did not levy a tax on ourselves, gas prices would rise anyway, due to OPEC action. On the other hand, if we took the initiative to tax ourselves and raise gas prices, OPEC would be unlikely to raise prices further, since its American-trained economists would be pragmatic enough to charge only what the traffic would bear.

But the great and lingering value of the gas-tax proposal was not just that editorial writers said, "Oh, that Anderson has a good idea to solve the energy crisis," but that they took this proposal as a symbol of Anderson's willingness to propose sensible ideas even if they were unpopular. The Anderson gas tax in time became a living advertisement of Anderson's political courage. The *Philadelphia Inquirer* called it the proposal of the "Presidential candidate who doesn't mind telling people things they may not want to hear." The *St. Paul Pioneer-Press* said "Anderson should be in line for nomination for Courageous Candidate of the Year." The *Washington Post* called him "courageous," the *Vancouver* (Washington) *Columbian* called him "gutsy." In the *Chicago Tribune*, columnist Michael Killian summed it up: "Anderson is candidly facing up to a serious unpleasant reality with an eminently workable if admittedly painful solution, just as he'd have to as President."

But the most dramatic word of praise came from an unexpected source. One day in November the famous "Herblock" cartoon of the *Washington Post* was devoted to the Anderson gas-tax idea. It depicted a couple driving up to three gas pumps, from which they were going to have to choose, as one usually chooses between "regular" and "high-test." One pump looked like a type of dispenser one would see behind the counter of a soda fountain. A pathetic looking Jimmy Carter was standing astride it. This first pump was labeled, "The Moral Equivalent of Frozen Custard" (in reference to Carter's labeling of the energy crisis as "the moral equivalent of war"). At the other end was a pump which featured an elephant's trunk for a hose. Manning this pump was a caricature of a rich Republican presidential candidate, complete with ten-gallon hat *à la* John Connally. So far, the alternatives looked equally unpleasant. But in between them was a third pump, one which looked to be normal. There, standing next to it, his face as shiny and wholesome as that of a schoolboy, was John Anderson. This pump was labelled "GOP Presidential Candidate John Anderson's Proposal for a 50¢ Gas Tax with the Money Used to Reduce Other Taxes." At the bottom of this elaborate cartoon was the caption: "ARE WE ANGRY ENOUGH TO WANT SOMEBODY WHO REALLY MEANS BUSINESS?"

This was the biggest shot of publicity the campaign had received to date. When a friend called at at 6:00 A.M. and alerted me to look in the *Post*, I was positively ecstatic, and wanted to tell Anderson about it immediately. He was on the road campaigning, but I had the phone number of the private home where he was staying with a family of campaign supporters. For some reason, I was under the impression that it was in Wisconsin. I waited until about seven-thirty, figuring that it would be acceptable to wake Anderson at 6:30 A.M. Wisconsin time, since he usually rose early. I dialed the number and it rang several times. An unfamiliar voice answered, and I asked for Congressman Anderson. "Is this an emergency?" came the reply. "No, not really," I said. "Well, do you know what time it is?" the person at the other end said. "Sure," I replied knowledgeably, "it's seven-thirty in Washington, and six-thirty in Wisconsin." "Well, I don't care what time it is in Wisconsin," the voice answered back, "but it's 4:30 A.M. here in Portland, Oregon, and Congressman Anderson is *not* up." With that, the phone clicked dead. Apparently the congressman was not in Wisconsin.

—from *Herblock on All Fronts* (New American Library, 1980)

To get even more publicity for the 50-50 Plan, which was certainly the biggest issue we had going for us, Anderson planned to introduce formal legislation, and on that occasion call a press conference announcing the action. This was finally done in December, after a twenty-three-page bill was drafted. Normally, scores of phone calls would be made to the various people on our press lists to induce attendance at Anderson's press conferences, and most of them would politely say that they would try to make it and then never show up. The gas-tax press conference was different. Anderson had been talking about the proposal quite a lot, and a large number of editorials in recent weeks had been creating a drumbeat in favor of such a course of action. At the same time, several high Carter Administration officials, in just the previous few days, had been rumored to be looking at such a gas tax themselves. All of this aroused a general new interest in our proposal, and brought out the media in unexpectedly large numbers (about thirty) to the press conference. That night on TV, and the next morning in the papers, Anderson's formal introduction of the gas tax legislation was treated as a major news story, one of the first times the campaign had really been taken seriously. Never mind that Anderson was the only congressman willing to support the proposal and that it seemed to have no legislative future. At least it was interesting and becoming much discussed. Candidates during campaigns often acquire strong images, fairly or not. In 1980, Connally was looked upon as the wheeler-dealer; Kennedy as inarticulate; Carter as mean; Bush as preppy; Reagan as prone to gaffes. Anderson was lucky to have established early on a rather heroic reputation as someone of intellectual integrity and political courage. Looking back, it was largely because of the gas-tax proposal that he acquired that reputation, and that it stuck with him in the eyes of many all the way to the end of the campaign.

From the beginning, the Anderson campaign was something less than a well-oiled political machine. It was not until the first week in July, 1979, that an office had been established and opened for business. It was located on Eighth Street, in the Southeast quadrant of Washington, in a part of town euphemistically described as "transitional." This meant, in practice, seedy and unsafe, but we could not afford a neighborhood closer to Capitol Hill. For convenience, however, a point had been made to locate the office within two blocks of a subway stop; this was particularly important if we intended to encourage college students to volunteer their services in the evening.

When I toured the office for the first time, my initial thought was that our campaign staff would never grow into it. As it turned out, we were to move two more times in the course of the campaign to progressively much larger offices, and even then, at the end, space was impossibly cramped. But for now, we were excited at last to be able to tell the press that we actually had an office and an address; it constituted tangible evidence that the Anderson campaign was not just the figment of our imagination they might have taken it to be. The office was on the second floor of an old building, right above the Metropolis Bike Shop. It was marked at first only by a little label above the buzzer at the front door, which identified the second-floor offices to be those of the "Anderson for President Committee." Later on, a makeshift cardboard sign would be hung in the second-floor window facing the street, but until then, it would have taken a Sherlock Holmes to find the Anderson office, even if he had come armed with the address. Immediately inside was a large front room with big picture windows overlooking the street. This was a not unimportant asset, insofar as it allowed employees to keep an eye on their cars below and make sure the time had not expired at the parking meters. In one corner, away from the street side, was an inner office, which campaign manager Bill Bradford made his own. He posted a small, hand-lettered organization chart on the wall, and a couple of other odds and ends for aesthetic effect, but otherwise the office had a perennial air about it as though someone were just moving in. Down a hall from the front room was a small utility area, used to brew coffee and to carve up pizza and sandwiches when those were ordered out; and then two more modest-sized rooms which came to be used, variously, for scheduling, press, accounting, and secretarial chores.

On July 6, at 5:00 P.M., while the office was still fairly vacant and only gradually becoming furnished and peopled, Bradford arranged to have a little opening ceremony, to which the staff members of Anderson's congressional office and the roughly ten employees and volunteers of the campaign were invited. At the appointed time,

Anderson came the one mile from the Capitol to the campaign office. As he entered his campaign office for the first time, the campaign staffers continued to go about their work as if he were not there. Evidently the intention was to show him what the office normally looked like, and perhaps not incidentally to impress him with their diligence. Anderson went from desk to desk to introduce himself; most of the staff members and volunteers had been hired by Bradford and had never before met John Anderson. Finally, Bradford called everyone together, and they stood in a circle around Anderson as he spoke. He began by thanking them all for their dedication and their effort. He told them he had just been traveling in New England and could feel in his bones that the campaign had a real chance. Then he asked if there were questions. He was ill at ease. It was an odd feeling to realize that all these strange new faces were working for him, many of them giving their time and effort free of charge, simply because they had been motivated out of a faith in what they had heard about him. Much later in the campaign, Anderson came to deal more comfortably with such situations, but for a long while he would feel a certain self-conscious amazement and humility.

Another advance made in our campaign efforts at this time was the preparation of a formal brochure about the candidate which could be distributed at his speeches and fund-raisers. This seems rather modest progress in retrospect, but at the time it was considered a major accomplishment. In the days of the exploratory effort, we had relied on handing out to interested parties a few hastily stapled-together clippings of favorable newspaper columns. Clearly, a prepackaged brochure would be much handier, and would lend us a marginal, but much-needed, aura of professionalism.

Unfortunately, while such an idea may have been an excellent one in its conception, its execution was so amateurish as to render the effort self-defeating. Given the precarious state of campaign finances, we were always interested in effecting economies in our operation. Though such an attitude was in the main commendable, one corner that was cut did not turn out in the long run to be such a bargain. It was decided to let a firm from Anderson's hometown produce the brochure, because it had offered to do so at a substantial discount. The finished product resembled nothing so much as a flyer one might have distributed in a hotly contested race for president of the student council. A stiff and obviously posed picture appeared on the front page of the brochure, the printing inside was scratchy, and the components of the text were set off by four unimaginative subheads: "Experience," "Character," "Leadership," and "Principle."

The brochure did impart some useful information. It made a point of citing some of Anderson's policy positions that were thought to have Republican appeal, noting, for example, that he was the chief sponsor of something called the Regulatory Reform Act, a piece of legislation that would seek to phase out unnecessary government regulation; and the Limits to the Growth of Government Act, a bill intended to constrain spending so that it corresponded to the rate of economic growth, and which would have required that the president submit a balanced budget to Congress by fiscal year 1982. For the environmentalists among our potential supporters, the brochure cited Anderson's cosponsorship of the Udall-Anderson Alaska lands bill, considered one of the major conservation bills of the century, seeking to preserve parts of Alaska from timber development.

Later on in 1979, we did manage to revise and upgrade the brochure. The new version would boast multiple colors, shinier paper, and fancier type. A picture of Anderson and his wife was added; it had been chosen quite memorably. One day Keke had said to me, "Mark, do you remember that wonderful picture that was taken of John and me when President Sadat was visiting?" I thought I knew what she was referring to and retrieved it for her from the files. She asked me for a pair of scissors, and proceeded to cut Sadat out of the picture. It was not that she had anything against President Sadat—indeed, she admired him very much—but merely that she thought it happened to be a good picture of her and her husband. It became the standard family photo for the rest of the campaign.

Our essential fund-raising goal during 1979 was to meet the so-called federal matching requirements, which would make us eligible for a certain amount of public financing. This consisted of raising at least $5,000 in each of twenty states, of which increments of no more than $250 per contributor would be counted toward the goal. The point of this formula was to ensure that money would be disbursed from the federal treasury only to candidates who could demonstrate a relatively broad base of public support, and thus avoid government subsidization of frivolous candidacies. Although Anderson's travel schedule concentrated increasingly in the four earliest primary states which we had targeted—New Hampshire, Massachusetts, Illinois, and Wisconsin—he would be readily diverted elsewhere as opportunities developed for raising money in other states. We went to great trouble one week, for example, to schedule a trip for him to St. Louis, where there was the prospect of raising a few thousand dollars that could be applied to our quota for Missouri. We considered it all-important to reach the threshold for matching. It was not only that all money raised after that point would be doubled by the federal government, but also that reaching such a point represented the bare minimum of respectability for a serious presidential candidate. John Connally and Ted Kennedy met matching requirements within weeks, if not days, of their announcements. It was a measure of the difficulty the campaign was experiencing in getting its fund-raising act together that Ben Fernandez, the GOP Hispanic candidate, and Lyndon La Rouche, the candidate of the offbeat United States Labor Party, actually met the requirements sooner than Anderson.

Anderson began to find what in the campaign trade were called "little angels" to shepherd fund-raising efforts in selected places: Max Stanley, an industrialist, quickly made arrangements for the money we needed to meet our matching quota in Iowa; David Kotek, an activist in Jewish causes in New Jersey, took a fancy to Anderson early on and promptly raised the money he needed from his state (for a while, the accountant in Rockford, who received the checks of contributors to Anderson's campaign, imagined that Vineland, New Jersey, must be the richest city in the United States, so many checks was he getting from its residents—of course, it turned out to be just David Kotek's hometown); Alphonso Bell, an oilman and former congressman in Los Angeles, helped to round up some California contributions; and in New York, a number of prominent people offered their assistance, including Robin Farkas (of the Alexander's department store chain), Andy Heiskell (chairman of the board of Time, Incorporated), John Sawhill (president of New York University and soon to join the Carter administration as deputy secretary of energy), and Larry Rockefeller (son of Laurance and nephew of Nelson).

In addition to these individual efforts, which generally took the form of fund-raisers our patrons agreed to host, the campaign experimented with a limited program of mass mailings to targeted groups of cause-oriented liberals who were thought to be particularly receptive to political solicitations. Peter Taggart of Santa Barbara handled the mailings, and urged Anderson to approve letters of a somewhat negative tone in the interest of inciting people to respond. Anderson demurred for a while, and the matter was debated internally in the campaign, but finally he relented in view of the campaign's financial desperation. Taggart prepared a letter which voiced alarm on Anderson's part about the onslaughts of the far right. In part, the letter read: "[If someone like Anderson is not nominated] it will be a Republican Party far different from those of Dwight Eisenhower or Gerald Ford—or even Richard Nixon. . . . It will be a Republican Party determined to destroy every humanistic federal program, roll back the progress we've made in civil rights, and carry on an ultra-nationalistic foreign policy and massive nuclear weapons buildup."

Still, finances remained a dependable source of frustration. One evening when we were in New York, Robin Farkas hosted a dinner for about a dozen people in Anderson's honor. (We had discovered Robin in the process of asking around for free overnight accommodations, to spare the campaign the hefty expense of New York hotel prices.) The dinner was held at the elegant University Club in midtown Manhattan, and was meant merely as a social gathering; no money would be raised. Just by coincidence, as we came into the club, Anderson spotted a marquee which announced that a reception was being held that same night in one of the large rooms for fellow candidate George Bush. Sensing Anderson's curiosity, I promised to scout it out and report back. By the time I arrived at the Bush reception, most of the guests had left, but the room was of such a size as to indicate that it had been, by our standards at least, a very large affair. Apparently it had been a stand-up reception with a cash bar. I bumped into someone and asked him how it had gone. He turned out to be one of Bush's brothers. He told me—somewhat gleefully, after I explained my affiliation—that the event had raised about $50,000. Bush had left early because he had had still *another* event to attend. I gulped as I heard all of this, and wondered whether I should tell Anderson the gory details; it was bound to produce only a sigh of frustration. With the exception of the "Salute to John Anderson" dinner held in Rockford the night of Anderson's announcement, we had not reached the point where we even charged admission to a fund-raiser. Our fear, probably well-founded, was that people would not otherwise attend. Working with a fund-raising department of about two-and-a-half people, it would have taken us several weeks to arrange anything on the scale of the Bush reception, and yet Bush was doing this sort of thing practically every night of the week. It did not surprise us when we learned later that the Federal Election Commission reports filed through June put Bush's total contributions to date at over $1.5 million, compared to something under $200,000 for ourselves.

The next morning, I arrived early at the Farkas apartment to pick Anderson up for our round of appointments. He looked very tired. He told me he had had a restless sleep thinking about the ease with which Bush was raising money, and the incredible difficulties we were experiencing. He just did not see how we would ever be able to make the grade. "We don't have any of those fancy Ivy League connections," he said.

Meanwhile, up in New Hampshire, Anderson's young pollster, Dick Bennett, conducted a survey in August of 300 likely Republican voters. He found that in terms of name identification, Reagan stood at 99 percent, Baker at 61 percent, Bush at 50 percent, and Anderson at 28 percent. (Anderson's standing was near the bottom of the totem poll, but it was encouraging to think that so many people had heard of him. Presumably this was a result of local newspaper stories about his numerous visits to the state, as well as news wrap-ups that were done regularly on the whole presidential field, although the cynical among us always suspected that the name "John Anderson" simply had a ring to it that made it sound familiar to people.) Bennett convinced us to run a newspaper ad campaign to improve Anderson's name-identification further. Newspapers were to be preferred to radio, he argued, because the type of younger, educated voters we wanted to target apparently listened mainly to the larger Boston radio stations, on which advertising would be quite expensive, rather than to local New Hampshire stations. Bennett maintained that much of what was being written or said about Anderson was not really registering with people, because they still did not recognize his name. Until they knew it, they would tend to skip over or ignore it. The newspaper ads would be placed on two consecutive Mondays in each of the eight dailies in the state. They would be written with extreme simplicity so that virtually everyone would see them, absorb them, and perhaps be intrigued enough to seek more information, or at least to tune in better the next time they ran across John Anderson's name. Each ad took up about a third of a newspaper page. The first advertisement had only two lines, but they were in big block letters.

"JOHN WHO?"
"JOHN ANDERSON, REPUBLICAN FOR PRESIDENT."

The sequel ran exactly one week later, only slightly elaborated.

"JOHN WHO?"
"JOHN ANDERSON."
"OH, YEAH. JOHN ANDERSON. HE'S RUNNING FOR PRESIDENT."

These ads did indeed succeed in their limited purpose of circulating Anderson's name, at least to judge from the number of people we ran into the following January who mentioned that they had seen them. Of course, it was merely an effort directed at elementary name identification, rather than one meant to project tangible political or intellectual information about Anderson. As a result, while Anderson's name identification improved, this did not immediately translate into better standings in the more important *preference* polls. It concerned us that the one candidate we assumed would pose our greatest competition for moderate voters, Howard Baker, was doing very well. But Bennett reassured us that Baker's standing was probably less a reflection of his own popularity than it was of widespread dissatisfaction among voters with the two other prominent Republican choices, Ronald Reagan and John Connally. His own conclusion was that the field was ripe for expanding.

The campaign took on a new flavor around mid-September, when our first field office was officially opened for business. It was located at 37 Warren Street in Concord, New Hampshire, just two blocks removed from the main avenue of business downtown. All the office consisted of at this time was the first floor of a slightly peeling yellow frame house, and on the morning of the grand opening, it could barely accommodate the contingent of ten or so local reporters who, along with several bulky TV cameras, descended upon it. Presiding at this outpost was Elizabeth Hager, a young and irrepressibly cheerful state legislator, whose unflagging spirits and enormous dedication typified that of our other state coordinators at the time: Jane Fowler in Massachusetts, Jeanne Bradner in Illinois, and Ann Peckham in Wisconsin. All were women of a moderate Republican stripe, active in state party politics. Far from attracting the cause-oriented liberals who would flock to the campaign late in its independent phase, it was representative of Anderson's appeal at this time that he should have working for him supporters more likely to be involved in League of Women Voters or "good government" type activities than in antinuclear demonstrations.

In conjunction with the campaign's heightened presence in the state, Keke had decided to move up there herself for a period of time, as a means of supplementing the campaign's efforts and of crossing paths with her husband, who was beginning to spend more time there than in Washington. A friend of the Andersons had offered the use of a vacation house in a small town about an hour's drive north of Concord, and so it seemed an ideal arrangement. What Keke had not bargained for, however, was the ramshackle quality of the house, its primitive amenities and desolate location, and the raw New England weather. But Keke showed herself to be an energetic and resourceful campaigner. One day, for example, as she was driving, she stopped at a house she happened to pass, because the mailbox out front said "Anderson," and she figured there might reside therein someone with a natual affinity for supporting her candidate-husband. Another time, she pulled into a trailer park to distribute leaflets, and, knocking at one door, chanced to come across the mother of Senator Bob Dole's first wife, with whom she then sat down and practically converted to supporting Anderson. Keke had the use of the Andersons' leased station wagon, which my fianceé Margot and I had driven up one weekend from Washington. It was bright red in color, plastered with bumper stickers, and driving around in it, Keke was the perfect picture of a political den mother, doing whatever chores were necessary to get her husband elected.

For the rest of the campaign, Keke would remain constantly on the go. She became actively involved in all aspects of the campaign effort, had strong opinions on how it should be run, and exerted a decisive influence in many of her husband's decisions. The Andersons had an eight-year old daughter to raise, but their other three daughters and one son were much older and fairly independent; this freed Keke to devote almost full time to her husband's political activities, something family responsibilities had never before permitted. She was ten years younger than her husband, slim, attractive, entirely unaffected, and down-to-earth. If her husband sometimes seemed academic and aloof, Keke was vivacious and occasionally even fiery, a trait she proudly attributed to her Greek heritage. She was generally more liberal in political disposition than her husband, and the two frequently engaged, even publicly, in heated political arguments.

Keke's exuberance was often a good influence on her husband, keeping him lively, but it did not please everyone. She insisted on supervising campaign activities closely, ruffling many a feather among campaign staff by the summary manner in which she tended to intercede in decisions; one short-lived campaign manager, Dan Swillinger, attempted at one point to withhold her airplane tickets in an effort to prevent her from returning to New Hampshire, where she had gained a reputation for having ideas on how to do things that regularly diverged from those of the local campaign staff. Keke's instincts, however, were often quite good, and she sometimes showed a flexibility and imagination that a more bureaucratic campaign headquarters tended to lack. Above all, Keke was supremely loyal to what she perceived to be her husband's interests. Indeed, she could become furious with anyone—particularly members of the press—who expressed criticism of him. But she and her husband enjoyed a close and affectionate relationship, and Anderson would not have had the motivation to keep running against all the odds had she not provided constant support and encouragement.

In New Hampshire, Anderson just kept plugging away: on campaign trips to Concord, and Keene, and Portsmouth, and Dover, and

Hanover, and Lebanon. He gave frequent issue-oriented speeches; we put out a never-ending stream of press releases; money was raised and media appearances were scheduled. Still Anderson remained obscure. One day a reporter asked him how he was ever going to attain enough publicity to become a major contender. He replied, with his tongue only partly in his cheek: "I call in my staff every morning, and I upbraid them. I say, 'What have you done in your sleeping hours or your waking hours to think up things that can make me famous?' And they sheepishly slink out of here saying they have not yet thought of anything." Neither had Anderson, so we were even.

Even when the press did cover Anderson, it never ceased to amaze us what they wrote about. When a candidate became famous, he could often set the terms: many of his statements, if they were made emphatically enough, would be reported. But when a candidate was unknown—and hence presumed to be of little interest to the public—he was often covered only when he did or said something extremely unusual, or perhaps funny, or when whatever he did or said lent itself to a preconceived point a reporter was trying to make. Later in the campaign, it was easy to empathize with Barry Commoner, the Citizens' party candidate, when he resorted to using foul language to attract press attention, so little did the press seem to be interested in anything more civilized he was saying. It is true that Anderson received a fair amount of one-shot national publicity at the time of his announcement in June, for his speech on the floor of the House against the antibusing amendment in August, and on the occasion of his formal introduction of gas-tax legislation in December. But other than that, it is revealing what episodes gained for him his greatest publicity during all his months of thoughtful speeches and hard work in 1979.

One major press story had to do with our Washington campaign headquarters having been robbed of several small electrical appliances. Jokingly, we prepared a press release dismissing the incident as a "third-rate burglary." Everyone saw the Watergate reference, thought it cute, and the report of the burglary and our reaction to it constituted network news that night. The other great splash we made was later in the fall, when Anderson made the offhand comment that his campaign had been so successful to date that he was no longer an "asterisk" in the polls, but had actually achieved a percentage. The "asterisk" comment, which seemed to sum up the poignant plight of the underdog, was widely quoted for months. Everyone in the world seemed to have heard these two stories. This may have been a reflection not merely of the volume of press copy they generated, but their placement in the "people" sections of magazines and newspapers, sections that are probably read much more than ordinary news articles. Anderson was not going to win as much attention saying anything else until the night of the New Hampshire primary the following February, when he was asked in an interview with John Chancellor whether in light of his 10 percent showing, he would continue as a candidate. Anderson replied, "I will go on, just as long as I have clean laundry." That, too, was a comment heard 'round the world.

But, in general, getting Anderson his due in the press was one continual exercise in frustration. He had been proposing his fifty-cent gas tax since early summer, for example, and talking about it at every opportunity. In early December, *Time* magazine ran a lengthy story on what the various candidates were saying about energy. Yet the conclusion the story reached was that the 1980 field was "producing no ideas that seem much different" from President Carter's, but only "an array of me-too remedies" that "rehash the safe, the secure, and the unexciting." How could *Time* have reached such an erroneous conclusion? Very simply. They did not consider John Anderson a real candidate. They talked about Jimmy Carter, Ronald Reagan, Ted Kennedy, Jerry Brown, John Connally, Howard Baker, and George Bush . . . but no John Anderson, no Phil Crane, no Bob Dole. This despite the fact that Anderson was an officially declared candidate, had been a leading congressman for two decades, and was something more, one liked to think, than a flake or a screwball.

In an effort to redress the oversight, I called several of the correspondents at *Time* to be sure they knew of the gas-tax proposal. A couple of them were particularly intrigued; because of a new interest the administration was showing on the subject, *Time* was thinking of running a major story. Our office provided them considerable information as to the theory and the numbers behind the gas tax. Eagerly we looked forward to the next issue of *Time*, expecting to see prominent mention made of Anderson's role in the new gas tax debate. Sure enough, a large two-page story appeared on the gas tax, but nowhere in the story did the name John Anderson appear. It was almost impossible to believe. It would have been like printing a story on a 30 percent across-the-board reduction in taxes, and not mentioning Kemp, Roth, or Reagan. The omission was so obvious as to seem virtually deliberate. I called *Time* to protest, and Keke called some *Time* executives as well. The answer was the same: We would have been happy to mention you, but we have space limitations. Why they could not find room for an integral two words— "John Anderson"—somewhere in such an unusually long story was not self-evident. Shortly after this episode, Margot received a letter from her parents, who lived in London but were avid readers of *Time.* "You know," they wrote, "what the U.S. needs is a big gas tax, like they have over here. Anderson could get a lot of publicity if he proposed one." Margot and I read the letter, and groaned.

Another remarkable instance of inequitable press treatment occurred in October and November of 1979, on the subject of the famine then taking place in Cambodia. Anderson, along with Congressman Stephen Solarz of New York, had introduced the first bill in the Congress to provide aid for famine relief. Anderson and Solarz were, at the time, the only public figures in Washington talking about the subject, and talk about it they did at every opportunity. Anderson went one day to testify before a House subcommittee, and gave his most impassioned plea. I had called no fewer than forty reporters to let them know in advance of the testimony. The reaction was virtually the same everywhere. "Oh, yeah, Anderson, he's running for president, isn't he? Well, we'll try to make it." Of course, no one showed up. Anderson was simply not yet newsworthy. On the other hand, three weeks later, Ted Kennedy decided to take up the subject. Suddenly, the Cambodian famine was propelled into the headlines. Lest Kennedy bask in all the limelight, Jimmy Carter was immediately moved to take it up as well. The headlines grew even bolder. Soon it was the biggest news of the day. For the entire previous month, I had been calling the morning news shows just about every other day, urging them to put Anderson on the air to talk about the Cambodian famine. "No, thanks," came the reply. "No one wants to hear about it." Now, the news shows suddenly decided it was newsworthy. The famine had not worsened. The only difference was the personalities who were talking about it.

In fairness, it should be said that the networks in late 1979 did each run one obligatory interview with Anderson, presumably so that they would be able to say that they had given every candidate his day in court, and had exposed the voters to all the choices. (Anderson did quite well in the interviews. After Anderson's five minute interview with Walter Cronkite aired in late November, Jack Valenti, the motion picture executive, penned Anderson a note in appropriate cinematic terms: "You were superb . . . poised, confident, and believable . . . a first-rate performance." And, after Anderson had finished taping a similar interview at NBC, John Chancellor was overheard to tell one of his colleagues that Anderson had given the best interview of any candidate.) The networks also made an honorable effort to air a number of preliminary "issues" pieces, illuminating the positions of the candidates on selected topics. But when it came to the Republican candidates, almost always only the Big Four (Reagan, Connally, Baker, and Bush) were covered. It is true that Anderson was fortunate by this time to have accumulated a large volume of excellent columns and editorials; but we soon learned that those were simply not the source of news to most people. John Anderson was not destined to "exist" until his name was repeatedly broadcast on the network news or emblazoned in newspaper headlines.

That we no longer found such treatment surprising made it no less galling. In time, realizing we could not lick reality, we gave in to the temptation to join it. Minor candidates soon discover that their chances of making news increase if they ride the coattails of others more famous. When Connally came out with his bold "peace plan" for the Mideast, for example, we lost no time in denouncing it, not only because Anderson genuinely disagreed with it, but because we knew that stories would be written about reaction to the plan, and our comments might fit in. So we took the kid gloves off and charged that Connally's remarks "displayed a shocking insensitivity to history and a cavalier disregard for true peace." When I phoned in this statement to the various people on my press lists, I could just sense their ears perking up. The stronger and more colorful the quote, the likelier it was to see the light of day. There is no question that the anticipated reaction of the press influenced our statements on matters like this; the press almost forced us to exaggerate our positions in order to win coverage. In one particularly explicit case, the producer of "Issues and Answers" hinted to me that whether Anderson was chosen as a guest one particular week was contingent on whether he would be willing to make a strong statement on the subject of Iran. With studied ambiguity, I implied that he would, and he got on. After the first few minutes of his interview proved disappointingly mild to her, she turned to me in the control booth and said, "Can't you slip him a note to say something stronger?" Even news show producers were interested in ratings.

In our frustration to be taken seriously, to break out of our anonymity, to contend with the other candidates on an equal footing, the campaign decided in late 1979 to make preliminary contact with a well-known New York media strategist named David Garth. I had taken the initiative to suggest to Anderson and Mike MacLeod, Anderson's administrative assistant, that we set up a meeting. Later I was to rue the day that we had ever done this, but at the time it seemed perfectly logical. The way for a dark horse candidate to obtain instant stature and credibility in the eyes of the political experts and the press would be to bathe in Garth's reflected glory. If he were to help us, it would be a sign to the outside world both that he thought we had a chance and that our campaign could be expected to shift in its style from amateur to professional. None of us had ever met Garth before, and probably would not have recognized him on the street. His name, however, was a different matter; we knew it very well. Garth was regarded with awe among political professionals as someone whose TV commercials and advertising strategies had accomplished the election of numerous major candidates, many of them at one time underdogs. We did not know anything, however, about his philosophies or his techniques.

Garth's offices on Fifth Avenue in New York were unassuming. They were modest in their decor and had the informal and occasionally frenetic atmosphere of a campaign. A couple of young women sat in the front office answering phones and, between calls, clipping newspaper articles. In some of the adjoining rooms, college-age young people could be seen using the Xerox machine, talking earnestly on telephones, rushing to and fro. When we arrived, we were asked to wait for some time, then ushered into a small, rectangular room which had a long table and some chairs arranged around it. Apparently this was the conference room. A TV set was at one end. Within a few minutes, a young man came in, somewhat chubby and disheveled, and without explanation said, "Well, I'll play for you some TV ads from our previous campaigns." We took this to be a part of the standard sales pitch for clients, even though we had not given any indication as yet that we were interested in purchasing Garth's services. We did not need to be convinced that Garth produced good ads; we needed to be told we could afford them.

In the meantime, Garth was still nowhere to be seen, and all we had been told was that he was being delayed at lunch. And so, for a while, the thought ran through our minds that perhaps this grand organization called Garth and Associates was in fact only a Wizard of Oz operation where Garth lent his name and reputation but where the real work was done by young people who looked like prodigies recently graduated from the Bronx High School of Science. An hour after we arrived, Garth finally came in. Looking back, one suspects it may have been standard operating procedure to keep clients waiting, to impress upon them who the important party was in the relationship.

Garth told us that he had been approached by every other Republican candidate with the exception of Reagan, but that of all the GOP candidates, he would be inclined to help only us. Although Garth was known for working with the campaigns of liberal Democrats, he hinted that he would prefer us even to Kennedy. We were flattered, and asked Garth his price for providing us a Boston-based media package directed just toward the crucial first two primaries, New Hampshire and Massachusetts. Garth turned to his young assistant, and asked him for a calculation. Well, they finally concluded, probably something in the range of $100,000 to $150,000, *plus* production costs, *plus* the standard 15 percent commission for purchasing time on TV, *plus* the TV time itself. We did not need time to contemplate the offer; such sums were well beyond our reach, and Garth did not seem like the type of person who would have volunteered to help us on a *pro bono* basis.

Sensing that we were not about to make a deal, we thought we could at least ask Garth for a few minutes of offhand advice on how our dark-horse campaign might proceed at this point. Garth—short, round, and cigar-chomping— leaned back for a moment and blew a few puffs. Then he came on in his rapid-fire way: "Well, you should schedule editorial board meetings with the *New York Times* and some magazines like *Newsweek.*" Of course, we had done exactly that long before; we had gone considerably beyond what Garth was recommending. Yet this was pretty much the sum of his advice. The rest of the time he gave us his general views on how the presidential race was shaping up. Everything he said he stated authoritatively, and in very pungent political terms, conforming to one's image of a clever consultant and strategist. And yet, after we left, having spent close to an hour with him, Anderson, MacLeod, and I had the same impression as we compared notes in the taxi to the next stop: Garth's political genius had not been immediately obvious. He had not imparted any exceptionally perceptive analysis, nor suggested to us anything particularly creative or original. That was the one thing Anderson had been hungering after: some new concept as to how we could run the campaign; some new ideas for what we could be saying; a strategy that would allow us to short-circuit the normal requirement of having to slog out the campaign on the primary trails, where organization and money, which we did not have, counted for so much. And yet, there was something about Garth, his cultivated air of importance and infallibility, and his undisputed reputation for success, which kept us intrigued. We could not do anything for now, but we resolved to get back in touch with him if the day ever arrived that we were able to afford his services.

Back on the ranch, things fell to a level of great discouragement in November. Howard Baker had declared for president around the first of the month. His announcement, held in the historic Senate Caucus Room, with crowds of spectators overflowing into the corridors, had all the aura of a president in-the-making. If a moderate had a chance in the GOP, conventional wisdom assumed, that moderate would be Howard Baker, not John Anderson. In the question and answer period, Baker was asked how he thought the Republican field looked at the moment. He replied that Reagan was the clear front-runner, he himself was second, John Connally was third, "and that's about the way it stacks up." No one challenged him on the point. From the perspective of the people in this room, John Anderson was no better than a fringe candidate.

Almost directly from his announcement, Baker flew to Maine to participate in a GOP convention at which a staw ballot would be held. (Straw ballots were informal polls occasionally taken of people attending party conclaves. Since they were the one item of hard news such gatherings produced as to where the candidates stood, they received considerable attention, and great efforts were made to stack or cultivate audiences accordingly. In consequence, the results were all the more unscientific; but that did not deter fierce competition.) The Baker strategy was that an expected landslide at the convention—the popular Senator Bill Cohen of Maine, after all, was a strong Baker supporter—would make for an auspicious beginning to his campaign. What happened, however, was a terrible upset for Baker: by a few votes, George Bush edged him out. The next day, Bush's name was catapulted into the headlines across the country. Everyone assumed that Baker must have been the most shattered man on earth that morning. Not so. At least Baker had won something like 400 votes. John Anderson had received four.

It was not as though Anderson had failed to try. He had been to the convention, given a speech, and had one of Maine's two congressmen, David Emery, working in his behalf. Something, however, had just not clicked. A couple of days later, when Anderson was back in Washington, he, Keke, MacLeod, and I went down for lunch to the crowded Longworth cafeteria, in the basement of his congressional office building. We stood in line for sandwiches, then found a table off to a side of the room where we could talk discreetly. The question did not have to be stated explicitly, because it was so obviously on all our minds: should Anderson stay in the race or get out? Was he just setting himself up for further humiliation if he stuck it out all the way until the February 28 primary in New Hampshire? What if he got only 2 or 3 percent of the vote? Would it not be better to leave gracefully right now? I made the argument for continuing to plug away a while, until more results were in. We could always withdraw in January, if things looked equally miserable then, if the polls looked bad, if we were not raising any money. Meantime, there was no need to burn our bridges immediately. Maybe, for some reason, things would brighten up. The others seemed to have similar sentiments. Anderson would keep going.

But this did not entirely improve Anderson's mood. Dan Balz of the *Washington Post* interviewed him in mid-November along the campaign trail in Evanston, Illinois. The story he did on Anderson was a sad and poignant one. It was prominently placed on page two in the *Post*, and, for many people in Washington, given the rarity of Anderson stories, may have been the first extended piece they had read on him. Anderson had the Maine convention on his mind. "I don't kid myself," he said. "I make a lot of speeches that don't make news. But I made a speech at that cattle show in Maine. The national media were there. I thought it was a significant speech, different than the others, in which I decried missile madness. Republicans aren't supposed to talk that way. But not a word of it appeared in print." So why was he running for president? Balz quoted him this way: "'After spending an adult life of unfulfilled dreams and promises, a man has to prove something to himself,' he says, finishing his Scotch. 'Maybe I'm trying to sum it all up to convince myself that everything I've been doing makes sense.' And so his real motivation is simply explained. 'I guess,' says Anderson, 'I just want to get it all off my chest before I close up the books.' "

Our depths of despair lingered, but gradually gave way again to campaign business as usual. Around Christmas, Margot and I joined the Andersons for a couple of memorable excursions. One evening we went over to the Maryland home of Gloria Steinem, the feminist, and Stan Pottinger, a former official of the Ford Justice Department, for a pre-Christmas dinner. Apparently they had been interested in meeting Anderson because of their admiration for the strong positions he was taking on women's issues. Gloria immediately struck us as being anything but the stereotype of a strident feminist. She came out to greet us in a red satin jump suit, wore long nails and a ring studded with diamonds, spoke in a soft and feminine voice, and acted as a very traditional hostess. The only sign that she might have had an occasional progressive tendency was that her maids called her by her first name. The evening was totally relaxed and informal. At one point, as we were assembled in the dining room, a dozen kids from the neighborhood who were out caroling came to the door. Gloria invited them inside, and they stood around our table and sang. Stan rushed into the kitchen and returned with extra eggnog and glasses to serve the visitors. Several of the youngsters recognized Steinem, but of course none recognized Anderson. After dinner, we retired to the living room and, sitting by a crackling fire, Gloria went through her address book and provided us with the names of celebrities she said she would be happy to call in our behalf to see if they would be interested in helping the campaign. Not so many of these ideas panned out, but it was a lovely gesture, and it made for just the right yuletide spirit.

A few days later, Margot and I drove out with the Andersons to Baltimore, to have lunch with Milton Eisenhower, younger brother of the late President. The occasion had an interesting background. Over Thanksgiving, I happened to come across a somewhat dated *Time* magazine on an airplane flight. In it was a Hugh Sidey column about Milton Eisenhower, in which Sidey quoted him as saying he thought the nation was in desperate straits, and that the times required a president of demonstrated independence and creativity. As yet, Eisenhower indicated, he had not seen a candidate on the horizon to fit that bill. It was obvious that we had to let Milton Eisenhower know about John Anderson. We wrote to him, suggesting that he need look no farther for a candidate. A correspondence was struck up. Soon, Eisenhower wrote back:

> I am waiting for a candidate who has the political courage to tell the American people the truth about the threatening problems this nation faces. Insidious inflation, tremendous imbalances in international payments, the energy problem, crime so serious it is changing the character of American life—these and other pressing problems—what are we proposing to do about them? I mean it: I await a candiate who is willing to speak honestly, even if some of the things he must say seem politically unpopular, especially with respect to selfish pressure groups.

We replied, citing Anderson's various positions and proposals. Eisenhower wrote again, indicating that he was giving Anderson some thought, and saying: "I am convinced that the people of this country are desperately worried and are looking for a leader who will have the courage to tell them the whole truth, and the hard, unpopular things we must go through to regain stability. Such a person might be swept into office."

After receiving this letter, we set up an appointment to meet him. Eisenhower lived in an unpretentious subdivision near the campus of Johns Hopkins University, where he had once been president. His modern townhouse was decorated elegantly. We sat first in the living room, surrounded by many mementos of the careers of both Eisenhowers, then joined him for a simple but gracious lunch. Eisenhower said many interesting things during the four hours that we were with him. He argued, for example, that it was difficult to support Reagan because he would be just about as old entering office as Dwight Eisenhower had been leaving office, and people, Milton noted, usually thought of his brother as being old. Reagan would not be agile enough to withstand the rigors of the office, he believed.

But the main message Eisenhower sought to leave with us was that, as he had said repeatedly in his letters, America was waiting for a president who was willing to make hard choices and to take independent stands. Commentators were already beginning to note such a strength of character about Anderson. But Eisenhower talked about it the most eloquently that day in Baltimore, and as the campaign season of 1980 was about to begin, at long last a clear sense was emerging of how John Anderson might eventually set himself apart.

4

January–February, 1980: The Primaries Begin

The Republican presidential debate in Des Moines, Iowa, on the evening of January 5, 1980, proved a clear turning point in the fortunes of the Anderson campaign. It was the sort of event we had all hoped would one day come along and afford John Anderson the opportunity he so desperately needed to be seen by a larger public. If people only had the chance to see him, we were sure, they would like what they saw and the campaign would begin to take off. The people who saw the Iowa debate on television were limited in number, but were sufficient to provide a core of nationwide support which would in time have the potential to snowball into much larger proportions.

Incredible as it seemed in retrospect, Anderson had almost not attended the Iowa debate. An invitation had been issued to him in December, but the campaign's political director, acting unbeknownst in his behalf, initially declined it. Virtually everyone else involved in the campaign had instinctively assumed that it would be an extraordinary opportunity for the candidate, given the heavy national publicity that participants could expect to receive, and the likelihood that Anderson, a skilled debater, would shine in comparison to the other candidates.

Not so the political director, a twenty-six-year-old former Anderson research assistant who had been tapped for the position in part because he was willing to travel in the field at subsistence pay and to sleep by night on folding cots in the homes of volunteers. He began with the same premise everyone shared: that no matter what

Anderson did, he would not win many votes in the Iowa precinct caucuses later in January, since a lack of resources and organization had prevented him from campaigning in the state. From that premise, he reasoned that it would look worse if Anderson appeared to be trying—for example, by participating in a major event in Iowa such as the debate—than if he were seen *not* to be trying, and therefore not participating in the debate.

Such an argument had a plausible logic, but in the end did not square with reality. We flattered ourselves to think that many people would notice whether or not Anderson had actively campaigned in Iowa; all they would see were the raw results the day after the caucuses. If he had 5 percent, it would look better than 1 percent. People would not say, "Oh, 1 percent, that's okay. Anderson wasn't even trying." Rather, they would say: "1 percent! That Anderson's really at the bottom of the heap." It seemed clear that participating in the Iowa debate was an easy way of gaining an extra few percentage points in our vote totals.

But even more importantly, the Iowa debate represented a rare opportunity for national exposure. Originally it was to have been televised on all three networks. This, however, was when both a Democratic and a Republican presidential debate were scheduled to be held. When Carter withdrew from the Democratic debate, citing his responsibility to mind the hostage situation, the networks decided that they might not carry the Republican debate either. The one of real interest was that between Carter and Kennedy. The Republican debate would not be so noteworthy both because front-runner Reagan had announced he would not be attending, and because there was not the element of excitement present in the Republican race that there was in the Democratic race, what with someone of the political stature of Ted Kennedy challenging an incumbent president of the same party. One sensed that the networks had agreed to cover the Republican debate mainly out of a public service obligation to treat both party debates equally. As it turned out, only the Public Broadcasting Service aired the debate live, although CBS carried it on a delayed basis beginning in some areas at 11:30 P.M. While this was nothing compared to the prime-time multinetwork coverage we had once envisaged, it still represented an audience much more vast than anything Anderson had addressed before; furthermore, reports of the debate could be expected to fill large newspaper stories the next day.

One weekend in late December, Margot and I happened to see the Andersons at their home in Bethesda. I told them that my parents, who lived in California, had sent me a clipping from one of their papers which indicated that only Reagan and Anderson had declined invitations to the Iowa debate. "Are we really declining?" I asked. This was hard to believe. "Who's declining?" Anderson asked. "I don't know anything about it." The Andersons had not been told. They could not believe it either. It did not take long to make a decision. "Of course we're going," Keke said.

On the afternoon of the debate, we arrived in Des Moines. As we walked off the airplane ramp into the indoor waiting area, a small but vocal group, much to our surprise, was awaiting Anderson's arrival. Several local boosters, who had signed up on the basis of having heard Anderson during a rare previous appearance in the state, stood with several makeshift placards and cheered their candidate as he approached. Even a TV crew from a local station was there to greet him. The other passengers from the plane, disembarking along with us, surveyed the scene quizzically, wondering what celebrity had been in their midst, or, if they had read John Anderson's name on our supporters' signs, wondering which one he was, or perhaps *who* he was.

Anderson, a briefcase in hand and a suitbag slung over his shoulder, nodded appreciatively toward his supporters, and paused for a couple of minutes to shake their hands and thank them for coming. The camera crew came forward, and Anderson told an interviewer how much he was looking forward to the debate that evening. I nudged him away, and we started walking toward the main terminal area. A husky farmer who happened to be nearby looking on, stepped across Anderson's path and stopped him. "Listen here," the farmer said, his denim overalls contrasting starkly with Anderson's subdued business suit, "I hope you don't believe in this here grain embargo of Carter's." In fact, Anderson had been supporting the president's embargo, having called it necessary to signal American displeasure with the recent Soviet invasion of Afghanistan. Indeed, Anderson had been one of the few Republicans to step forward in Carter's defense on this issue. Midwestern farmers, however, were irate, contending it would hurt them rather than the Soviets, who could turn to other sources of supply. In this particular circumstance, something told Anderson that discretion was the better part of valor, and so he politely thanked the farmer for his opinion, said he would reflect on it, and then walked away, for once thanking his lucky stars that his name and his stands on the issues were still so obscure.

We collected our luggage, walked out of the terminal, and then jumped into what for us was an impressive two-car caravan that would take us to our lodgings. Anderson, Keke, and I crowded into the back seat of one of the cars, and were briefed on some of the logistical arrangements for the debate by our driver, Luther Hill, who for a long time would be the mainstay of our campaign effort in Iowa. Luther was the scion of a local newspaper family, and always seemed to have a new luxury car at his disposal whenever he met us. It reassured us to think that our support was of such high quality, in the same way that one might consider one's money particularly safe if it were housed in a grand and prosperous-looking bank building.

Luther took us straightaway to the downtown Ramada Hotel, where rooms had been reserved. We felt disappointed not being able to stay at Hotel Fort Des Moines, a fancier hostelry where most of the other candidates, as well as two of the network news operations, were being quartered, and which was also in closer proximity to the civic center where the debate was to be held that evening. Unfortunately, by the time Anderson had accepted the debate invitation, few rooms in Des Moines remained available, and if the management of Hotel Fort Des Moines did in fact have some flexibility in rearranging guest accommodations, the Anderson campaign clearly did not have the clout to persuade them to do so.

In any case, Anderson's first requirement was to have a hotel with an indoor swimming pool; although his discipline would flag a little, of necessity, as the campaign wore on, this was still a time when he made a strong effort to maintain his long-time regimen of swimming a half a mile a day. The other candidates, for their part, were less interested in immersing themselves in water than in briefing books. Anderson always took a much more casual attitude toward such preparation. This concerned me somewhat, because it was reminiscent of the overconfident way Richard Nixon was said to have treated his ill-fated debate in 1960 with John Kennedy. Like Nixon, Anderson seemed to feel that, after all these years studying national issues, it would be an acknowledgment of inadequacy to have to prepare. And so he had spent valuable time the night before at a party in Boston, and then consumed his entire morning in traveling to Des Moines, when instead he might have been reading in a relaxed environment, resting, and otherwise psyching himself up for the night's big event. When he reached his hotel room, with just hours to go, it was clear that he had a few natural first-night jitters. He expressed regret that he had not come out to Des Moines sooner. But he cleared his mind with a swim, and returned to his room, ready to spend at least a little time with a large black briefing book we had brought along. He glanced through it for five or ten minutes, then put it aside somewhat impatiently as if he knew all he wanted and now only wished to get on with the debate.

The story behind the preparation of the briefing book was one that revealed a good deal about the needs of a candidate and the often divergent imperatives of his own campaign organization. Knowing that Anderson would appreciate reading material in advance of the debate, several members of our staff had prepared short question-and-answer sheets on various topics in the fields of defense, foreign affairs, energy, the economy, politics, and the like. Two weeks before the debate, all the necessary papers had been collected and were about to be turned over to Anderson for his leisurely perusal. Just then, however, we got a call from Cliff Brown, our part-time director of research, who had been out of town, had not yet seen the material, and requested time now to review it. He wanted to be sure it was in tip-top form, and, this being a Thursday, promised that Anderson would have it by Saturday, as Anderson had requested.

Cliff was highly intelligent and hardworking, but he also happened to be a perfectionist. As a result, he created for himself the task of rewriting every single question and answer that had been prepared, as well as completely reorganizing their order. This may have been an improvement, but the problem was that he had to stay up two consecutive nights to do it, and still, by 1:00 A.M. Saturday morning, he had not completed the task. He phoned me at that point and apologized that the briefing book would not be ready when Anderson wanted it, but endeavored to justify this on the grounds that it would be unworthy to give a candidate something that was not impeccably professional. As a result I had the duty on Saturday to inform Anderson that the briefing book was still in preparation. He was mystified. He could not have cared less that the questions and answers were not perfectly phrased; all he wanted was something he could thumb through quickly as an exercise to put himself in the right frame of mind for a debate. Whenever Anderson used a briefing book, it took him only a few minutes to realize that he knew just about everything it contained already, but that was an important realization, for it gave him a self-confidence which was often what he was really seeking. For this purpose, he generally would have preferred an imperfect book sooner to a perfect one later. He could never understand why the people working for him were often much fussier than he was.

In the late afternoon, I went with another Anderson staffer to the Des Moines Civic Center to scout the physical situation which would await Anderson that evening at the debate. We were handed badges that identified us as representatives of the Anderson campaign, so that we would be admitted by security personnel to otherwise private areas. Suddenly it was sinking in that Anderson was to be treated, at least for purposes of the debate, as a serious contender like all the others. He would share the same platform on stage, and have exactly the same amount of time to speak. The same number of people would hear him as would hear John Connally or Howard Baker or Bob Dole or George Bush. Of course, the other candidates were still heads above us in some departments. Several of them, for example, had already had big teams of advance men breeze through the civic center paving their way and creating a general aura of expectation. I remember wondering at the time whether there was something I was neglecting to do to help prepare for Anderson's arrival. What had all those advance men been doing for the other candidates? Whatever they had been doing, it seemed, was superfluous. All Anderson needed to do was to come in the right door, and from there one of the hosts of the event would escort him the rest of the way. The fact that his staff had not prepared for him a minute-by-minute schedule or a detailed map of the dressing room area hardly seemed likely to upset his equilibrium or impede his debate performance.

I returned to the hotel, and not much later we were all in Luther Hill's car again, heading toward the debate. Large numbers of policemen were ringing the streets around the civic center as we arrived, but Luther rolled down the window and explained to one of them that our car needed to pull up to the entrance because we were carrying a debate participant. The policeman leaned in to look, and all of us in the car found ourselves pointing at Anderson, as if the policeman would have difficulty identifying which of us was the candidate. The policeman, probably feigning recognition, nodded, and waved us through. At first our instinct was to find a parking space and then walk as a group indoors. But the lights and cameras waiting at the entrance for arriving candidates—a scene vaguely reminiscent of academy awards night in Hollywood—made us think that it might be more in style to pull Luther's Cadillac right up to the throng of newsmen and let their flashbulbs pop as Anderson emerged grandly from his pseudo-limousine and walked in the door of the civic center. We followed this battle plan, and, much to our delight, Anderson was instantly recognized and, for a fleeting moment, the center of attention until he was safely inside and the newsmen resumed their waiting for the next candidate.

We went immediately to the dressing room area backstage, where each candidate had been assigned his own room to wait until the moment before the debate began, when everyone would march onto the stage together. A make-up woman was due to stop by Anderson's dressing room to touch him up for the benefit of TV, but until then we had quite a lot of time to pass without much to do. We decided to find the press room, where Anderson might recognize some familiar faces and get into a more relaxed mood by exchanging pregame banter. Keke joined us, and we walked through catacomb-like basement corridors until we found the right place. Hundreds of reporters had coverged in a large and noisy room, standing around talking among themselves and, like us, waiting for the show to begin. Anderson came in a side door, and a number of reporters quickly gathered around him. They were startled to see him so seemingly at ease, and charmed to see him, in contrast to a Kennedy or a Connally, so accessible to the press. He chatted a bit, then looked at his watch, and we headed back. Once we were in the dressing room again, Howard Baker poked his head in to say hello, a warm gesture that touched the Andersons. It was not often that the better-known candidates treated John Anderson as an equal.

When the debate was finally to begin, and the candidates were walking out of their staging area, a photograph happened to be snapped of them, showing five of the six off to one side, and Anderson very distinctly on the other. When this picture subsequently appeared in the Washington papers, one wag at the campaign cut it out and captioned it with an expression which Anderson had frequently been using in his campaign speeches: "The other Republican candidates in the race are bunched up so closely on the right, you can't even slide a piece of paper between them." The picture could not have been a more graphic illustration of the proposition.

As the candidates filed out on stage, they saw before them a cavernous room and a vast sea of people, probably a much larger live audience than most of them expected. In the middle of the auditorium a battery of TV cameras had been mounted on a platform; around the edges of the hall, it was standing-room only. Keke and I sat in the very front row, in an area of seats reserved for the immediate parties of the candidates. We wondered whether it might not have given us a more realistic sense of the debate to watch it from the control room and see how the scene came across on a TV screen, but front-row seats were too tempting to pass up. Besides, Keke wanted to be close enough to give her husband occasional facial expressions of moral support. We were nervous as announcements were made that there were five minutes, and then two minutes, and then thirty seconds left before the debate was to begin.

The debate format consisted largely of the candidates giving brief answers to questions posed by a panel of reporters. Throughout the debate, Anderson tried his best to make his responses prompt, direct, and specific. Partly this was meant to contrast with the more political and rhetorical approach of his rivals; partly to help smoke them out on their own specific positions, which Anderson guessed to be more conservative and traditional than his own, and perhaps even identical among all the other candidates; and partly because this was the style which came naturally to a one-time college debater.

The Iowa debate. Left to right: Phil Crane, Howard Baker, John Anderson, moderator Jim Gannon, John Connally, Bob Dole, and George Bush. (Wide World Photos)

The other participants each showed a unique personality. Phil Crane talked in an earnest and scholarly way like the history teacher he once was. Howard Baker seemed intent on projecting the image of country lawyer, nice guy, and GOP conciliator; his voice was soft and the words he chose folksy. George Bush seemed slightly nervous and quite reserved; probably he had been advised that his up-and-coming status in recent Iowa poll standings required him to play things low-key and avoid controversy. At one point, when questions from the audience were permitted, he was quizzed as to his views on "homosexuality and other forms of immorality." He gave a flustered reply, saying repeatedly the one thing that seemed to come to his mind: "I'm against codification," presumably referring to the making of explicit laws forbidding homosexuality, but somehow sounding embarrassingly awkward in the context of the question. Connally's presence on the stage was a commanding one.

But when it came to the closing statements, Connally misjudged his time. He was in the middle of making a sweeping statement about the evils afflicting America, when he asked the rhetorical question "And how did all this happen?" The moderator was forced to interrupt. "I'm afraid we won't be able to find out," the moderator said, "because, Mr. Connally, your time is up." It was reassuring to know that despite all the money he was spending, there were at times limits that applied even to the Connally campaign.

Bob Dole seemed the most relaxed. He was in top form, turning on the sarcastic quips and one-liners that made him fun to watch but, as a result, hard to take seriously as a prospective president. At one point the candidates were asked what single thing they regretted most in public life. Dole replied. "Well, I once called Jimmy Carter a chicken-fried McGovern." The audience laughed. "But I regret that," Dole continued with a straight face, "because I've come to respect Senator McGovern." The audience roared. At another point, George Bush made the comment that he had served as a congressman for two terms in Washington, but then left to work in the private sector. And so, Bush said, "I was in Washington long enough to learn about the problems, but not long enough to become one of the problems." Dole was the next speaker. He could not resist a crack. "Well, George *tried* to become one of the problems," Dole said, alluding to the two Senate bids which Bush had made, "but he was defeated." The audience roared again.

When the debate turned serious, most of the candidates stuck to conventional wisdom and popular positions. John Anderson was the exception. When it came his turn to say what he most regretted in his public life, he, alone among the candidates, was quite specific: the vote he had cast in favor of the Gulf of Tonkin resolution, the legislation Lyndon Johnson used to justify prolonged American participation in the Vietnam War. When he was asked how it would be possible to cut taxes, raise defense spending, and balance the budget all at the same time, as other Republican candidates had pledged, he answered with accustomed honesty: "You do it with mirrors," a line which was often to be recalled during the rest of the campaign. When he was asked how he would address the energy crisis, he pulled no punches and recited the fifty-cent gas-tax proposal he had been advocating for a half-year, but with which most people were still unfamiliar. Finally, when it came to the question of whether he supported the president's grain embargo against the Soviet Union, he distanced himself once again from his Republican rivals. Anderson voiced unhesitating support; the others criticized it sharply. This prompted Anderson to make one of the evening's more memorable statements.

> It's not easy sitting here in the heart of Iowa, in farm country, to support an embargo on the shipment of grain, but it seems to me that it is passing strange that those who are critical of our foreign policy as being deficient on the grounds that it is weak, when the first real test comes of responding to the kind of overt aggression that has just been taken by the Soviet Union against Afghanistan, are unwilling to accept any measure of sacrifice.

Of course, Anderson was not contesting the Iowa caucuses, as the others were, and therefore had the luxury of playing to a broader national audience, but, interestingly enough, he managed to impress many Iowans in the process. More and more, we were coming to see that people often had a grudging respect for politicians who were candid and forthright, even if they told them things they did not particularly want to hear. Anderson struck a responsive chord in talking about the tough things, the painful things, that he said would have to be done to revive the American economy and America's traditional hope and optimism. Deep down, a lot of people knew he was right: that the necessary course would not be easy. In a cartoon which appeared just a few days after the Iowa debate, the cartoonist Herblock summed up the difference between Anderson's approach and the hypocrisy of conventional politicians. The cartoon showed a crowd of all the candidates but Anderson, raising their fists and shouting, according to the caption, "We shall fight in the speeches, we shall fight on the flagpoles, we shall fight on the bumper stickers . . .." In the background of the picture, a placard was visible: "But we're against sacrifices like cutting grain shipments or raising gasoline taxes . . . and we're against John Anderson, too." Everyone talked tough, but only Anderson seemed to have the courage of his convictions.

The Iowa debate had allowed Anderson the opportunity to display a number of specific positions that stood out in bold relief from those of the other candidates. But it remained for Anderson's closing

—from *Herblock on All Fronts* (New American Library, 1980)

statement at the debate to establish Anderson's overall philosophy. Mary McGrory, the *Washington Star* columnist who was one of the panelists, had asked Anderson early in the debate a question as to why he felt he was different from the other candidates. He had made a reply that mentioned several specific points, but a dissatisfaction lingered with him throughout the rest of the debate that he had not answered the question as pointedly as possible; his comments had been too mechanical. The three-minute closing statement he was allowed offered him a chance to make amends. He discarded the somewhat wooden and conventional statement with which his campaign staff had supplied him, in favor of his own extemporaneous remarks.

Just before it was his turn to make a statement, Keke turned to me in the audience. "He's really got to shine now," she said. "If I could tell him what to do, I'd tell him to stress the economy, and let people know that he's the only one who's really willing to do the things that have to be done." It was practically an instance of mental telepathy. Anderson sounded just those themes. He noted that everyone agreed the country had terrible problems, but that when he dared to suggest things like a gasoline tax or support of the grain embargo, he was ridiculed. All the other candidates could do, he said, was propose bigger spending for arms. He wanted to make an appeal, he said, for self-discipline at home. "*That's* the meaning of Iran," he said. "*That's* the meaning of Afghanistan." His voice rising with passion, his arms gripping the table at which he was sitting, he said, "We've got to pull up our socks in this country, we've got to be willing to sacrifice something today in order to secure a better future and a better tomorrow." His father had been an immigrant from Sweden, he said, and it was not easy for him. "It won't be easy for us either," he concluded, "but we can do it."

It was the only one of the closing statements which the audience applauded. Anderson had clearly stolen the show. As he left the stage, and Keke and I joined him in departing the auditorium, he was mobbed by well-wishers from the audience, and by radio and TV interviewers. From the civic center, we went to a reception our Iowa campaign volunteers were hosting at Hotel Fort Des Moines. We had been afraid that postdebate partygoers would skip our reception room in favor of the fancier spreads put on down the hall by the better-known candidates. Instead, the Anderson reception seemed the place to be. About 1:00 A.M., we returned to the hotel, overcome by the excitement of the evening. No one was sleepy, and we stayed up exchanging animated views on all the questions and answers we could remember from the debate. About 1:45 A.M., I put in a call to Margot, who was in Washington and had watched the debate on TV. It was an hour later in Washington, and, amazingly, she had already found a morning *Washington Post* delivered to the front door. The central article on the front page was a report on the Iowa presidential debate. Anderson's name was mentioned frequently; he had parted company so often from the other candidates on the issues that his positions always had to be noted separately. I put Anderson on the phone with Margot, and she read to him some of the article, then congratulated him on his masterful closing statement. "Oh thank you, thank you, my dear," Anderson replied in his familiar paternal tone. "You know," he said, "I had a closing statement prepared. But suddenly I thought, 'I just can't say that,' and I put it aside, and I took off, and I think I just went right on going."

For the first time, Anderson had been visited by a genuine burst of national attention. Particularly important were the beginnings of an intellectual groundswell of support from politically informed and active people, the type likely to spend Saturday evening watching a presidential debate on public TV. A number of liberal Democrats who did not like Carter but were skeptical of Kennedy found themselves intrigued by this iconoclastic Republican. It became almost radical chic for long-time Democrats to confide in one another a feeling that a candidate named Anderson seemed to be the one person talking sense in an otherwise dreary campaign season. Anderson held a fascination for intellectuals in general because his answers seemed to be more fact-filled and his analyses of issues more sophisticated than one normally expected from politicians. Whereas the debate had found George Bush quoting former Yankee baseball player Yogi Berra ("Don't make the wrong mistake"), Anderson in his quotations had invoked the likes of Yale historian C. Vann Woodward.

But Anderson captured the imagination of viewers for more than the fact that many of his positions were different from, and generally more liberal than, those of his Republican colleagues. There was, in addition, something unusual about his whole approach. He seemed so sincere, so straightforward, so candid, somebody who could be counted on to tell it like it was. He seemed to value honesty more than popularity, and to be someone who might just prefer to be right than to be president. Even at the White House, we later heard, Jody Powell had been impressed enough with the contrast between Anderson's courage on issues like the president's grain embargo, and the seeming political cowardice of the other candidates (Connally, Baker, Dole, Bush, Crane, Reagan, and Kennedy), to begin referring to President Carter's opponents as "Snow White and the Seven Dwarfs." (The reference was to Anderson's shock of snow-white hair, which was later to make him so recognizable, and to become the cartoonists' delight.)

It was not that Anderson was liberal or moderate per se as much as that he was someone who cared about issues, or "ideas," as he would sometimes say. He had at one point in the debate repudiated what he called the "old politics," by which he meant a catering to special interests and a tendency to propose vague and inoffensive solutions to the nation's problems. It seemed obvious: the name for the attitude which would guide the Anderson campaign ought to be "new politics." Anderson liked it at the time, Keke did not; she thought voters were so disenchanted by politics in general that any phrase which even contained the word "politics" would fall flat. But within a few weeks Anderson began using the expression, and by the end of the Republican campaign it had gained great currency. It did seem to sum up the notion that the Anderson campaign had as much to do with an overall approach toward politics as it did with specific content. During the primary campaigning in New Hampshire in February, our first media consultant, Bob Sann, was to put commercials on the air which coined another term that also became a leitmotiv of the campaign: "the Anderson difference." It said the same thing, and in a nutshell it explained the phenomenal success the campaign was to enjoy in the coming months.

As we walked through the Des Moines airport the next morning en route back to Washington, a number of people recognized Anderson and came up to him warmly offering their congratulations and support. We stopped to eat in the airport coffee shop, and two of the waitresses bashfully approached our table seeking Anderson's autograph. "We like what you're saying," people told him at every turn. When the Iowa caucuses were held two weeks later, Anderson ended up doing better than expected: 6 percent. This was impressive, considering all the factors: a total absence of campaign organization in the state; the image of many Iowa voters that Anderson was not really interested in their vote or at least was not a serious contender in this particular primary; and the fact that it was a caucus state where other candidates like Bush and Reagan—who were personally known to precinct-level activists who so heavily influenced the result—had a natural advantage. Out of the seven Republican candidates, we managed at least to avoid scoring the worst: that distinction was left to Bob Dole, who received only 2 percent and was soon forced to drop out. We were thankful for small things.

A few days later, on a swing through Manhattan for interviews at networks which had become newly interested in Anderson's activities, we had an early evening engagement at a private midtown club with George Ball, the former undersecretary of state who was now a partner with a major investment banking firm. Following the Iowa debate, he had sent to our campaign headquarters a personal contribution of $1,000. Ball was not only relatively well known—and therefore a rare and valued commodity among our supporters—but someone, like Anderson, with a reputation for taking unpopular and outspoken positions on issues. (He had been somewhat renowned during the Johnson administration, for example, for his in-house opposition to the Vietnam War.) It seemed an honor that he would bestow his support on our campaign.

Anderson was running late, and so I went ahead to let Ball know. I met him, and we went upstairs to have a drink in the club's paneled library. He told me he had been terribly impressed with the bold positions Anderson had taken in the Iowa debate, and applauded his courage in the face of such obvious political risks. For his own part, Ball, though a prominent and established Democrat, did not feel comfortable supporting either Carter or Kennedy, the competence of both of whom he questioned. I told Ball that, from what I knew of his general political philosophy, he would feel at home with Anderson. On the other hand, I volunteered, Anderson took a very traditional (i.e., pro-Israeli) line on the Arab-Israeli dispute, in contrast to what I knew to be Ball's reputation for having strong sympathies with the Arab point of view. Ball replied calmly, "I'm not surprised, but don't worry: I'm not a one-issue voter."

After twenty minutes or so, Anderson arrived, apologized for the delay, and, with a glass of Scotch in his hand, soon settled comfortably into conversation. Ball repeated his praise for Anderson and said he would be happy to help him raise money. He made a point early on to note for the record his controversial views on the Mideast. Anderson said he was aware of them, but that, if it were all right with Ball, they could simply agree to disagree. As for Ball's endorsement and his help, Anderson said he would welcome it openly. "It wouldn't be consistent with my principles to try to hide you," Anderson said. During the rest of the conversation, Anderson solicited Ball's views on the subject of the crisis in American relations with Iran, where American hostages had been taken just months before, and on the recent Soviet invasion of Afghanistan. Ball argued for a more urgent United States focus on growing Soviet influence in the area, rather than the ongoing fixation on events in Teheran. Anderson admired Ball's cogent and deeply informed advice. In the future, we would carry Ball's telephone number with us, and on numerous occasions consult him when a difficult (and non-Mideast) question of foreign policy arose.

The Ball endorsement represented a major coup for the campaign. A couple of days later, we put in a call to Milton Eisenhower to see what he thought about the idea of appearing together with George Ball at some point and making a joint endorsement of Anderson. He replied that the idea sounded like a wonderful one, and so symbolic: a prominent Republican and a prominent Democrat joining ranks in behalf of John Anderson's "new politics." Unfortunately, the idea of a Ball endorsement ran afoul of Keke. One of the staff members in the congressional office, who identified strongly with pro-Israeli causes, was aghast to hear about Ball, and convinced her that our association with Ball would forfeit any prospect of Jewish support in the campaign. Plans for a public endorsement came to a halt. This was probably a mistake. Low in the polls as we were, it seemed inappropriate to be so cautious. Moreover, it was difficult to square this pragmatic attitude about Ball with our self-avowed campaign theme of candor and forthrightness. Later, as it turned out, Ball's endorsement was inadvertently announced. He appeared one week on a Sunday morning news show, and at the tail-end of the questioning, was asked whom he would be supporting in the 1980 presidential race. He had time for just a five-second answer: John Anderson, he replied. The next day, his comment was reported in the newspapers, and his support of Anderson became widely known, despite the campaign's efforts to soft-pedal it.

It was later that evening, following our meeting with Ball, that the reception was held which was described in the prologue to this book. It was also on this night, by coincidence, that one of the networks (CBS) ran the first extended piece on the Anderson campaign. It was well-placed, in the middle of the broadcast. It began with Walter Cronkite saying, "Not long ago, John Anderson was so obscure that he was the subject of a spoof on 'Saturday Night Live.'" A clip from the well-known television comedy show was then played. It had been part of the show's Weekend Update segment, a regular "Saturday Night Live" feature which was itself a spoof on news shows. A picture of Anderson had been flashed on the screen behind Jane Curtin, the actress who played the role of anchorwoman. Explaining the picture, she said, "The man shown above is said to be a Republican candidate for president of the United States. He is described as a white Caucasian male, fifty-seven years old. If you have seen him, please call the following toll free number." But such comedic days of obscurity were past, Cronkite said, because Anderson had done quite well in the Iowa debate (a clip was shown of Anderson's performance to prove it), and the campaign had achieved a new recognition. Pictures were flashed on the screen of a cramped but thriving campaign headquarters, where large numbers of volunteers had been coming in off the streets all week to offer their services. Cronkite's portrayal of the campaign was extremely sympathetic. With a spot on his news show we were indeed taking off.

There were soon other symbols as well. Marty Peretz, editor of the *New Republic*, donated a thousand dollars to the campaign and invited Anderson to a meeting with his editorial board which Anderson afterward characterized as a "love feast." Father Healy, the president of Georgetown University, hosted an elegant dinner for Anderson and prominent Washington journalists. Bob Scheer, the well-known *Los Angeles Times* journalist who had conducted the famous "lust in my heart" interview with Jimmy Carter for *Playboy,* decided Anderson was his next hot property, and besieged us for appointments. Sally Quinn's warm portrayal of Anderson appeared in the *Post.*

But one of the most telling signs of Anderson's new stature could be seen, interestingly, in the more critical way the press treated him one Tuesday morning at a round-table interview in Washington. The occasion was the breakfast which Godfrey Sperling of the *Christian Science Monitor* regularly hosted for Washington reporters and news sources and at which Anderson had appeared several times before. The atmosphere in the past had been unfailingly sympathetic, and any controversial comments Anderson had made were always treated with kid gloves. Today, midway through the breakfast, the press struck a different tone. Anderson was asked a seemingly straightforward question: how would he respond as president should Soviet troops, which had already invaded Afghanistan, move next into Pakistan. Anderson replied almost instinctively. Well, he said, we have to draw the line somewhere, and such a move would require a military response. Ears in the room perked up. *"Military response?"* someone said. Anderson realized the pitfall. He was not about to propose a new Vietnam-like involvement in South Asia. So he backed and filled a bit, and tried to qualify his answer. While the United States should always reserve the right to send troops, he said, probably just a supply of military aid to Pakistan would suffice. How else could we respond, he asked, if such an important friendly nation were aggressively attacked? Anderson had barely escaped making a very serious statement he might have regretted. He was beginning to discover that success could be a two-edged sword: it would mean not only new publicity, but also increased scrutiny and criticism.

On Sunday, January 19, while the other Republican candidates were campaigning down to the wire in Iowa, the Anderson campaign headed west once more to Los Angeles. Though we had not wanted to divert ourselves again from the main arena of the early primary states, we had decided to fly out briefly for a remarkable fund-raising dinner that was being hosted by a wealthy and politically active Democrat named Stanley Sheinbaum. Sheinbaum had written the campaign several weeks before, and one day when I was in the campaign office, I happened to see his letter buried on a desk unanswered. I was from Los Angeles and recognized Sheinbaum's name. It took some prodding of the finance staff to get in touch with him. Sheinbaum had guaranteed the campaign treasury receipts of $10,000 to $20,000 if Anderson would come out personally and address a small $1,000-a-plate dinner Sheinbaum would arrange at his Bel Air home. He would even promise the attendance of such celebrities as author Irving Wallace and producers Grant Tinker and Norman Lear. No one had made such offers to the Anderson campaign before, and the finance staff had apparently taken Sheinbaum for a crackpot. In fact, he turned out to be true to his word.

The Sheinbaums lived in a massive modern home, whose front yard resembled a sculpture garden and back yard opened onto dramatic views of West Los Angeles and downtown. For one day, the Andersons took a mini-vacation and sunned on the patio; nothing would budge them from their well-deserved rest. In the afternoon, the Sheinbaums were joined by their close friends, Ted Ashley, chairman of the board of the Warner Brothers motion picture studio, and his attractive wife. Today was Super Bowl Sunday, and they were all congregating to watch the game on TV. I was invited to watch with them. We went in to the Sheinbaums' oversized master bedroom, and they switched on the television. The Sheinbaums and the Ashleys proceeded to slip their shoes off and prop themselves up on the giant bed which faced the TV. I discreetly demurred and seated myself on the floor off to one side of the bed. Casting a sideways glance at this arrangement of four adults lying side-by-side face-up on the bed reminded me of nothing so much as the famous scene from the movie, *Bob and Carol and Ted and Alice.* Of course, in this case, all four had their clothes securely fastened about them, and the purpose of the exercise was only the perfectly innocent one of watching a Sunday afternoon football game. But something about it did look like the quintessential Los Angeles lifestyle. They were even passing around among them a huge barrel of popcorn, divided into four color groups, including cheese, caramel, chocolate, and regular. The life of the rich looked like fun. How far the Anderson campaign had come from its candidate's humble beginnings in Rockford, Illinois, I thought.

The dinner that evening turned out to be brief but intimate. It was served buffet style, with the guests eating in the living room from TV-trays that they pulled up to their couches and chairs. Anderson gave a short statement, but tried to leave most of the time for questions and answers. Norman Lear, sitting off to one side of the room, asked him the first question. "Congressman," he said, "Teddy Kennedy had a problem answering that question Roger Mudd asked him as to why he wanted to be president. What's your answer?" It was a perfect opportunity for Anderson to display his self-confidence and ability. But he was a little nervous about the occasion, and even if his answer proved more articulate and coherent than Kennedy's, still it was a roundabout one, which hardly left the audience breathless, as Anderson sometimes could. Anderson simply repeated his standard explanation that, after having served "front row and center" for twenty years in the Congress, he felt he had some ideas and some knowledge that could be usefully applied in the office of the nation's chief executive; and that things were going so poorly for the country, and the field of candidates this year was so bleak, that he felt an obligation to step forward and try to make a contribution.

Lear must have been satisfied with the answer, for within a few weeks he had become one of Anderson's most enthusiastic supporters. Even more enduring and active a supporter proved to be Sheinbaum himself. Hereafter, he acted as impresario whenever Anderson came to Los Angeles, and in between visits he worked indefatigably raising money and convincing prominent Democrats to switch their support to a liberal Republican. Sheinbaum considered himself an economist, but he seemed also to be a well-connected politico-about-town. He had the luxury to be one, since he did not seem in need of spending his time making money. We wondered how he had made his Hollywood contacts, and only later learned that his wife was the daughter of the late movie titan Jack Warner. Sheinbaum had been appointed a regent of the University of California by Jerry Brown. This was an important and prestigious position, and indicated Sheinbaum's prominence in California Democratic circles. Why he had breached his relationship with Jerry Brown, foregone Ted Kennedy, and opted instead for John Anderson he never quite explained. But it seemed clear he was having fun in the limelight as Anderson's key California supporter, and he proved an effective organizer.

After the Iowa debate, the next large shot of publicity for Anderson came from a personal appearance he made in late January on "Saturday Night Live." Everyone under the age of thirty in the country appeared to have seen it, judging from the huge numbers of young people who started swelling Anderson's audiences in the days immediately afterwards and who made references to us about it. The idea for getting Anderson on the show had occured to us in December, when "Saturday Night Live" had done the spoof on Anderson which Walter Cronkite later excerpted. I put in a call to the producer's office and discussed the possibility of Anderson's doing a walk-on, cameo appearance on some future edition. I remembered that Gerald Ford had once participated in a skit, and I knew that Anderson would be happy even to be joked about for the sake of the name recognition he so urgently needed.

The people I spoke with liked the idea, but told me the show was going out of production until later on in January. I was disappointed, but made a note on my calendar to get back in touch at the appropriate time. Weeks passed, and the time arrived to check in again. Rather than calling myself, I persuaded Keke to do so, on the thought that she would have more influence. She had written a thank-you note, and sent a picture, to actress Jane Curtin back in December when the original Anderson spoof appeared. I suggested that she talk directly to Curtin. The two got on the phone, and Keke took it from there. She spoke earnestly. "My husband would be very good," she said. "He's had lots of oratorical experience on the Hill. And when he was a senior in high school," she added, to clinch her argument, "he once played the part of Abraham Lincoln." We heard later from someone in the cast that Jane Curtin had just about bowled over laughing at the last remark, but apparently the call did the trick. The next day, I got a call from Lorne Michael, the show's producer. He said they had decided they would indeed like to do something with us, though they were not yet sure what it would be.

A skit was finally written. In an effort to avoid potential legal problems and demands by other candidates for equal time, the part created for Anderson simply placed him in the audience of the show.

At an appropriate point in the script, a camera would zoom in on him. It would be a nonspeaking part, and he would be on camera for only a few seconds, but it would be made clear that it was John Anderson.

The show's assistant producer called the campaign to work out details. The show was done live at 11:30 P.M. in New York. Anderson was asked to arrive early in the afternoon for rehearsals. The scheduler at the campaign did not question why it was necessary for Anderson to rehearse for a nonspeaking role that required him only to sit in the audience. Arrival time presented a problem. Anderson had long been scheduled to appear at an important fundraiser in one of the North Shore suburbs of Chicago late that Saturday afternoon. If he really had to be in New York when the show said he did, he would not be able to make both engagements. The campaign scheduler therefore decided that, since money-raising was so important, Anderson would have to do the Chicago reception, and the "Saturday Night Live" appearance would have to be canceled. This was an odd judgment. In the first place, it seemed clear that the program was much more important to Anderson in the long run than a single fund-raiser. He was not going to get anywhere without substantially more national publicity. As for the possibility of rescheduling the appearance on "Saturday Night Live," it seemed unlikely: a script had already been written, and the show was going to great pains to accommodate us. Most of all, our philosophy regarding media opportunities had long been that one in the hand was worth two in the bush. As it turned out, the show's request for rehearsal did turn out to be negotiable, after we pressed the case, and Anderson was ultimately able to attend both events.

The "Saturday Night Live" skit was a takeoff on the Iowa caucuses, which had been held the previous week. An Iowa farm family was being besieged by the various candidates for its vote; the candidates were willing to go to extraordinary lengths to get it. George Bush assiduously folded the family laundry, and pleaded to be assigned more chores: "I see so much that needs to be done, and I want to do it." John Connally asked the little daughter whether he could do anything for her, such as buying her a pony. Ted Kennedy offered to drive her to her music lesson. Ronald Reagan was upstairs asleep. The only reference to Anderson was made when a policeman came to the door and asked whether anyone had seen him; no one recognized the name. At the end of the skit, an epilogue was done on what happened to all the candidates. Most of them had met up with unlikely fates ("Howard Baker was arrested in a motel room with Phil Crane"). John Anderson, however, was different: he was said to have been elected fortieth president of the United States. With that, the cameras zoomed in on the real John Anderson, sitting in the audience laughing. The picture was held momentarily, then the show switched to a commercial. The crowd around us, most of whom had not noticed or recognized Anderson until now, roared its approval. Anderson was famous.

Anderson's status as a student folk hero was confirmed days later on Thursday, January 31, in Cambridge, Massachusetts. Nothing had prepared us for the spectacle we witnessed driving up that evening to the MIT student lounge. Hundreds of students were converging on the building from all directions. We wondered what event would be taking place there. We knew the students could not be coming for Anderson's speech, because there were too many of them, and they were arriving too early. We were wrong. Fifteen hundred students (Keke would insist it was 2,000) were packing themselves into the lounge area to hear the hottest new candidate around. Many of them had to be turned away, and so the spillover crowd filled a large cafeteria nearby where a sound system was quickly set up to pipe in Anderson's voice; later on, Anderson came over to the cafeteria, stood on a table, and addressed this other crowd separately. The corridor between these rooms was lined with students hoping to catch even a glimpse of Anderson's white hair. Jerome Wiesner, the president of MIT, who met Anderson and escorted him around, told us it was the largest turnout of students he had seen at the school since the kids took over the administration building in 1968. He was as astonished as we were.

Frequently throughout the campaign, the assertion could be heard that Anderson's college support grew out of the coverage he received in the comic strip *Doonesbury*. Surely that contributed substantially to Anderson's renown and popularity among young people, but the *Doonesbury* series on Anderson had not yet begun by the time of his speech at MIT. The MIT students were responding, evidently, to other things: the Iowa debate, "Saturday Night Live," the increasing coverage local Massachusetts papers were giving to the intensifying primary race, and the not infrequent editorials and columns which lauded Anderson as the best candidate for president. People were simply curious to see him in person.

Following the MIT speech, we went out to the Boston suburb of Dedham to spend the night with Keke's brother and sister-in-law, John and Mary Machakos. They were to put us up many times again before the Massachusetts primary was over. The Machakoses lived in a split-level tract home on a quiet street, in a house, as a matter of fact, that resembled the Andersons' own. They always treated us—myself included—with the utmost hospitality. It was a warm and comfortable environment, and, while it was not always the most convenient place to stay in relation to the campaign schedule, the Andersons much preferred it to a hotel. We were also still practicing the frugality required by our meager campaign resources, and it did not hurt that the accommodations were offered free of charge.

On this night, as on so many, Mary prepared salads and sandwiches, which we ate off our laps in the den as we talked and watched the late-night local news. We told and retold the story of the evening to John and Mary, and never tired of repeating Wiesner's comment about the size of the MIT crowd. It was clear that something in the campaign had ignited. The next day, large crowds again greeted us at both Brandeis and Tufts Universities. Nonetheless, after an initial euphoria about this new popularity, it began to dawn on us that students were to some extent a world apart from the vast bulk of people who would actually be casting ballots on election day. That Anderson was now recognized or revered among students did not at all imply that adults had yet tuned in to his campaign. Indeed, it would be a long time before the political fashion that was beginning to sweep the New England campuses would spawn imitation in the adult world. That night, for example, we ended up at a Lincoln Day dinner in Southboro, Massachusetts, and the middle-aged group in attendance did not seem to regard Anderson as anything special, and generally looked as though they had come more for the social occasion than for the speech.

On Saturday, February 2, we spent the day campaigning in Vermont; its primary would be held a month later on the same day as the Massachusetts primary, and we would visit Vermont several more times before then. Congressman Jim Jeffords, a liberal Republican who had endorsed Anderson, met us in the morning at a TV station in Burlington and escorted us around the rest of the day. We were delighted by his efforts. He was an affable companion to have as we made our stops, and, as Vermont's sole representative in Congress, his endorsement carried a great deal of weight in the state. He guided Anderson into shopping malls to pass out brochures and shake hands; through several more radio and TV stations; to a Burger King near Lake Champlain for lunch; and then to picturesque Middlebury College in the evening, where he introduced Anderson as "the one man other congressmen stop and listen to when he rises to speak." The chapel of the college was packed with cheering students.

Later, Anderson expressed bewilderment that there could be such a degree of public interest, and yet not one TV crew interested enough to cover what he was saying. Whenever we saw the evening news, there seemed to be a major story about another candidate, and we would at best be mentioned as an afterthought. Were the other candidates getting crowds this size? It was not that Anderson wanted publicity merely to satisfy his own ego; he simply realized that it was an essential requirement for his campaign to succeed. I reassured him that all the networks and local TV stations had been notified every day of the crowds. Most of them politely replied that they would try to send a crew, but somehow no one ever seemed to make it. Finally, in exasperation, Anderson agreed to sit down one day and personally call a number of network correspondents and assignment editors. Shortly thereafter, about mid-February, small, but perceptible, changes began to occur in the television coverage we received. But by then, reporters generally were coming out in larger force anyway, as the date of the New Hampshire primary approached. It was difficult to say whether, in fact, we had been the beneficiary of the affirmative action coverage we had requested.

On Sunday, we returned for the day to Washington both for a network television interview and so Anderson could catch up on paperwork at his desk in the congressional office. He asked me whether I would be joining Keke and himself that night in returning to New Hampshire. I was tired, and had not been planning to. Until then, I had been traveling only half-time and returning frequently to Washington because it was easier to do the speechwriting and press work there for which I was still responsible. The Andersons were leaving on a flight in the early evening. Up until the very last minute, I debated whether to join them. Suddenly I decided that it was not fair to expect the Andersons to go back on the campaign trail while I stayed at home; their misery deserved company. Margot dashed me out to the airport, and I ran into the terminal. Somehow I managed to get a ticket and walk on board just as the stewardess was about to close the door. The Andersons saw me coming down the aisle and let out a shriek of surprise: "You came!" I was glad I had.

These were the classic days caricatured in the *Doonesbury* comic strip. When I decided to join the Andersons on this particular trip, I had assumed I would be gone for only two or three days. Accordingly, I had packed only the limited supply of shirts and underwear that would fit in a briefcase. As it turned out, I did not come back during most of the several months of primary campaigning. I continued wearing the same suit, and had to rely on Margot to meet me on alternate weekends to replenish my stock of clean clothes. My shoes developed holes, and since I had neither the time to get them repaired, nor the opportunity to buy new ones, I did the next best thing: I purchased a pair of rubbers which I wore permanently on my shoes to cover the soles.

Most of the time we traveled, it was just Anderson, myself, often Keke, and perhaps a local volunteer to do the driving. After a while, we acquired the company of two volunteers who eventually stayed with us much of the campaign: Jim Scales and Bill O'Donnell, both of them originally from our Massachusetts office. They took turns driving and navigating, and assisted uncomplainingly with many other thankless odds and ends; Bill also served energetically as my assistant coordinating press matters in later days when the contingent of reporters traveling with us grew larger. I functioned as best I could in most of the rest of the roles: press secretary, speechwriter, political advisor, issues advisor, confidant. My plethora of responsibilities did not enhance the efficiency of our organization. Speeches were written on yellow legal pads as we bumped along on the road, to the occasional chagrin of the candidate who could not read them; at every stop, I had to call Washington to collect messages and coordinate plans, causing frantic searches to be undertaken at the end of events when Anderson could not find me in the remote room or building where I had located a phone; and in my spare moments, I had to divide my time evenly between caring for the press and conversing with my boss, though both generally expected full-time attention. We rented cars or vans, usually requiring just one such vehicle to transport everyone in the party, and we took wrong turns almost as often as we took right ones. The Andersons and the rest of us did all our own checking into hotels, baggage handling, meal fetching, and a million other things that later in the campaign would be taken care of by battalions of assistants.

When we arrived in Boston from Washington this particular evening, Bill O'Donnell was at the airport to meet us with a shiny new van the campaign was renting. We were impressed by its size: it could seat nine, though we would rarely need it for more than about four. But having graduated from a sedan to a van was tangible progress. As we drove from the Boston airport up to New Hampshire, where we would stay for the night at the Nashua Howard Johnson's, Anderson and Keke debated the merit of President Carter's newly declared "Carter doctrine," a pronouncement that the United States would stand ready to defend the Persian Gulf against Soviet aggression. Keke argued that the country should not lift a finger until it was assured of full allied cooperation; in her opinion, our allies were not as yet doing enough. Anderson rejoined that we would be damaging our interests if we let the Soviet Union deprive our allies of their oil, since we would surely be affected by any economic hard times they suffered. Keke went further: she said—and was to repeat many times in future months—that no son of hers would go off to fight for the sake of oil in the Persian Gulf. Again, Anderson replied that, as much as he believed that we used too much oil, unless we changed our ways, the Persian Gulf would continue to be vital to our interests, and we could not remain indifferent if it were threatened by enemy power.

But the more we thought about Keke's point, the more we realized that it contained the kernel of an important theme Anderson should be sounding: that the United States ought to be willing to accept some degree of inconvenience at home (i.e., higher gasoline prices) in preference to taking the risk that its young men would have to be sent to the shores of the Persian Gulf to fight and die for the sake of a natural resource. Anderson would thereafter make this argument in defense of his energy conservation positions and his gas tax. His repertoire for speeches was expanded to include two lines he frequently repeated throughout the primaries: "national security begins at home," and the United States should be as "hawkish at home" as Carter wanted it to be abroad.

The next two days were fairly typical of our schedule for the coming several weeks in New Hampshire. One morning we attended a reception of about forty or fifty people at a charming old frame home, surrounded by a white picket fence, in Hollis, New Hampshire. At lunch, Anderson gave a tough, orthodox conservative economic talk at the Manchester Rotary Club. The following day, in Dover, he attended an editorial board meeting at *Foster's Daily Democrat;* we were visiting all the local weeklies and dailies we had time to see, hoping we might win endorsements. It was a small, family-run paper, and an editorial board meeting in this case consisted of an informal chat with a political writer, a senior editor, an associate editor, and Mrs. Foster. Later that afternoon, we stopped in at the nearby law office of a supporter where wine and cheese had been put out for the benefit of townspeople who wanted to stop by and meet candidate Anderson. During a lull in the proceedings, we slipped into a back room so Anderson could make some telephone calls I had been pestering him about. One of my duties was to collect names and numbers of academic, political, and business figures whom we felt it would be profitable for him to contact for one reason or another. This particular afternoon, he was able to reach literary figure Norman Cousins in Los Angeles about the possibility of his support (Cousins subsequently sent in a large contribution); former ambassador George Kennan at Princeton, to ask his opinions on the crises in Iran and Afghanistan; and Professor Larry Seidman at Swarthmore, to talk over his ideas on a tax-based incomes policy, which it seemed to me Anderson might find it intriguing to propose.

Many nights we returned to the Concord Ramada Inn, a chain motel, replete with boxy rooms, slightly seedy-looking corridors, and room service that tended to deliver cold hamburgers and french fries and even to forget the silverware and ketchup. But we stayed there enough during the New Hampshire primary that it grew on us, and one now recalls nostalgically the almost pleasant sensation that the sight of this nondescript home-away-from-home gave us as we pulled up in our van at the end of a wearying day of campaigning. We did occasionally have other quarters—notably the modern and relatively fancy Hilton at Merrimack—but what would our campaigning have been without the experience of the plainer motels that Walter Mondale once so eloquently described as the reason he withdrew from presidential campaigning?

Generally the Anderson party rented just two or three rooms. This contrasted somewhat with the arrival of Ted Kennedy's party, with whom we shared the motel on a couple of occasions. The Kennedy party usually booked a block of thirty to forty rooms, enough to house three shifts of Secret Service, a flotilla of personal aides, and a busload of reporters. We could always tell when Senator Kennedy was somewhere in the vicinity. We would be walking through the lobby on the way to our van in the morning, and the scene would be wall-to-wall crush. Usually we tripped over at least one television camera wire or had to say "excuse me" a dozen times to get to the front entrance. Oftentimes, one of the young Kennedy workers would recognize Anderson, come up and confide to him that he was their "next favorite candidate," and then look longingly after us as we left, as if to admire the more intimate and easygoing nature of our campaign compared to theirs. Once or twice we went down to the Ramada Inn bar in the evening, and, over a beer with Anderson, some of the Kennedy workers expressed this latter thought directly.

One by one, Anderson was managing to speak at most of the colleges of Massachusetts and New Hampshire. From Keene State College to Dartmouth to Clark University to Boston University, Wellesley, and a dozen others, we found large and fervent audiences. We had no advance men setting up our engagements. All that we needed at a college were a few on-campus volunteers to pin up mimeographed notices on the bulletin boards, and the largest auditoriums would be jam-packed. The first TV crew that finally covered one of Anderson's college speeches was one from CBS's "Sixty

Minutes," which met up with us at Amherst and the University of Massachusetts. On that occasion, Anderson was introduced by historian Henry Steele Commager, who told the students that the Republican party had not been a party of new ideas since Abraham Lincoln and Teddy Roosevelt, but that under John Anderson's influence it might be able to change. Anderson gave one of his tub-thumping speeches to prove it, denouncing the "old, conventional politics" and promising bold, innovative, honest reforms in policy. The audience loved it, a hundred students signed up to help, and several times as many filled out forms to reregister their party affiliation so they would be eligible to cast a vote for Anderson in the Republican primary. People often expressed skepticism to us about the value of support from college students, noting that they were notoriously unhelpful in campaigns since relatively few of them bothered to vote. We found the reality very different. During the early primary days, when the students were so enthusiastic about the Anderson candidacy, they put themselves in the vanguard of the campaigning, distributing leaflets and doing an enormous amount of other foot-soldiering that had to be done, and, in fact, turning out in large numbers at the polls. At the same time, they gave the Anderson campaign an air of glamour and success, when people finally had a chance to see on TV the large crowds Anderson was drawing—even if a closer examination revealed their faces to be all rather young.

After the speeches in the Amherst area that evening, the Andersons, Bill O'Donnell, and I left by van for a reception in Longmeadow, Massachusetts. What ensued was a comedy of errors worthy of Laurel and Hardy. Why Bill functioned as our driver was a mystery to all of us, most of all Bill; he would have been the first to admit that his powers of navigation were something less than perfect. Of course, none of us really had a right to complain; we were free at any time to help in the driving or navigating chores, but we had always readily delegated them to Bill. The directions this evening called for us to find a certain road and take it several miles until we came to the entrance to a highway. We drove on and on, and saw no entrance to a highway. "Are you sure this is the right way?" I asked. "Yes, I'm sure," Bill said. On and on we kept driving. The Andersons were, of all things, giggling in back, sure we were driving the wrong way. It had been a dark, lonely road. Suddenly, a gas station came into sight. "Why don't we stop here and ask directions," I suggested calmly. "We don't need directions," Bill said, "this is the right road." "STOP HERE!" I screamed. Bill knew when I was serious, and lurched into the gas station. I jumped out to consult the gas station attendant. From the van, the Andersons and Bill could see the scene plainly: the attendant stood there conversing with me, and then suddenly stuck out his arm and pointed it in the opposite direction from which we had been heading. I got back in, and we turned around. No one spoke for several miles. Then the Andersons started giggling again. Bill and I did, too. We had finally found the right road.

The adventure was not over, however. When we reached Longmeadow, the directions again became unclear. We stopped in a pizza parlor while I ran in to call the hosts of the fund-raiser. I told them we had arrived in town, but that we were having a little difficulty finding their street. They gave me painstaking directions. I got back in the van and we tried to follow them. We went down a couple of streets, made a turn, and made another turn. We had found the street. Now we needed only to find their house. We squinted our eyes and looked for addresses. Just as the numbers got close to the one we wanted, the name of the street changed, and the numbers were entirely different. Around and around the block we went, thinking we had narrowed it down to where the house had to be, but then being completely unable to find it. We were already an hour late to the reception, and our impatience was growing by the moment. Suddenly I spotted a police station. We drove up to it, and again I hopped out. I ran in and identified our van as one which contained presidential candidate John Anderson. "We are very late to a fund-raiser, and we just can't find it." I showed the officer the address. "Why, that's just a block away." "Maybe," I said, "but we can't find it." He began to give me directions. It had already been a long night, and we had had our share of difficulties following directions. "Please," I said, "give us a police escort." The officer looked at me as though I were slightly deranged. I repeated my plea: "Please!" He shrugged. "Meet me around the front," he said. I returned to the van, and we waited. A minute later, the policeman drove his squad car around from the back lot. He started the red light on top of his car flashing, and we followed him. He drove us a block, and pointed with a flashlight out the car. "This is it," he said. "Thanks," we said, much relieved.

The pace of campaigning stepped up. One Friday was spent making a sort of whistlestop tour by car of small New Hampshire towns: Exeter, Chester, Raymond, Derry, Nashua, Milford, Peterboro, Dublin, Keene, and Walpole. Everywhere along the way, Anderson would speak at a town hall for a few minutes, or walk down a main street, popping into shops and saying, "John Anderson . . . appreciate a vote." That weekend we spent campaigning in Vermont. Margot joined us, and along with Bill Glew, our Vermont coordinator, the five of us drove around much of the state, from Brattleboro to Rutland to Bennington to Burlington. The scenery was lovely and the long drives between towns were relaxing and fun, even if the conditions in the car were somewhat cramped. Sunday night, Anderson spoke in the noisy cafeteria of the University of Vermont. He was not pleased that, for the umpteenth time in recent weeks, no microphone had been provided, and he was forced to shout himself hoarse to the audience. That night, we took our dinner in the restaurant of the high-rise Burlington hotel in which we were staying. The status of our campaign was obviously on the rise: when we explained to the maître d' who Anderson was, he recognized his name, and admitted us without reservations.

The next day, we had an engagement at the *Burlington Free Press.* The editorial board was interested enough in hearing Anderson to convene a special Sunday meeting. At the end of the hour-long conversation, Anderson was asked whom he might support if he failed to win any primaries and had to drop out before the nomination. Anderson gave a standard reply. "I don't think there's a dime's bit of difference among them." For example, Anderson said, they all opposed the SALT treaty, whereas he strongly supported it. "I just don't see how I could endorse someone who opposes something so important." This comment was picked up on the wires and appeared the next day in the *Washington Post.* The image was beginning to build that Anderson was irreparably at odds with his own party.

On February 16, we traveled to Milford, New Hampshire, where the Jaycees were holding a statewide meeting at which most of the

Republican candidates would be speaking. The site for the occasion was a converted high school gymnasium, and the place in which the candidates had to wait their turn to speak was the locker room. We arrived a few minutes before we had been told it would be Anderson's time at the rostrum. Just as we were waiting, a motorcade arrived, Ronald Reagan alighted, and came in the locker room to join us. He shook hands with everyone in the friendliest fashion, as he would the several future times we ran into him at joint events. He thanked Anderson graciously for allowing him to go ahead and take Anderson's speaking turn. Anderson nodded, but after Reagan left, we all puzzled about what he had meant. I found someone in charge and asked. "Well," we were told, "the Governor had another engagement and asked if he could go before you." Anderson had not been consulted; there were still very definitely two classes of candidates. As a result of the change, Anderson was left standing in the chilly air of the locker room for quite a long time, and when he was finally called out to speak, he felt a cold coming on and was quite irritated besides. His speech, naturally enough, fell flat. That day in Milford proved a miserable one for him, and he was forced to wonder at times like this whether, for all the student support he had aroused, he would ever really have a chance.

But every so often an event would occur in the campaign that seemed to have been designed to boost our sagging fortunes and spirits. One of the most memorable such events was the night of February 18, when the New Hampshire Gun Owners Association hosted a candidates forum at the Highway Hotel in Concord. Our campaign's political director had at first declined the invitation without telling Anderson about it, just as he had done in the case of the Iowa debate. Then when Anderson found out, and indicated he wanted to go, the political director argued strenuously against it, on the grounds that the subject was one on which Anderson's views were too controversial. But Anderson would not be deterred. We were attending another candidates' forum earlier in the evening, at Yoken's Restaurant in Manchester. At the end of the speeches, all the candidates except Anderson went scurrying out; he remained behind shaking hands. "This is ridiculous," Anderson finally said. "If that other forum is good enough for them, it's good enough for me. I'm not going to be left out." With that, we found the van, jumped in, and raced to Concord, just in time to file in with the other candidates. The entire GOP field had come.

One by one, the candidates were given an opportunity to express their views on the subject of gun control, and one by one they took turns vying to denounce it. All of them, that is, except Anderson. He took the podium, and began to give a qualified and relatively restrained statement of support for gun control. "I'm not talking about the legitimate right of hunters and sportsmen to keep rifles and long guns. I'm just saying that, in the case of concealable handguns, we ought to be able to license owners in the same way as we require drivers of motor vehicles in Illinois to get a license." Loud boos rose up from the audience. "Throw him out of here," some shouted. Anderson was genuinely taken aback. He had not been naïve enough to suppose, of course, that his views would be popular, but he had hardly expected the reaction to be so emotional; were not the candidates simply supposed to state their position on the issue? He shook his head and went on. "Now, the only intention of such a law would be to weed out the drug addicts, convicted felons, and mental defectives. If that doesn't apply to you, you have nothing to worry about. I'm sure you're all law-abiding citizens." "Not if I catch you in a dark alley at night," one member of the audience yelled back. For the first time, we wished we had Secret Service for reasons other than status. Finally, after all the candidates had finished speaking, they were asked one by one whether they would be willing to veto any legislation that in any way restricted the ownership of guns. Again, one by one, they said yes, they would. Again, except for Anderson. He said it would have to depend on the particulars of the legislation. He was booed roundly and, after the event concluded, we did not feel particularly safe until we were back inside the van and driving away.

Anderson said, "Can you believe it? All those big, strong men, afraid to lose a single vote." The rural character of much of New Hampshire created a large progun constituency; it was the natural reaction of a candidate to adapt his views to the political environment. Anderson had resisted the pressure, and we congratulated him proudly. He had not hit anyone over the head with extreme views; rather, he had stated only moderate views, with which a majority of Americans probably agreed. But in the context of this particular forum on this particular night, he had demonstrated a willingness to voice an unpopular position, which seemed to run against his own self-interest. Aside from the gun owners, we hoped, the larger public would respect him for it. Sure enough, the next day, the TV news shows were full of sympathetic clips from the event showing Anderson being booed. He seemed heroically to be facing a den of lions. Though this had not been his design, he had never received such large-scale and favorable national attention.

Although Anderson was eventually to win over voters in part on the basis of his unusual political style, in the first instance he had to appeal for support on the basis of his actual political positions. In this respect, his nemesis during the New Hampshire primary proved to be George Bush: many voters who might have supported Anderson regarded Bush as being almost equally moderate, yet as having a better chance to win. Anderson's tack was to use every opportunity to draw differences between himself and Bush; he tried to make the case that, despite an Ivy League look of moderation, Bush was in fact quite conservative. Anderson delighted in noting that Bush himself had recently been quoted as saying that he would find it difficult to point to any "real philosophical differences" he had with Ronald Reagan; and that Phil Crane, the candidate who perhaps more than any other set the standard for conservatism in the campaign, had said recently that he had looked over Mr. Bush's position papers and felt he could have written them himself. Anderson attacked Bush as well for "fuzziness on issues" and derided him for justifying the generalities he used on a theory that there was not time during a campaign for "fine-tuning." Anderson also quoted Bush's chief political operative, David Keene, as acknowedging that, while the Bush campaign had deliberately avoided issues to date, once it began to address them, "people will begin to see that the guy is really a conservative. But by then all the moderates will be locked up." Once when the *Manchester Union Leader* publicized some old charges about alleged financial improprieties in which Bush had been engaged, we all fairly squealed in delight. "Bushgate!" we said. There was no love lost between these two rivals.

Had George Bush been able to capitalize on his momentum coming out of Iowa, and scored better in the New Hampshire primary than a relatively disappointing 25 percent, the Anderson campaign probably would have been on its last legs by the time of the Massachusetts primary. But because Bush had not proved as invincible as the image he had created for himself, it is likely that significant numbers of moderate Republicans in Massachusetts decided in the final week before that state's primary that they might as well try John Anderson. The reason Bush had not done very well in New Hampshire had to do, more than one imagined, with John Anderson. For John Anderson was very much involved in the story behind the fateful Nashua debate.

When we heard in early February that a one-on-one debate between Reagan and Bush was being arranged under the auspices of the *Nashua Telegraph,* Anderson immediately called the newspaper's publisher, Herman Pouliot, to request an invitation. Pouliot said he would like to include Anderson, but that Reagan and Bush were insisting on a two-man format. Anderson was disbelieving; he knew that Pouliot personally favored Bush, and had a hunch that the two were in cahoots in trying to make it look as though there were really only two candidates left in the GOP field. The point of this, Anderson assumed, was to convince moderate voters that, if they wanted to stop Ronald Reagan, it was time to rally behind one candidate, and that the strongest and most natural such candidate would be George Bush. We determined to do our best either to be included in the debate, or to stop it. Anderson called Common Cause in Washington to enlist its support. Within days, Common Cause called press conferences in Washington and in New Hampshire to voice protest. Anderson next got in touch with Bob Dole, who was also upset about being excluded, and agreed to join him in filing a formal complaint with the Federal Election Commission. Finally, we drafted an ad which ran in the *Nashua Telegraph* and then several other New Hampshire newspapers. It read as follows:

An Issue of Fairness
Has the New Hampshire primary already been decided?
Then why are only Ronald Reagan and George Bush being invited to the February 23 debate sponsored by the *Nashua Telegraph?*
There are seven candidates in the Republican race, not two. Yet this debate leaves the impression that the contest has already been narrowed to only two serious candidates.
This is both untrue and unfair. New Hampshire voters have always

prided themselves in their independence. Their votes will only be known on election day.

And candidates in the New Hampshire primary have always looked upon the primary as an opportunity for even a dark horse, on the strength of character and ability, to come to the fore on election day.

This is the way it should be, and this is the way it should remain. The *Nashua Telegraph* should invite all the candidates, or none of them.

The ad was signed, "New Hampshire Citizens for Anderson."

We proceeded on another track as well. Anderson placed a call to John Sears, then Reagan's campaign manager, and expressed his feeling that the debate should be opened up, and that Reagan should take the initiative of doing it. Sears said they were working on just that idea, and that he would let us know as soon as possible before the debate whether participation might be expanded. Saturday afternoon, the day of the debate, we were in Concord. Since we had not heard anything yet, we were working on the assumption that the debate would go on as arranged. Anderson was doing an interview with a local cable-TV station, and I was in the wonderful old Victorian mansion on Main Street into which our New Hampshire headquarters, now teeming with volunteers, had moved. A call came in from Sears, and I took it. He said that the debate would be opened up after all, and that every candidate would be coming, except John Connally, who was detained campaigning in South Carolina. Reagan would now be paying for the hall, Sears said, and that is why the rules were being changed. Sears said everything was 98 percent sure; the uncertainty came from the fact, he said, that Bush had not yet made a public comment, and it was conceivable he might not agree to it. In fact, he did not.

I rushed over to the cable-TV studio to let Anderson know. We got dressed, had a snack, and drove in the van down to the Nashua gymnasium where the debate was being held. It was not going to be broadcast live on TV, like some of the other debates, so we were not quite as concerned about being there well in advance. By the time we arrived, a large crowd had already gathered. We were directed by a policeman to a back entrance, reserved for the candidates. We walked in, asked where to go, and someone pointed to a back room that looked as though it might have been in real life an office of one of the gym coaches. Reagan, Baker, Dole, and Crane, along with their wives and one or two aides each, were already huddled in the room. Anderson, Keke, and I squeezed in. The group was debating whether everyone should walk out on the stage together and have Reagan refuse to debate unless the others were included. Meantime, Bush was already sitting on stage waiting for his opponent to appear. The crowd was growing restless, and no one knew what was going on.

From what I could hear, Reagan sounded as though he agreed with the excluded candidates that they deserved to participate. Everyone seemed quite irritated with Bush, whom they viewed as acting like a spoiled child. Reportedly, two emissaries had been sent out to talk to Bush but had been rebuffed. It did not seem as though any clear conclusion had been reached, but forty-five minutes had already passed since the debate was supposed to have started, and everyone seemed eager to go out on stage and bring the matter to a head. Reagan said, "All right, let's go." It was not obvious what Reagan planned to do. Just then, Gordon Humphrey, the conservative New Hampshire senator who was helping to spearhead Reagan's campaign in the state, came up to him and said, quite loudly, "Governor, you've got to debate Bush. If you boycott, it will look as though you're backing down and are afraid to debate. If you don't debate, you'll lose the election!"

All the candidates marched out on stage. Reagan took his seat, while the others lined up behind him and Bush. The atmosphere in the auditorium broke into pandemonium. The moderator quieted everyone down, and proceeded to explain the debate format as if the original rules for a two-man contest were unquestionably going to be observed. Bush said he wanted to go on with it, because those were the rules under which he had been invited, and which the *Nashua Telegraph*, the original sponsoring organization, had prescribed. When it came Reagan's turn to say something, he began to speak about the unfairness of excluding his colleagues. Everything seemed to be leading up to Reagan's saying, "And therefore, I won't debate." But he looked unsure of himself, as though he really did not know what decision he would make. He cast a glance to the side of the podium where a number of us were standing, including Gordon Humphrey and Reagan's wife, Nancy. Suddenly it looked

Confrontation at Nashua. Left to right: Reagan, moderator, Anderson, Baker, Dole, Bush, and Crane. (Wide World Photos)

as if he had had a change of heart, and he concluded by saying he was willing to have a two-man debate after all, but did want to make clear for the record that he personally would have wanted the others included.

The excluded candidates marched out of the gymnasium into a back room. Half of the TV crews followed. In a dramatic atmosphere of anger and confusion, they lined up, one-by-one praising Reagan and denouncing Bush. The scene foreshadowed the way that, during the Illinois debate weeks later, several of the candidates would gang up on Anderson. He would be a front-runner at that time; but for now the "heavy" was George Bush. When the dust had settled, Bush seemed to have lost great ground from the debate, and Reagan seemed to have emerged with the magnanimous, fatherly image that throughout the campaign would serve him so well.

But John Anderson, too, was emerging with a positive image. It was one that paradoxically he had not connived for nor coveted, but one which he had earned simply by being himself. It was more than a coincidence that he won far more editorial endorsements from the newspapers of New Hampshire than did any other Republican candidate. And it was more than a coincidence that the endorsements were all made on the same stated premise: that John Anderson had the honesty and the courage America needed to address its difficult problems. The *Concord Monitor* wrote: "Anderson is not only eloquent, he is forthright to the point of bluntness. He has been saying what he thinks without regard to whether or not it is politically expedient." The *Peterborough Transcript* said: "Today public figures worry more about image than reality. How refreshing it is to have someone who cares about the reality. . . . Anderson tells the truth, bluntly if necessary, however unpopular." And the *Daily Dartmouth* summed it up: "Unlike most candidates, Anderson does not run a slick, image-oriented campaign. Instead . . . he is running on the issues. . . . As the New Hampshire primary draws near, voters who are not impressed with sophisticated, Madison Avenue candidates will find John Anderson the best alternative in the 1980s."

Anderson got 10 percent of the vote in New Hampshire on February 26, thus placing fourth in the Republican primary, and Ronald Reagan trounced George Bush to take first. As we sat and watched the returns from the garish suite which had been reserved specially for the Andersons that night at the Concord Ramada, we considered the results a relative victory. Anderson was ahead of Crane, Dole, and Connally, and only two or three percentage points behind the much better known Howard Baker. At one time we had been afraid of ending up with only one-tenth of what we did. We could now go on to Massachusetts for the primary there March 4 with our heads held high. But more than the 10 percent, Anderson had won something else during his January and February campaigning: he had won increasing respect for being the unusual person that he was, willing to say what he believed and to let the chips fall where they may. It was ironically this willingness to lose that gave him his best chance to win.

5

March, 1980: Success, Frustration, Opportunity

The week between the New Hampshire primary, February 26, and the dual primaries in next-door Massachusetts and Vermont, on March 4, was a moment of high intensity for the Anderson campaign, the time during which we made the startling transition from the status of also-ran to that of one of the front-runners. The audiences we encountered at college campuses had been large and growing for almost a month, but their influence was to be felt particularly in Massachusetts, where certain areas, such as Boston, have highly concentrated student populations. Wherever Anderson went, he seemed to be mobbed; wherever our campaign needed volunteer help, unlimited supplies of enthusiastic young people seemed to be available from local schools. All our simmering resentment the past months about not having achieved due recognition from the press evaporated almost overnight, and it would not be long before some began lamenting exactly the opposite problem: the threat of overexposure, and a rise of such a meteoric nature as to make people suspect that it might be, like a shooting star, ephemeral in its duration.

The two days following the New Hampshire primary had been unexceptional. Columnist Bob Turner of the *Boston Globe* interviewed Anderson over breakfast one morning in a suburban Holiday Inn, and the sight of John Anderson strolling through a crowded dining room turned no heads. That afternoon we flew on our first chartered plane to Westfield, Massachusetts, where the occasion for our visit was an invitation to tour the headquarters of Friendly's

—from *Herblock on All Fronts* (New American Library, 1980)

Ice Cream. Anderson donned a white paper hat, affixed an incongruously serious look to his face, and followed his guides around a large plant as they explained the various machines and stages of the ice-cream-making process. Our scheduling department back in Washington had agreed to put Anderson through this exercise on the thought that it might afford a compelling "photo opportunity" for the photographers traveling with us. It did. The next day, in the *New York Times* and around the country, an Associated Press wire photo graced a prominent spot on the inside page, showing Anderson, in his hat, campaigning earnestly in western Massachusetts. Anderson was philosophical: "Well," he said, "at least it will let people know that I don't just spend my time with college students."

There was more than a kernel of genuine sentiment in Anderson's statement. Commentators were beginning to note that Anderson's support seemed confined to college campuses and were drawing comparisons already to the days of Eugene McCarthy's so-called "kiddie crusade." Throughout the campaign this would be a dilemma that dogged us: it was always tempting to arrange speeches for Anderson on college campuses, because that is where he drew his largest and most responsive crowds; but, on the other hand, if he were to inspire the support he needed from the general public, he would have to demonstrate a more broad-based appeal. We always pledged to ourselves that we would make greater efforts to schedule noncollege appearances: at factory gates, before business groups, at old folks' homes. But every time we witnessed the massive outpourings of student support, our disposition toward student audiences was reinforced. Politicians, be they practitioners of the "old politics" or the "new politics," like to be cheered.

But on the weekend of March 1, we sensed for the first time that the tidal wave which had been building on college campuses was beginning to spill out into other communities as well. Why this happened so suddenly was not clear, other than that the fact of an impending primary may simply have begun to concentrate the attention of voters. Whatever the case, a quick succession of fund-raising receptions had been arranged along the coast of Massachusetts, and everywhere that Anderson stopped—Ipswich, Gloucester, Manchester, Beverly, Marblehead, Peabody, and Hingham—he was awaited by throngs of fanatical adult supporters, crowded elbow-to-elbow in local living rooms, hoping to hear the wisdom of a new political prophet. What had been a voice crying in the wilderness had now made itself heard; suddenly people wanted to learn the details of Anderson's program for oil conservation, for "reindustrializing" the American economy, for negotiating a saner state of relations with the Soviet Union.

Monday, the day before the Massachusetts primary, the Andersons acquiesced to staying at the stately Copley Plaza Hotel in downtown Boston, instead of staying as usual with Keke's brother in Dedham. This was intended by the Washington office to cast the candidate in a more presidential mold as interviewers and supporters came to see him in the waning hours of the campaign. (The presidential aura may have suffered somewhat from the presence at night of a certain itinerant staff aide slumbering on a couch in the sitting room; the campaign was not yet in a position to afford *two* expensive hotel rooms.) The local TV stations were invited one-by-one to come to the suite for interviews. They did so obligingly, conducted half-hour interviews, and that evening the airwaves were filled with "exclusive" Anderson interviews on all the Boston news shows. The newspapers, too, needed something for the next morning—and the TV crews expressed an interest in action shots as well as interviews—and so the Andersons agreed to make a brief walking tour of the nearby Italian area of Boston, a colorful backdrop for spontaneous street campaigning. The press were gratified, and flocked in great numbers with us as Anderson walked down narrow side streets looking for local hands to shake. The extensive press coverage Anderson received from this Monday campaigning may well have given him an important boost in Tuesday's close election results.

Monday night, March 3, proved to be the highlight of our Massachusetts campaigning. A grand finale had been planned in the way of an election eve rally at the historic Quincy Market in downtown Boston. We arrived as usual in one car, that of a volunteer, found a parking space, and proceeded somewhat nonchalantly toward an entrance. A crowd of fifty or sixty was waiting outside, waving placards. It turned out that these were just the stragglers; most of the Anderson supporters who had turned out for the rally were already making their way upstairs into the Great Hall of the market, where Anderson would be speaking. As we moved indoors, the long corridor of open-air food stands on the first floor was packed with people, some of them regular Monday-night strollers, even more of them, it seemed, Anderson boosters heading where we were heading. Anderson was jostled by enthusiastic well-wishers as he proceeded on; I was relegated to the role of makeshift bodyguard, blocking a path through the crowd. More and more, we realized what a help a genuine Secret Service contingent would be at moments like this. It was not that Anderson was in danger of someone jumping out at him poised to attack, but the aggregate physical experience of walking through a jungle of people thrusting their hands out even in a friendly way was enough for a candidate to feel manhandled by the time he had finished. Acting alone, I was not able to keep people at any real distance.

When we reached the Great Hall, the sight was electrifying. What looked to be a thousand or more people, predominantly students, were crowded into a hall that was probably meant to accommodate only half that number. So many jam-packed people, along with the bright klieg lights required for the half-dozen TV cameras stationed on a platform in the middle of the crowd, made the atmosphere a hot and sweaty one, a decided contrast from the cold March night outside. As we surveyed the situation from the back of the room, we could see John Buckley, the Middlesex County sheriff who had been one of our most avid organizers in the state, and Si Spaulding, a former GOP chairman in Massachusetts, and now our own state chairman, standing at the podium, making remarks intended to warm up the crowd. I waved my arm to let them know Anderson had arrived, and over the microphone they asked the crowd to let him through. We advanced to the podium amid a cacophony of screaming fans. Anderson introduced several members of his family who were with him, then launched into a speech about the "new politics," and told of the enthusiastic reaction he had encountered for it during his campaigning in Massachusetts. Tonight, Anderson's every line was a bell-ringer, and his speech was interrupted repeatedly by lusty shouts of approval. "Something has happened in recent weeks," he said. "We have struck a responsive chord with the people we talk to, especially the young people who are concerned about the future."

Once again, Anderson explained the secret of his appeal. People are tired of traditional politicians, he said, who promise tax cuts and balanced budgets and increased defense spending as if it is enough to wave a magic wand to accomplish these goals; or who say the energy crisis can be solved merely by deregulation, or inflation cured by cutting just a little fat from the budget. The time has come, Anderson said, when people are looking instead for a "new politics," for candid talk about the urgency of national problems, and about the specifics and the sacrifices that will be required to deal with them. People are ready for a new national self-discipline, he said, and a call to commitment, the kind that John Kennedy had proclaimed in the early 1960s. Anderson said he could feel that something had happened in Massachusetts, that citizens had palpably responded to his campaign, and that the results of the next day would surprise many people. When Anderson finished, he made his way haltingly through the crowd out again to the car. In the mad rush, I lost him, and ended up hitching a ride back to the hotel with Si Spaulding. We agreed in the car that Anderson had been magnificent, and that however the Massachusetts results turned out, he had left his mark: the campaign had exercised a true magic on young people. I found Anderson back at the hotel, and we sat a while sipping Scotch and savoring the satisfaction of at last feeling we had accomplished something. The next day would truly tell.

Tuesday morning, we checked out of the Copley Plaza, to move to the Sheraton Boston, the hotel which would be the site of our postelection reception later that night. In the lobbies of both hotels, we could see out of the corner of our eyes guests pointing Anderson out to others as he walked by; many of them came up and wished him good luck. Today, finally, was to be Anderson's one occasion for rest. He had been offered the use of Si Spaulding's large home on the Massachusetts coast, an hour or so outside of Boston. He asked me to come out, and we left for Si's house about noon. On the highway, several people in passing cars looked into our window, recognized Anderson, and flashed him a thumbs-up signal. Anderson commented that if as many people who expressed support for him would actually vote for him, he would win every primary in a landslide.

Keke had decided to stay behind shopping, but Anderson was looking forward to using this spare time to catch up on his reading and even, given the day's mild temperature, to lounge on Si's sunny patio, overlooking the water. Si was at work, but his wife was at home and laid out a spread of soup and other snacks on the kitchen table. Later on, she absented herself, and we were left to our own devices to while away the time. Midafternoon, Anderson grew restless sitting outside, and suggested we take a walk into town; he seemed to remember seeing a tiny business district a couple of miles away, and wanted to find something at the pharmacy. We set off on a leisurely two-hour walk.

The road from Si's home led us in winding fashion through a lush area of large homes, some of which appeared to be summer estates still closed for the winter. Virtually no one was around, and with the air brisk, the sky bright blue, and the neighborhood still, Anderson found it easy to forget he was still immersed in the thick of a hotly contested campaign. He talked reflectively. He was hopeful of doing well, but admitted he had no real way of knowing, and would not be surprised by virtually any result. And yet he had an instinct, reinforced the night before, that something miraculous might happen. For the first time, he could disabuse himself of any lingering doubts as to the wisdom of making his exhausting run for the presidency. Even if it ended tomorrow, it would have been worth it. He had learned a lot about the country, about people, and about himself; and he had registered an impact on the political scene. He had kept plugging away, despite all the naysayers, and, despite the pressures to parrot the positions and styles of the other candidates, he had stuck up for what he believed. This uniqueness had paid off. He resolved to continue campaigning just as long as people continued listening to what he was saying. He was glad he had not taken a job Gerald Ford had once offered him as an appellate court judge; he was less remorseful now that he had not made a run for the United States Senate in 1970, as he had once considered. He was glad he had not forsaken a career in Congress for the lures of a lucrative law practice, or the occasional offer of a highly paid lobbying position. He had found his calling. He was comfortable with himself. He was embarking on a new phase in his life, and glad at last to be doing so.

By the time we got back later that day to the Sheraton Boston, darkness had fallen, and we resumed our anxiety as to what the evening of election returns would hold. Anderson went up to join

Keke in their hotel suite, during which time I searched out the ballroom that we had rented for the evening. Already a half dozen or more television crews had arrived to set up their cameras and lighting equipment; our own volunteers were working to decorate the room with banners and to set up large TV sets off to one side, from which network election coverage could be monitored by the audience throughout the evening. I rejoined the Andersons in their suite, where we ordered some food from room service, and began the vigil of watching television reports of the voting figures that were just now starting to trickle in. As the evening wore on, I began commuting between their suite and the ballroom downstairs, keeping tabs for the Andersons on what sort of crowd and atmosphere were developing, and, at the same time, keeping the waiting press informed as to the candidate's own mood and reactions.

By nine o'clock or so, it was becoming evident that Anderson had been doing extremely well in both the Massachusetts and Vermont balloting. He and Reagan and Bush were fluctuating at the top of the lists, but it was still too early to be able to gauge a clear outcome. I sat flipping the channels of the one TV set in the suite, looking every minute for the most up-to-date results. We paused for a moment watching one particular station as the anchorman began to announce fresh results. "Based on partial returns," he began, "the Associated Press is projecting John Anderson the winner in both Massachusetts and Vermont."

We fell off our chairs. Everyone had been excited as Anderson's tally had been mounting throughout the evening, and he had been showing consistent strength compared to the other candidates. But we were so unaccustomed to victory that we had almost assumed our luck would run out. If ever something were dreamlike, this was it. The Andersons simultaneously jumped up and hugged each other. They reached out and grabbed the hands of the two of their children who were with them, then my hand. They had made it. Everything they had done was worth it. All the hours, all the travel, all the speeches, all the pains, all the doubts—these were behind them. The campaign, in an instant, had been transformed. The days of a dark horse were no more; now we were a campaign to be reckoned with. We had achieved recognition and credibility.

I went downstairs again to the ballroom, where the scene was one of intermingled chaos and ecstasy. By now, a thousand or more people, a large proportion of them local students, had crowded into an area that could barely hold them; scores more were still trying to get in, but contenting themselves for the time being with remote vantage points in the corridor immediately outside the ballroom entrance. Every time an announcement was made over the TV as to the latest candidate standings, a hush would fall over the audience. As Anderson's impressive vote totals were mentioned, a deafening roar would rise up from the same crowd. Many of these supporters had been active until the last moment ringing doorbells, telephoning voter lists, handing out literature. They felt it to be their victory as much as Anderson's and hugged and kissed one another as if it surely were.

Anderson was planning to arrive at the ballroom about 10:00 P.M. to make a victory statement. It occurred to us suddenly that he would barely be able to make his way to the podium through the wall-to-wall mass of humanity that would greet him in the room. We notified the hotel manager, who agreed to provide two or three sturdy security officers to help us out. We knew they might also come in handy in preventing a mad crush from separating Anderson from his wife and children. I returned to the suite one last time, suggested to the Andersons that it was about time to go down, and together we all walked out anxiously and excitedly as if we were about to enter a new world.

I had warned the Andersons en route what a large crowd awaited them, but when they saw it in person they were fairly staggered by the sight. As Anderson approached the entrance of the ballroom, the people in the corridor began to clap and yell, and soon it was evident to the crowd inside that the conquering hero was in their midst. Waves of applause began undulating over the audience as Anderson made his way through the door and then up to the stage. I crowded onto the platform with him, and then made sure that Keke and the children were up front at his side. Minutes went by before the crowd quieted down, and then Anderson began to address it.

"People have accused me during this campaign of being a 'spoiler,'" Anderson said, referring to charges that he had no chance to win and would succeed only in splitting the moderate GOP field and contributing to the nomination of Ronald Reagan. Anderson would not take such a charge lying down. "Is it spoiling the race to be talking seriously about the issues of energy, the economy, and our foreign policy?" he asked rhetorically. "Is it spoiling the race to be saying honestly and specifically what programs have to be put in place to overcome our nation's grave problems? Is it spoiling the race to be reinvolving young people for the first time in years in the political process of their own country?" The crowd went wild expressing its support. Anderson went on for a few minutes and then concluded by quoting Ralph Waldo Emerson in an effort to sum up what had accounted for the campaign's remarkable Massachusetts success: "Nothing astonishes men so much as common sense and plain dealing." It was a quotation we had found quite by accident thumbing through a reference book just a few hours earlier at Si Spaulding's, and which we had decided to use as a centerpiece of the speech tonight. Notwithstanding its mundane origins, the quotation soon became a standard one in Anderson's repertoire, and came to be widely associated with our campaign. Finally, Anderson put his remarks aside and fished out of his coat pocket a small lapel button. He held it aloft, and explained that it had been given to him a few days earlier by the students at Tufts University, and that he had been carrying it around for good luck ever since. The button was all but invisible to most of the audience, and so Anderson read its message aloud: "You Gotta Believe!" The room vibrated with the greatest roar of the evening.

Anderson paused a moment on the stage by prearrangement; he was passed a little earpiece by a CBS technician nearby, and was now tuned in to New York for a live interview with Walter Cronkite, who was conducting his regular primary night election coverage. This rite of passage accomplished, we exited to a small anteroom close by, where ABC had put up a makeshift set for a quick interview. When that was finished a few minutes later, we sneaked out a side door, since much of the crowd remained in the ballroom still enjoying the victory atmosphere, to the outside of the hotel. There a police car was stationed, waiting to take us across town to Boston City Hall where NBC had set up an election night studio to which Anderson was now invited for his final interview. Anderson, Keke, and I climbed in the back seat, and I told the two officers driving us that the congressman was in a hurry. No more needed to be said. As if rushing to the scene of a crime, the driver flicked on

Photo © 1980 Richard Sobol

Massachusetts primary night: moment of success. John Anderson holds aloft "You Gotta Believe!" button. Keke Anderson applauds, while Mark Bisnow (upper right) stares off to distant horizons.

the sedan's flashing red lights, sounded the siren, and sped through occasional red lights to deliver us in record time to our appointment. We were as excited as kids. Everything tonight was electric.

Once we got to City Hall and walked into the NBC studio, the familiar face of John Chancellor greeted us. Whenever we had seen Chancellor before, we were in the position of supplicant, hoping that this great media personage who could decide Anderson's fate would choose out of the goodness of his heart to air even a few seconds worth of news about him. This evening was different. Anderson was a bona fide hot news item, and as he walked in he could hold his head a little higher, knowing that it was he himself who could now bestow the favors. But our pride and ebullience were not to last long. "Congressman," Chancellor began, "I must tell you that we see you coming in second in Vermont, because the rural returns aren't in yet. And we're not positive you're going to be first in Massachusetts, either. AP called this race prematurely. We're not projecting you a winner yet."

Everything is relative, and as Chancellor was uttering his reservations, our hearts were sinking with defeat. It can't be, we thought. We've just come from a victory speech; they can't deprive us of our prize. To lose by a hair would be too much to take. Why didn't we campaign a little harder! Were we going to have to keep playing second fiddle to Bush and Reagan? And Massachusetts was our best state! It seemed like a hoax.

Anderson performed stoically through his interview, as Keke and I watched him close by from the sidelines, but underneath we could all feel ourselves nervous to get back to the hotel. Would all those supporters who cheered Anderson just minutes ago turn now to despair? Had the campaign's glory evaporated so quickly? The police car had stayed at the curb and now rushed us back. We arrived at the Sheraton expectantly, wondering how sour the mood had become. Anderson did not want to return to the reception, thinking it would now be almost inappropriate, if it were really true that he were coming in second, and no longer first. We went back to the suite instead, to catch up on the TV news reports. We were soon relieved. Even though more and more reports were coming in that technically Anderson had not won either primary, still he was being treated as the moral victor: no matter how one sliced it, he had pulled off a stunning upset to have scored as well as he did. Though he came in second in both states, he had still managed to beat Reagan in Massachusetts and Bush in Vermont.* All the news and commentary seemed to be about Anderson. Until about 2:00 A.M., when we finally turned in, the phone in the suite rang every other minute. Just about everyone who had ever known Anderson, it seemed, was calling to offer congratulations. The mood was upbeat once again.

The next morning, before the sun was up, I went to fetch Anderson from his room and accompany him on his rounds to the three

---

*The final Massachusetts results were: Bush, 32%; Anderson, 31%; Reagan, 29%; Baker, 5%; Connally, 1%; Crane, 1%.

network morning news shows, something that would become a regular postprimary ritual. At each place, Anderson had a heavy dose of coffee, and managed to fortify himself enough so that, even on a bare four hours sleep, he looked alert and spoke confidently about his new political status. The question asked repeatedly was how he would be able to parlay a couple of near-victories in friendly territory into the streak of successes elsewhere that would be required ultimately to secure the nomination. Anderson responded, in effect, that now that he had come to public attention, his appeal would broaden and one success would lead to another. The alternative, he reminded his interviewers, was a conservative, Ronald Reagan. Many moderates were already sympathetic to his own candidacy, he pointed out, and now that they saw he could win, they would at last declare themselves. Whether this is what he believed, or merely what he hoped, was not clear, but for the time being the interviewers seemed to find it persuasive.

When we returned from our last interview at about 8:30 A.M., Anderson's fatigue had caught up with him. He still had two hours before a press conference, the next event on his schedule, and he felt like taking a nap. But there was so much noise in his hotel suite, with his wife and kids up there too and the phone and doorbell ringing incessantly, that he did not think he would be able to get any more sleep. I had an idea and told him to follow me. I led him across the hotel into another wing in which the tiny economy room where I had been staying was located. "You can sleep right here," I told him. "I'll come back in an hour or so and get you up." It was a perfect arrangement. I went back to his suite and then down to the lobby, telling a dozen inquisitive reporters only that I had seen him leave his room but was not sure where he was at the moment. To his children, I said only that I thought he had gone downstairs and would be back in an hour. Nobody knew where he was but me, and I would keep the secret until he had had his nap.

When it came time for the press conference, I went back to the room to get Anderson up, and to go over with him a prospective opening statement. It had occurred to us earlier that this would represent a perfect opportunity, given the large number of press bound to attend, to demonstrate the difference in approach between John Anderson and more typical politicians, such as George Bush.

Bush had a reputation for always talking politics; Anderson was known, rightly so, for his true love of issues. What better way to highlight this than for Anderson to present an opening statement at the press conference not on the predictable matter of the primary, but on a more substantive national or international issue.

The ploy would not be strictly for the purpose of public relations. Anderson had long lamented that politicians paid little interest to issues other than the very biggest ones in which they knew people were interested. He felt that a campaign had an educational potential, which was usually neglected, to bring numerous important but unheralded issues to more general public attention than they might otherwise receive. A president would have to take positions on a million and one issues; as a candidate, he might as well start getting used to it. Anderson was quite opinionated on most subjects anyway, and during the long dry spell on the campaign trail when no one had seemed to be listening, we frequently resolved that if the day ever came when at last we had the ear of the press, we would not let it slip by. Throughout the primaries, we made every effort to fashion our press conferences as a forum for Anderson to express strong views on a wide variety of specific and timely new subjects. So it would be today. We found the press conference room downstairs chock full of reporters and cameras. Anderson stepped up to the podium, got out his notes and began. "I want to make a comment about the election held yesterday—," he paused for effect, "in Zimbabwe."

The day before, an important election had also been conducted in that fledgling new nation in southern Africa. Robert Mugabe, the Marxist candidate who had opposed the coalition favored by the white establishment of Ian Smith, had won handily, and the United States would soon be forced to decide a posture toward the new government. Anderson expressed his strong concern about some of the hostile statements Mugabe had made in the past regarding the United States, as well as about Mugabe's brand of politics in general, but said that the best course for our own foreign policy would be to extend an olive branch and see whether we could establish a constructive new relationship. This was Anderson in his best light, talking about specific issues, and the press read the clear message once again that this Anderson was indeed a different type of candidate. The exercise may have been contrived, but its meaning was real. It was a good foot to be getting off on, as we began a new phase of our campaign: Anderson would now be very much in the lime-light, followed by platoons of press, every word of his listened to, weighed, and reported.

DOONESBURY by Garry Trudeau

DOONESBURY by Garry Trudeau

DOONESBURY by Garry Trudeau

From Boston, we flew to New Haven for an appearance at Yale. So many reporters had suddenly signed on to travel with us that, for the first time, we had to rent buses to transport them to and from the airport. In the two weeks between the Massachusetts and Illinois primaries, the traveling press would number anywhere from forty to sixty, a corps the size of which the campaign would never equal again, even during its independent phase. Anderson was rapidly on the rise, and therefore the one to watch.

Our first stop at Yale was for a talk with a small group of professors who tendered Anderson their assistance in his campaign. From there we walked across a spacious green to the chapel, which, despite its immense size, was by now overflowing. A large crowd had even positioned itself outside the entrance chanting to get in. As Anderson continued walking, he was immediately spotted everywhere, and students by the score came running up to join him in his walk, to shake his hand, to take pictures. He looked every inch the part that some had in recent days been ascribing to him: a latter-day Pied Piper of student politics. As he entered the chapel, a jubilant crowd was waiting. It jumped up as one, and gave him a full minute's ovation. It was clapping, one suspected, not only for Anderson, but for the fairy-tale-come-true he represented. He was a David conquering Goliaths.

By the next morning, we were in Chicago. There we began without a breath to embark upon the intensive two weeks of campaigning we would have before the critical Illinois primary on March 18. It was Anderson's home state, and while he had never been well known outside his own region of northwest Illinois, he was assumed to enjoy the advantage of voter pride in a native son, and therefore was expected to do very well.

The campaigning got off to a dramatic start. At De Paul University downtown, our first stop, a woman in the audience stood up and loudly challenged Anderson's position in favor of liberalized abortion laws, accusing him of wanton disregard for human life. Anderson took up the gauntlet and entered into a lively exchange. The woman persisted. Finally Anderson, in his most stentorian voice, reprimanded her: "The question, madam, is not whether you are for or against abortion; the question is whether or not you are for the right of the individual to choose!" Applause and cheers rolled across the college audience; such a position was popular. To the TV cameras, however, it made great theater which would look to viewers at home as if Anderson once again had stood up for his beliefs in the face of hostile inquisitors, such as he had done so memorably at the New Hampshire gun owners forum. An image of Anderson was becoming fixed in the public mind, and events would repeatedly tend to be interpreted in such a way as to corroborate it. Most of the networks carried a clip of his statement that night on the news, and Anderson's refrain was to be much-remembered throughout the campaign.

Other outspoken statements contributed to Anderson's growing reputation for candor and courage. A day or two later, for example, he used the occasion of an otherwise routine news conference at Naperville College in central Illinois to issue a remarkably specific proposal to cut the budget. All candidates of both parties had seemed to be competing over the months in the toughness of their rhetoric on the subject of fiscal responsibility. Anderson felt it was time for the candidates to put their money where their mouths were, and to say specifically what they would cut and trim. He, for one, was willing to do it. Our Washington office prepared some pertinent material and shipped it out to us. We carried it around waiting for an opportune moment to employ it. We had had more than enough to say at all our recent press conferences, but it struck us on this particular occasion that the time had come for an infusion of something even more daring than usual.

And so Anderson offered a list of twenty or more highly specific spending cuts totaling $11 billion in budget savings for the federal government. Reporters were predictably impressed that a politician would do such a thing, particularly since Anderson was enjoying virtual front-runner status these days in Illinois; conventional wisdom held that front-runners ought to do everything possible to preserve their fragile position. Keke was upset that Anderson had gone out on a limb, but he reassured her that it was just this courageous attitude which had served the campaign so well in the first place. Keke was doubtful; she argued that the campaign had entered a new phase where its strategy had to be more circumspect and traditional. Yet days later, Anderson won much-coveted endorsements from both of Chicago's major daily newspapers—the

Tribune and the *Sun-Times*—explicitly on the grounds that, alone among the candidates, his campaign had demonstrated the type of outspoken honesty that would be required of an effective president.

It was in the middle of the Illinois primary that the Secret Service began traveling with the campaign. Candidates became eligible for this protection only after their campaigns had raised one million dollars, or a presidentially appointed board had certified them as requiring immediate protection (as was the case with Senator Kennedy). Our fund-raising efforts had boomed along with our poll results, and we were now over the necessary threshold to qualify. The Secret Service offered presidential candidates just one package of protection; there were no high and low options. Whether you were a Kennedy or a Reagan or an Anderson, you got pretty much the same thing. Three shifts of eight agents each were assigned to follow the candidate around at all times. Extra agents were detailed as necessary to help handle the unusual crowd situations. Untold others performed advance work in the field, arriving several days before each engagement to scout out sites and plan appropriate security arrangements. Still another contingent guarded the candidate's home around the clock, whether or not he was in it. The Secret Service provided a sedan to transport the candidate, a specially equipped station wagon crammed full of agents and weapons to tailgate it, and still another car full of agents to lead the way. Sometimes there was a fourth car of agents as well to bring up the rear. Local police were invited to supplement this motorcade; depending on the city, they might provide anywhere from one to five squad cars and occasionally even a battalion of motorcycle escorts. In addition, foot patrolmen were sometimes assigned to control downtown intersections or freeway entrances as the candidate's convoy swept past.

Such Secret Service protection struck us, certainly at the beginning, as remarkably extravagant. We would have been happy with a couple of bodyguards who could help move Anderson through crowds. But the Secret Service insisted on providing enough manpower to be prepared for virtually any contingency. Given that their reputation was on the line, and that the government was willing to pay almost any cost related to candidate security, the Service evidently preferred to err on the side of overprotection. At times, we did not mind the presence of such a large entourage, walking almost in lock-step with the candidate: it made Anderson look like an established candidate, which was useful at a time when some still questioned his ability to compete with the bigger campaigns. At other times, the presence was an obtrusive one. Spectators were kept at a distance and supporters were resentful at not being able to mingle with their candidate. Moreover, the image of the Secret Service, insofar as it did suceed in giving us more of a professional and big-league look, at the same time robbed the campaign of its original easygoing and small-scale charm. Anderson himself was skeptical for a long time about the value of the protection. He did not think he was in any mortal danger, and he often felt like an animal in a cage, so closely was he guarded and observed. For a campaign which not long before could barely afford to support the travel of a single full-time aide, the advent of the Secret Service came as something of a culture shock.

One day, during our campaigning in Chicago, Anderson ran out of the Tiparillos he occasionally smoked, and could not suppress a craving for more. As we were driving along Michigan Avenue, he spotted a drugstore, and asked the Secret Service to pull the motorcade over. Within moments, a crowd had gathered on the sidewalk, wondering what a number of cars with flashing lights were doing at the curb, and why several husky men with sunglasses had just jumped out, surrounded the sedan, and were now staring back at them so coldly. Suddenly Anderson decided he did not want to be the one to alight from the sedan in the midst of all this attention, and so he asked me whether I would mind running into the drugstore to get him his cigars. I was happy to oblige, but I had never felt so self-conscious opening the door of a car and climbing out. Once I got in the store, and was standing in line at the check-out counter to make my purchase, a new feeling overcame me. I could not believe I was waiting in a five-minute line for a simple package of cigars, when outside an armed multicar motorcade was stalled at the curb with engines running and guns practically drawn. The temptation was great to break into the front of the line and offer the explanation, "Excuse me, but I have a motorcade outside waiting for me." Somehow I could not muster the courage to express the thought, and so the Secret Service, the police, and the candidate just had to wait.

At times like this, the Secret Service seemed more trouble than it was worth. Anderson at one point considered striking a blow for the "new politics" by canceling them, but before long they had grown on us. All told, they did their work very competently and smoothly, and as individuals they were amiable and discreet. Moreover, having them reponsible for our transportation spared us a lot of logistical headaches. Anderson was happy not to worry anymore about having drivers who did not know where they were going, and also happy not having to tender assistance himself in reading road maps.

The single most influential event during the Illinois primary was a debate among the candidates sponsored by the League of Women Voters and held in the final few days of campaigning. By this time, only four contenders remained in competition: Reagan, Bush, Crane, and Anderson. The headlines Anderson had earned from his upset finishes in Massachusetts and Vermont were enough to make him, at least for the moment, the man to beat. As a result, many of his positions seemed to be opposed almost automatically by his rivals, as their way of drawing the clearest distinction between their candidacies and his. Knowing the past checkered history of front-runners, there seemed to be an expectation among onlookers that at any moment this new kid on the block would stumble as everyone else had. No one seemed above giving him a little push.

I watched the debate from a vantage point in the audience at the Continental Plaza Hotel in Chicago, where it was being held. Several of Anderson's family members were seated next to me. Most of us fidgeted. Bush accused Anderson, misleadingly, of wanting to cut Social Security payments; Anderson had proposed reducing slightly the *rate of increase* in benefits so as to correct a statistical discrepancy in the cost-of-living index. Reagan asked Anderson whether he truly meant what he had been quoted as saying in a recent interview: "Now, John," Reagan said, "you wouldn't really prefer Teddy [Kennedy] to me, would you?" And Crane suggested, none too subtly, that Anderson was doing his politicking in the wrong party. At all these charges, Anderson struck back. He raised his hand furiously to be recognized by Howard K. Smith, the moderator. When called upon, he spoke at great length, in great detail, and at great speed, rebutting every argument. When not called upon, he tried to interrupt. By any measure, it was an intense performance. (Fortunately, it did not look quite as bad on TV as it did to the studio audience, since the cameras focused on him only when he was speaking; the rest of the time, the home audience did not see him, as we did, sitting on the edge of his seat, wound tight as a coil.)

Reagan came off best of all, remaining above the fray, and speaking in an avuncular tone of voice. He made several self-deprecating jokes which lightened the atmosphere, such as quoting an ancient Greek philosopher, and then adding, "Of course, I'm the only one here old enough to remember." Anderson, for his part, rather than calmly deflecting the salvos fired against him, escalated the conflict, and called attention to his differences. He seemed uncomfortable in his own party. The impression he left was that if Reagan were the nominee, he would not feel bound by party loyalty to support him. Such an attitude was bound to offend large numbers of Republicans who were watching. This was not fatal in itself— not all voters find party loyalty an overriding concern—but it was combined with a general style that made Anderson come across like an angry young man, determined either to get his own way or to go home and plot mischief.

As many differences as Reagan, Bush, and Crane had among themselves, they had realized it to be in their common interest to cut Anderson down to size, so as to make the field more competitive. As commentators were to say afterward, it was clear that the tactic they took in the debate, consciously or unconsciously, was to "gang up" against Anderson. Of course, this did not necessarily have to hurt Anderson: too overt an aggressiveness might have backfired, making Anderson the object of sympathy and the others look like bullies. But Anderson, who at times loved nothing more than to score debating points against opponents, took the bait and acted defensively. George Bush had been quoted in a local newspaper the morning of the debate as saying that his strategy would be to get Anderson hot under the collar, on the assumption that he was high-strung and would not take it well. I pointed out the article to Anderson, and he promised to guard against overreaction. When push came to shove, however, he did not prove successful in his efforts at self-restraint. Anderson's "hotness" before the cool eye of the TV camera was to recur as a major problem during the campaign, giving him a certain image of stridency which many voters found unappealing.

On Friday, March 14, Anderson made his first return to Rockford since his illustrious exploits back in New England. He had hoped his homecoming would have a triumphal air about it. The first stop as Anderson's motorcade rolled into town was a vacant lot downtown, where a makeshift stage had been set up from which Anderson would address a throng of hometown supporters. Only three or four hundred people showed up, not the thousands of which one might have dreamed; with a full busload of national press on hand to record the event, the turnout was an embarrassment. Some laid the lukewarm reception to poor advance work. Others suspected that Anderson's considerable popularity in Rockford was more in the way of respect than love. Whatever the underlying reasons, the treatment Rockford accorded its favorite son on this day was conspicuous in its restraint.

Equally stinging were arrangements made for a large dinner to be hosted by the local GOP organization later that night. An invitation to address the dinner had been extended not only to Anderson but, we were informed at the last minute, to Phil Crane as well. Anderson was repelled by the idea of having to share the platform with Crane. It was not merely that Crane was a conservative ideologue who made no secret of his contempt for Anderson's brand of moderation. It was not only that Crane had, just a few days before in the Illinois presidential debate, crudely impugned Anderson's credentials as a Republican. What Anderson found hardest to take was that, after twenty years of serving his town and his party so faithfully in Washington, the Rockford Republican establishment was going to make him share the spotlight on this extraordinary night with someone who was not even from the district.

Back in Chicago the Sunday evening before the election, our mood vacillated between nervous and discouraged. Despite polls a week before showing an Anderson lead, we had sensed that such standings were inflated from Anderson's Massachusetts showing and were not destined to last. The latest polls seemed to bear this out. And so, as the day of the primary approached, the question in

our minds became not so much whether we would beat Reagan—
we were growing resigned to the prospect that we would not—but
whether our margin of loss would be respectable enough that Anderson could remain a major contender in the next primary, two
weeks later, in Wisconsin. That was important, because we had
convinced ourselves that Wisconsin was fertile ground for our campaign, and might prove a place where we could reclaim any lost
fortunes.

Anderson was troubled that his success had been acknowledged
by political pundits in almost a grudging way. In some quarters, it
was being treated simply as an aberration, or even something as
lowly as a passing fad. An editorial on March 17 in the *Washington
Post*, for example, was entitled "The Anderson Phenomenon," and
an article the week before in *Newsweek*, "The Anderson Craze."
True, our biggest boosters at the moment seemed to be college students, Cambridge professors, young professionals, newspaper edi-
torialists, Hollywood celebrities, New York cafe society, and generally what one commentator dubbed the "brie and chablis" set, in
reference to its urbane tastes. But we looked upon this as only a
preliminary accomplishment, and an impressive one at that, considering how little we had had only weeks before. It was a base we
would broaden and build on over time. In any event, we wondered,
why should the fervor of college kids always be assumed superficial
and ineffectual? Had they not, in recent times, frequently anticipated fundamental social change? Had they not constituted the vanguard of many a movement that eventually swept past the confines
of college campuses?

As if to suggest just such a possibility, the same people who were
labeling Anderson as merely a "phenomenon" were also beginning
to talk about whether he ought to consider harnessing the energies
of his supporters to an independent bid for the presidency, outside
the bounds of the traditional parties. Hardened political observers
could not bring themselves to see how a flock of college students
would be able to decide the outcome of a Republican convention.
Perhaps they could be of use in a McGovern-style insurgency
against the Democratic party. But the rules, the attitudes, and the
traditions of the GOP were very different. At the same time, these
observers recognized that, having tapped such a vast reservoir of

support, Anderson would be reluctant to quit the race for president. What would be left but an independent run? Anderson's own frequent talk of a "new coalition" and a "new politics," not to mention his studied refusal at the Chicago debate to pledge his unquestioned loyalty to the Republican nominee, were interpreted as hints that the thought of an independent candidacy was already percolating in his mind.

The truth is that Anderson had thought about it very little, and, to the extent he did, had pretty much rejected it. He was preoccupied with the Republican race, and refused to believe that he did not still have a chance. The last thing Anderson wanted to do was encourage speculation that he might bolt the Republican party. His credibility among Republicans, whose votes he needed, was already tenuous enough. Still the speculation would not die. The questions became ever more incessant. The subject was being taken seriously enough that, by the final days of the Illinois primary, major newspaper columns were being written about it. The consensus seemed to be, however, that while Anderson might be tempted to take the plunge, the water was deep and pretty much uncharted. The usual conclusion was that such a campaign, as Anderson said himself, would be almost a practical impossibility, given the financial and legal requirements, as well as the traditional public prejudice in favor of established parties.

Taking its cue from Anderson himself, the campaign staff had not given the idea of an independent candidacy any systematic thought, but in light of the intense public discussion of the subject eventually decided it would be remiss not to look into it at least casually. At first glance, an independent campaign did indeed look to be an exceedingly difficult undertaking. Cursory research uncovered a number of illustrative problems: the filing deadline for independent candidates who wanted to be listed on the ballot in Ohio, for example, fell on March 18, and we obviously were not prepared to submit the requisite petitions; missing the Ohio ballot would mean forfeiting the possibility of twenty-five electoral votes. And in the case of California, a state law seemed to prohibit anyone who had filed as a candidate for a party primary from filing also as an independent candidate for the November general election. These problems were interpreted as forbidding signals that an independent campaign would confront all sorts of similar obstacles; no one gave much thought at the time to the possibility that such rules might be amenable to relatively easy legal challenge.

Anderson himself came to cite these examples when pressed by reporters about an independent campaign. He tried to mention them in an offhand way, as if he had just read about them in the newspaper. He was afraid that if people learned the campaign had actually done research, it might give the impression that the option were under serious consideration. Overall, Anderson's reply to questioning was simply that the issue was moot, because he expected to become the Republican nominee.

But we could not help feeling flattered that the press was taking the whole subject so seriously. It had been exciting enough to have done so well in New England, and to be in such good standing in the Illinois race. But now the realization was sinking in that the success of the campaign had been broadcast well beyond the original primary states. There was support and enthusiasm for the Anderson campaign among people all across the country. In the space of a few weeks, a new candidacy had sprouted up in the national consciousness, so much so that it now possessed, at the least, the potential to damage the established parties. The gravity of our position perhaps registered with us most when commentators began observing that the possibility of an independent campaign by John Anderson could threaten to deny Jimmy Carter reelection. As of mid-March, such speculation could already be heard.

As the days of the Illinois primary campaign drew to a close, George Bush was fading from sight, and for the first time we no longer considered him the prime threat to pick off our would-be supporters. Having been the beneficiary of the momentum (he called it the "Big Mo") which he had generated in Iowa, he now became the victim of a snowballing reverse momentum, when he failed to live up to expectations. Freed from concern about Bush, Anderson used the opportunity to zero in on Reagan. He did so not because he expected to wrest away any of Reagan's conservative supporters—it was not as though many people were wavering between Reagan and Anderson—but because he felt it would create the impression that John Anderson had become the chief spokesman of the alternative point of view to Ronald Reagan's. He could then turn the tables on Bush and argue that Republicans interested in stopping Reagan should jump off the faltering bandwagon of George Bush and rally instead behind the more viable candidacy of John Anderson. To some extent, it may have worked. Increasingly, we picked up reports that we were making substantial inroads among moderate Republicans in the North Shore Chicago suburbs, for example, who had originally been thought to constitute a Bush constituency.

Most of the day before the primary we spent on a last-minute campaign blitz around the state. We splurged and chartered a plane; the large number of press traveling with us helped underwrite the expense. Our purpose was to appear in as many media markets as possible on this last day, and leave an impression of Bush-like momentum. Our first stop was Moline. The air was chilly, the sky was bright blue. We walked off the plane, across the tarmac, and into the modest terminal of the airport. A microphone had been set up and a crowd of 100 or so had gathered for a rally. It was not a large number, but they were charged up, and Anderson's blood started circulating. He told his audience that the campaign was neck and neck with Reagan, but that he would win only if people who did not usually vote could be motivated to come to the polls.

"The Republican party," he said, "should not be considered just the privileged preserve of a few. It is not a closed reservation, but an open one." For a moment, he sounded as though he were back battling the forces of the new right which he had encountered two years before in his own congressional primary, when he had stood up to the intolerance of some of his fellow Republicans who wanted him read out of the party for his supposed liberalism. "You know," Anderson said, "usually Republicans wait until *after* an election to broaden their base, but in this campaign it has been my intention to do it *before* the election." Anderson was anything but apologetic for the efforts he had been making to attract Democrats and independents into the Republican primary. He quoted a *Sun-Times* poll which indicated he would be the strongest candidate the Republicans could field against Jimmy Carter, implying that his appeal to Democrats was a virtue, not a vice. "People shouldn't have to be 99.99 percent pure to get the nomination," he said, citing his twenty years in the Congress as a Republican, and his six successive elections as chairman of the House Republican Conference as proof enough of his party credentials. What people wanted this year, he concluded, was not so much the tired partisan rhetoric to which they were usually subjected, but the "straight talk" of which Adlai Stevenson had once so eloquently spoken.

From Moline, we went on to Peoria. Anderson told another airport rally that those who questioned his Republican credentials were simply resorting to a desperate argument because they were lagging in the polls. He said that if he were to win in Illinois, the shock waves would go out across the country and "be picked up by a lot of seismographs." Asked whether he was gearing back his expectations, however, he conspicuously avoided the prediction of a first-place victory, and instead contented himself with saying only that he expected to do "very well." Next it was off to Springfield. Turning to the subject of Ronald Reagan, Anderson accused his chief rival of advocating "Coolidge economics" and of making "strident, warlike" statements during the campaign in proposing blockades of Cuba and Iran.

We returned late to Chicago, and headed directly to an auditorium at Lincoln Park. A crowd had been waiting for Anderson to arrive for the last one-and-a-half hours, but had been kept satisfied by the presence of former Massachusetts Senator Ed Brooke. Brooke had agreed to do a little campaigning in Anderson's behalf, and had fortunately been at this particular event, available to substitute as a speaker until Anderson's arrival. Anderson thanked him, took to the stage, and then gave a dramatic election-eve speech. "The people are disillusioned," Anderson said. "They are waiting for a voice to speak to them in clear and honest terms. They are looking for candidates who don't just speak to them in promises, or speak to special interest groups, but to the nation as a whole." Then Anderson said, summing up the philosophy that had succeeded so well in setting him apart from the rest of the field:

> The great premise that has undergirded this campaign is that we think the American people of all parties, of all political persuasions, are hungry for candidates who are willing to take specific stands on even the most controversial issues. I have tried to practice common sense and plain dealing . . . . If I win the nomination on that basis, I will be very happy; if I lose the nomination on that basis, I will be

just as happy, because I think that's the basis on which a campaign ought to be conducted.

Primary day was clear and brisk in downtown Chicago, with temperatures in the low 40s. The questions on which many assumed the election would turn were what the voter turnout would be, and how many Democrats and independents would ask for Republican ballots, something voters could do in Illinois up to the moment they entered the polling booth. One complication expected to work against Anderson was that a major state's attorney race was taking place in Chicago, one in which Mayor Jane Byrne had become involved. Consequently, Democrats interested in that race would be discouraged from taking the Republican ballot which they would need if they wanted to vote for Anderson. Crossover voting might not occur to the extent we hoped.

Anderson spent much of his day in Rockford, where he cast his vote and spoke to campaign workers and supporters. In the car en route back in the evening, we heard over the radio that Anderson was leading Reagan, 45 percent to 40 percent, with about 6 percent of the vote in. We knew this was an unreliable early figure, but it momentarily boosted our hopes. Yet almost as soon as we were back in Chicago, and had flipped on the TV, we saw the networks beginning to project that Ronald Reagan would win. We assumed it must be a substantial margin if the networks were going out on a limb this early to make a prediction simply on the basis of exit polling. As we were watching the local CBS affiliate, network news broke in at 8:45 P.M. to allow correspondent George Herman to announce a CBS projection that Reagan would beat Anderson 51 percent to 33 percent. (The final outcome was Reagan, 48 percent; Anderson, 37 percent; Bush, 11 percent.) At first, great disappointment fell over the room. Oddly enough, however, one sensed that Anderson felt suddenly relieved of a ten-ton weight. With such a big margin, he would not be able to kick himself that had he only done this thing or that thing, he could have won. It looked as though Reagan would have swept to victory in any case.

At 9:45 P.M., it was time to leave for the ballroom of the Marriott Hotel, where supporters had gathered to watch the returns. Anderson had practiced a statement in between glances at the TV screen. It summed up his philosophy about the campaign, and when he delivered it a short time later, it came from the heart. "Politics is more than a game of winning or losing. It represents instead an opportunity to address a society's problems and to begin to focus the efforts of a nation in surmounting them. Nor is a Presidential campaign merely an exercise in vote-getting or a contest of organization and money. It is instead a chance for an honest effort to chart a new course for the nation." As for the new politics, he said: "Beginning tonight let us spread it to Wisconsin, to New York, to Connecticut, to Ohio, to Michigan, to Kentucky, to Indiana, to California, to every other state where a primary remains. We will spread it wherever people will listen, wherever people will change, wherever people will hope. We have just begun to fight." His supporters cheered. At this point, Anderson had a marvelous inspiration, and, in reference to the next primary, two weeks later, asked the crowd to join him in singing "On Wisconsin!" The audience responded exultantly. Anderson may have lost the primary, but he was continuing to win the hearts of a new and expanding constituency of people looking for something different.

Before going on, as promised, to Wisconsin, we detoured briefly to Connecticut both for fund-raising purposes and to make a token appearance in advance of the state's primary the following week. Anderson continued to argue, albeit with less certitude than before, that the GOP convention would not ultimately choose to nominate Ronald Reagan, because it would recognize his "unelectability" come fall. Anderson was still fighting gamely. Indeed, he wondered whether he ought not remain longer in Connecticut, rather than rush back to Wisconsin for a primary that would not take place until the week after Connecticut's. It seemed to us that a Bush victory in Connecticut—something quite possible since it was his home territory—could be a great danger: he would be able to ride the crest of its momentum right into the Wisconsin primary the following week. On the other hand, were Bush to be frustrated in his own home state, his campaign would truly be on the verge of collapse, and Anderson might stand to inherit some of his support. All in all, extra time spent campaigning in Connecticut, given the headlines it could produce in Wisconsin if Anderson proved at all successful, might well be worth several days, or even weeks, of slogging around Wisconsin itself. But when Anderson checked with his Washington staff, he was told it was too late to change the schedule, and so we thought no more about it—until, of course, our fears came true, and both Bush and Kennedy did unexpectedly well there.

On returning to Wisconsin, we stopped briefly in Racine for two evening campaign events. At 8:30 the next morning, a Saturday, I walked down the hall from my room, past the Secret Service command post, and knocked at Anderson's door. He had been up some time, and had already ordered room service. He needed some clean underwear, and asked me whether I thought there was any place to buy some near the hotel. I asked the Secret Servicemen outside, and they seemed to think there might be a store open a couple blocks away in a small downtown shopping district. Shortly thereafter, with seven Secret Servicemen in tow, we set out to find the store. The streets of downtown Racine were deserted. To an occasional car that passed, the sight of us must have looked bizarre. Anderson and I were dressed very casually, but we were surrounded by a small army of men in business suits and sunglasses. We stopped first in a drugstore, looking for newspapers. Then we found the clothing store, about the only other thing open in sight. Anderson brought up to the cash register about $6.00 worth of purchases, and presented the clerk his American Express card. The store did not take American Express cards, and Anderson was out of cash. He turned to me. The only thing I had on me was a Mastercharge. Unfortunately, it was a Mastercharge which I knew was many times over its limit of charges; I had not had time to go home and pay my bills in the previous two months, and yet I had no choice but to charge things constantly anyway. I handed over my card, sure that it would be checked on some fancy machine to see if it were valid. With seven gun-toting law enforcement officers surrounding me watching my transaction, I was sure alarm bells would soon be sounding. The irony was exquisite, but no one checked the card after all, and I ended up making the purchase and getting stuck with the bill.

Later that day, we set out in a chartered plane along with a still large press corps, on a tour of the Wisconsin north country. Our state coordinator had scheduled us to spend time in several very small cities. Her reasoning was that the other candidates were ignoring them. We soon found out why. They were remarkably out of the way, and not important enough to justify the diversion of so much time. In a couple of the areas, the political environment was anything but congenial. Clearly, we would have been better served spending the time in more densely populated areas such as Milwaukee County (and in particular in some of its receptively moderate suburbs). Our press contingent was mystified as to the strategy which compelled us to travel where we did, and began to report about it in tones of thinly veiled sarcasm. But on we went to La-Crosse, Ashland, Rhinelander, and Wausau.

On a Sunday morning in the course of this excursion, Anderson flipped on the Charles Kuralt news show on CBS. Kuralt spent ten minutes summarizing the state of the 1980 campaign. His report was disconcerting. He analyzed it, in effect, as already being a closed matter: Carter versus Reagan. The rest of the day, Anderson was a little more subdued and reflective than usual. By the time we reached Rhinelander that night, he was in just the right frame of mind to deliver one of his most memorable speeches of the primaries. The forum was an unlikely one: the Oneida County Republican dinner. Anderson seemed to be thinking aloud as he spoke, discarding the unimaginative notes I had prepared for the occasion. He recalled to his audience the early days of the campaign, and the philosophy which had inspired him. In running for president, he said, citing a phrase from his original announcement speech in June of 1979, he had wanted more than anything to appeal to the "conscience and the reason of Americans." It was time, he said, to step back and view national problems not through the lenses of special interest groups, but from the perspective of the whole nation's interests.

Anderson noted that he had run in almost a dozen elections for public office, and admitted to having generally employed a traditional approach in doing so. Usually the way politicians get elected, he said, is by saying things that people like to hear. They go before groups of farmers and pledge to fight for higher price supports; they speak in a United Auto Workers meeting hall and voice support of legislation dear to labor; they attend meetings of the National Educational Association and make a point of explaining why, more than other candidates, they will bring benefits to teachers. Over the years, he said, he had discovered that there was one great problem with such politics-as-usual. "Promising people that you're going to take them up on the mountaintop and deliver this, that, and the other thing is not going to work. A politician who does that and is elected in November is going to reap the whirlwind when he takes office in January and finds that he can't possibly carry out the promises he has so extravagantly made." The country was now in deep trouble, Anderson went on: dangers in Afghanistan and the Persian Gulf, chronic and debilitating inflation, an energy crisis that was changing our way of life. Only a different political approach would be equal to the challenge. "I made up my mind that there was something even more important than winning or losing, and that was to try to articulate a new policy, a new politics, that would be based on a willingness to endure the slings and arrows—and, yes, even the insults—of those who disagree with you; but to try to speak in perfect honesty on each and every issue you address, even though it may be in an environment where it would not be received with great acclaim." The Anderson difference was never stated better.

After this event in Rhinelander, Anderson spent considerable time talking privately about the pros and cons of an independent bid for the presidency. We avoided letting anyone else hear about it, concerned as we were that something might leak to the press and cause people to think Anderson was not still dedicated to his Republican campaign. He was entirely uncertain about the independent idea, and frankly wanted to postpone a decision as long as he could. The situation was one of excruciating frustration. The size and fervor of his crowds were at their peak; the country seemed to be clamoring for an alternative to the likely nominations of Carter and Reagan. But most of the voices beckoning Anderson seemed to be coming from outside the Republican party, and winning his party's nomination now seemed increasingly unrealistic. A defeatism was spreading among political commentators about his campaign that caused him more and more to ask himself what the point was of prolonging the effort. We had not organized in primary states beyond Wisconsin, due to our original shoestring budget and limited hopes; we had concentrated our resources exclusively in the early states thinking that if we did well, by some stroke of luck, we would cross our next bridges as we came to them. While Anderson had never entertained illusions about appealing to the conservative heart of the GOP, he had hoped that by means of reregistration drives and open primaries he could enlist the help of independents, Democrats, and former nonvoters in tilting his party back in a more moderate direction. But now, as he looked ahead, he had to wonder: How would we be able to do any better in states like Indiana and Kentucky and California than we had done in Illinois, where we had applied so much energy, and in Wisconsin, which we thought would be such a congenial environment but where things were now beginning to look so bleak?

The idea of running as an independent did not come naturally to Anderson. True, he did not feel he owed the sort of blind allegiance to his party that other candidates did—indeed, given his treatment in recent years at the hands of his party's conservatives, he felt increasingly alienated and resentful—but he *had* always been a Republican, and he had a fear that abandoning his party in the middle of a campaign would be taken as fickle or opportunistic. Even so, it was a hard thing to hang it all up after such an expenditure of effort as he had made, and just at the moment when he had become a major force in politics. Even Kennedy and Bush, later in the primaries, were to find it hard to stop when their efforts proved futile; and they, at least, had parties that would welcome them back and likely political futures beyond the 1980 election. For Anderson, calling it quits might mean never being heard from again. Anderson began to think more seriously about an independent campaign.

Several of Anderson's Washington advisors pressed him to let the campaign start proceeding on two tracks. Bob Sann, then our media advisor, and Tom Mathews, our direct mail expert, both seemed to think that a great potential existed for a third party movement which would dissipate quickly if it were not soon tapped. Anderson agreed to convene a meeting in Milwaukee of various people whose advice he wanted to weigh as he came to a decision. I sat down with him and we considered systematically who should be invited to this potentially critical discussion. Certainly Norman Lear, the television producer; he had been in touch with us repeatedly to express what he said was his growing intuition that the public would soon be hungering for an alternative to Carter and Reagan. Lear was someone who we assumed had his finger on the public mood, given his success at creating entertainment of mass popular appeal, and so his sentiments carried considerable weight. Lou Harris, the pollster, was someone else we hoped would join the discussion; he had already indicated to Anderson his own feeling—corroborated, he said, by his polling data—that public attitudes would be favorable to a third party bid. (Harris, alone of those we contacted, declined to participate, citing a professional responsibility to avoid formal political involvement.) David Garth, the media specialist, seemed a third obvious choice. Both Anderson and I assumed that if a third party candidacy were to be taken seriously, it would be extremely helpful to show the press that someone of Garth's stature had confidence enough in the enterprise to be taking it on, and would be applying his talents to running it. Finally, several staff members would be included: myself, Mike MacLeod, Cliff Brown (our director of research), as well as Tom Mathews and Roger Craver, the campaign's direct mail specialists. We talked with the Washington office Sunday evening on the phone, and asked that a meeting be arranged for Tuesday afternoon at the Pfister Hotel in Milwaukee, where Anderson would be staying at that time.

While visions of an independent bid began to preoccupy our thoughts, we continued on our Republican campaign schedule at a hectic pace. Sunday night, we flew to Wausau. I joined Anderson for hamburgers and ice cream in his motel room, and we sat up late into the evening talking about the days ahead. We agreed that while a Reagan/Carter contest was being treated as virtually inevitable by much of the press at the moment, such a perception could soon change. Surely the press and the public would be looking for more excitement, more suspense, to carry them through the campaign season, we reasoned; it would be extremely dull to close the book on the campaign at this early date. An Anderson candidacy might provide just the spark people were looking for.

Two days later, the Andersons were together in Milwaukee, having dinner and discussing a syndicated Lou Harris column in the local paper which concluded, on the basis of poll results, that John Anderson was a "striking new political force in this country." They could not but be moved by such characterizations. We sat and talked for a while about some of the considerations that would govern a decision about an independent bid: How much money would be needed, and where would we get it? How would we be able to meet the difficult filing deadlines of some of the states? What would sustain public interest in the campaign through the remaining primaries and the conventions when Anderson would not be competing and would therefore have trouble claiming media attention? Would it be possible to win the presidency encumbered by controversial positions like the fifty-cent gas tax? Would we be able to broaden the campaign's appeal beyond students and intelligensia? Was it possible that large numbers of people who did not usually vote could be excited enough by the Anderson candidacy to turn out at the polls? Would Anderson in the end prove to be only a "spoiler" and throw the election to one of the other candidates?

The next morning, at a routine press conference following a speech at Marquette University, questions focused on whether Anderson would quit the Republican race and launch an independent campaign. Interest had been fueled by an article in the local Milwaukee paper that morning which indicated that Anderson was leaving the door open on the matter. The report was based on comments he had made the night before on a radio phone-in show. Anderson contested the newspaper's interpretation. A woman, he explained, had called in to urge him to run as an independent. Just to be polite, he said, he had told her that he would "reflect on it." "But I mull many things over all the time," he reassured the press, "and the fact is I am still bound and determined to fight for the GOP nomination." He admitted that, in response to questions several days before, he had indeed given a flat no when asked whether he would consider undertaking a third party bid. But he appealed for understanding that it was simply tempting to try to end speculation which one thinks exaggerated, yet about which one keeps getting pestered.

About 11:45 A.M., when we were back at the Pfister Hotel, I went to the lobby to await the arrival of Norman Lear, who needed to be ushered up to the Andersons as promptly and as inconspicuously as possible. We were not going to go to great lengths to hide the fact from the press that the congressman was holding an important meeting this afternoon, but we did not want to advertise it. The press would be suspicious anyway, we assumed, that Anderson had nothing on his schedule for several hours, and that unusual pedestrian traffic was flowing to and from his room. If quizzed, we were prepared to say only that we were having a general strategy meeting.

This would have seemed natural, given the general perception that our fortunes were fading and that we needed to revise our strategy if we were to pull out a victory in Wisconsin. Lear arrived with his wife, Frances, as well as his friend Stanley Sheinbaum. I took them up from the lobby, and for an hour we joined the Andersons over lunch in their suite. At that point, others began arriving for our formal meeting, which was to begin at 1:00 P.M. The one person still absent was David Garth, and we wondered if he had made his plane from New York. I went down to the lobby again, checking for signs of his presence, and, sure enough, he was just walking in. I brought him directly up to the suite, holding my breath that someone would recognize him and wonder what he was doing in the same hotel as John Anderson; nobody did.

The meeting convened, and almost from the outset an unstated premise began to take hold that it would be a good thing if Anderson ran as an independent. The main question seemed to be what had to be done. Anderson himself sat listening almost impassively, taking notes, but not revealing his own sentiments on the subject. Keke, Lear, and Mathews made the most forceful arguments in favor of running. Cliff Brown was about the only one to voice concrete reservations, arguing among other things that, in his opinion, winning the Republican nomination was still an active possibility. Garth made a point of saying more than once that Anderson's chances of winning as an independent were smaller than one in a hundred. For a moment, I took that to mean that he did not think Anderson should run; but in fact he did support an independent candidacy. Looking back, his statement was perhaps another example of his standard operating procedure: by making something look extremely difficult, one gets great credit if it suceeds, yet has a built-in explanation if it does not. Garth also argued that Anderson should run not as the candidate of a formal third party—because, he said, this would scare voters accustomed to the two-party tradition—but, rather, as an independent candidate who would technically retain his Republican party registration. Heretofore, most of us had not made this distinction between a third party candidacy and an independent candidacy, but, after hearing Garth amplify on it, we found outselves in agreement with his conclusion.

Finally, Garth argued that running an effective independent campaign would cost only about $12 million, not the $30 million that each of the nominees of the major parties was expected to spend. When other participants asked how this would be possible, he explained that the campaign would have to be run very frugally, and eschew the extravagances of a customary big-time campaign. Lear said he sensed that people would be eager for just such a choice as Anderson could offer, and even suggested as a theme for the campaign the old musical tune "High Hopes." It was easy to get caught up in the spirit of the meeting, but I could sense that Anderson himself had not been completely sold as yet on the idea of stopping his Republican campaign in its tracks and starting another campaign from scratch. Given the gravity of the decision people were recommending, I argued that Anderson make no final judgment until he had slept on the matter for several days. It seemed unnecessary to reach a definite decision, or even a tentative one, this particular afternoon. Although ballot drives and other organizational efforts needed to be put in motion if Anderson were really going to change course, time was not slipping away so quickly that he should feel under the gun to make an impulsive decision.

For the next several days, Anderson was peppered incessantly with questions from the press about the possibility of his undertaking an independent candidacy. Editorials appeared widely supporting or opposing the idea. The Carter White House was reported to be worrying about the prospect; polls showed Anderson increasingly popular with Democrats. Meanwhile, Anderson kept mum as to his thinking, but refused to rule anything out.

The primary situation looked more and more discouraging. Though we had once hoped Wisconsin would be the state which would bring Anderson to the fore in the Republican field, the latest polls showed him likely to come in third behind Reagan and Bush. If that happened, he would soon be faced with a profound choice between quitting a campaign in which he had invested two years of his life and taking a plunge into an uncertain new adventure which carried great risk, not only for his own future, but for the course of the 1980 presidential election. Anderson requested a speech for the night of the primary which would neither commit him to a particular course of action nor foreclose anything either. And so, when the returns came in Tuesday night (Reagan, 40 percent; Bush, 31 percent; Anderson, 28 percent), and Anderson's hopes for some semblance of success in Wisconsin had collapsed, he came before another ballroom full of the faithful and addressed them with calculated ambiguity.

> I believe we have made ourselves heard . . . . It has been our purpose to convince Americans of a new urgency about our problems, and to rally them to new goals . . . . The question is not whether you are a conservative or a liberal, a Democrat or a Republican. The only question is whether you care about your country in its hour of need, and whether you are willing to join hands to do what needs to be done . . . Are the American people ready for a new politics and a new course? I believe they are.

Then Anderson quoted Carl Sandburg.

> The people will live on.
> You can't hinder the wind from blowing.
> In the darkness, with a great bundle of grief,
> The people will march.
>
> In the night, and overhead a shovel of stars for keeps,
> The people will march and ask, "What to? Where next?"

And so he concluded: "For my part, I will keep marching, too. And I ask you to join me. We will not give up in our quest. We will not cease in our efforts to say what needs to be said, to do what needs to be done." His supporters cheered; they were willing to travel a new road.

6

April, 1980: From Republican to Independent

Anderson's third place finish in Wisconsin was widely interpreted as dashing his hopes for the nomination. Given its lenient provisions for crossover voting, the Wisconsin primary had been regarded as peculiarly well-suited to a Republican candidacy that appealed in large measure to Democrats. Besides, the state had a reputation, rightly or wrongly, as more receptive than most to liberal politics. In the end, however, Democrats flocked across party lines as much to Ronald Reagan as they did to John Anderson; moderate Republican suburbanites pulled their levers in large numbers for George Bush; and great masses of students whose support Anderson had sought chose to remain more than expected in the columns of Ted Kennedy and Jerry Brown.

But third place was third place; and whatever the explanations, the press found it convenient to report the outcome of the race in terms of sheer ranking. It appeared the wind had leaked quickly from the Anderson balloon. At first it seemed unfair. After all, but for the unanticipated resurgence of Bush and Kennedy in primaries the week before in Connecticut, their heretofore disappointed supporters might have considered lending Anderson their votes in Wisconsin. Had Jerry Brown dropped out of contention, as he had been contemplating seriously since the Massachusetts primary, his supporters, too, might have switched over. In a real sense, quirks seemed responsible for Anderson's defeat. How, then, could the press leap to the generalization that his showing in Wisconsin revealed an inability to succeed in future primaries and ultmately to capture the nomination?

On more objective reflection, however, we recognized increasingly that the conclusions being drawn in the press were not without warrant. Probably the press had been kind to withhold its judgment as long as it had. The Anderson campaign had done considerable spadework in Wisconsin; it had put a serious organization in place; and the candidate himself had made numerous visits to the state. He still had the benefit of a fresh image and exciting headlines from the recent New England primaries; and his showing in Illinois, while disappointing to us, had nonetheless proved respectable. None of these propitious conditions obtained for future primaries. We barely knew what the next ones were. We would not be able to coast into them on favorable publicity. We had not enlisted precinct workers in those areas, established offices, compiled telephone lists, or studied voting patterns. Crossover and reregistration practices were less flexible. Student populations would not wield as much influence. And more and more, Republicans would scoff at the idea of choosing a standard-bearer whose loyalty to party seemed so uncertain.

But the biggest single nail driven into the Anderson campaign coffin was something more mundane: the failure to gain a spot on the ballot in the Pennsylvania primary, to be held in late April. Incredible though it later seemed, the Anderson campaign organization had not been able to gather the mere 1,000 signatures required to qualify. This had happened back in February, when the campaign office in Washington was relatively small and there were no field offices to help shoulder the work. The matter of collecting signatures had been delegated to a volunteer out in the state. No one knew him well enough to attest to his reliability, but he was relied upon nonetheless. There was much else to occupy the attentions of the headquarters, and so it was tempting to make the vague assumption that things were in order.

All of a sudden, less than forty-eight hours before the deadline for filing signatures, our lone volunteer in Pennsylvania phoned the Washington office frantically. He confessed that he had barely collected any and appealed for immediate help. Given the importance of the Pennsylvania primary, the size of the task to be done, and the urgency with which the campaign needed to do it, the action to have been taken at this point was obvious: every available resource should have been thrown instantaneously into the effort to get signatures. Inexplicably, the campaign took a more relaxed approach. Mike MacLeod, the latest in our series of campaign managers, detailed four young Washington office workers to drive up to Pennsylvania the next morning and lend a hand. Not surprisingly, the solution proved to be too little and too late. The hapless four workers returned to Washington that night sullen and dejected. They had managed to scrape together only 800 signatures. For want of 200 more, the Anderson campaign would be excluded from competing in one of the most important primaries to date. It did not boost morale when we learned later that a number of lesser known candidates had managed to qualify, including one whose chief distinction was that he had been a certified mental patient at a Pennsylvania insane asylum.

And so, while most of the other candidates left Wisconsin set to plunge into three weeks of intensive campaigning in Pennsylvania, the Anderson campaign was not even sure what its next move would be. After the deadline was missed in February, and thought was first given to the "Pennsylvania problem," we had worked up a consoling scenario: either we would be beaten decisively in the primary competition by the relatively advanced stage of Pennsylvania, in which case our status in that state's primary would not matter; or, if we had survived that long, the campaign would be so flourishing as to be able to do well simply on a write-in basis, something that the primary rules in the state permitted. April had seemed so far away, and we were able to put Pennsylvania out of mind virtually until it was the next primary and staring us in the face again.

In the cold light of the post-Wisconsin dawn, however, we realized how difficult, expensive, and, in the end, uncertain a write-in effort would be. We made one brief stop in Philadelphia, but then decided to regroup in Washington. On an inspiration, we took a three-hour train ride back, not only boosting the energy-efficient virtues of Amtrak, but feeling for a splendid moment as if we were campaigning back in the romantic era of the whistlestop tour. When we arrived at Union Station in Washington, a motorcade took us quickly back to Anderson's congressional office. There, on the steps of the Longworth building, a group of fifty campaign workers waited to greet their candidate. It was the first time Anderson had been back in a long while. And it was the first time he had been back with the big four primaries—New Hampshire, Massachusetts, Illinois, and Wisconsin—behind him. He deserved a welcome home, and he was touched to receive it.

In a speech that night at George Washington University, Anderson vowed he would not abandon his race because of seeming electoral realities. He admonished the press and the public for an excessive poll-consciousness. "If polls were always believed, Carter would have bowed out of the race last fall, Kennedy would have bowed out of the race this spring, Ronald Reagan would have given up after Iowa, and Thomas Dewey would have beaten Harry Truman." For his part, Anderson said, he would stay in, and continue to fight for the principles of his campaign. Drawing from memory, he ended by invoking the famous line from Abraham Lincoln, "I desire to conduct the affairs of [an Anderson] administration that if, at the end, when I come to lay down the reins of power, I have lost every other friend on earth, I shall at least have one friend left, and that friend shall be down inside of me." The crowd of 1,500 students burst into applause. This was a classic, and moving, statement of the courage which had come to be associated with John Anderson during the primaries. The Anderson magic was still winning hearts.

On Thursday, April 3, Anderson went to Los Angeles for a three-day respite on the beach at Malibu. Bud Yorkin, a prominent TV producer, had offered Anderson the use of his beach-front hideaway. Anderson was scheduled to begin several days of campaigning in California the following Monday, and so it seemed a convenient and appealing way to spend the weekend. Anderson had not had a vacation since the campaign officially began almost a year before. Now, more than ever, he needed a quiet moment to reflect.

I flew out to Los Angeles on Friday, using the opportunity to visit my parents; I would be accompanying Anderson on his campaign rounds the coming week, but did not plan to see him over the weekend. It seemed clear to me that he and his family could use some privacy—Keke and two of his daughters were to be joining him—

and that this would be a time for staff members to assume a low profile. Nonetheless, I did have a memo which I wanted to deliver, reflecting my own ambivalent thoughts on the advisability of an independent campaign. It seemed important to get the memo to Anderson as soon as possible, since he was planning to spend a good part of his leisure time mulling over campaign options.

I drove out to Malibu Saturday afternoon, intending only to leave an envelope at the door of the house where he was staying. Although it had been announced publicly that he would be spending the weekend in Malibu, we had gone to great pains not to disclose his address or telephone number to the press or even to most of the campaign staff, in an effort to protect his solitude. Nonetheless, enterprising reporters soon began driving along Pacific Coast Highway looking for the telltale evidence of Secret Service guarding a beachfront home. It was not hard for them to find. The Secret Service had set themselves up conspicuously by parking a trailer in the driveway, perfectly visible to passing motorists, and then allowing their agents to congregate in large numbers on the sidewalk out front.

I arrived at the house, paused at the curb, and asked the Secret Service to pass along an envelope to Anderson. They reacted with surprise that I did not want to disturb him, telling me that, far from having been a recluse, Anderson had distinctly been up and around. He had walked along the beach that morning, for example, cheerfully stopping to greet strangers. I should have anticipated that. Despite Anderson's occasional attempts at obtaining privacy, he would soon grow restless and want very much to see the world again. I went up to the door and knocked. He answered, and broke into a great smile, pleased to see a familiar visitor. Evidently he was feeling isolated and was only too happy to change his pace. He had been sitting in the living room, staring out at the ocean, and intermittently glancing at newspapers. We talked a few minutes, and then, learning that I had brought a friend who was waiting outside, insisted that I bring him in to have some tea and chat. We had our tea, but took our leave fairly quickly; he said Keke was napping, and I feared that if we woke her, she would not be pleased to see her husband entertaining guests.

But Anderson asked me to come again the next day, to talk at greater length about the future of the campaign. And so on Sunday morning I drove out again to Malibu. I came to the door, but it was a while before my knock was heard. Anderson, Keke, and Diane, their twenty-year-old daughter, were sitting on the patio deck in the back of the house, absorbing a mild morning sun and reading the Sunday newspaper. Somehow they had even managed to find a *New York Times.* They passed me several sections of a paper, and I joined them in reading. The air was tranquil except for the regular, muffled crash of ocean surf in the distance, and the occasional interruption of someone who had just run across an interesting article in the paper.

About 11:00, Anderson asked me if I wanted to take a walk on the beach. We rolled up our pants legs, kicked off our shoes, and walked along the sand close to the surf. The Secret Service followed along: one lead agent scouting things about fifty feet ahead, another three agents keeping pace a discreet distance behind, and a station wagon loaded with reinforcements slowly driving along an access road above the beach in the distance.

Anderson indicated he was still wrestling with the question of an independent candidacy. He said he was sorry that the press had inflated the significance of his Malibu weekend the way it had, predicting that he would arrive at a decision by Monday and then announce it with great fanfare. Anderson had invited such speculation by making the jocular comment on leaving Washington that he planned to "sit under a eucalyptus tree" and contemplate his future. Unavoidably this left the impression that a decision was in the making. But Anderson did not now see the urgency of it. Would it not be possible only gradually to explore an independent race, raise money, and test public opinion?

As we walked along, he lowered his voice, and cast me a sidelong glance. "Well, at least I've decided that the Republican race is over." I was surprised by his statement, but not jolted. He had not expressed this sentiment before, but it would have been hard not to reach such a conclusion. For a while it had seemed possible that Reagan could falter in the coming weeks and months; nonetheless, it was difficult to imagine party regulars permitting Anderson to fill the vacuum. They would much sooner have resurrected Howard Baker, George Bush, or Gerald Ford. Whether or not Anderson had a chance as an independent candidate, it was clearly fruitless to continue his Republican candidacy. As far as the independent campaign was concerned, I argued that even were he genuinely undecided, it might still be necessary to set the wheels in motion, simply as a means of preserving the option. He seemed to agree.

Anderson's uncertainty at this point about running as an independent appeared to stem from practical considerations: could money be raised, and an organization be put together, on the awesome national scale that would be required, and quickly enough to make him an effective competitor of the party nominees? The political wisdom of the move no longer seemed to give him trouble. He had begun to see the situation in almost historic terms, that the parties had proved inadequate in solving the problems facing the country, and that extraordinary remedies might now be the only answer. A conjunction of circumstances had arisen which might not be repeated; this could prove an election like no other. Not only might an independent candidate be capable of winning the presidency, but, in the process, he might help usher in a reinvigorated party system and a whole new approach to the conduct of political affairs. 1980 could be looked back on as the beginning of a new national era. These thoughts were equally sobering and stirring, and one had the sense that if only Anderson could be satisfied on the mechanical questions about running, he would be set to take the plunge.

When we returned to the house forty-five minutes later, Diane was in the mood for lunch. She was about to take our orders and go off to find some hamburgers. I suggested to Anderson that we all get out of the house and go with her. He was happy to be nudged. We walked out front and informed the Secret Service of our objective. They loaded us into an armored Cadillac limousine—it was hard not to be self-conscious riding around an informal beach area in something so enormous—and we headed off down the street. After a minute, it became obvious to Diane that we were going in the wrong direction. I intervened with the driver. "You know, I think McDonald's is the other way," I volunteered. "Oh," he said, "I thought Jack-in-the-Box would be okay." This was a reference to another popular hamburger chain. Diane took strenuous issue, and, quite partial myself, I helped her to stand her ground. Two-way radios began buzzing, and slowly the motorcade ground to a halt.

We waited for traffic to pass, and then the motorcade snaked across the highway and headed back in the opposite direction.

During our ride, and in between our bites of Big Macs, we resumed discussion of Anderson's prospects as an independent. I raised several points from the memo I had given Anderson: that an independent campaign would represent another exhausting effort which might produce only embarrassingly modest levels of public support; and that if enough support developed to keep us going until election day, the campaign might miscalculate its strength and not only lose, but have on its conscience that it had elected one of the other candidates inadvertently. On the other hand, I said, these problems could be avoided if Anderson pledged from the beginning to pull out of the race if it became evident he could not win. My overall recommendation was that he begin actively testing the waters for an independent campaign and launch whatever organizational efforts were necessary, but that he not lose perspective and pursue such a course blindly. To the contrary, he should be ready at any time to reverse course; the rational among his supporters would recognize that the best is sometimes the enemy of the good. But for the time being, it did indeed seem that much of the public considered a choice between Carter and Reagan no choice at all and sought a third way out.

Early that afternoon, we were joined by a young campaign specialist from Massachusetts, David Thorne, who had flown in at Anderson's request. His purpose was to present findings on research he had conducted into the practical aspects of an independent campaign. The first important filing date for such a candidacy, Thorne reported, would be April 24. On that date, eight hundred signatures would have to be turned in to qualify for a spot on the ballot in New Jersey. On May 6, forty thousand would be needed to secure a place on the ballot in Massachusetts. Because election officials typically invalidated a large number of signatures, we were informed, the rule of thumb was to submit twice the required number. Every state had different provisions for filing, and a battery of lawyers would be needed to make sense of the crazy quilt of legal regulations. Fortunately, an independent legal effort had already been begun on Anderson's behalf. It was being spearheaded by a Maryland lawyer named John Armour, someone who had assisted in a similar way in the 1976 independent campaign of Eugene McCarthy, and financed by Stewart Mott, the liberal philanthropist who for several months had taken an interest in the Anderson candidacy.

While we were talking, Norman Lear dropped over at Anderson's invitation, still in his Sunday tennis clothes. He was convinced that the state of the country called out for another choice in November, and he was prepared to do whatever he could to advance an independent candidacy. Anderson listened intently. He appreciated the gravity of the decision he was being called upon to make, even if he was getting conflicting advice from many sources. The day before, he said, former Massachusetts Senator Ed Brooke had called to urge him not to make an independent run. Brooke argued that Reagan's probable nomination meant it was all the more important for people like Anderson to remain in the Republican party in order to help revive its moderate wing. Anderson liked and respected Brooke, who had given him a valuable endorsement in the Massachusetts primary, but felt it was an illusion to think the moderate wing of the party could be strengthened. The problem was not one of numbers—there were many Republican liberals and moderates in high positions, such as Governors Milliken, Ray, Thornburgh, Thompson, and Quie—so much as one of will. These same people had had their chance to step forward early on and support John Anderson. Had they done so, he might have had more success, and there would not now be a reason for his having to seek another route to the presidency. But they had not stepped forward, and so it seemed ironic to be hoping he would try again to help the moderate wing of the party when, partly on its own account, his first such attempt had failed.

At about 5:00 P.M., Tom Mathews arrived. His purpose was to discuss with Anderson the financial potential and pitfalls that faced an independent effort. It concerned me somewhat that we were turning for advice to people who had a vested interest in Anderson's decision. Looking back, it seems no coincidence that our various "vendors"—professional fund-raisers such as Mathews, media specialists such as Garth, and lawyers such as the one we were to retain later, Mitch Rogovin—were among the independent campaign's most enthusiastic proponents not only at the beginning, but even at the end, when it had no chance. This is not to impugn their motives, but only to question whether a candidate should permit himself to rely on advisors whose views are unavoidably colored by commercial personal perspectives.

On "CBS Evening News" that night, a feature about Anderson was run with the theme, "Will he or won't he?" A CBS camera crew had been stalking the Malibu beach all weekend looking for the Anderson retreat, and an opportunity to take furtive pictures of the candidate huddling with advisors. When we were out on the deck in midafternoon, we had spotted a crew coming up on us from a hundred yards down the beach. Feeling intruded upon, Keke said, "Quick!" and we promptly slid out of our chairs and moved inside. On the news segment CBS aired, taped footage was shown of several shadowy figures on the Anderson patio, making suspicious-looking moves into the house. One would have taken Anderson for Howard Hughes or Robert Vesco, the way an air of mystery was created about his comings and goings.

At seven the next morning, I met Anderson again back in Malibu. It was a beautiful day as we headed along the ocean and made our way into downtown Los Angeles. As if a several-car motorcade were not conspicuous enough, the armored limousine screamed for attention; it was much different from the Chrysler sedan the Secret Service normally provided. I asked the driver if it were not possible to change cars. Anderson was to be speaking in the afternoon at UCLA; the sight of a candidate who espoused energy conservation blithely riding in such a vehicle would be an embarrassment. It was not a particularly pleasant car to ride in anyway. The bulletproof windows were so thick as to distort one's vision of passing scenery and make us feel like inmates of a mobile prison. The Secret Service detail leader promised to check into the possibility of a change. As it later turned out, there was reason for this particular car and a change could not be made. In the aftermath of President Carter's recent speech announcing the termination of United States relations with Iran, sporadic incidents of violence had occurred among local Iranian students. The Secret Service, for the protection of its own interests as well as ours, insisted that an armored car be employed. As a compromise, however, it was arranged that we would be able to pull up to an inconspicuous back entrance for the UCLA speech that afternoon.

We arrived a little before 8:00 A.M. at the Sheraton Wilshire where Anderson had a breakfast meeting with local black leaders, then a second breakfast meeting with local reporters. From there we headed to the Biltmore Hotel, where the major event of the day would be held: an 11:00 A.M. press conference, at which reporters for the first time would be able to quiz Anderson about his weekend reflections. The room Anderson entered contained wall-to-wall press. The podium was so jammed with microphones that it was impossible for him to lay out his notes for an opening statement. Cameras were aimed at him from every direction.

"I had a very restful vacation in Malibu the last three days," Anderson began. "Unfortunately, I was not able to find the eucalyptus tree after all, and therefore did not do all the contemplating I would have liked regarding the possibility of an independent campaign." There was amusement at this line, but also disappointment that Anderson would not be issuing a dramatic announcement of intention. Instead, Anderson went on to say that he would not be making a final decision for several weeks. In the meantime, he said, he would be consulting widely with friends and supporters, and would also continue campaigning for the Republican nomination. Nothing would be ruled in; nothing would be ruled out. When he finished his statement, the press pounced on him with questions but could obtain no further enlightenment.

We returned to Anderson's hotel suite at the Biltmore where he was hoping to read the newspaper and rest a few moments. The physical situation we encountered there epitomized the burgeoning bureaucracy of a successful campaign. The suite consisted of a small bedroom and a much larger, elegantly appointed sitting room. On a table in the sitting room, the local campaign organizers had thoughtfully provided an array of croissants, fruit, orange juice, and coffee, presumably meant for the candidate and his wife. At least six or seven campaign aides, however, had crowded into the room, evidently thinking it their solemn duty to remain at all times near the candidate. A couple of local workers, for example, had been assigned to sit in one corner to answer the telephone and take messages. It did not seem to matter that the telephone was not ringing, and was not expected to; they were there "just in case." The practical effect of this large group of well-meaning assistants was to force Anderson into the bedroom for the duration of his free time. Instead of sitting comfortably in a chair and reading his newspaper, as he wished, he had to prop himself up by an elbow and read awkwardly on a twin-sized bed. Anderson was reluctant to have his supporters cleared abruptly from the room, and so he simply resigned himself to the inconvenience.

Later that afternoon, Anderson spoke at UCLA. In the car, we agreed he should make a point of mentioning his famous gasoline tax. Campaigning in California presented another Daniel-in-the-lion's-den situation. Of all places, it was here that energy consumption needed to be curtailed, and Anderson should say so. Over 2,000 students were assembled in the ballroom of the Ackerman Student Union as Anderson walked in. "When I told people I was coming out to California," he began, "they asked me whether I would be continuing to advocate my fifty-cent gasoline tax. These people were cynical about politicians and assumed I would tailor my message to fit the audience. Well, I do not plan to do so. For if we really have an energy crisis, which I believe we do, is it any less real in California? Of course not." Far from being hostile to this message, the students offered thunderous applause.

That evening, the campaign had a fund-raising reception at the Beverly Hills home of movie agent Jennings Lang, and Anderson busied himself circulating among southern California's beautiful people, taking soundings about an independent candidacy. The soundings were all quite favorable. Meantime, however, there was also concern expressed to him about the importance of announcing his intentions early. Technically, a reregistration drive was still under way in California, intended to qualify as many pro-Anderson Democrats as possible to vote in the June Republican primary. The deadline for reregistration was closing in. Anderson supporters needed to know whether their candidate would, in fact, be competing in the primary. If not, they would just as soon remain eligible to cast their ballots for Democrats. Anderson's public pronouncements remained Delphic.

From the reception, we headed off to the Santa Monica Civic Auditorium for a heavily advertised rally, intended to kick off the Anderson campaign in California. Anderson had been traveling around the city and speaking all day long, and, as any mortal would have been under the circumstances, he was by now quite tired. In the car, he complained that too many events were being scheduled. Clearly this was true. Now that he had exalted status with the media, they would give him about the same-size stories each day whether he did one event or twenty. He did not have to go around marketing himself in "retail" fashion anymore, speaking to every group that wanted to hear him. What mattered was to be seen for a minute or two on TV, or to have a good story in the newspaper— not to be seen in person by 500 people here or 1,500 people there. The principal effect of putting too many items on the schedule was to exhaust the candidate so that he did not do as well as he might have at times when it counted.

As we pulled up to the auditorium—a large arena traditionally used for the annual Academy Awards presentation—a prominent marquee outside announced tonight's event: "JOHN B. ANDERSON COMES TO CALIFORNIA!" At last, Anderson remarked, he really did feel like a celebrity, seeing his name literally up in lights. Outside the entrances appeared to be huge lines of people waiting to get in. This was an irony. The Washington office had been so concerned about having the rally make a good impression, that it had requested the removal of several hundred seats in the auditorium, to guard against the embarrassment of seats going empty. Now people were being turned away.

Anderson was ushered into a room offstage, from which he could hear the strains of a seven-piece Dixieland band providing "pre-game" music as the audience continued to file in. The atmosphere was lively, reminiscent of a political convention; there were large numbers of banners, placards, and noisemakers in the crowd. But as he waited, Anderson was melancholy, honestly wondering whether he had the reserves of strength to go out on stage and rouse his audience. He knew that expectation in the air was high. Not until an hour before had he been told the size and nature of the rally he would be addressing; now he realized its importance. It was hard to imagine firing others up at this point; he was just not fired up himself. Making a decision about going independent was taking its toll.

Twenty minutes later, when he was due to be introduced, he emerged from his room. He looked impatient to get the engagement over and done with; he had decided to use some shopworn notes prepared for a previous appearance, ones that rehearsed basic campaign themes. But when he got out onto the stage, and saw the sea of cheering people greeting him, his adrenaline started flowing. Instead, he gave a hearty extemporaneous speech. The audience responded so fervently that the atmosphere switched from resembling that of a political convention to something more akin to an old-fashioned revival meeting. This was Anderson's element. Perhaps there *was* something to what commentators occasionally said, that his unusually religious upbringing was a deep-seated, if unconscious, reason for his enjoyment of politics.

Following several more engagements, we flew to northern California, primarily for two college appearances. At Stanford, Anderson asked 1,500 students, "Is American democracy inherently incapable of providing a genuine, meaningful choice for the American people in presidential elections?" This was a reference to what he later called the "dreary" choice of Carter or Reagan, who seemed destined now to be the nominees of the party conventions. "I have been committed during this campaign," he said, picking his words carefully, "to offering people a choice. And that is what I will continue to do." People were free to interpret this as a clear signal of intention to run as an independent; or they could assume he was giving only a standard rhetorical justification for continuing to remain at this time in the Republican race. As usual, Anderson wanted to preserve an ambiguity. Whatever their preferred interpretation, the students burst into applause.

The next morning, we set out across the bay to the University of California campus at Berkeley. Anderson was particularly proud of this appearance, having been told that it was the first time a presidential candidate had dared to set foot on campus in many years. Two thousand students jammed into Zellerbach Auditorium, and an overflow crowd of 1,500 more, disappointed at not being able to get in, crowded into Sproul Plaza outside, where they listened attentively to the sound of Anderson's voice booming out over a public address system. Anderson began by noting that it had been over fifteen years since the free-speech movement began on the campus at Berkeley, and since then the students' message had been heard. The movement, he said, had not been just a narrow one, addressed to First Amendment rights of personal freedom. It had had a larger significance as well: a revolt against hypocrisy, an attack against conventional wisdom. To some extent, Anderson said, those were principles which he liked to think were guiding his own campaign.

En route back to Washington, the commercial plane we were taking experienced several delays and we did not land at Dulles International Airport until 2:00 A.M. After we had come to a stop, the pilot announced that everyone was to remain seated while the Anderson party disembarked first. Whether this was requested by the Secret Service or intended as a courtesy by the airline, I did not know. But whatever the motive, the announcement was an obnoxious one to most passengers. Everyone was anxious to get off the plane after such a long flight. Yet the pilot repeated his announcement one or two more times. Those of us in the Anderson party found ourselves cringing in embarrassment. Finally, I felt compelled to stand up and announce to the people around me: "On behalf of the 'Anderson party,' please vote for us anyway!" As we filed out, we nodded sheepishly to Eunice Shriver, the sister of Ted Kennedy, whom we had spotted sitting in the coach section of the airplane; she had a knowing look of amusement on her face, as though she could empathize perfectly with our embarrassment. Finally, as we were passing through the first class section, I heard someone call out to Anderson. It was Mike Curb, the Republican lieutenant governor of California, also traveling on the same plane. "Please make sure the 'Anderson party' is not confused with the Republican party," the conservative Curb said. "Happy to," Anderson replied.

On Saturday morning, April 12, I went into the Washington campaign office. It was my first visit since it had moved from its original four-room suite on southeast Capitol Hill. Now it was several times bigger and located in another area of Capitol Hill, behind the Union Station train depot. The office had been used formerly as the headquarters of Howard Baker's presidential campaign; just at the time we were looking for larger quarters, his campaign had folded. I was astounded by the scale and appearance of the new place: compared to the last one, it seemed enormous and much more businesslike. Numerous work areas were partitioned off, and several campaign departments (finance, accounting, press, and the like) now had separate offices unto themselves. The campaign had the air of a mini-corporation.

But along with the physical growth of the office came an alarming bureaucratization of its operations. Instead of the five or ten or fifteen people we had employed on the payroll up until a couple of months before, the paid staff had now expanded to something in the neighborhood of 150 or 200. Some of the people were located in new field offices that were springing up around the country, but most were concentrated in the Washington headquarters. In addition, streams of volunteer workers were still coming in every day off the streets, and so the office, as large as it was, had already become crowded. Because so many more people were now available to do work, assignments and job descriptions were becoming much narrower. Originally, there had been an esprit de corps among our campaign workers; since there were so few, everyone was happy to lend everyone else a helping hand. If anything had to be done, everyone would stand ready to help do it. People were constantly busy and excited.

Now things were changing. If something fell outside the immediate jurisdiction of a campaign worker, he or she would not rush to do it, for someone else might complain. On the other hand, if someone felt overburdened, rather than working longer and harder and asking others to pitch in, enough money was available that it was tempting just to hire a new person to help. Most everyone who worked in the office was highly dedicated and competent, putting in long hours and often not leaving until late at night. But the campaign had become overstaffed. During the day, if one walked through the office, it would be common to observe much of the staff congregated in small groups telling stories and trading gossip, or talking on the phone at great leisure with field workers at the other end. Many would have preferred greater responsibility.

Mike MacLeod had been the campaign manager since early January. Keke and Bill Bradford had had their differences over management style, and he had left in the fall, succeeded by two further campaign managers who also had their limitations; by the beginning of the year, the Andersons were anxious to find a replacement who was a better known quantity. MacLeod had worked for Anderson a number of years in administrative capacities both in the

House Republican Conference and in Anderson's congressional office. He was in his late thirties, tall, thin, graying at the temples, always punctilious in manner, and never a hair out of place. He had no experience at operating an enterprise of the campaign's magnitude, and admitted as much. His immediate prior experience had been to supervise the few employees of a small and low-key congressional office. He was highly intelligent, witty, and articulate, and, since he was older than most of the other staff, presented a good image as campaign manager. Probably he would have been better cast as campaign spokesman, however, than as someone making major operational decisions. A campaign manager must be a particular type of person: someone with a sense of clear priorities and a dynamic ability to follow through on them. He has to be able to say, "This is our number one priority; we've got to get this done right now." MacLeod was good at keeping orderly lists of projects and objectives, but sometimes he seemed not to discriminate among them. He was not the type of person to demand immediate action. On the contrary, he was extremely cautious and disliked tension and conflict; one reporter likened him to a schoolmaster. The sprawling bureaucratic quality of the campaign was in part a reflection of this disposition; imposing effective financial or organizational discipline did not come naturally to him. Many came to regard the serious budget problems which later burdened the campaign as a consequence of Mike's inexperience. In Mike's defense, it must be remembered that the tasks were awesome; the scope of the campaign's efforts grew monstrously overnight. Moreover, he had come to the job reluctantly, out of a sense of duty to fill a vacuum that existed, not because he enjoyed the prospect of such a thankless role, or because he considered himself particularly qualified for it. Thereafter, both he and the Andersons felt that another change of managers would serve only to confirm a notion in the press that the campaign operation was amateurish and unstable.

On Monday morning, April 14, I went out to the Andersons' home to discuss with them an article which had appeared that morning in the *Washington Post*. It was a criticism of a new style the campaign seemed to be taking on, and it concerned me not least because I considered the charges to contain an element of truth. It seemed to be something we needed to sit down and talk about. The article had been written by Kathy Sawyer, a *Post* reporter who had traveled with us briefly in recent days. She said, in effect, that success had spoiled the campaign. What had once been a charming, small-scale operation had now become a proud, big-time one. To a large extent, this was unavoidable and, in certain respects, an improvement. But at the same time, she warned, it presented new dangers. First, the campaign risked becoming impersonal. Already, the candidate was being whisked in and out of events by the Secret Service; isolated in suites, holding rooms, and limousines; and so put upon with new demands that access to him by reporters was becoming noticeably curtailed. Second, Sawyer warned, as the press gave Anderson more attention and the campaign desired to broaden its appeal to voters, we would experience the temptation to trim our sails and avoid controversial aspects of issues. She noted an instance the previous week in which Keke had barred her husband from talking with reporters on a plane about a potentially controversial idea he had for the United States to share oil with its allies to induce their participation in an embargo against Iran.

To all of this Keke replied that much of the press retained an unspoken sympathy for Ted Kennedy, and that their complaints were largely groundless ones intended to bring her husband down to size. Such a theory struck me as excessively conspiratorial. I had not seen any great evidence that the press was holding a brief for Ted Kennedy. Moreover, I had seen abundant evidence that many in the press had strong personal sympathies for John Anderson. I urged Anderson to undertake a sort of affirmative action program designed to reassure reporters who shared Sawyer's perceptions. He should make a special point, I said, of meeting reporters on an informal basis, agreeing as much as possible to requests for interviews, and being perfectly candid in his conversations. Concerning issues, Anderson should continue to take positions right out front; he should continue to express himself without inhibition and say simply whatever he felt was right on a subject. If he toned down now, it would be noticed and resented. Anderson agreed, on reflection, and said he would try to show more sensitivity to these potential problems.

We drove back to the Congressional office about noon, continuing to discuss this and other subjects, and decided to have lunch in the Members' Dining Room. Just as we were about to enter, the bells rang, signifying a vote, and Anderson said he would have to detour a few minutes to the House floor. Keke, Margot, and I, rather than finding a table, thought it might be fun to go quickly up to the visitors' gallery and watch Anderson's entrance on to the floor. He had not been back since before the primaries, and we were curious about the reception he would be given. He got a very warm one, from both Democrats and Republicans, though he seemed in a hurry to position himself on the Republican side of the aisle, lest anyone read too much into the fact that he was talking to a lot of Democrats. Subsequently, they could be seen walking over to him which, from our vantage point, looked like just the right touch of symbolism. As we saw Anderson leaving, we got up ourselves and hurried back to the dining room. He must have been detained talking with passers-by, for we beat him there by a few moments. Suddenly he walked in. He was all alone, without his Secret Service. We were so accustomed to the retinue, he practically looked naked. "Aren't you missing something?" Margot asked. He thought a moment, then said, "Oh, my gosh . . ." As he later explained, he had, by force of habit, walked out of the House chamber through a certain door used by Republicans, rather than the one at which he promised to regroup with his agents; the Secret Service were not allowed to accompany him onto the House floor itself. I was detailed to go back and find them. The agents were embarrassed, when I told them what had happened, and came scurrying down the stairs to catch up. It was about their only slip-up of the campaign, though, of course, it was hardly their fault.

Tuesday night, the Andersons asked Margot and me to join them for dinner. We went to Gusti's, an inexpensive Italian restaurant downtown, and found a corner table. The Secret Service, as always, occupied a table nearby. Once again, we discussed the prospect of an independent campaign. Anderson was inclined to go forward with it, at least in a tentative fashion. But if he did so, he pondered the idea of changing the nature of his campaigning. Rather than running around the country every day for the next six months, perhaps he could headquarter himself in Washington, and spend only two or three days a week on the road. He could use his time in Washington to hold highly publicized briefings, and to spend more of his personal time doing the reading and writing which he had long regretted not having had an opportunity for during the last year. The distinction of his campaign would continue to be its orientation to issues; such a campaign style would seem thoughtful and reflective. On his forays into the field, he could make major, hard-hitting, well-researched speeches on important issues which the other candidates were neglecting. He could set a new tone in campaigning: talking issues rather than shaking hands. Moreover, he would not have to exhaust himself in the process. As for the campaign staff, it could be reduced to a fraction of what it was; a certain minimum number of accountants and lawyers might be required, but otherwise, the crew could be skeletal. Most campaign money needed to be preserved for media, or channeled to volunteer organizers in the field. Altogether, Anderson found such a scenario very appealing. But that was as far as it ever got, for David Garth—who a few days later was to be given control of the campaign—had very different ideas.

On Wednesday, April 16, Anderson agreed to an interview with Dan Balz of the *Washington Post.* Balz was someone whom Anderson knew well and with whom he enjoyed talking. The press was finding it odd that Anderson had become in the last several days virtually incommunicado, and this at precisely the time when the world was clamoring to know what progress he had made toward a decision on the independent campaign. Anderson recognized that it would be a good idea to allow the press some access, lest they think him arrogant for his aloofness. Besides, he was getting restless sticking by home and the congressional office; Keke had insisted that the campaign schedule be canceled for the entire week and her husband be allowed to "unwind."

Anderson was quite relaxed when he spoke with Balz. He went ahead and told him that, yes, he had thought about it, and, why not, he was going to make a run for president as an independent. Balz knew he had a hot news story: the first time Anderson had told anyone from the press, categorically, that he would be running. Balz gave him an opportunity to reconsider his statement, and asked him whether it was definitely okay to print it. Anderson reflected, and said he saw nothing wrong; he thought he should be honest with the press. His only concern at this point was that other news people not feel we were playing favorites with the *Post.* Interviews were quickly scheduled for several other journalists, and still more were informed by phone that Anderson had indicated he was "strongly inclined" to run. Finally, I made a point to call the congressional staff, so they would not have to find out about their boss's plans by hearing it over the news. That evening, all the networks carried stories about it; and the next morning, it constituted major, "above the fold" stories on the front pages of many of the country's large newspapers.

David Garth had been asked by Anderson to join the independent campaign as its chief strategist; he would not officially assume the reins of authority until Anderson formally declared his candidacy. As a preliminary exercise in muscle-flexing, however, Garth called me the morning the story broke. He was furious, and shouted nonstop into the phone for several minutes. Oddly enough, he was not directing his fury at me, but at Anderson, whom he excoriated in a number of colorful, if unprintable, ways for the fact that he had granted an interview without consulting him. To a lesser extent, Garth also employed his rich vernacular against Norman Lear. Garth felt, to put it mildly, that Lear was interfering with Garth's own prerogatives. Apparently this was because Lear had called both myself and Anderson to suggest ideas for an announcement speech. (Lear was to become a regular caller and visitor to the campaign, and Garth just as regularly reacted in this same vein.) Thus was I introduced to the famous "Garth treatment." I was lucky: the "Garth treatment," so others told me, was often reserved for less reasonable hours of the day.

I found this first encounter with Garth somewhat disconcerting. It seemed incongruous that someone like Anderson, whom I had never heard utter other than the King's English, could feel comfortable in the company of someone given to such a different language. I soon learned, however, how that could be: Anderson never heard Garth swear. To the contrary, Garth was on his best behavior when it counted, and different in his relations with subordinates. Garth seemed to be upset on this particular day because he did not want it revealed until the last minute that Anderson would be declaring his candidacy. Anderson had jumped the gun.

Garth, however, had never informed Anderson that he was not to give interviews; indeed, it had never occurred to Anderson that giving interviews required permission. If Anderson's instincts could not be trusted in an interview situation like this one—one where he was rested, reflective, and deliberate, and given a chance to reconsider any of his statements—then he probably did not deserve to be president. Of course, his instincts turned out to be excellent. Had he remained in total seclusion that week, he risked looking Hamlet-like about his presidential plans. Instead, the coverage from his interviews boosted his stature. None of it was negative in any way. It only served to heighten the drama and the nationwide interest in his announcement the next week. Morton Kondracke of the *New Republic* called at one point and said, "What a brilliant strategy: you got a double whammy, front-page stories two separate times for the same news!" The strategy had been anything but deliberate, yet given that much of the public was still quite unfamiliar with Anderson, it did not at all hurt.

This incident proved a harbinger of things to come. Garth was prone to become quite upset about minor things, and to fly off into rages over anything that did not happen precisely as he had determined it should. He did not believe in the collegial style of decision-making, and often did not even inform others of his decisions, let alone consult with them. It was to be an interesting six months with such a captain at the helm. Certainly it would be quite different from our previous experience.

On Monday, I had lunch with *Time* magazine correspondents Eileen Shields and Larry Barrett, who told me they were working on an Anderson feature for the coming issue, and hoped it would be chosen as the cover story. For their editors to decide to put Anderson on the cover, they explained, it was necessary for them to be able to indicate that his announcement of candidacy the next week would be the real thing: a somewhat dramatic, full-scale, formal statement that he was really going through with it. The reason for their apprehension was that Garth had been telling journalists privately that the announcement might be much more modest; Garth thought Anderson should simply release a short written statement announcing the formation of an exploratory committee. Were this the case, the *Time* reporters told me, they did not think we would get the cover. I felt the cover was extremely important. One of the things we still needed most was basic name recognition and public exposure. Moreover, Anderson did not see a purpose in playing coy and delaying. He had decided to make the run, and he felt he might as well admit it loud and clear. That was just his natural inclination. But Garth kept down-playing Anderson's decision in his conversations with *Time* reporters and others. Therefore, I asked Anderson to talk directly with the *Time* people to reassure them. They were reassured, and work on a cover story went forward. The very same situation developed with *Newsweek;* ultimately, they, too, began work on a cover story, despite Garth's objections.

At the same time as I was having this luncheon, a more important meeting was going on at the Madison Hotel a few blocks away. Anderson, Keke, MacLeod, Garth, and several of Garth's associates from New York had convened to discuss campaign strategy. A reorganization was decided on; Garth insisted on calling all the shots from here on out. MacLeod would continue to administer internal campaign office details, but political strategy would be decided entirely by Garth, who would operate out of his New York office, while making frequent visits to Washington. As for myself, Garth demanded that I be moved from the candidate's side back to the congressional office. Here I would be less likely to contradict Garth's directives to the candidate, toward which I was already known to harbor some suspicion. Garth wished to curb, rather than encourage, Anderson's predilections toward spontaneity, toward easy access to the press, toward outspoken statements on issues. I had gained a reputation as prodding Anderson somewhat in all these departments.

The Andersons very much wanted Garth's help in the campaign; he was allowed to state his conditions, and they were accepted virtually without protest. Everyone assumed that personal feelings could be smoothed over, that before long the campaign would be humming, and Garth's celebrated genius would be evident. After Anderson returned from the meeting to the congressional office, I went in to discuss with him several new requests for press interviews. He turned to MacLeod, who was also in the room. "Mike," Anderson said, "why don't you explain to Mark what we've just decided." With that, Anderson hastily excused himself to catch a vote on the House floor.

I was not at first as upset by this decision as Garth probably expected me to be. I even called him that evening to say I understood. He was hired in part to take charge of media, and would surely want his own people in place. Of course, I had been much more than a press secretary at Anderson's side, and it was not clear to me why I could not continue to perform other functions on the campaign trail, if not that role. But if the truth be told, I had a momentary sense of relief. The idea of waging an independent campaign, and truly taking it to the White House, was intimidating to someone like myself who had never before worked in even a single political campaign. Perhaps our inexperienced operation had been good enough to get us where we were, but did we really know what it took to go all the way? Like others, I had an almost childlike faith in experts; I was awed by Garth's reputation, overwhelmed by his personality, and did not think it unreasonable that control of the campaign should now be turned over to the political pros. We were all very excited about the new campaign, and while I would have preferred to stay in action on the front lines, it did not seem too much to ask individuals to subordinate themselves to the larger interests of the cause. We would all share in the fruits of victory if Anderson won. Later I found it hard to believe that I could have been so naïve and docile, and accepted Garth's abrupt changes so uncritically, but at the time it was easy to hope that everything would work out.

I did suffer a little embarrassment in the press. Al Hunt wrote in the *Wall Street Journal*, "One sign of the changing nature of the campaign is that Mark Bisnow, the disheveled young Anderson aide who became a folk-hero in the popular comic strip *Doonesbury*, has been dropped from the campaign staff." And Mary McGrory, the columnist, wrote: "Garth's influence has already been established. Mark Bisnow, the gentle, gangling press secretary who personified the 'Doonesbury' flavor of the first campaign has been transferred to the back room to work on issues. He will be replaced by a successor of Garth's choosing."

Garth immediately ordered that no information be given to inquiring reporters as to what Anderson's plans were for a formal announcement of candidacy. Thursday, April 24, had been set by Garth as the day of the announcement, but this was to be revealed publicly only one day in advance. Why Garth demanded such secrecy was unclear. In the meantime, press calls flooded into the campaign office, and most of them went unanswered. The campaign took on an aura of being sloppy and disorganized. Reporters immediately began circumventing the campaign bureaucracy and reaching me at the congressional office. They wanted to know what was happening, and why their calls were not even being returned. I could not explain. I did not know myself.

Tuesday, two days before the announcement, Anderson sat down at his kitchen table about seven in the morning, and began to draft a speech. Four hours later, he called me. He wanted me to come over and discuss it with him. It was Anderson's personal effort to justify the extraordinary adventure on which he was about to embark. In deciding whether to run as an independent, he had written, he was forced to reconsider the reasons that had motivated him ten months before to declare his original intention to seek the presidency. In that time, he said, the signs had only multiplied that the country confronted, as he had thought then, "a crisis of governance of truly alarming proportions." The Carter administration, he said, "has demonstrated an incompetence to chart a clear, common sense economic policy," and not surprisingly this had "contributed to a worldwide feeling that a nation unable to deal with its problems at home is relinquishing its role as a leader in foreign affairs." Where self-doubt and confusion among Americans existed, Anderson had written, "it is not because people have lost confidence in themselves or in the inherent strength of the country, but because they do not believe they have been told the real truths about our basic problems." They have been led, Anderson said, "by men more interested in perpetuating their own political power than in telling the plain unvarnished truth." To the telling of such truths Anderson would dedicate his campaign.

As the day of the announcement approached, great expectation filled the air of the campaign office. Opinion had been hotly divided at first about the change in course from Republican to independent. Many campaign workers and supporters were registered Republicans who felt an enduring loyalty to party. Others, inexperienced in presidential politics, clung to the unrealistic hope that Anderson still had a chance to capture the nomination, perhaps by some strange backroom scenario that would unfold at the GOP convention. But gradually, most supporters came to recognize that conditions were as auspicious as they ever would be for an independent run: there was an increasing sense of inevitability that Carter and Reagan would be nominated by their parties, and a sense that these nominees would be immensely unpopular among the public at large. Kennedy supporters were still smarting from the rude treatment their candidate had received all campaign long at the hands of Jimmy Carter. As for moderate Republicans, it was still not clear what enthusiasm they would be able to muster for such a standard-bearer of conservatism as Ronald Reagan. Finally, a large group of voters, not identified with either party, threatened to sit out the election unless a candidate of greater appeal arrived on the scene.

Combined with this public attitude about Carter and Reagan, there seemed to be a large, and growing, body of support for the style, philosophy, and positions embodied by Anderson himself. The image of courage and candor he had projected during the primaries was taken as a breath of fresh air by large numbers of people who generally regarded politicians and political parties with a degree of suspicion and disdain. Liberal Democrats admired the sense of compassion Anderson seemed to convey, as well as his essentially progressive opinions on important social issues, such as civil rights, women's rights, and gun control. Republicans admired his tough stands on economic issues. It was in such propitious circumstances that Anderson stepped forward to offer his candidacy.

Early Thursday morning, Anderson came with his wife into the congressional office. At 11:00 A.M., he would be proceeding downtown to the National Press Club, where he was to deliver his announcement. In the meantime, he wanted a chance to reread his text, and to reflect on prospective questions that might be asked by the press. At one point, Anderson asked me to prepare a brief memo outlining a reply he could use as to why the effect of his candidacy would not simply be to throw the presidential election into the House of Representatives, which would happen if total electoral votes were split in such a way as to deny any one candidate a majority. Evidently, Anderson had been called by Jerry Ford the night before, and Ford had made a strong argument in this vein in urging Anderson to abandon his plans. Many commentators had been making it as well, and I was surprised that Anderson would need a memo on the subject at this late a stage. Garth had boasted to me during the week how rigorously he was preparing Anderson for questions;

I believe he meant to leave the implication that it was now "professionals" who were taking charge. I knew that Anderson found such practice exercises tedious, and often tuned out lectures others tried to give him on how to behave. Still, it was striking that this particular question had not been fully examined and rehearsed.

As it came time to depart for the Press Club, the Andersons asked if I cared to join them. Perhaps they were feeling a tinge of guilt about my reduced status. We rode across town together. Keke joked in the car that while this was Anderson's second presidential announcement, there might even be a third one. She explained that this would occur when Anderson was given the Democratic nomination, and had to announce a final change in his party registration. As for Anderson, he was concerned about how he looked in his new suit. Keke had insisted he get one for the occasion. "I get a new suit before every announcement," he said proudly.

The announcement went smoothly. The turnout was much larger than had been the case for the Republican announcement ten months before. A hundred or more press people were in attendance, a dozen camera crews, and enough campaign supporters and curious onlookers to fill a large ballroom. Each time Anderson made a gesture during his speech, every camera in the room seemed to click, hoping to catch an interesting pose. He was being treated presidentially. That evening, the story of his announcement topped the news on all the network TV broadcasts. NBC titled its story "Indy Andy." A new campaign was galloping out of the starting gate.

That afternoon, I took a couple of important calls in the congressional office. Both *Time* and *Newsweek* phoned in to say that Anderson had definitely been chosen for the covers of their next editions, which would come out Monday. Of course, they added, that was barring any unforeseen contingency.

At 1:15 A.M. that night—or, technically, Friday morning—I was awakened at home by a phone call from a reporter for the *New York Post*. "Does the congressman have a comment on what's happened?" she panted. "What's happened where?" I said, perturbed at being awakened. "In Iran," came the reply. The abortive Iran rescue mission had just been announced by President Carter.

I managed to get only intermittent sleep the rest of the night, turning the radio on regularly to catch the latest details of this extraordinary event. Among other thoughts that passed through my mind was the obvious, if cynical, one: "There go our covers!" Sure enough, Anderson's great moment in the sun had been eclipsed. Had Anderson made the covers—and had people been buzzing about his announcement the next several weeks, instead of about the rescue mission—it seemed possible he would have surged in the polls several more points. So much of our ratings, I was convinced, had to do with sheer publicity, and the degree to which Anderson's name was on the tips of people's tongues. It was an unlucky way in which to start out the independent campaign.

At 10:00 A.M. Friday morning, someone from the campaign reached me in the congressional office, and requested that I prepare a statement in Anderson's name commenting on the rescue mission. It seemed an easy task. I had talked with Anderson at length about it that morning and knew exactly what he would want to say. I prepared such a statement:

> My heart goes out to the families of the brave men who have given their lives in the attempt to rescue the hostages. That these men knew the risks of their dangerous mission and willingly put their lives on the line is no consolation. They will be honored in their memory.
>
> The timing of the mission was unfortunate. It came just at the moment that we had finally succeeded in winning the support of key allies for a concerted set of economic and diplomatic sanctions, intended to force the early release of the hostages. It will be another tragedy of the episode if that effort is now set back.
>
> I am also concerned about what seems to have been a lack of consultation with the Congress on this matter, though the mission apparently constituted a potentially major military undertaking of the kind contemplated under the War Powers Act.
>
> Nonetheless, in this difficult hour, I think the President deserves our support as America's course of action toward Iran is reassessed. And I believe it will continue to be an obligation of the Presidential candidates to display the patience and restraint that may ultimately be necessary for a successful resolution of this terrible crisis.

At about 10:30, I had the statement ready. In the old days, it would have been a simple matter to release. I would have phoned Anderson and read it to him; he would have said fine or suggested corrections; then the Xerox machine would have started churning out copies.

But Garth had now instituted a new procedure. I was required to send my draft first to the campaign headquarters, which involved

From Republican to Independent

a delay, and from there it would be telecopied to Garth's office in New York for the approval of his staff. I sent the draft off and put the matter out of mind the rest of the morning. Time passed, I went out to lunch, and when I came back about 1:30 P.M., someone in the congressional office was just then receiving by phone a statement that had at last been approved by one of Garth's New York assistants, Maureen Connelly. This chain of events mystified me. It had taken three-and-a-half hours to prepare and approve a statement that should have taken only a half-hour. In the meantime, the press office at the campaign had been flooded with calls, and no one could understand why Anderson did not have a simple statement available. Was this "professionalism?" I wondered. Moreover, the statement had been stripped of its original content and the prose itself had taken on an air of hasty composition. Let the reader judge. This was the revised statement:

> There are a great many questions and concerns on the minds of the American people relating to the rescue attempt. I share those concerns. These questions will be the subject of the discussion in the coming weeks. But right now, my heart and deepest sympathies go to the families of the brave men who gave their lives in an attempt to rescue the hostages. In this difficult hour, the President deserves our support. I give him my support, and I know the American people will do the same. I also believe that all segments of our society, including the Presidential candidates, must show patience.

I called Maureen Connelly in my irritation and said: "You want to know my honest opinion about this statement? It's insipid, yes, that's the word: insipid." I expected her to argue. Instead, she said, "Exactly. That's the point. We don't want Anderson to step out of his box . . . we don't want him to say anything controversial or he'll be vulnerable." And I said, "Well, if that's so, I don't want to be a party to it," and I hung up.

Later that day, I explained to Anderson what had happened and admitted I had been rude, for which I apologized. He said he regretted Maureen's attitude, but felt it was just a bug in the new operation that would be ironed out. He said he would not allow such a practice to become the norm if he had anything to say about it. I expressed the concern that, given the demands on his time, a lot of things could be done that he would not know about, and that the same sort of thing could easily be done in his name again. He said he would make every effort to prevent it. Poignantly, he said he had just read an editorial in the *New York Times* that morning which he would try to abide by. The *Times'* editorial was entitled, "Mr. Anderson's Independence," and it said: "A present question is whether Mr. Anderson will keep expressing his convictions. It is easy to sound Lincolnesque when the polls read (*)—it's even easy to risk offending people when they read 20 percent. . . . The test of Mr. Anderson's candidacy and his independence will be whether he keeps on talking about sacrifices as he gropes for 30 percent or 40 percent or more." That would indeed be the test. We were already being tested, and we would be tested more and more every day.

7

May–June, 1980:
The Campaign Changes
Character

It might have been obvious from the episode of the Iran statement that the nature of the campaign was changing. Further events only reinforced the impression. Shortly after his announcement, Anderson was invited by the *Washington Post* to a meeting with its editorial board. Instinctively, he accepted. He was delighted, as always, to have the opportunity to air his views. Garth saw it quite differently, and was furious when he learned what Anderson had done. To Garth's mind, the press was a natural adversary which needed to be kept at a distance and provided only carefully screened information.

The arrangements had been made, however, and Anderson went to the meeting. One of his remarks to the editorial board attracted particular attention. He indicated that he would consider withdrawing from the race if, at some point, it looked as though his candidacy might contribute to the election of Ronald Reagan. This remark greatly upset Garth, not because he disagreed with it necessarily, but because he considered it foolish for Anderson to spell out his thinking on a future course of action; this was just the sort of indiscretion Garth had been afraid Anderson would utter. By usual standards, Garth may have been right: rather than talking openly, it was often shrewder to keep quiet. But evading questions had never been Anderson's style; that is why people seemed to like him. And on this particular matter, Anderson felt that people would understand his reasoning. Many Democrats, gravely concerned about the possibility of Reagan's election, would be more likely to support Anderson if they knew he would be realistic in his pursuit than if he looked as though he were committed to waging a fight blindly to the end.

Garth's *modus operandi,* however, was to keep his clients on a short leash; he did not want them speaking too intimately or frequently to the press, or taking positions which would offend potential supporters. He preferred to rely on the controlled environment of paid television commercials to project their image; critics considered him the ultimate political packager. But variations on this approach had proved eminently successful, sometimes against long odds, in the many campaigns Garth had conducted throughout the 1960s and 1970s. His most notable experience had included mayoral campaigns in New York (John Lindsay, Ed Koch) and Los Angeles (Tom Bradley); United States Senate campaigns in Pennsylvania (John Heinz) and California (John Tunney); gubernatorial campaigns in New York (Hugh Carey), New Jersey (Brendan Byrne), and Connecticut (Ella Grasso); and even the foreign presidential campaign of Venezuelan Luis Herrera. His experience in American presidential elections was much more limited: he had produced ads for Eugene McCarthy during a short period in 1968,* and had made a short-lived effort in 1972 promoting John Lindsay for president.

Garth set about supervising the Anderson campaign by implementing his usual techniques. First he hired a new press secretary who would, as Garth explained it to me, serve as a "vacuum cleaner, not a thinker." The metaphor was obscure, but Garth's essential meaning was clear: the press secretary was to take orders only from Garth, and to function as his eyes and ears at the candidate's side. He was also to keep the press and the candidate at a distance from one another; this was thought to provide protection for the candidate from the needling questions of reporters and prevent him from making precipitous and unguarded remarks. The person Garth chose for this function was Michael Rosenbaum, a young reporter from the *New York Post.* He was tapped by Garth and subsequently

---

* Apparently it was long enough, however, to inspire a one-time McCarthy speech-writer, Jeremy Larner, to make Garth the model for a cynical campaign consultant in the movie *The Candidate,* for which Larner wrote the screenplay.

introduced to Anderson. He had no past association with Anderson, with the campaign, or with Washington; and it soon became clear that he possessed little knowledge of the campaign's history or of Anderson's positions and philosophies. Anderson, for his part, barely talked to Rosenbaum, and sometimes had difficulty remembering his name. Garth did not seem to find this unusual or inappropriate. Despite nearly universal complaints from reporters traveling with Anderson, Garth kept Rosenbaum entrenched in his position at Anderson's side. He instructed him to treat the press with at best a studied reserve. Only mundane information was to be shared. Rarely were requests for interviews to be granted. Those who wrote good stories were to be rewarded with attention; those who said anything negative were to be paid back in kind.

To the average person, such an attitude toward the press may have seemed insensitive and unwarranted, but seen from Garth's perspective, it had a logic, which many veterans of political campaigns might have understood. In Garth's view, the object of the press covering a campaign was to find color and drama, to provoke injudicious comment on the part of the candidate, and to report contradiction and conflict. That is what people liked to read about in their newspapers and see on their TV screens, and reporters were happy to oblige them. The press were determined to trap a candiate, Garth felt, and the only way to elude their grasp was to put up a tough front and remind them who was boss. In this context, Rosenbaum was a good choice: he had a hot temper and raw nerves, and carried out Garth's instructions effectively.

A second element of Garth's strategy was to discourage, for the time being, Anderson's discussion of controversial issues. Garth had no objection to his making strong speeches denouncing Carter and Reagan, as long as he stuck to generalities or to positions previously expressed. But he did not want Anderson staking out new positions or addressing, more than necessary, unpopular topics. Although the campaign had advertised itself as being one of "new ideas," and although Anderson was beginning to express frustration that his campaign staff was of little help in supplying him with any, Garth did his best to steer the campaign away from uncharted waters. He argued that the time would come in the fall for Anderson to go on the offensive again, but that for now he needed to concentrate his efforts on basic organizational tasks, such as encouraging the petition drives that were being launched around the country to qualify him for spots on all the fifty state ballots. Intensive issues-oriented campaigning, Garth believed, would distract attention from these activities; Anderson needed first to consolidate his gains before stepping out on further limbs. Why invite unnecessary scrutiny or criticism six months before the election, when the unpopularity of the prospective party nominees, Jimmy Carter and Ronald Reagan, might be enough by itself to send more and more voters scurrying into Anderson's camp?

Anderson, of course, did not swallow whole the prescriptions of Garth to avoid controversy; he listened to Garth and respected his political judgment, but ultimately Anderson had too independent a will to be muzzled. Nevertheless, it was a tiring business to campaign eighteen hours a day and, unless he were offered constant new material and affirmatively encouraged in using it, there was a natural tendency to lapse into rhetorical and repetitive speeches. Other than Rosenbaum, the only campaign staff who traveled regularly with Anderson during the first several months of the independent campaign were minor press assistants and Jim Scales, who functioned as a sort of personal valet. No substantive advisors accompanied him, although in other campaigns several such positions were standard. Anderson could often be something of an introvert, and needed prodding at times to break out of his isolation. Now he was virtually alone on the campaign trail, and that is precisely the way Garth wanted it.

As for the issues shop back in Washington, Garth reinforced the authority of research director Cliff Brown, an amiable college professor whose academic bent it was to supply the candidate with speeches and memos which reflected exceedingly cautious and highly qualified positions; borrowing a phrase, observers dubbed some of the material to be "as exciting as a mashed potato sandwich." As if Cliff's supervision did not suffice to keep a lid on intellectual ferment, Garth also proved capable of squelching issues quite directly. One day in May, for example, I was contacted by a scholar of East Asian affairs who was volunteering part-time in the campaign as a research assistant. He believed strongly that Anderson should take a position in opposition to arms sales to the People's

Republic of China; rumors were circulating that the Carter administration was preparing to undertake a new military supply relationship. The issue was timely, because the Chinese defense minister was about to visit the United States. At my direction, the researcher prepared a briefing paper and a short speech on the subject for Anderson's consideration; I knew the arguments accorded with his general notions on arms sales. I sent the materials along to Garth and then phoned him. "Absolutely not," he said. "We shouldn't be for arms sales or against them. We should just say we are concerned. But I wouldn't even bring up the subject, because if Anderson's pressed, he'd have to say yes or no." That was that. No consideration was given as to whether Anderson should be consulted personally on the issue, and allowed to decide for himself.

Besides new approaches to press relations and to issues, there was a third innovation which Garth introduced into the campaign, perhaps the most consequential. He believed that Anderson, having achieved such a sudden rise to prominence, was faced with a danger of overexposure, or, in campaign jargon, of "peaking too soon." The answer to this problem would be to reduce Anderson's visibility over the spring and summer so as to preserve his "freshness" for the fall. To this end, Garth did what he could to discourage certain national media coverage of the campaign. He curbed Anderson's appearances on morning news shows, declined to allow interviews with important columnists, and postponed plans for major, newsworthy speeches. The week of the independent announcement, for example, Barbara Walters of ABC requested an interview with Anderson. She indicated that a seven-minute excerpt would be shown on the network's evening news. Most of us regarded the opportunity as one sent from heaven. Garth thought it anathema, and laid down the law that Anderson would not do it. "Let her wait until September," he said. In the meantime, Garth directed Anderson to spend his time campaigning around the country, from city to city, seeking press only in local media markets. While he would continue unavoidably to be accompanied by a large corps of national press, the emphasis in speeches prepared for Anderson would be on topics of interest mainly in the local areas which he was visiting.

Garth's strategies may have been well suited for conventional candidates running conventional campaigns in conventional circumstances. Anderson's entire reason-for-being, however, was that he was seen as unconventional. In the matter of press relations, for example, Anderson had been treated sympathetically by reporters in large part because they found him unusually open, direct, and plain-spoken. His easy accessibility impressed them. Of course, Anderson's intelligence gave him an advantage over other politicians: he could handle himself adeptly and had no real fear of the press, as do some public figures; indeed, he rather enjoyed reporters. Garth may not have been used to dealing with such clients and so perhaps did not fully appreciate this. Journalists, too, are people, with their own sets of prejudices and sensibilities. When Anderson seemed straightforward and uncalculating, many wrote about him in almost saintly terms as an honest and incorruptible politician. When they sensed that press relations were becoming "managed," however, a certain cynicism developed toward the campaign which eventually was projected onto the candidate, even though he was not directly responsible for the change.

Anderson's statements and positions came to be treated more skeptically, as if they were now motivated by political considerations. Having portrayed himself as "different," Anderson could expect to be held to a higher standard than other politicians, and to be judged more harshly. Some members of the press even looked back and began to suspect, unfairly, that the original, seemingly courageous, stands which had made Anderson famous during the primaries constituted, in fact, only "media hype." Such personal disillusionment crept unavoidably into some of the reporting, and, as press relations soured, so too, after a certain lag, did the general tenor of press coverage that reached the public. And the strategy of keeping reporters at a distance not only caused resentment, but denied Anderson a chance to be seen in his warmer human dimension. One-on-one, Anderson was easy-mannered and charming; but behind a lectern and in front of a large audience, he often adopted a somewhat stiff public pose. Reporters who saw him in this light sometimes labeled him "preachy" and "strident." From these observations, it was a short leap for them to characterize his entire campaign as being a mission of religious zeal or personal egotism, as some occasionally implied. This was unfair, but the antidote of letting reporters see Anderson up close in frequent personal interviews and social exchanges had become unavailable.

The strategy of avoiding issues was another one that, in the long run, backfired. Anderson's appeal stemmed from a sense people had that he was leveling with them. He had shown a willingness to enunciate specific and potentially controversial positions on issues, even at personal political risk, an unusual approach which had merited extensive press coverage and dramatic public response. People seemed to think of him as a "non-politician," someone who had the guts to tell it like it was. Packaging him into something more soothing would create an aura of the conventional and risk sacrificing his much-vaunted "Anderson difference." Since that was the characteristic that had set him apart from the others, and given his candidacy its original appeal, a new approach would be self-defeating. And yet, over time, reporters noticed a change in Anderson's demeanor on the campaign trail. His speeches and press conferences began to lack a cutting edge; they became rambling and occasionally platitudinous, and more oriented to politics than to issues. Some observed that Anderson had now come to sound like George Bush, who had been accused during the primaries by Anderson himself, among others, of seeming quicker to discuss election strategy and poll standings than serious matters of national policy. It was an irony that Garth sought to tone down Anderson's presentation of issues on the notion that this would prevent him from saying anything which would engender bad press or public reaction; for now Anderson began to get bad press, and gradually to lose supporters, precisely for the fact that he was no longer saying as much as people had become accustomed to hearing from him. There was also a certain poignancy in the situation. Some of us remembered how frustrated Anderson had been a half-year before, or more, when the public kept turning a deaf ear to the important things he was saying, such as calling attention to the famine in Cambodia. Back then, when he had something to say, nobody was listening. Now that everybody was listening, he did not seem to have as much to say.

Finally, Garth's efforts to prevent Anderson's "overexposure" also proved short-sighted. At the time Anderson declared as an independent, the most critical thing he needed was sheer publicity. True, he was already drawing 22 to 26 percent nationwide when voters were asked their preference in a hypothetical three-way race among Carter, Reagan, and Anderson. And yet a remarkable 46 percent of the public continued to tell pollsters that they lacked sufficient information about him to form an opinion of his candidacy. Clearly he had enormous opportunity to improve. If Anderson managed to cross the threshold of about 30 percent, many felt his status as a serious candidate would become enshrined and irreversible. Rather than fading from the national spotlight, he needed more than ever to be seen, to inch his way up in the standings, the sooner the better. This meant availing himself of every major media opportunity that came his way, and losing no opportunity to speak out forcefully. He needed to draw new supporters and to retain the enthusiasm of his original ones as well; the last thing he needed was to enter into a period of enforced political hibernation.

Of course, Garth was used to conducting campaigns where strong party organizations were already in existence, and where large amounts of money were available to finance television commercials. In our case, he had neither. It was the extensive and favorable coverage of the press, free of charge, which until now had given the Anderson campaign its boost. And yet the effect of Garth's strategy was to keep Anderson largely out of the public eye unless and until he passed through a particular area where he would be covered by local press. Throughout much of the late spring and early summer, one would hear from people in various parts of the country much the same thing: "Oh, yeah, Anderson was here a couple weeks ago . . . but other than that he seems to have faded from sight. What's he doing?" By the time he got to his twentieth media market, he had been forgotten in the first fifteen. Moreover, unless he said something unusual, the national press accompanying him had difficulty turning out stories that editors back home considered worthy of prominent coverage. Newspaper stories in major papers were relegated to inside pages, and network stories—given intense competition for hard news—often failed to air at all. All of this was at a time when Carter, Kennedy, and Reagan continued to receive regular headlines. The result of Anderson's noncontroversial and low-visibility program of city-hopping was little progress in positive publicity and a steady decline in preference polls. Instead of rising to something on the order of 30 percent, he fell, steadily, about 1 percentage point every week and a half, down to 22 percent, then 20 percent, then 18 percent, and progressively worse. Garth argued that Anderson could recoup everything in the fall. Many of us worried that by then it would be too late.

The changes in the character of the Anderson campaign after it turned independent were abrupt, but to the naked eye their consequences would be seen only gradually. For the time being, the campaign management was known to be in transition, preoccupied with urgent and difficult tasks of organization, and so Anderson enjoyed a certain honeymoon period with the public during which time he was given the benefit of the doubt that he was the same candidate as he had been before. It was only in time that people began to appreciate that his press was not as favorable, that he sounded different in some of the things he talked about, and in general that he was not heard from as much. Even then, not everyone followed the political scene closely enough to notice, but enough did notice to make the difference in whether he went up in the polls by 2 percent, or down by 2 percent. Over the months, this quiet, incremental decline took its toll.

In the first weeks, few in the campaign felt in a position to quarrel with Garth's methods. He had been vested with full authority by the Andersons, obviously had their confidence, and remained in firm control. Even among those who harbored misgivings, Garth's reputation as a grand master at the game of politics was such that one was easily induced to make the leap of faith that he knew exactly what he was doing. Moreover, there was a tendency to regard concern about the "character" of the campaign as somewhat naïve and sentimental; only amateurs did not accept that compromises and expedients were a necessary part of "playing to win." Were we seriously interested in getting to the White House, or interested only in giving nice speeches? It was also easy to dismiss concern about Garth's tactics so long as things continued to go well. A great optimism was in the air; one Harris poll showed Anderson winning 29 percent nationwide if respondents assumed that he had a real chance to win and that votes would therefore not be wasted. Indeed, a breakdown under the assumption of the "real chance," showed Anderson leading in the eight states with the largest number of electoral votes; leading in the eastern states, as a region; and second only to Reagan in the West. As for ballot access drives, these were succeeding beyond expectation; in Michigan, for example, the campaign quickly filed petitions containing more than three times the required 18,000 signatures. Even the number of reporters assigned to Anderson, and the seriousness with which they wrote their stories, seemed to indicate that the press considered it not inconceivable that Anderson could win.

Rarely did observers see the connection between the new nature of the campaign and the practical political consequence that it might lose Anderson support; usually the question of Garth's tactics was seen as strictly an ethical concern. The conventional wisdom had taken hold in the campaign that it was necessary to be tough and traditional to win. Like generals fighting the last war, many assumed that the campaign needed to employ techniques which had proved successful in previous political campaigns. Garth's overall objective was to build for Anderson a coalition of groups normally oriented to the Democratic party which he felt were ripe for plucking away from an unpopular Jimmy Carter: labor, black groups, Jewish groups, big-city voters, and the like. He assumed that other groups which Anderson had already begun attracting in large numbers—students, moderate Republicans, young professionals, for example—would, given their distaste for the major party candidates, have no choice but to stick with him. As a result, he endeavored to have Anderson take as many popular positions as possible before these new groups, and to have him avoid giving offense to any other significant group which he felt could potentially be attracted to him.

It was an approach which might well have been successful were Anderson the nominee of a traditional party; but it was destined to backfire in the case of someone who had earned acclaim on the basis of refusing to be just another politician. Anderson was admired precisely for those attributes which in other candidates might have been considered liabilities. He had made a point of addressing what he called the national interest, rather than special interests. In addition, the objective of an independent campaign was unique: to convince voters to buck the two-party tradition and to take a chance on something new. To do so, Anderson would have to make more than a *good* case for his candidacy; he would have to make a *compelling* case. He would have to show himself as more than just the best candidate; he would have to excite people, motivate them to choose the historic path of an independent candidacy, challenge them to undertake a major experiment in American democracy. All of this required a continuation of the style of campaigning Anderson had pioneered in the primaries.

Saturday night, May 3, I went to the Washington Hilton for the annual White House correspondents' dinner. The Andersons also attended and were cheered enthusiastically when a spotlight focused on their table and they were introduced to the crowd of one thousand or more. An even greater measure of Anderson's celebrity was the number of jokes told about him by the after-dinner speakers. Presidential press secretary Jody Powell, for example, reported that little Amy Carter had come up to her father recently and—in a takeoff on the question usually reserved for a "spoiler"—asked him whether he would be taking more votes from Reagan or from Anderson.

At the dinner I ran into Bob Sann, the low-key media advisor we had retained during the primaries. Bob had done a remarkably good job in producing Anderson's commercials; despite only modest financing from the campaign, he had created several catchy and effective ads, in the process coining the term "the Anderson difference." Garth had been hired for the independent campaign not out of any dissatisfaction with Sann, but only because Garth was in a category by himself in terms of fame and reputation, an association which we thought would profit us. The Andersons' idea had been, however, that Sann would remain involved, and assist Garth in media projects. We should have known better. Garth always insisted on exclusive control. Sann had not heard a thing from the campaign since the independent phase began, not from Garth, not from Anderson, not from anyone. Meantime, he still had a number of assistants employed on his payroll, specifically for purposes of the campaign. All they could do was wait patiently for assignments. Sann's repeated phone calls to Garth were not returned. It reached the point where Sann would have been satisfied just to hear that he was not wanted anymore. But he never heard anything. The silence lasted many weeks more, and finally Sann disbanded the staff.

Sunday afternoon, Margot and I went out to the Andersons' home in Bethesda. It was less than two weeks since the independent campaign had been launched, but I wanted to discuss with them a troubled sense about the course on which it seemed headed. The day was a warm and sunny one, but the Andersons remained, as usual, isolated indoors. Partly this reflected Anderson's disposition to sit at home reading when others would have preferred getting outside for fresh air; partly, it had to do with the inconvenience the Andersons now experienced whenever they traveled with their cumbersome security escorts.

Keke answered the door, and brought us back into the den. We talked a few minutes. Then Anderson came into the room. We did a double take. He was dressed in little white tennis shorts, a T-shirt that read "MICHIGAN STATE," and on his face sported oversized Mickey Mouse Club sunglasses. "How do I look?" he asked proudly. Anderson was capable of even slapstick humor on occasion; had more people seen the lighthearted side of him, which he usually kept well hidden from public view, his appeal as a candidate might have increased considerably.

It was in this almost festive atmosphere that I chose to give the Andersons a lengthy and solemn memorandum detailing my concerns about Garth's recent actions. I felt something like a party-pooper addressing such negative opinions to him, just at a time when, to all appearances, the campaign seemed to be going so well. But my concern was what could happen down the road. It seemed to me that we were still coasting on the image and the publicity we had received during the primaries. If Garth continued on his present tack, Anderson would risk losing his "difference," and voters would be inclined in November to return to their traditional party folds.

Anderson gratefully accepted the memo, promised to read it, and Margot and I took our leave. After going on for many pages in specific detail, the memo concluded:

> If we practice too much pragmatism at the expense of our original idealism, then we are sowing the seeds of our own destruction . . . because the thing that has struck the most responsive chord with the public . . . is that people have the sense that John Anderson doesn't think winning is everything. David Garth may have been in tune with what it took to win campaigns before, but he has missed the boat if he doesn't see the profound revulsion people have today against packaged and over-cautious politicians.

The next day, Anderson was in the congressional office. I summoned up my courage, and walked in to ask his reaction. He was steely eyed and cool. The memo had upset him. He told me he and Keke had read it twice, and discussed it a great deal. He said to me, "Mark, we can't go back to the *Doonesbury* days. Things are different now. We're in the big time." These were phrases he was to repeat on more than one occasion when the question of Garth's tactics arose again. But there seemed to be a difference of opinion as to what the *"Doonesbury* days" implied. I certainly would not have argued that we abandon our larger and more sophisticated campaign organization in favor of the awkward and amateurish one that we had used to muddle through in the early days. On the other hand, it did seem a mistake to extinguish the spontaneity, candor, and accessibility which had originally proved so appealing to the press and the public. Anderson reacted strongly, however, to the suggestion that an excessive pragmatism might sooner or later raise the question of whether there were an "Anderson difference" after all. "That hurts me," Anderson said. "Of course there is, and there always will be."

It was heartening to see Anderson so determined to maintain his integrity, and I felt embarrassed now ever to have questioned it. At this point, it seemed appropriate to step back and suspend further judgment about the campaign's new direction; I wanted very much to be part of the team, and would try my best to get along with Garth. In practice, this meant strict deference. Garth did not seem the type of person with whom one could quietly reason; he had his own set of ideas, and at times seemed to regard even constructive criticism as a mark of insubordination. In all the rest of the campaign, I never did speak my mind to him. Even when he spoke to me vituperatively, and I felt strongly that his views were wrong, I hesitated in fighting back. Now I see this was a mistake, and unduly fainthearted on my part, but at the time I sensed that challenging Garth directly would result only in escalating the decibel level of the conversation and that, in practice, the only chance of prevailing in an argument with Garth was to have him overruled by Anderson. I would make increasingly strenuous arguments to Anderson about Garth's practices, but I always felt it was decidedly Anderson's right and duty—not mine—to change the ways of the person whom he had chosen to run his own campaign.

Early in May, I met one of Garth's chief assistants, Zev Furst. Garth had a number of younger people working for him in his New

York office, and typically each one would be assigned to assist him with a particular campaign. Garth always had several contracts for his consulting services going on simultaneously, and often when a candidate claimed to have Garth working for him, in fact much of the work would be done by one of these younger assistants, acting under Garth's only occasional supervision. In the case of the Anderson campaign, Garth involved himself much more than usual, given the magnitude and importance of a presidential campaign, but frequently, when he remained up in New York working on other business, Zev would be his Johnny-on-the-spot down in Washington. Although Zev had no formal title, position, or responsibilities, the fact that he acted with the imprimatur of Garth made him second only to Garth in the campaign hierarchy. Zev was in his thirties, tall, thin, quick-witted, articulate, and constantly in a state of motion. If "Pigpen" in the Peanuts comic strip always traveled in a cloud of dust, Zev always seemed to bring with him a cloud of commotion. He acted as a sort of gadfly about the campaign, except that he rumbled like a tank, roaring in and out of offices, asking what people were doing, reversing decisions that had been made, issuing orders. His reactions to events were often exaggerated—he never hesitated to label a "crisis" what others took to be a minor snafu—and, despite a redeeming sense of humor, he generally seemed to feel that the most effective means of dealing with problems was to groan in exasperation and prophesy the end of the world. He had a favorite expression—"done!"—which he used to respond to suggestions that he liked. Presumably it was meant to imply that action would be accomplished promptly, although, as it happened, this was not always the case. The general perception of Garth and Zev was illustrated by a joke that made the rounds among the campaign staff: "How many David Garths does it take to screw in a light bulb?" "None. Zev will do it." "And how many Zevs does it take to screw in a light bulb?" "None, it's done!"

Incredibly enough, this was Zev's first real campaign experience; his immediate previous employment had been as Jerusalem representative of B'nai B'rith, a Jewish service organization. Nonetheless, Garth entrusted him with major authority in the campaign. What appealed to Garth was less Zev's professional experience than his personality and temperament, which apparently were judged to be well-suited to managerial responsibilities. Garth and his associates were proud of a reputation they had acquired over time for being tough-minded and bold. Since many of their decisions were, in point of fact, surprisingly cautious, I realized after a while that this reputation had more to do with a trait that might be called "pseudo-decisiveness." Garth and Zev liked to be seen making decisions. Rarely would either of them pause a moment and reflect out loud on the pros and cons of a situation. The premium seemed to be on coming up with an answer to a question within three seconds. Never mind if the answer were wrong, and their minds changed back and forth every day for a week. As long as each time they were forceful in stating their decision, the content of the decision itself was almost secondary.

One day in early May, I overheard Zev talking about a speech on the subject of Israel which Anderson was to be giving in the next couple of days. I had not heard about it, though I had recently been designated to supervise foreign affairs speeches and research, among other campaign duties. I stopped and inquired. Garth, I learned, had decided Anderson needed to burnish his credentials as a supporter of Israel, and so had arranged for him to fly to New York and address the prestigious Council of Presidents of Major Jewish Organizations. An acquaintance of Garth's from the West Coast had been asked to prepare a text. Zev had just received it. I asked if I could read it.

The speech took a vigorously pro-Israeli position on the gamut of Mideast issues, a point of view generally in accord with Anderson's past record, but on one issue it ventured beyond what I knew to be Anderson's sentiments: a pledge was made that Anderson, as president, would recognize Jerusalem as the capital of Israel and, accordingly, move the United States embassy there from its present location in Tel Aviv. I was taken aback. This was a position widely regarded as an untenable one for a president to take if he were genuinely interested in promoting a Mideast settlement. There was a good reason that no administration, Republican or Democratic, had seen fit to take these moves. Sovereignty over Jerusalem is among the most delicate and intractable of issues dividing Arabs and Israelis. Both consider it an integral part of their respective domains, and neither in the least recognizes the other's claim. At best, it was something that would not be resolved until most of the other issues of a Mideast peace were settled first. For the United States to take sides was unnecessary and would look gratuitous to the Arab world. Our position would be prejudiced and our effectiveness as an honest broker in the Mideast peace process would be seriously damaged.

On the other hand, it was easy to understand Garth's motivation in wanting Anderson to make the speech. Anderson had long been considered a "friend of Israel," and it did not seem too much to hope that the right approach to American Jews could win considerable support. As a group, they seemed disenchanted with Carter, the firmness of whose commitment to Israel was considered uncertain, and yet, given a traditional political disposition toward the Democratic party, unlikely to move toward Reagan. Anderson seemed a plausible third way out, except for one serious obstacle: Bob Strauss, the Carter campaign chairman, was beginning to circulate information about a long-forgotten skeleton in Anderson's closet. It seemed that as a first and second-term congressman, in the early 1960s, Anderson had introduced a startling proposal to amend the Constitution of the United States so as to enshrine America as a "Christian nation." Anderson had long since repudiated the effort, claiming that it was done only very casually and carelessly as a favor to district constituents. But it was hard to explain away. The born-again religiousness of Jimmy Carter had left many uneasy, but nothing Carter had done held a candle to Anderson's proffered Constitutional amendment. Combined with what some considered to be at times a sanctimonious demeanor, evidence of this kind about Anderson's religiousness was bound to put off certain more secular voters.

Still, that he had made one mistake hardly seemed reason to compound it with another. Swinging to the other extreme might give the air of a candidate protesting too much. I got back to the office and talked about the matter with Bob Walker, who saw it from the same point of view. We decided to broach the issue with Anderson, bypassing Garth, whose reaction, we suspected, would be defensive and unbending. We went into Anderson's office and laid before him our feelings. He listened and agreed that the language needed to be changed. Bob volunteered to call Zev and negotiate. Zev was not persuaded. "No, absolutely not, no changes!"

he said. Bob persisted, as did I. Subsequently, Anderson overruled Zev and agreed to qualify his statement somewhat to say that he would recognize Jerusalem, and move the embassy, *"at the end of the peace process."*

In a technical sense, he figured, no one could quarrel with such a formulation. For, by definition, the peace process would not be concluded until the parties agreed on all of the terms. This meant, in turn, that either the peace process would be ended, and the Arabs would be satisfied with Israeli control of Jerusalem; or, the peace process would not be ended, and the United States would not have to change its policy and extend recognition. While this new language was definitely an improvement, I expressed to Anderson a continued uneasiness about it. It seemed to me that such a qualification would in all probability escape most audiences. On the other hand, to the extent it were noticed, it might well be considered specious or obfuscatory. I was outvoted on the matter, and Anderson went ahead to use the line the next day in his New York speech. He won resounding applause from his audience when he spoke it. A week later, he delivered essentially the same speech in Washington, before a conference of the American-Israel Public Affairs Committee. The speeches were reported only slightly in the newspapers, and the Jerusalem issue caused little fuss for the moment.

I remained concerned, however, about what might happen down the road, and on May 15, I gave Anderson another memorandum, this one addressed to his recent speeches. In part, it said:

> I am afraid that for every voter you may be pleasing by taking this stand, you will end up losing one or two other voters who become disillusioned if they sense you are just playing to a special interest and practicing politics as usual.

And it tried to call to mind what had served him so well before:

> I know you got a wonderful reception in both New York and Washington, and it will be tempting for you to think: "What a great speech Garth's people gave me! It really went over big!" But that's a short-sighted way to look at it. For consider what a wonderful ovation you could have had if you had given an anti-gun control speech before the New Hampshire gun owners, or a fiery anti-grain embargo speech to the farmers of Iowa. But that has not been your style, and that is why people have supported you. You have to remember that you are ad-

dressing an audience that is not just confined to the one hall where you are speaking, and where people are applauding you. You are not just speaking to narrow groups. You are speaking to all Americans.

Later, when we talked about it, Anderson replied that he had no intention of changing his colors for the sake of winning votes. He reassured me that he had been careful to use the qualifying phrase—"at the end of the peace process"—when he discussed recognition of Jerusalem, and that he thought I was exaggerating the problem. He would stick to his guns, he promised, and continue to say whatever he wanted, irrespective of Garth's advice.

Eventually the Jerusalem position did attract attention, and lent a widespread impression that Anderson was willing to adapt his positions to suit an audience. It was ironic that this issue went farther than almost any other in creating the very controversy Garth sought to avoid. Of course that had been anything but Garth's intention. He had simply misjudged potential reaction, thinking it would be popular to those immediate audiences which heard it, and pretty much go unnoticed by others. Certainly, Anderson, for his part, should not have flinched from stating important positions merely because they were controversial; unfortunately, he never gave evidence that this was a deeply held belief and, in fact, the more he came to consider it, the more it became a source of regret. Giving speeches that were 100 percent in accord with the opinions of an audience was a perfectly acceptable and time-honored form for a conventional politician seeking to win votes. But in the case of someone who had become known for scrupulously honest and balanced presentations, a speech purposely filled to the brim with applause lines had the potential, to the ears of a wider audience, ultimately to ring false.

In late May, I noticed one day on an advance schedule that Anderson was going to be passing through Princeton, New Jersey, for a fund-raising reception. One of my responsibilities was to arrange occasional issue-oriented seminars for him, and this seemed to be an excellent opportunity for him to sit down and chat about foreign affairs topics with George Ball, who lived in the area. Given the clear differences between them on the subject of the Mideast, I assumed from the beginning that a discussion on that score would be excluded. But Ball was an expert in many other areas. He had been commissioned not long before by President Carter to prepare an elaborate options paper on the situation in Iran during the fall of the Shah. He had been the last Westerner to meet with President Park of Korea before Park's recent assassination. And, as a former undersecretary of state and a frequent author and commentator, he would be capable of giving Anderson a *tour d'horizon* on just about any other current issue as well.

I called Ball, and he was eager to be of assistance. He offered the use of his home. Ever discreet, he said he would understand if Anderson wanted the meeting to be an entirely unpublicized one, and kept quite informal. In addition, he suggested including several other notable residents of Princeton: Nicholas Katzenbach, the former attorney general; William Bundy, editor of *Foreign Affairs* magazine; George Kennan, elder statesman of the American diplomatic corps; and perhaps a couple of Princeton professors. They could be useful, Ball implied, not only for the obvious contributions they would make to an informed discussion, but also because they would help camouflage the fact that Anderson was meeting with Ball, if anyone were really so concerned about that.

Ball was being very generous with his help, and I knew that Anderson would enjoy enormously the intellectual stimulation such an evening would afford; Anderson had a particular fondness for exchanges on foreign policy. I phoned the campaign scheduler to clear a time for a meeting, subject, of course, to the various approvals that were now required from the campaign hierarchy. Cliff Brown quickly phoned me back. "Oh, no, you can't let Anderson see Ball. Garth'll go through the roof!" Cliff then proceeded to lecture the scheduler on the political implications of such a meeting, and together they decided to assert unilateral authority and scotch the proposal. I knew an appeal to Garth would be fruitless; he would be even more adamant. Time was short, and it seemed impossible to reach Anderson quickly. Moreover, Garth would be furious if he thought I went around him to check with Anderson. The situation struck me as incongruous. I was really the only one close enough to Anderson to know his preferences. The others were virtual strangers. They were making decisions now not on what they imagined to be Anderson's inclinations, but on what they assumed to be Garth's.

I had the unpleasant duty to phone Ball back, and make a lame excuse in Anderson's behalf. Several days later, I explained to Anderson the decision that had been made in his name on a meeting with Ball. He seemed somewhat concerned by it, but not overwrought. He continued to believe that Garth knew what was best, that certain practical concessions were required in the interest of running a professional campaign, and once again pledged that, "where it really mattered," Garth would not be allowed to run roughshod over the campaign. I could not but wonder where the line would be drawn.

On Tuesday, May 27, when I got home from work in the evening, a bulging envelope awaited me in the mail from Stewart Mott, the activist liberal and philanthropist who had taken a large interest in Anderson's independent campaign. I knew that Mott had been helpful in the beginning by initiating legal research into the requirements of an independent candidate's qualifying for the fifty state ballots. I had not heard much about Mott in the intervening month or so, except the report that Garth was trying to keep him at arm's length from the campaign. Knowing Garth, my assumption was that Mott's ideas about the campaign must have differed somewhat from his own. In any case, Mott was someone of stature who might prove a competitor for the ear of the candidate, and Garth was not one to brook such competition.

I opened the envelope from Mott, and inside was a copy of a several-page memo to Anderson from Mott, which listed scores of concrete ideas for improving the organization and performance (not the ideology or positions) of the campaign. I was quite astonished. Almost every suggestion seemed an excellent one, many of them simple and even mundane. But no one else had been making such suggestions. Garth was too wrapped up in grand strategy to bother with many organizational details. And Mike MacLeod was not the type of manager who would have taken the initiative to change established routines without considerable prodding. Mott seemed to have precisely the "get up and go" which others in the campaign lacked. I had never talked to Mott, but was moved to do so now. I knew nothing of his perspective beyond that disclosed in his memo, and did not think it would hurt to talk to him directly.

I was not sure how to reach him, but after a moment it occurred to me that MacLeod would probably have his number. I called

Mike's secretary and asked if she could find it in her Rolodex. She had it, and gave it to me. No more than twenty seconds later, before I had had time to sit down and place the call, my phone rang. It was MacLeod. This was an irony. I had been trying to reach him for several days on another matter, and he had begged off each time that he was too busy to talk; now he could not have been more eager. He said he had overheard my call to his secretary, and wondered why I wanted Mott's number. I explained that I had received his memo, and wanted to call him about it. Mike began calmly by saying that he did not think it was a very good idea to do so. Mott, in Mike's estimation, was a "troublemaker, a loose cannon." I recognized those terms as ones that were frequently applied to people who did not fit into the scheme of things as laid down by Garth. I protested that, at least as to organization, Mott's suggestions seemed good ones, and I did not see what he was doing wrong. It seemed to me it would be quite useful to involve a person of such energies in the campaign, rather than isolating and antagonizing him. Mike said that many of Mott's ideas had already been implemented; I knew that not to be true. Mike became increasingly agitated. "The guy's flakey, don't talk to him." Mike's attitude mystified me; I had never heard him speak so forcefully. "I don't want anyone in the campaign talking to him, and if you do, there are going to be problems," Mike finished. At this juncture, I hardly wanted to create problems, and so I reluctantly acquiesced and agreed not to make my call.

The next day, at a little before three in the afternoon, I was at my desk in the congressional office and received a call from Garth. He was at the campaign headquarters a couple of miles away. "I want to talk to you," he said, with his inimitable gruffness. "Come over here immediately." Thus summoned, I drove over promptly. I walked into the bustling headquarters and found Garth back in MacLeod's office. Garth said hello matter-of-factly, and then escorted me down a couple of aisles until we found a small room that was unoccupied. For the next hour-and-a-half, we sat facing each other across a table. I had once received the "Garth treatment" over the telephone, but now I was to have the honor of getting it in person.

Garth began by saying he had heard I tried to contact Mott. He asserted that Mott was mentally unbalanced and unstable. "He's crazy, and no one in this campaign is going to associate with him." Garth informed me, though I had already heard it, that Mott was planning to convene a meeting of people interested in the Anderson campaign, for the purpose of discussing how the campaign might improve its effectiveness. "Anyone from this campaign who attends that meeting," Garth said, "will be fired on the spot." Garth further informed me that he had had a meeting just recently with the Andersons, and that they had agreed, too, never to speak again with Mott. More than that, Garth said, they had vested in himself the authority to deal with campaign staff who transgressed in the matter. At this point I should have argued. It was not that communicating with Mott was in itself an important issue. But the idea that I could not choose with whom to converse on the telephone—just as Anderson could not be allowed to decide with whom to meet in Princeton—bespoke a paranoia which was difficult to accept. Garth's manner intimidated me, however, and once again I retreated from direct confrontation; my silence caused me later regret.

Garth told me I was naïve about campaigns. Everything depended, he said, on "striking the right tone." The reason he had not wanted Anderson to make a highly specific statement about the Iran rescue mission, for example, was that "you have to know how it's playing before you comment." Garth seemed impatient at having to give someone such a remedial lesson in politics. He said that tactics were paramount. "We're sitting on the story of the century, and John Anderson is going to be the most sought-after person in the country by the end of the summer if we play things right." For a moment, I found myself captivated, and wondering whether his approach was the right one after all. He *had* elected Ed Koch mayor of New York City, he *had* elected Hugh Carey governor of New York, he *had* elected all those others. Maybe he was able to see things the rest of us did not.

Before excusing me, Garth sought to put me firmly in my place, in the event his more dispassionate explanations had not quieted my concerns. Frankly, he said, it was not his inclination to be nice to me; he said I struck him as too wedded to the past campaign, and reluctant to play ball with the new team of which he was the captain. Nonetheless, he said he was forced to be nice to me because the campaign did not have many smart people around, and I was one of the more useful people among the slim pickings. Garth was remarkably adept at the backhand compliment. Then he held out a carrot and a stick. "You'll notice," he said, "that I haven't said anything bad about you to the press. I could say lots of things, if I wanted. I've done it to other people. I'm a very colorful speaker. As long as you play ball, you're safe." He went on: "Now, if you want to be part of the team, and you agree to play by my rules, your life'll be a lot happier. I'll make you an integral part of this campaign again." To be a team player, he said, would mean that I curb my direct communications with Anderson, and that I start taking orders only from Garth. "Everyone else is agreeing to it," he said. "You'll be sorry if you don't."

My thoughts at this point were filled with confusion and disbelief, but I sat nodding and trying my best to look nonchalant. I had signed on with Anderson when his chances were one-in-a-thousand and had come through thick and thin with him for two years. Now, when we had at last achieved success, Garth was permitted to come in and take over lock, stock, and barrel. I could not deny a personal resentment. But more important, after all the thousands of hours I had spent with John Anderson, I thought I knew his purposes and philosophies. Now someone who had barely arrived on the scene was summarily trying to impose an entire new mindset on the campaign. It seemed incredibly wrong. I kept thinking: "This is a bad dream. It's a scene straight out of Watergate. I didn't know things like this really happened."

I did not know where to turn. It was obvious that MacLeod considered it his duty not to question Garth's strategies, but to carry them out. Garth indicated he had read my memos to Anderson about the direction of the campaign. I had given copies only to the Andersons and out of courtesy, to MacLeod, and asked them all very distinctly not to share them. Later I learned that MacLeod had immediately passed his copy to Garth. So, too, had he informed Garth in an instant about my attempted phone call to Stewart Mott. As for Anderson himself, he seemed to have occasional vague doubts about Garth, but basically he was inclined to leave the details of campaign management in his hands. He was hearing from Garth even more than he was hearing from me, and Garth's explanations tended to sound authoritative and convincing. Anderson was traveling on the road a great deal and, with much else to concern him, did not care to upset himself unduly about what he saw as initial organization problems that would in time be ironed out. There was still no clear evidence that Garth's approaches were, other than offending a few people's sensibilities, actually impinging on the campaign's chances to win. Just the opposite: to the extent that one's appetite for victory had been whetted, there was all the more reason to listen to Garth, the one person associated with the campaign who had a proven, and impressive, track record. Who was a wet-behind-the-ears twenty-seven-year-old to be challenging the wisdom of Madison Avenue's premier political strategist? And what, in any case, was the alternative to Garth? If he left the campaign—and his departure would probably be explosive—it would look as if he thought the campaign did not have a chance after all, or as if the candidate had exercised bad judgment in having originally brought him on. Unless he could be replaced with someone of equal stature—and who was of equal stature?—it would be taken as an acknowledgment that the campaign was floundering in management problems. Under the circumstances of such limited options, there was a great temptation to give Garth the widest latitude to work his magic, and for everyone else simply to reserve judgment and wait and see.

I felt increasingly presumptuous going against the tide of opinion at the campaign, and continually wrestled in my own mind in deciding whether to bother Anderson about my personal feelings. Perhaps I over-dramatized the situation, but, having grown up in the era of Vietnam and Watergate, I could not avoid thinking how conventional wisdom often proved so fallible. If I had criticisms, it seemed particularly important to voice them at an early stage; I remained close to Anderson—even if I now talked to him more on the phone than in person—and I knew he would want me to be honest with him. So I determined to talk to him even more bluntly than I had to date. At the end of May, when he returned for a few hours to the congressional office, I walked in to discuss the situation with him still one more time. He gave me his full attention, and listened until I was done. I told him how troubling I found Garth's philosophy and practices and that, if I knew Anderson, he might well be troubled, too. Garth, I said, was assuming total control of issues, and not just confining himself to political strategy or media. More to the point, I said, he seemed to regard issues as distinctly secondary, and had freely announced that he would reserve the right to approve or disapprove the candidate's positions.

Garth, I continued, was working by intimidation. He had threatened to discredit anyone who did not go along with his orders, and promised to reward those who did. I said it would not surprise me if this were more bark than bite, but that, whatever the case, it ill became Anderson to have someone acting like this in his name. The campaign office had changed, I said, and was reminiscent now of nothing so much as the "invasion of the body snatchers." People were walking around in familiar bodies, but they had been "Garthed" into acquiescence.

"These are the realities," I said. "You may be dismayed by them, but they will not change so long as Garth is around." Garth had been given his chance, I said. We thought he was a genius who would turn the campaign into an incredible fighting machine. Perhaps he was a genius, but not for this campaign, which was a unique one. He had begun to do things which were not the way to win, but to lose. It might be a blow, I said, but in the long run, the campaign would be best served either by having him leave or by sharply curtailing his influence. "You have my loyalty," I told Anderson. "If you do not agree with what I have said, and if you think I will just be an irritant from here on out, a thorn in your side, I am prepared to leave, and leave quietly. You tell me what you think is best."

"You don't have to leave," Anderson said quickly. "I think things will work out. Garth's run a lot of campaigns before, and he's *won* them. He knows what he's doing. You've got to give these things time to work." He went on. "We can't run a campaign the same way we did when we were unknown. There's a totally different set of circumstances now. We have petition drives, we have legal battles, we have money to be raised, we have to compete in fifty states, we have to broaden our base. We have a million and one things to do," he said, "and you're sitting here fretting because we're not the nice, little campaign you used to know, where we could go around saying anything that popped into our head. Well, we're not amateurs anymore." His eyes fastened hard on mine, and he spoke softly. "Now, look," he said, "just try to show some patience. Garth is not going to change me."

Having come this far with Anderson, I was not going to leave unless he wanted me to; I would gulp hard and try again to become part of the team. If Anderson did not sense the danger of the Garth influence, then perhaps I was being unduly sensitive or naïve. Perhaps my reaction was simply one of wounded pride that I had lost to Garth my long accustomed place of influence at Anderson's side. I reminded myself that it was not *my* campaign, but Anderson's. And what experience did I have, compared to Garth, to prejudge the results of his strategies at this early stage? He was the expert; that is why we had hired him. Surely there was good reason that the press and the political world held him in such awe. Perhaps I could learn something by working with him.

One day the following week, with Anderson back on the campaign trail, I returned from lunch to the congressional office. A telephone message awaited me, with the ominous words scrawled out: "Garth called—he sounds upset." I sighed, wondering what it was this time, and placed a call to his New York office. Zev came to the phone. "We've blown it," he said, "it's all over, we've lost the election." "What on earth are you talking about?" I asked. "Anderson, now he's done it," Zev said. "David's thinking of quitting." "Over what?" I repeated. "What's the problem?"

As it turned out, Anderson had made a comment that morning out in Portland, Oregon, before a group of students, that the United States should consider apologizing to Iran if it could be proved that our government had complicity in criminal acts of the Shah. Zev and Garth were upset because this comment had been blown up into a full-page banner headline in the afternoon edition of the *New York Post:* "ANDY DROPS BOMBSHELL!" I thought it odd that they could be so quick to judge Anderson's behavior on the basis of a story in a newspaper which was notorious for sensationalistic journalism. In point of fact, Anderson's statement had been quite qualified. He had been asked whether, if it were clearly proven that the United States Government had conspired with the Iranian SAVAK organization to perpetrate murder and torture, the United States might owe the Iranian people an apology. He answered in his usual direct fashion that, yes, were such a thing clearly proven, we would; but he hastened to add that, in the meantime, we should not in any way kow tow to the Ayatollah.

Garth apparently had visions of Anderson's statement being compared to a controversial one Ted Kennedy had made a few weeks before, also concerning Iran. At the time, Kennedy had casually remarked to a TV interviewer that the former regime of the Shah had been one of the most brutal governments in history. Kennedy was widely disparaged by commentators for making such a sharp statement at a time when American hostages were being held and President Carter was trying to maintain a tough policy toward the Ayatollah. The Anderson comment was very different, and, not surprisingly, drew little notice the next day in most reputable national papers. But this did not prevent Garth from threatening to quit over what he had rashly dubbed a "crisis." He was to declare many such crises in the months ahead, and to brandish the threat of his resignation with at least equal frequency.

Another "crisis" occurred when *Newsweek* finally turned out its delayed cover story on Anderson. To most of us, such publicity was just fine. To Garth, anything that was not packaged in his own production shop gave cause for worry. For days preceding publication, he nervously wondered how Anderson would be portrayed, and what, in particular, would be said about his chief campaign strategist. Anderson, as usual, was a model of nonchalance. He was happy to get a needed splash of publicity, and quite prepared to take any accompanying lumps. He would read the article once over lightly, and then thumb through the rest of the magazine to see what else was in the news. Garth, on the other hand, went to great lengths to get a prepublication copy, and to scour every detail.

On the relevant Monday morning, I got a call from Garth. "You're the one who told them," he said, "I know it was you." "Told them what?" I asked. "You know what I'm talking about, and I know it was you." What Garth turned out to be referring to was the mention in *Newsweek* that, behind his back, campaign workers had taken to sneering at him as "Garth Vader," a takeoff on Darth Vader, the villain in the movie *Star Wars*. Actually, I had never heard that reference to Garth before, but thought it was marvelously funny. No, I told Garth, I had not been the originator of that expression. But, to myself I thought: If only I had been that clever.

Keke was also concerned about something that had appeared in *Newsweek*. Within the larger story on Anderson, there was a small box that contained a story on herself. She was described as being someone of great spunk. As if to provide evidence for such a description, she was quoted as having said about her husband, presumably in a lighthearted vein, "Oh, yes, John had such cute wavy brown hair when I met him . . . I married John for raw sex." Actually, I sensed that Keke was rather proud to have been quoted in that way; she liked being thought of as uninhibited, direct, and young. At the same time, however, she did not want people to think she would allow herself to be quoted saying something indiscreet, especially since she had criticized others for such lapses.

One morning, as I walked into the congressional office, Keke was already there, sitting on the couch in her husband's office, rereading the *Newsweek* story. She asked me whether I had been the one who reported her "raw sex" comment to the magazine. I suspected someone was planting the idea in Keke's head that the occasional negative stories the newspapers were carrying about the campaign were coming from disenchanted staff members like myself. That was, of course, untrue. In fact, far from defaming the campaign or anybody in it, I made a point of speaking to friends in the press in an upbeat fashion, always putting the best interpretation on matters. I felt great loyalty to John Anderson, and did not want to do anything to hurt him. At least Keke was making her accusation a little more playfully than Garth had. She said, "Oh, come on now, admit it, you told someone that story." "No," I said, "it's the first time I heard it." "No, I bet it was you," Keke persisted, with a smile. "I think you heard me say it one day when we were at home in the kitchen." "No," I said, "I just don't remember that at all. Besides, I have a witness to prove my innocence." With that, I called Margot, who worked upstairs in the office building for another congressman. I knew that had I ever heard such a memorable line, I would have repeated it to Margot. She could testify that she had never heard such a thing.

Margot came down. "Believe me, Keke," she said, "Mark didn't say that. Mark would blush even to say the words, 'raw sex.'" Keke thought about that a moment, impressed by the evidence. Then she turned back to Margot and said, "Dear, you ought to get a new boyfriend!"

One afternoon in mid-June, Anderson invited Mo Udall to drop by for a private chat; they got together every few months for conversation over a Scotch. Afterward, Anderson told me he had asked Udall again about being his running mate. Udall again had declined, but Anderson still had a hunch that if the polls turned around, Udall, like many others, would suddenly become available. Keke, for her part, had a suspicion that Carter would offer Udall a cabinet position in a second Carter administration to keep him in line. Udall had apparently suggested to Anderson that he consider someone else who had been a colleague of theirs in the Congress: Brock Adams, the former secretary of transportation. Anderson seemed to be mulling it over. I had reservations about Adams, and expressed them. "Well, who would you pick?" he asked. We discussed a number of names, including such random inspirations as former Interior Secretary Stewart Udall, Illinois Senator Adlai Stevenson, West Virginia Governor Jay Rockefeller, Eastern Airlines President Frank Borman, former Massachusetts Senator Ed Brooke, former Massachusetts Governor Michael Dukakis, and others. Each one seemed to have obvious liabilities as well as advantages. But what surprised me was that this seemed to be a subject to which Anderson had given very little thought, despite the fact that much of the rest of the world was thinking quite a lot about it. Indeed, I had had more searching conversations about the question with friends at the dinner table than we were having now.

My assumption had been that Garth by this point would have prepared thick black briefing books on each of fifty potential candidates, and that opinion-makers and political leaders would have been carefully surveyed for their suggestions. My assumption was ill-founded. One day about this time, flying back from New York with Zev Furst, I observed him taking out a yellow legal pad, jotting some vice-presidential names very spontaneously, intending to present this casual, longhand list to Anderson as his thoughts on the subject. I glanced at the names, noticed some omissions, and metioned them to Zev. "Oh, yeah," he said, "let me add those, too."

This mode of operation was an irony. The one thing the campaign staff had looked forward to when Garth had been hired was the advent of a more streamlined organization; we readily recognized our shortcomings as amateurs. Garth was assumed to be the consummate professional. Apparently we had a misunderstanding of what "professional" meant. One had assumed it meant organized, efficient, systematic, comprehensive, thorough. It did not. Garth may have been experienced, creative, and clever, but his focus was on the "big picture," not the little details. As a result, there was a startlingly slapdash quality to many of his efforts. He did not, in short, introduce new efficiency into our operation; we did not become the lean and tough campaign many assumed we would.

Instead, much time was spent reinventing the wheel. As a reflexive action, Garth stopped many of the practices which had been established during the Republican campaign. Columnists, for example, who had become used to quick and direct access to Anderson, now could barely get their calls returned. Joe Kraft, the widely syndicated columnist, called me one day in complete exasperation. He was a great admirer of Anderson's, and had already written many complimentary things about him. He had been trying for weeks to reach him on the phone. None of his calls to the press office were returned. I told him not to worry, and I called Anderson myself. He had no idea Kraft had been trying to reach him, and wanted me to put him through right away. Subsequently, Kraft wrote a piece about Anderson so flattering that the campaign found it suitable for reprinting and distribution to campaign contributors. Unfortunately, Kraft concluded the column by noting that Anderson was carrying his campaign virtually alone, and needed a better organization in the worst possible way.

Also before Garth arrived, Anderson had requested the formation of task forces of outside experts on a number of issues. These panels would draft and circulate briefing materials, position papers, and proposed speeches on their respective topics. Several of us began collecting the names of prominent people in various fields we might ask to serve on the eight to ten task forces that were envisaged. For my part, I was responsible for putting together a foreign policy group, and thus spoke to numerous specialists at Washington think tanks, on college faculties, and the like. It was not long before a hundred or more prominent names had been suggested to me; these were people well regarded in their fields, and thought to be friendly toward Anderson and willing to help out. I contacted a sampling of them by phone, and it turned out that they were indeed quite agreeable. Some expressed the caveat that the help they provided not be construed as an endorsement per se, but it surprised me how many well-known people were perfectly amenable to contributing their services to an independent candidate. So long as Anderson had stature, they would be agreeable; when his prospects for success began to sag, more than a few of our one-time advisors would crawl back into the woodwork.

One day, I called Garth in New York and asked for his consent to establish some of the groups on a formal basis, since Anderson had recently inquired into their status. He told me to fly up and talk to him about it. Notwithstanding the expense—covered, of course, by the campaign—Garth preferred to see people in person, even if the conversation could be conducted in no more than a few minutes. I went up to Garth's office, and sat down with him and Zev. Cliff Brown also joined us. I laid before Garth my proposal for the task forces. "This is exactly what we need," I said. "Anderson wants it. He suggested the task forces himself. And he keeps asking where the 'new ideas' are. Since you don't want him to start proposing new ideas yet, at least we can use this time to develop them. When the press asks us where the new ideas are, we can tell them they're percolating in our task forces. It will buy us some time until fall."

Garth looked over the foreign policy list. He did not seem to recognize most of the names, who were recognized in their fields, but not well known to the general public. "We don't need all these people," he said. "Let's just take a few. Zev will give them a call and get them on board." I was awestruck that Garth, right before my eyes, had so quickly whittled down the list. He may have been right that this would be more workable, but it seemed a tragedy to lose both the names and services of so many distinguished people. We had contemplated asking for a variety of papers from the foreign policy group—on Iran, arms sales, United States–Soviet relations, nuclear nonproliferation, and many other topics—and it seemed to me that we could put to good use the talents of virtually anyone who would serve. The Reagan-Bush campaign, for example, was later to announce a national security task force of ninety or more experts. But, determined to get along, I put up only the most perfunctory protest, and that was that.

A few days later, I called Zev to see what progress had been made. "Haven't been able to reach them yet," he said. I called again the next week, but, again, the same answer. Still another week later, I tried him, this time posing my question a little more bluntly. "Well," he said, "they can't do it." I couldn't believe it. I knew, to the contrary, that some of them were interested. It was obvious to me that Zev had not called them. For some reason, Garth simply did not want any outside advisory panels. This changed all of a sudden, however, in late June, when *Time* magazine mentioned that the campaign might be gearing up a number of task forces; a reporter had apparently heard the rumor. It looked good in print, as if the campaign's arrangements for developing "new ideas" were really quite solid. Unfortunately, when reporters from other publications called in that morning to follow up on this news story, no one knew what to tell them. The task forces we had hoped to have were nonexistent. They had been put "on hold."

Garth and Zev were alerted to this sudden new press interest. For the first time, they became concerned. Zev ordered Cliff and a couple of others to scramble around for some names, and told the press department to announce that a list would be released later in the day. All Zev and the others could come up with on the spot, however, were some very few people we had been dealing with informally. This did not make for an impressive list. There was not enough time to contact the scores of others we had wanted. Nor would we be able to show any fruits of labor from these groups. The campaign seemed amateur again.

For several days in late June, I traveled with Anderson on the road. This was the first real campaign swing I had been on with him since late April. I flew from Washington to Hartford, Connecticut, along with Keke, who was also joining him. On reaching Hartford, we were taken to the state capitol where Anderson was giving a speech. It was a gorgeous day, and at the scheduled time, Anderson emerged onto the square outside the capitol to address a noontime crowd. About 800 or 1,000 people had congregated to hear him. After an opening line or two adapted to the occasion, Anderson concentrated the rest of his speech on what seemed to be a well-rehearsed litany of criticisms against Carter and Reagan. This was disappointing. He came across sounding quite negative, and did not seem to have anything particularly positive to say on his own behalf. Nonetheless, Anderson got a rousing round of applause at the very end when he concluded by saying that he could feel it in his bones that the nation was going to elect its first independent president. The statement had an air of historic drama and proved a bell-ringer.

From the state capitol, we went to a local TV station, where Anderson was scheduled to tape a half-hour news interview. The program was to be shown only statewide in Connecticut, and only at 7:30 P.M. on the following Saturday. I could not understand why such a thing warranted Anderson's time. He was tired from a heavy round of appearances already, and would have profited much more by having the time off. Indeed, as I sat with the press watching the taping on closed-circuit TV, he looked fidgety and impatient, and the impression of most of us was that he had not done a particularly good job. It was as though time had stood still all these months: Anderson was still being forced to do the minor and relatively unproductive things that he had so disliked doing in the early days of the campaign. Then, however, he had been obscure, and had had no other choice.

I was quite curious as to why this event had been scheduled, and started asking around. Large organizations may have their advantages at times, but they have disadvantages as well. Most of Anderson's campaign events were now being set up by people far removed from him, who had little idea of his own preferences. In the old days, someone from headquarters would have called news stations directly to set up interviews, only after first asking Anderson whether it was something he wanted to do. Now, large teams of advance people swept into the field, were urged to do things by local coordinators who saw matters only from their own parochial points of view, then had to report to "lead" advance people who would sift through options, call deputy schedulers back in Washington, consult with the press office, and finally arrive at an itinerary. The reason Anderson had been scheduled to do this particular interview, it turned out, was that a local coordinator thought it would be helpful if Anderson met one or two of the panelists on the program, who were important local reporters. Of course, Anderson could have arranged simply to have drinks with them in a more relaxing atmosphere, or have called them on the phone. Indeed, it later turned out that one of the prima donnas on the panel was miffed because he had not been given the opportunity for an exclusive interview, and had to share Anderson with the others. Such were the vicissitudes of a big campaign.

From Hartford, we drove on to Bridgeport for a speech at a local college, then arrived in late afternoon in fashionable Greenwich, where a major fund-raising dinner was to be held that evening. In the meantime, Anderson had an hour to take his shoes off and unwind. Right before the reception began, Donald Kendall, the chairman of Pepsico, and a long-time Republican activist, came by to talk about helping. I was glad to see that we still had an occasional Republican supporter.

The next morning, June 22, we had to get up before six to catch a plane to Cleveland. As we assembled at the airport gate, waiting for the flight, members of the press were buzzing about an article which one of them was informed had appeared that morning in the *Washington Post*. I immediately called Margot to get more information. On the front page of the *Post* was a story with the headline, "Anderson Could Win, Pollsters Agree." A consensus of prominent pollsters, the story reported, did indeed feel that the Anderson candidacy, far from being just a temporary aberration, represented a serious challenge to President Carter. John Anderson, they felt, had a real chance of being elected the next president of the United States. Quoted to this effect within the article were numerous pollsters, including George Gallup, Lou Harris, Mervin Field, and Daniel Yankelovich.

What the pollsters added, however, was that for Anderson to be successful, he needed to translate the negative feelings about Carter and Reagan that were so widespread in the country into specific positive feelings about himself as an alternative. He had to develop and project more of a program; he had to give people more reason to vote for him than just as a vehicle of protest. Nonetheless, the publication of this story gave the campaign a shot in the arm. There is nothing like a good word from pollsters to impress hardened reporters. The optimism they regularly heard Anderson express in his speeches could be discounted as self-serving; the pronouncements of pollsters were taken as more objective. Suddenly, the campaign moved up a notch or two in the estimation of the press. Whatever Anderson said assumed a new significance: one day he might really be president.

We arrived in Cleveland in the morning, where Anderson was to address a national convention of the United States Jaycees. As we alighted from the plane, and boarded the motorcade, we had the honor of our first exposure to Cleveland's unique hospitality. Nowhere else did a city provide Anderson such an elaborate welcome. Hereafter, all other motorcades were to be measured against the standards set by what we dubbed this "Full Cleveland." Leading the procession were eight to ten motorcycles riding in formation in two columns, followed by two police cars, a lead Secret Service car, the limousine, a Secret Service station wagon, a staff car, another Secret Service station wagon, three police cars, an ambulance, the press bus, another police car, and some more motorcycles. Every freeway entrance was blocked off as we passed, and motorists backed up at these entrances had stepped out of their cars to see what was the problem. When we passed, some of them waved enthusiastically (although others, apparently irritated, were provoked to make gestures which were less polite). When we reached the downtown area, all the intersections we drove through were blocked off as well. With all this extravagance, it hardly seemed surprising that the city of Cleveland was teetering on the brink of bankruptcy.

After the Jaycees speech was finished—it consisted of Anderson's reading, with a hoarse voice, a fairly subdued campaign-prepared text on general campaign themes—we stopped off at the Bond Court Hotel nearby for lunch. The Andersons took their meal privately in a suite that had been made available. It was a beautiful day, and I went walking around the area near the hotel. A couple of blocks away was a large square, with a grassy field, a fountain, a view of the river and Cleveland Stadium, and a lot of people out walking.

A little later, Anderson came out and joined me. As we walked around, and in between the fifty hands that were thrust out for him to shake, he mused aloud as to how on earth he was ever going to overcome the public skepticism that he was a spoiler. We agreed that he needed to shift the burden on the spoiler question, and suggest that it was *Carter,* not Anderson, who might well be the ultimate spoiler. This had a real plausibility, since a Lou Harris poll had just been released that day, indicating that when people assumed Anderson to have a real chance, he and Carter were tied nationwide at 31 percent, compared to Reagan's 35 percent. We also agreed that the campaign needed to get across more effectively than it had to date that Anderson did not require anywhere near a majority of the popular vote to win. Rather, a clever, highly targeted campaign in a certain number of states could give him the requisite electoral votes. If voters understood this, they might concede him more of a chance.

But, finally, we discussed one other strategy, which he seemed intrigued by, but predicted that Garth would strongly oppose. The proposition was that if Anderson were still considered a spoiler about late September, he might make a dramatic statement in which he explained the situation to people and pledged to withdraw unless he were at least number two in the polls by the end of October. In return for this he would ask voters to suspend their judgment, and to tell the pollster, when he came around, their real preference. Clearly, if Democrats, for example, thought Anderson would withdraw at the end if he were a spoiler, they would not have to worry anymore that a vote for Anderson might only help elect Ronald Reagan. They might be more willing to support Anderson for the time being, knowing that, if his candidacy did not work out, they could easily turn back to Carter, and Anderson would take himself out of the picture. The same would be true for moderate Republicans, who did not wish to reelect President Carter.

That evening, we arrived in Pittsburgh from Cleveland. The Andersons asked me to join them for dinner in our hotel restaurant. Midway through the meal, I was summoned to the phone. It was Zev. He had heard that Anderson had made an extemporaneous comment at a news conference that morning on the subject of a sale by the United States to Saudi Arabia of parts for F-15 fighter airplanes. The fact was, of course, that Anderson had handled himself adeptly, and that nothing went wrong. Zev found this a very delicate subject, however, and even though he approved of Anderson's position, ordered me not to allow him to speak extemporaneously again on that subject. I was not in the mood to protest. When I went back to the table, I reported the conversation verbatim. Anderson laughed. He did not take Garth or Zev seriously half the time. He was accustomed to their overreactions. "Tell him fine," he said, and laughed some more. The incident had been a tonic, putting Anderson in a great humor. He said that perhaps I should tell Zev that he was thinking of introducing the Christian amendment again.

The next morning, Anderson got a 5:30 wake-up call so he could throw on some clothes quickly and leave for a plant gate by 6:00. I was not required to be in attendance, and so I slept until a more reasonable hour. Later, however, Anderson told me in some irritation that in the course of a half-hour at the gate, he had met only seventeen people. Despite dozens of new campaign advance people, somebody had goofed: it was the wrong gate at the wrong time.

That turned out, however, to be one of the more successful events of the day. At 9:15, in a conference room of our hotel, Anderson was to have a major breakfast with local labor leaders. The scene was memorable. A long table had been set up, covered by a satin tablecloth. Twenty-five place settings lined the table. On one side of the table was a rope to keep the press at a distance. Thirty or more reporters and cameramen were assembled on the other side of it, waiting to get pictures and comments as the breakfast meeting opened.

Unfortunately, none of the labor leaders had yet arrived. I took a seat in a corner of the room, on the press side of the rope. The appointed time for the breakfast to begin came and went. At last, Anderson walked in the door of the room. For some reason, he had been brought up without anyone's having checked to see whether his guests were there to be greeted. He looked in the room puzzled, and the same expression came over his face as the rest of us had all been wearing: Where is everyone? Anderson suddenly felt awkward, and did not know where to go. He spotted me, and, mine being the most familiar face, walked over. "Well," I said, "make yourself comfortable," and with that I pulled up another chair and handed him the *Pittsburgh Post-Gazette.*

Another five or ten minutes passed, and finally two people showed up. They were casually dressed, and had not even been formally invited; they said they were representing a couple of guests who could not make it. I huddled with Mike Rosenbaum and suggested that we just invite the press to sit down and have breakfast. Perhaps they would be willing to overlook the campaign's clumsiness if they got a free meal out of it. Besides, it seemed such a shame letting all those breakfasts go to waste, and it did not seem necessary for Anderson to have to sit for forty-five minutes just conversing with two uninvited guests. Rosenbaum did not like the idea. The press was quickly ushered from the room, before they could record too many embarrassing pictures, and the doors were closed. We never did find out whether Anderson had been sabotaged by a deliberate boycott or simply by incompetent staff work.

From Pittsburgh, we went on to Philadelphia, where Anderson campaigned in the colorful Italian Market, reaching his hand over piles of fruit and vegetables to greet all the sellers and merchandisers who jammed into this large outdoor area. Meantime, Keke moved through the crowd too, shaking hands of people her husband missed. She was an effective addition.

One evening, back in Washington, Keke asked me to escort her in place of her out-of-town husband to a Georgetown party hosted by former Senator John Sherman Cooper. On the way out of my building, I ran into Barry Commoner, the Citizens' party candidate, who was apparently staying with one of my neighbors. We talked for a moment, and he said he was hoping that Anderson would debate him. He drove off with a single aide in a small Volkswagen station wagon. It was all so reminiscent of the early days of the Anderson campaign. It was a pint-sized campaign, which thought it was much more important than it was. And yet, it should have been more important. Commoner, like Anderson before him, was speaking very seriously and creatively on issues, but was being almost studiously ignored by the press. The only way they would ever cover him would have been if he zoomed up in the polls. But he never would because he was never covered. His obscurity was secure.

Meanwhile, Anderson campaigns, here at a typical university appearance in Chicago. (Wide World Photos)

When I got to the Andersons', Keke was all set to go. She was wearing a summery white dress, perfect for an outdoor party. As we walked out the door, we passed the Secret Service trailer in the driveway. The door was open, because of the heat, and we could hear the sounds of the "CBS Evening News," which a couple of agents were watching. We decided to step in and watch with them. Just as we did, an Anderson story came on the air. It was a story about how the campaign was experiencing foul-ups in its scheduling, noting not only the abortive Pittsburgh labor breakfast, but also a speech that a luncheon group had waited for Anderson to give in one city, when, in fact, he was at that very moment giving a speech five hundred miles away. It was an irony that while overall scheduling practices had improved under a larger and more experienced staff, such as had been acquired by the independent campaign, the advent of a more "professional" image caused the press to judge the campaign's performance much more harshly than before. Keke went back into the house to call Garth and complain that the campaign could not afford more such publicity.

At the home of the Coopers, Keke spent every available minute speaking with the various senators, columnists, and other VIPs in attendance. I encouraged her to do so, introducing her to everyone I recognized who passed by. She was a marvelous ambassador of goodwill; everyone admired her spirit. At one point, we ran into South Dakota Senator George McGovern. He told her that he was glad her husband was running: in his own case, he said, he expected that Anderson's presence on the ballot in his state would bring enough Democrats to the polls—who otherwise would stay home if they only had a choice of voting for Carter—that it might make the difference in his senatorial election. It was a remarkable irony: the incumbent Democratic president dreaded the Anderson candidacy, but most other Democratic officeholders, up for reelection in 1980, thought the Anderson candidacy might very well have a beneficial effect on their own fortunes.

Anderson's popularity among disenchanted Democrats at times seemed an embarrassment of riches. A fear developed in campaign quarters that such an obvious appeal to Democrats would transform the perception of Anderson as a centrist candidate with whom Republicans could comfortably identify into a new perception that he was merely a liberal Democrat in independent's clothing. The campaign needed to demonstrate, in whatever symbolic ways it could, that members of both parties were still welcome.

In the course of the summer, a fortuitous opportunity arose to win over to our camp a notable member of the Republican establishment, Mary Dent Crisp, cochair of the Republican National Committee. Shortly after Anderson announced as an independent, she had been quoted in a Chicago paper as admitting that she very much admired Anderson's moderate positions and in particular his progressive record on issues of women's rights. The article erroneously left the impression that she was actually leaning toward an endorsement. This, of course, did not sit well with the hierarchy at the RNC and, despite her protestations of continued Republican loyalties, she began to feel frozen out of her accustomed party circles. At one point, Anderson called to thank her for her warm comments, but otherwise the matter sat idle. Subsequently, in the process of helping to draft the Republican party platform, Crisp resigned her position; in an emotional statement, she said she could not accept the stoutly anti-ERA language it incorporated. After time went by, I asked Anderson why he had not called to seek her support; he said it was because he assumed the campaign had already tried in his behalf. To double check, he agreed to call her. It was the first she had heard from anyone. The two hit it off, and after some negotiation, she accepted an invitation to join the Anderson campaign as national chairperson, a largely honorific position which meant, in practice, traveling the country almost full time giving speeches. Through the rest of the campaign, Crisp worked tirelessly and effectively in behalf of her new cause, applying the skills she had developed in years of organizing for the Republican party.

The first week in July, I went up to New York to join Anderson for some meetings. While I was there, Garth summoned me over to his office. The ballot-access efforts were moving toward a very successful conclusion, and Garth had decided it was time for Anderson to make still another presidential announcement speech, indicating formally that he was definitely going ahead with his candidacy. This was something that, until now, at Garth's directive, Anderson had been careful to say remained contingent on overcoming legal and financial obstacles. Garth wanted my help in drafting an announcement speech. Someone in the Washington office had written one, but Keke had read it and thought it was not eloquent enough. I thought it was well suited to the occasion when I read it, and was not sure I could improve on it. It was short, but that had been Garth's conception of the speech: that it was really to be just a formality, and an opportunity for the press to ask questions.

I sat at the typewriter in one of Garth's offices and wrote five or six pages of text. I turned it in to Garth. He looked it over and said, "Good work." Then he added, "I'm going to have someone else look at it and do some editing if necessary." With that, he gave it to Ron Maiorana, one of his partners in the firm, whom he frequently described as being a "whiz" of a writer. In the meantime, I went down to the street below to buy some souvlaki from a sidewalk stand and take a walk. Garth's offices were located on Fifth Avenue

near Central Park, and it was a pleasant summer day to be out-
doors.

When I returned an hour later, Maiorana had just turned in his
product to Garth, who passed it to me. I read the revision, and
thought to myself it must be a bad joke. Everything seemed deliberately rephrased in a flatter and more prosaic way, as if the object
were to say as little as possible in the most general and inoffensive
manner. The speech now appeared trite, sophomoric, and in places
barely literate. Yet this is what Garth wanted to put out in Anderson's name. Indeed, Garth said he liked it, and asked me what I
thought. My nerve failed; I did not feel like arguing. I rationalized
to myself that perhaps I was obtuse in some way and did not understand the art of crafting political statements. The gap between
us seemed unbridgeable. I answered that the speech looked fine,
and that I had to leave for the airport.

The whole way home, I wondered what to do. My feelings at this
moment were illustrative of the dilemma I felt almost constantly
throughout the independent campaign. Was it my duty to accept
Garth's judgment and instructions without quarrel and simply put
my own disagreements out of mind; or did my responsibility remain
to the Andersons on whom Garth's activities and decisions would
reflect? When I got to Washington National Airport, I put in a call
to the campaign, and happened to reach Ed Coyle, the deputy campaign manager. He said that Garth had just telecopied down the
speech Anderson would be using for the announcement. Coyle
asked if I was familiar with it. I said yes, but that I thought it had
some "rough edges." Coyle said, "Rough edges! It was unbeliev-
able!" I was relieved to hear Coyle's opinion. Coyle told me he had
conveyed his opinion to Garth, and had had a conversation with
him at a high "noise level." I reached Keke, tried to relate a sim-
plified version of the story, and suggested that for convenience we
just go with the first text that had been drafted by the campaign.
This was accepted and proved to be perfectly adequate.

And so, one morning in early July, Anderson marched into the
Caucus Room of the Cannon House Office Building, to a cheering
crowd of several hundred people, including many who could not get
in and had to line the halls to catch a glimpse of him walking in
and out.

The independent campaign had languished somewhat since it was first christened in late April, and to some extent had yet to define its reason for being. But for all the challenges and uncertainties it faced, the campaign was still young, and, with a little effort, one could continue hoping for the best.

8

July–August, 1980: Losing Ground

It had long been Garth's belief that if Anderson wished to be treated as one of the "big boys," he would have to act like one. This did not seem unreasonable in theory. It was the execution of the idea that raised the problems. Although the campaign knew from the beginning that its finances would be extremely limited, Garth encouraged a rapid and large-scale growth of campaign operations. In this he was assisted by Mike MacLeod who, despite repeated admonitions by the Andersons that money had to be preserved for later use in field organization and media, permitted relatively unrestrained spending habits to develop, which over the months depleted precious campaign resources. Few expenses would be spared to provide the professional look an important campaign needed: coordinators were brought on to harmonize relations with every variety of outside interest group; numerous additional press assistants were hired to clip newspapers, monitor news shows (Betamaxes were acquired for the purpose), and tape speeches; battalions of advancemen were organized; a large traveling party began accompanying Anderson. Frugality would be looked upon virtually as a sign of weakness; wags said the new motto was: when in doubt, spend. Whether expenditures benefited the candidate directly was not of overriding consequence; the important thing was to create an air of prosperity.

It was in this frame of mind that Garth decided a grand tour abroad to be a *sine qua non* for a serious presidential candidate;

250

Anderson would need to burnish his credentials as a world-class statesman fit to be president. Certainly the idea had a logic: seen in the company of foreign heads of state, greeting him as if he were a prospective equal, Anderson's stature could be notably enhanced and voter concern about entrusting high office to a formerly un-known congressman could be greatly relieved. Another considera-tion was the upcoming GOP convention. In light of Anderson's declining poll standings, Garth seemed to be rethinking his strategy of having his candidate maintain a low profile, and seemed increas-ingly concerned that massive coverage of proceedings in Detroit might for a period edge Anderson out of the political picture alto-gether. A glamorous trip abroad would be timed to remind voters of John Anderson just as they would otherwise be saturated only with coverage of Ronald Reagan.

And so, hearing no objection from Anderson, who was consulted briefly, planning for a trip began to move forward quickly. As usual, the decision-making process was concentrated in Garth's office in New York, although, at Anderson's request, Garth involved me early in the planning. Some of us from the campaign argued for a trip of short duration, perhaps one week or less, and focused clearly on a common set of countries, most logically the major European ones. Anderson had had experience decades before as a foreign ser-vice officer in Berlin, and felt most at home with issues related to Europe. Among other options, a trip to the Far East seemed too ambitious; an excursion into Third World areas, such as Jerry Brown had made in the recent past to Africa with singer Linda Ronstadt, too exotic; and the Mideast a quagmire to be avoided.

Zev had a different opinion. He felt strongly that Anderson should give Israel the preeminent place in his itinerary. This would send a clear signal to Jewish voters that Anderson was one of Israel's most ardent American supporters, which indeed he was, though this had become obscured in the attention that had been paid in-creasingly to Anderson's one-time sponsorship of the so-called Christian amendment. Zev also felt inclined to highlight a visit to Israel because, due to personal contacts, he knew he could orches-trate a near-royal reception.

Zev recognized that a visit to Israel alone might seem unduly one-sided, and that it would need to be complemented by a visit to an Arab state as well. The only such state in which someone of Anderson's outspoken pro-Israeli positions could be assured of a gracious welcome was Egypt. A visit there would be tacked on. At the same time, so as not to seem inordinately preoccupied with Mideast issues, Zev accepted the wisdom of having Anderson stop also in major European capitals. Altogether, this would be a taxing trip for a candidate to take in the midst of a campaign; chances of a highly publicized misstep would be multiplied by too arduous a schedule. Some argued for circumscribing the trip and eliminating the Mideast component. Zev insisted, however, that this was precisely the most important part.

In preparation for the trip, Anderson suggested that we consult several high-ranking diplomats of his acquaintance. They could help plan meetings, contact officials abroad to arrange appointments, provide the candidate with briefings, and perhaps accompany us in our travels. Garth resisted this. "We can do this without the help of State Department types," he said, by which he seemed to mean those whose concern for politics might be subordinated to an appreciation of diplomatic sensibilities; both Garth and Zev wished to circumscribe the influence of anyone who might tamper with their plans for Anderson to assume a highly visible pro-Israeli posture.

One day, thinking it would be helpful, I spent several hours trying to track down the precedent that existed for travel abroad of presidential candidates in prior campaigns. I learned that the only candidate in recent memory who had made a major trip, designed for its campaign effect, had been former Senator Edmund Muskie. At a very early stage in his unsuccessful effort to win the 1972 Democratic nomination, he had conducted a whirlwind visit to the Mideast, the Soviet Union, and Europe. I talked to several people who had traveled with him, and asked in detail about the preparations which had been made and what pitfalls they had encountered which we might try to avoid. This inquiry yielded useful information, which I assumed Zev would want to hear about. I was wrong. He said he did not care what Muskie had done; we would do things our own way. I tossed my notes out.

The time arrived in mid-June when we needed to lock an itinerary in place and secure meetings with leading officials. Through personal connections, Zev had already arranged a series of high-level meetings in Israel. As for the other countries, he hastily scheduled appointments at the embassies in Washington of those he had decided Anderson should visit: Egypt, Britain, France, and Germany. I accompanied Zev to the embassies, and at the time we made our rounds, absolutely no meetings had yet been scheduled for Anderson, nor had even any preliminary approaches been made. This did not prevent Zev, however, from exhibiting his usual self-confident manner. In requesting a meeting with German Chancellor Schmidt, for example, he told German embassy officials that meetings had already been agreed to by Prime Minister Thatcher of Britain and by President Giscard of France. To the British, at a subsequent meeting, he said that Chancellor Schmidt and President Giscard had already agreed. To the French, he said that meetings were already arranged with Chancellor Schmidt and Prime Minister Thatcher. At each embassy, the officials nodded as if impressed, and promised to cable their foreign offices accordingly. The trick seemed to work, because most of the requested appointments with heads of state, foreign ministers, parliamentary officials, and others came through within a couple of weeks.

Despite the campaign's seat-of-the-pants manner in arranging some parts of the trip, preparation in other aspects was much more elaborate. Several weeks before the trip, Zev delegated two or three campaign advancemen to jump on a plane, head to Europe and the Mideast, and make a preliminary survey of such things as the availability, cost, and location of hotels and restaurants. Apparently travel agents, embassies, and phone lines were deemed inadequate to the task. These early trips were referred to, in the inimitable jargon of a campaign, as "pre-advance." Within a few days, the advancemen returned home to report the results of their scouting. Only at this point did the real advance begin: several campaign workers were detailed back to Israel, Egypt, Britain, France, and Germany to make actual arrangements. In the week or two before Anderson actually left, phone lines between these advancemen and the Washington campaign office buzzed day and night. Nonetheless, Zev decided he needed to double-check personally on arrangements, and so, a week before the trip, he summoned all the advancemen, scattered around the five countries, to meet him in London. Not wishing to waste any time, Zev himself traveled on the supersonic Concorde. Zev's determination to engineer a flawless trip was laudable. But a short time later, as the campaign began experiencing financial difficulties and had occasional trouble meeting its payroll, grumbling could be heard among staff members about campaign spending priorities.

On the morning of departure, Monday, July 7, Anderson slipped over to the law office of Sol Linowitz in downtown Washington, there to receive a last-minute briefing on the state of Israeli-Egyptian negotiations from Carter's chief emissary to the Mideast. In the course of the previous few days, Anderson had had a number of briefings not only from academic experts, but also from several high-ranking Administration officials. He did not wish to complicate American foreign policy, and felt it would be only proper to cooperate gracefully with those who were actually in positions of responsibility. Knowing Jimmy Carter's antipathy toward Anderson at this point, some had suspected that the White House would exert pressure on its State Department and embassy officials to turn a cold shoulder toward the trip, but, in fact, they displayed considerable solicitousness at almost every turn.

Our traveling party left from Baltimore-Friendship Airport in the afternoon. A Boeing 707 had been chartered for the trip from Icelandic Airlines. Someone realized that the plane's foreign logo would not look appropriate in the background of trip pictures shown back home, and, after high-level huddling, it was agreed to paint over the offending words. This was still much cheaper than hiring an American carrier. The plane did not have a large fuel capacity, and required two refueling stops in each direction. The interior was spare, the service modest, and all in all the ambience resembled that of a cut-rate flight to Europe on the airline of Sir Freddy Laker. Given the occasionally tenuous financial condition of the campaign, such a style was perfectly appropriate.

Still, a certain esprit de corps developed on board which compensated for the absence of amenities. The plane took off crammed full of campaign staff, reporters, and Secret Service, as well as the can-

didate and three of his children whom he had brought along; Keke
stayed at home with the two youngest girls. Since our logistical
arrangements were being handled by numerous staff members already on the ground in the cities we were going to visit, it was not
obvious why the presence of so many others was required on board.
There were, for example, a dozen press and scheduling assistants,
in not very different proportion to the number of people they were
intended to serve. In addition, there were three staff members (myself included) who ostensibly were along to provide help in preparing speeches and to offer Anderson advice on his conversations with
foreign leaders, but whose larger purpose in practice seemed to be
to surround him in his meetings so as to lend him an appropriately
presidential aura. (Zev, in his offhand way, referred to us repeatedly
as the "substantive people," even, to our embarrassment, in front
of other lesser mortals who did not appreciate such crude social
distinctions.)

When we arrived Tuesday morning at Ben Gurion Airport in Israel, United States Ambassador Samuel Lewis was standing on the
tarmac waiting to greet us. It was 11:00 A.M., but already a steamy
hot day. Anderson made a short and prosaic arrival statement, then
we all boarded a long motorcade for the forty-five minute drive into
Jerusalem. When we pulled up to the entrance of the magnificent
King David Hotel, where we were staying, Anderson was quickly
recognized by American tourists, and mobbed for autographs, as he
would be every time he entered and exited the hotel the next several
days. Following a briefing from Lewis, we departed in the motorcade
again for the Knesset (the Israeli parliament), where Anderson received his official welcome from Deputy Prime Minister Yigal Yadin, substituting for a hospitalized prime minister. Anderson commented that he had seen in a local paper a caricature of both himself
and Yadin, comparing Anderson's independent campaign with the
third party Yadin had created back in 1976, and which he still headed today. Yadin recalled that at the beginning, conventional wisdom
had said it was doomed. While it had clearly not yet become a major
party, he noted, nonetheless it had accomplished the election of
fifteen members of parliament, and become an essential component
of the present governing coalition. Yadin added that he had been

asking Americans passing through Israel recently what they thought of the Anderson campaign. He said that many of them answered, "Well, you know, he just might have a chance." With that exchange of diplomatic pleasantries, the conversation turned to more traditional foreign affairs issues: Carter's policy toward the Persian Gulf, American plans for a rapid deployment force in the area, the possibility of joint American-Israeli use of new air bases being constructed in the Negev Desert.

This first diplomatic *tête-à-tête* was somewhat stiff, and it was obvious that the participants were as much concerned about conveying the right impression of knowledge and *savoir-faire* as they were about actually deriving enlightenment or agreement from their meeting. As Anderson emerged from the room, dozens of photographers and reporters who had been waiting outside closed in on him, shouting questions, demanding to know what had been said. Finally, Anderson was escorted to a prearranged spot at which he stood with Yadin and made a few noncommittal remarks. It was not as though anyone expected a major communiqué to be announced; but the making of a brief statement seemed a natural accoutrement of solemn diplomatic proceedings. In the countless instances in the coming week that Anderson met with foreign officials, this curious ritual would be repeated. After a point, Anderson became well rehearsed in making vague and flowery statements. "I'm a born diplomat," said the ex-foreign service officer.

Within the next several days, we had additional meetings with Moshe Dayan, the former Israeli defense minister; Yitzhak Rabin, the former Labor prime minister; President Navon, the head of state in Israel, whose functions were ceremonial; and numerous other well-known Israeli public figures. Elegant meals and receptions were hosted in Anderson's honor, and excursions provided into the Sinai and the West Bank. One afternoon, during a rare free moment back at the hotel, several of us decided to take a swim. Anderson's participation necessitated the presence of large numbers of Secret Servicemen, supplemented by Israeli security personnel. Some of them toted machine guns, and stationed themselves around the perimeter of the pool and at other points in the area. Two of them swam a few feet away from Anderson, changing directions whenever he did, and leaving the impression to a casual observer that some sort of synchronized swimming class was being conducted in the pool of the King David Hotel. Try as the Secret Service did to seem inconspicuous and unobtrusive, by the nature of things, they did not always succeed.

On the final evening, Anderson met the press. Up to this point, he had deliberately avoided mention of his position on the delicate subject of Jerusalem, except in passing, afraid it would look to the American press as if he were too uncritical a visitor and prospecting too transparently for votes. At his press conference, however, the question of his position was asked directly, and he was forced to acknowledge that he favored recognition of Jerusalem as the Israeli capital, although, as usual, he was careful to note that it would be appropriate to take such an action only "at the end of the peace process."

As feared, his statement quickly caught the attention of the American press. Bob McNamara of CBS News, traveling along with us, produced a piece for television which accused Anderson, in so many words, of changing his colors to suit his audience. McNamara had long liked and admired Anderson, and made little secret of his sympathy for the campaign, but since the arrival of Garth had begun to suspect a more crass political motivation behind Anderson's statements and positions. Other reporters filed similar stories. The image of the trip as projected back home to the States became a negative one. It looked as though Anderson had come over to Israel not to learn, but to advertise his pro-Israeli feelings. By far the worst blow came in a *Washington Post* editorial a few days later. In scathing tones, it accused Anderson of having become a conventional politician, like all the others he had been running against, and asked rhetorically, "What has become of the 'Anderson difference'?"

This was an inauspicious beginning for the trip and, in a sense, an unfair one. The press was correctly reporting Anderson's positions, but incorrectly implying that they were new, when in fact he had repeatedly said the same things back in the United States, where they had not provoked much notice. Perhaps they simply stood out in bolder relief when he made them on location in Israel. Overall, the Anderson trip abroad was a highly productive one that went quite smoothly. Hereafter, however, despite his impressive meetings with leaders in other countries, the image of his first stop in Israel lingered. A sour impression of the trip stuck in the minds of many voters long after we returned home.

As we prepared to leave Israel, the only missing ingredient of our visit remained a meeting with Prime Minister Begin. We appreciated that his bedridden condition kept him from a normal schedule, and yet we had read in the local papers that he was seeing top-level visitors in his hospital room. We brushed off questions as to why Anderson had not been included among these select few, but privately we were perplexed and not a little annoyed. Anderson, after all, was voicing strong support of many of the prime minister's policies, and it seemed appropriate that he should be rewarded at least with the right to make a modest courtesy call.

Zev had been working for weeks to set up an appointment. Only on the morning we were to leave did word come through that the prime minister would see us. The schedule had to be changed quickly. Drama filled the air, as we announced to the press that the prime minister had summoned Anderson to his bedside, just at the moment we were about to leave the country. We drove out to Hadassah Hospital. A crowd of photographers had gathered to record Anderson's arrival. Three of us proceeded with Anderson to the prime minister's suite. It was not the posh sort of setting one might have imagined would be accorded a national leader. Begin's room was a spare and simple one. The hospital was quite modern, however, and the room seemed to be equipped with the latest medical gadgetry. On one side was a standard-issue metal-framed bed. Several pillows were propped up at the head of it, and a number of pieces of fruit set out on a nightstand beside it.

Begin greeted us as we entered the room. He was wearing blue pajamas and a satin bathrobe, and we were immediately impressed that his condition was good enough for him to be walking around. A small monitoring device was strapped to his chest, reminding us that he was still under medical treatment, something also evident from the presence of several doctors hovering about. For a half-hour or more he and Anderson conversed, touching on several serious subjects, such as Jerusalem. On that score, Anderson made the point that, given the intractability of the issue, it would seem wise to defer it until other, more manageable matters were negotiated. Probably Anderson felt compelled to say this so that later he could indicate he had addressed issues frankly with the prime minister, and not simply succumbed to expressions of mutual admiration.

Toward the end of the conversation, Anderson casually mentioned to Begin that he would be seeing President Sadat of Egypt the next day, and asked whether he had any messages he wished Anderson to convey. Begin thought a moment and said: "Well, yes. Tell him that I am sorry I was not able to talk to him when he called the other day, due to my condition, but that I hope to call him Sunday morning." Anderson promised to do so. A doctor interrupted to say that Begin needed his rest. Begin waved him away. He was having a good time. Finally, however, having been a warm and gracious host, Begin bid Anderson off, and we went back downstairs.

In the lobby, scores of reporters and cameramen engulfed Anderson as he came in, quizzing him about his conversation. Anderson's responses remained general. The press were trying to ferret something interesting out of him. Finally, someone asked, apparently out of the blue, whether the prime minister had given Anderson any messages to take to President Sadat. Anderson paused. "Why, yes, as a matter of fact," he said, proud to be able to say so. "What was it?" he was pressed. Anderson thought a moment, and answered that probably it would be only proper to deliver the message first to President Sadat before disclosing it publicly. The press buzzed. "Can't you give us some idea what it's about?" someone asked excitedly. "No, no," Anderson said, "I think I better talk to President Sadat first." The next day, Israeli papers ran headlines: "AN-DERSON CARRYING BEGIN MESSAGE TO SADAT." Such is how news is made.

At 3:30 that afternoon, after a short flight from Israel, we found ourselves passing over seemingly endless stretches of sand dunes and descending into Cairo. We wanted to do at least the nominal sight-seeing during our short stay in Cairo, and the only time on the schedule for seeing the Pyramids was immediately after our arrival. And so we sped directly from the airport to the outskirts of the city, there to take a tour. One could not help thinking, as we walked around the Pyramids, and then the Sphinx, how far we had come from the coffee klatches of New Hampshire, the days of riding around in a Volkswagen van in Massachusetts, and all the other decidedly unexotic venues in our past that had led now to the unlikely environs of the Arab Republic of Egypt.

To and from our appointments, the Egyptian government provided such elaborate security and motorcade arrangements as to rival even the fabled extravagance our hosts traditionally showed us in Cleveland, Ohio. The traffic in Cairo was, under the best of circumstances, chaotic; horns blared, cars darted in and out of lanes, and generally no one showed the least concern for the observance of traffic lights and regulations. Our presence on the road only compounded the confusion. Several motorcycles and police cars, sirens screaming, led the charge. These were followed by the limousine, on either side of which rode an additional police car. This may have been symmetrical, but it was not very practical: the roads we traveled often narrowed into one lane in each direction. The police cars were not deterred. They simply drove into the incoming lane, trusting that cars coming from the other direction would veer out of the way.

Our major adventure in Egypt was a visit to President Sadat at his seaside villa in Alexandria, a large port city on the Mediterranean coast. We used a helicopter to get there. It was a big and noisy one, and equipped with no air conditioning to offset the desert heat. Evidently it was normally used for military transport purposes, not for ferrying important visitors. Our ride was taking place just ten weeks after the abortive American rescue mission in Iran, and, as the helicopter bumped around en route, all we could think of was the unhappy fate of those other helicopters. It did not help matters when we were told that they were, in fact, the same model.

After an hour-long ride, we landed on the lawn of Sadat's villa. The press had preceded us by bus. They had been required to spend over four hours winding their way along primitive roads to get there, and could look forward to going back the same way. This was not calculated to put them in a good mood. For all their trouble, their only reward was a fleeting opportunity to see Sadat greet Anderson in the living room of the house, and then, after waiting two hours while Sadat and Anderson conversed, to record the short press conference they held at the front door on Anderson's departure.

But for Anderson, the visit was much more memorable. We had wondered in what vein Sadat would receive him, given Anderson's by now well publicized advocacy of hard-line Israeli positions. Sadat could not have been more gracious. He welcomed Anderson warmly, talked with him much longer than had been expected (impressing Anderson with the broad-mindedness and insight of his views), and afterward showered effusive praise on him in front of reporters. He did not press Anderson on Jerusalem, and indicated to reporters that he was not upset by Anderson's differences of opinion with him on some issues. (This was in great contrast to an editorial in the English-language newspaper of Cairo which had greeted Anderson's arrival the day before with a blast of sarcasm entitled "The Meddler.") As a final personal touch, Sadat made a conspicuous show of walking us back across the lawn, up to the helicopter, and waving from the ground below as we pulled away. All in all, he had rescued our trip from potential disaster.

From Egypt, we traveled to Berlin. After a briefing at the United States Mission and a courtesy call on the mayor, Anderson made the obligatory pilgrimage to the Berlin Wall, where he delivered suitably stirring remarks about the great conflict between communism and democracy. Our advancemen had been unable to produce a crowd for this event—Anderson was relatively obscure in this part of the world—and so one witnessed the curious spectacle of a group of reporters gathered around Anderson to cover his ringing speech to the people of Berlin, which none of the people of Berlin were in attendance to hear themselves.

In Bonn the next day, fully eleven events were scheduled for Anderson. Among these were a brief meeting with President Carstens, the figurehead chief of state, and longer and more substantive discussions with Foreign Minister Hans-Dietrich Genscher as well as opposition leaders Helmut Kohl and Franz Josef Strauss. The schedule culminated in a lengthy meeting with Chancellor Helmut Schmidt. Schmidt offered a strikingly gloomy view of the world—"Schopenhauerish," as Anderson described it—and was critical of Jimmy Carter in a surprisingly unguarded way. The press had been able to get some pictures of Anderson and Schmidt greeting each other at the beginning of the meeting, but, losing patience during the long wait afterward, had pretty much disappeared by the time the meeting was over. This disappointed us, because the duration of a meeting seemed to be taken by the press as a measure of Anderson's success in hitting it off with his hosts. We imagined the reporters would have been impressed to see him emerge after two full hours with Schmidt, but now they would have to rely on my word to learn about it. I hoped fervently they would believe me.

As our two days in Germany wore on, just about all of us were beginning physically to wear out. We would have preferred to go straight home; the basic purposes of the trip had been accomplished, and the once glamorous meetings with foreign leaders were becoming almost tiresome. Traveling through Europe started now to seem alien to our real interests back home. The Republican National Convention was just getting under way in Detroit, and public attention was shifting to a scene of action from which Anderson would be very much absent. It was, however, too late to extricate ourselves; we continued on.

The red carpet was not rolled out in Paris quite as much as elsewhere. Despite persistent requests, and for protocol reasons that remained obscure, Giscard declined to see Anderson. Down on the totem pole somewhat, Anderson's first appointment was to pay a courtesy call on the president of the French Senate. He was a rotund, loquacious, Tip O'Neill-like character, given to making sweeping rhetorical statements which rivaled the grandeur of the lavish office where the meeting took place. It was hard enough for Anderson to have to sit through such a dry exercise in diplomatic small talk. To make matters worse, the official spoke no English, and so everyone had to endure long periods of translation following each statement. The Senate president would go on at great length, before pausing to give the translator an opportunity to tell Anderson what had just been said. Anderson used the opportunity to turn in my direction and make faces of exaggerated pain and boredom. As we were listening to one translation, however, Anderson saw his opening. The Senate president made the point that communication among leaders was vital in the modern world, and that they needed to keep in close and constant consultation. I saw a gleam in Anderson's eye. After the translation had finished, he spoke his piece. "I quite agree with the gentleman," Anderson said, pausing for just the right effect, ". . . and had I been given the opportunity to consult and communicate with President Giscard directly, as I had requested, why I would have made the very same point." The Senate president's face, which had been smiling and rosy as he sat listening to Anderson's incomprehensible English, turned into a look of puzzlement, then consternation, as the interpreter informed him what Anderson had just said.

From the Senate, we moved to the Assembly, and spent a half-hour with the leader there, former Prime Minister Jacques Chaban-Delmas, an extremely dignified presence who looked every inch the aristocrat he was. At intervals he rang a bell, signaling a young boy in a white smock to enter the room for the purpose of stoking the embers in the fireplace. This would have seemed unbearably stuffy had Chaban-Delmas not quickly indicated a less serious manner than first met the eye. As Anderson was discoursing at length at one point, Chaban-Delmas looked across the room in my direction, and, as if to imply our shared appreciation of such pointless diplomatic ritual, rolled his eyes toward the ceiling in mock-weariness. I rolled mine back. He smiled and nodded. He knew just what we were going through.

Other meetings were more productive. Prime Minister Raymond Barre spent an hour exchanging views with Anderson, largely on the economy. He applauded Anderson's proposal for a tax on gasoline, and urged more concerted action on the part of the West to stabilize the prices of oil and raw materials. Jacques Chirac, the conservative mayor of Paris and a leading critic of Giscard, welcomed Anderson graciously, and impressed him in sounding a note of toughness toward the Soviet Union which one had not heard from other French officials. And on our last night in Paris, Jean François-Poincet, the American-educated foreign minister, hosted a memorable "working dinner" for our party at the Quai d'Orsay, the French foreign ministry. The rooms were impossibly large, grand, and historic, and, we realized, an embarrassing contrast to what would be available to Anderson if he wished one day to reciprocate the hospitality.

It rained constantly in Paris, but we managed to have fun. Our accommodations were at the Paris Intercontinental, one to a room. This was one of the most expensive hostelries in town, which was to say, by any measurement, expensive indeed. Such a standard of living was no different, of course, from what had been afforded us at the King David Hotel in Jerusalem, or the high style we would enjoy at the Savoy Hotel in London. Poor as the campaign was—or soon would be—Zev felt strongly that Anderson's international image virtually depended on the class of accommodation his party was seen to be staying in; others of us were too delighted with the unaccustomed luxury to complain. Yet at this time fund-raising letters were practically begging supporters for $10 or $25 contributions— on the stated grounds that money was desperately needed to wage legal battles, and to support rudimentary organizing efforts.

Our stay in London was shorter, and the schedule much freer, than in previous cities. Anderson had useful, if brief, meetings with Foreign Minister Carrington and Prime Minister Thatcher. As we walked out of 10 Downing Street, the prime minister's official residence, a large crowd of tourists and reporters stood behind ropes that had been set up, waving hands and cameras in Anderson's direction. Anderson held court for a few minutes, standing at the front door, as if he were already a major world statesman who had just emerged from an important summit. Later, we went to the houses of Parliament, where an extracurricular group of MPs had arranged for interested colleagues to come and hear Anderson speak. An astonishing number, perhaps 200 or more, did so. They seemed genuinely excited to see the latest political fashion from America, a fashion which they apparently felt might in due course make its way across the Atlantic. Anderson parried their interrogation with ease, displaying a sophistication which some of these British politicians later expressed surprise at finding in an American counterpart.

On our last night in Europe—at about 2:00 A.M. London time, which was 8:00 P.M. the previous evening in Detroit, site of the Republican convention—we rode over to the ABC studio in London where Anderson was to listen to a live audio broadcast of Ronald Reagan's acceptance speech, and then give an interview about it to the network's Pierre Salinger, who sat there with us. The interview would be beamed back live to the United States, to be incorporated as part of the instant analysis which followed Reagan's speech. It was a measure of our position—how other events were now passing us by—that we were only too happy to hitch ourselves to the Republican National Convention in an effort to stay in the public eye. Our trip itself was no longer making news.

Soon after we returned to the United States, and had absorbed the reality of Ronald Reagan's nomination for president, we went off to California, eager to contest Reagan on his own turf. The response we encountered demonstrated that Anderson still exercised a hold over large groups of people. At the Marin County civic center, north of San Francisco, he walked out on stage to find an auditorium packed with a thousand people of all ages, cheering and clapping and stomping their feet in tribute. Marin County, of course, was well known for its pockets of avant-garde liberalism, and the audience that night may not have been particularly representative of American public opinion. But it was enough to reinforce Anderson's optimism that, despite polls which showed continuing slippage, the

Paul Conrad, © 1980, *Los Angeles Times.* Reprinted with permission.

campaign was still very much alive. During the next several days, standing-room-only crowds gathered to meet Anderson at every fund-raising reception on his schedule, at the homes of wealthy California supporters in Pacific Heights, Concord, Bel Air, and La Jolla. A party one evening honoring him in Beverly Hills attracted numerous Hollywood movie stars, from Ed Asner to Barbra Streisand. Anderson was not himself a fanatical moviegoer, and he did not recognize some of the celebrities. At one point, Norman Lear, who was taking Anderson around and introducing him, brought him up to Margot Kidder, the actress. "Hello, how are you," Anderson said in perfunctory fashion, moving on quickly to the next person who reached for his hand. Lear, realizing that Anderson did not appreciate whom he had just met, brought him back and said, "You know, Congressman, Margot played Lois Lane in the Superman movie." Anderson, who was probably only barely aware who Superman himself was, could only think to say, "Oh, for Pete's sake." Once again he moved on to the next guest. Even if Anderson was not particularly familiar with them, the stars of Hollywood were still flocking to him.

Still there was continuing discouragement. At one point during the trip, as we were sitting in a motel room about to depart for a Contra Costa County fund-raising breakfast, Anderson took me aside where no one else could hear. "This thing is killing me," he said, referring to the grueling pace of the campaign schedule. "And what's the purpose of it? I just don't feel we're making any new headway." I told him I thought he had been doing quite well. The crowds had been big and enthusiastic. "Yes, but it's the same people all the time. And I just can't stand the fund-raisers. Isn't there a better way to go around campaigning? I'm going to be a zombie by the time this thing is over." Anderson was experiencing the most natural feeling in the world, one that he had been warned of repeatedly even before commencing his first tour as a presidential candidate. Campaigning very plainly could be a dehumanizing, utterly exhausting experience: having to force smiles, give impassioned speeches even at moments when one had been drained of all emotion, having to sell oneself like an insurance policy, and to do all this sunrise to sunset, day in and day out, and always feel the pressure that not to do it would cost all-important votes. A campaign simply was not worth it if the candidate came to consider it such an impossible burden. Anderson did not want to give up, of course; but he did think his campaign activities could be made more manageable and more intrinsically rewarding.

The improvident spending habits of the campaign in effect had obliged Anderson to attend more and more fund-raisers; and the strategy of restricting national publicity over the summer was forcing campaign schedulers to compensate by sending Anderson to a superabundance of local events. The net result of this was to exhaust the candidate as he scrambled to avoid being left behind. And yet, many of the difficulties of campaigning were unavoidable. However one sliced it, a great deal of money had to be raised; unlike the nominees of the major parties, an independent candidate did not receive a free disbursement from the federal treasury of $29 million to use during the general election campaign. As an underdog, Anderson had no choice but to keep in circulation; if he stopped even momentarily, speculation would ensue that he was dispirited and perhaps throwing in the towel. And, finally, as much as he might prefer to talk about issues, it would not be possible, even if Garth gave the green light, to invent bold and path-breaking new ideas every day of the week. Ultimately Anderson agreed: the only healthy attitude would be to show patience, take events in stride, and wait the results out. If he won, that would be great. If he did not, well, he really had never had a right to expect it.

In midsummer, the campaign headquarters moved location once again, this time to the fashionable neighborhood of Georgetown. At first it seemed an unlikely place for a campaign that needed to watch its pennies, but MacLeod ultimately prevailed in his argument that it was the only available office space large enough to house a still burgeoning campaign staff. Apart from higher rents, the physical cost of the move itself came to tens of thousands of dollars. At the beginning, the new office provided a much improved environment over the previous one, which had been bursting at its seams; but, as usual, a variant of Parkinson's Law came into play, and the number of bodies at the new office quickly began to expand so as to fill the space available to accommodate them.

The political complexion of the staff was becoming predominantly liberal Democratic; few of our original moderate Republicans remained. The campaign needed experienced workers, and it seemed to be only those who had worked in campaigns of the McGovern, Udall, or Kennedy variety who were enthusiastic enough about Anderson to offer their services. The campaign was happy to take refugees from other campaigns, but some irritation was evident among longtime staff members that outsiders, who until recently had actively worked for other candidates and not Anderson, could transfer so readily into major positions in the Anderson campaign without having had to climb through the ranks. Anderson's traveling party was also growing, as it became increasingly obvious that Anderson needed speechwriters, political advisers, and others, both to lend an aura of professionalism to the campaign and to prevent the feeling that sometimes seemed to come over Anderson, that he was shouldering the entire campaign alone. Still, Garth made a point of assigning to these coveted berths people who did not know Anderson and were considered safe bets not to contradict Garth's line.

Over time, the Washington office did succeed in acquiring the services of several people of independent stature who, while their authority did not compare to that of Garth, were able in certain circumstances to balance his influence and weigh in on important decisions. Not only were they older and, more than the rest of us, actual peers of Garth and Anderson, but they had each come from a major position in the outside world and knew they could return any time. As a result, they seemed to feel more comfortable speaking up and standing their ground than young people who depended for their employment on strict obedience to Garth's directives. Generally these graybeards were consumed in their own spheres of activity—legal battles, issues development, direct mail—and did not have a long-standing close relationship with the candidate himself; but in the later days of the campaign, as Garth's strategies failed to produce positive results, their influence in the campaign's overall direction increased, and much to the good, even if it turned out to be too late.

Mitch Rogovin, the campaign's chief lawyer, had been hired in a roundabout way. One of Garth's first actions during the independent campaign had been to retain the Washington law firm of Arnold and Porter to handle the myriad and complex legal activities relating to ballot access. Garth felt that, to show the seriousness of the ballot access effort, and to ensure its success, the campaign needed to associate itself with one of Washington's most prestigious law firms. This was a costly move, considering that major law professors and lawyers all over the country were at the same time writing the campaign to offer their help without fee. But despite the campaign's shoestring budget, Arnold and Porter was retained, and proceeded to ring up several hundred thousand dollars of bills within a few weeks. Unfortunately, their work was said to be of uneven quality.

One day, the Andersons asked me to see Rogovin on their behalf concerning an unrelated campaign matter; they had known him for many years, having once been neighbors. Rogovin asked about helping out in the campaign, and I encouraged him to talk with the Andersons directly to renew his acquaintance. He did so, and offered his services. Arnold and Porter had been charging $160 an hour for its work; Rogovin, who headed a small but well-regarded firm, offered a "discount" price of $95 a hour. While he seemed to charge for a lot of hours, the rate was enticing, and, at the Andersons' insistence, his firm was hired to replace Arnold and Porter. By the end of the campaign, Rogovin had done a masterful job in fighting court battles and handling other legal odds and ends designed to secure Anderson's access to all fifty state ballots. The firm earned enormous amounts of money in the process ($1.5 million was one estimate), not to mention invaluable publicity, but in the final analysis no one could complain about a job well done.

Alton Frye, who joined the campaign in July as director of policy development, was someone who had known Anderson on a casual basis for many years and whom Anderson had often turned to for advice on issues of national security. Washington director of the prestigious Council on Foreign Relations, Alton combined substantial staff experience on Capitol Hill with distinguished scholarly credentials in a wide variety of fields. He was just the sort of sober, mature, and genuinely intellectual counterweight who was needed at times to balance the occasionally impetuous instincts of others. Alton worked prodigiously in fashioning the campaign's formal platform and on many major speeches; as a moderate Republican himself, he used what influence he could to help keep Anderson in the mainstream at a time when others sought for him to assume positions which would appeal to disenchanted liberal Democrats.

Like Rogovin, Alton came relatively late to the campaign. I had known him for some time, and one night asked him over to discuss my concerns about Garth's strategies and influence. Alton indicated he had been toying with the idea of volunteering to help the campaign as a policy advisor; I urged him to speak with Anderson at once and consider joining full time. He did so, and Anderson, despite initial balking from Garth, delightedly welcomed him on board. The intelligence and integrity Alton brought to the issues operation of the campaign fully justified Anderson's confidence.

Tom Mathews, originally hired as the campaign's direct mail expert after we achieved our first successes in the primaries, gave Anderson some of his strongest encouragement in the direction of running as an independent, but otherwise did not advise Anderson closely until he began traveling with him in the last two months of the campaign. Mathews was a jolly, blunt-spoken, imperturbable ex-newspaperman, who had a keen eye for public attitudes especially insofar as they were reflected in response rates to his mailings and the size of revenues flowing into the coffers of the campaign. His concerns about campaign style and strategy not surprisingly mounted, as fundraising efforts experienced difficulties.

As the summer wore on, Anderson could not avoid the problem of having to find a vice-presidential running mate. Ever since he had declared as an independent, the matter had weighed on him. He had always been inclined to put it off as long as possible, largely on the argument that the pool of available prospects would increase as the campaign went on and well known political figures came to spurn their parties' unpopular nominees. At the same time, it was presumed, the Anderson campaign would attain such a standing in the polls that these same people would be enticed to jump on a new bandwagon. Of course, it turned out to be just the reverse. The longer we waited, and the lower we fell in the polls, the more unrealistic it became that established politicians would take leave of their parties to participate in the potentially disastrous experiment of an independent candidacy. It was a measure of our changing fortunes that, at the outset, names as prominent as Walter Cronkite and Pat Moynihan could have been floated and taken very seriously by the press as prospective Anderson running mates, and, more remarkably, that some in the campaign could have been so presumptuous as to assess their merits and decide that, no, they were not good enough, and that we should keep looking. Others of us felt that, if there were really any chance of people so prominent accepting a place on the ticket, we should immediately make the offer.* By August, the prospect of getting many of the people we had at one time discussed had faded; and yet, hopeful as we were of rebounding in the fall, as Garth continued to insist that we would, we were prepared to rule out no one as willing to serve. Indeed, there was a feeling that acquisition of an imposing enough running mate might itself go a long way toward restoring the credibility, and the fortunes, of the campaign.

Failing that, some hoped the campaign would turn to a relatively untraditional choice (Archibald Cox, the former Watergate special prosecutor, was one suggestion; others proposed various leading figures of the business world), whose known ability would have reassured voters, but at the same time given them a chance to vote for another "nonpolitician." One continued to sense that great numbers of people would have liked nothing more than the chance to thumb their noses at the normal choices their system produced.

---

*Cronkite usually stuck to his anchor booth, but one afternoon during our early campaigning in New Hampshire, he had donned an Irish derby and, in the style of a cub reporter, followed Anderson at a discreet distance as the campaign toured a shopping mall. Others at CBS later told us he had returned quite charmed by the dark horse he covered. Months later, on a lark, a reporter called Cronkite and asked him what his reaction would be to an approach from Anderson regarding the vice-presidential spot. To the reporter's surprise, Cronkite sounded intrigued. He said he very much admired Anderson and even joked that, because he himself was not registered as a Democrat or a Republican, "it would be the right party." This remarkable interview was soon reported widely. Although entirely inadvertent, it was perfectly timed from our point of view. Cronkite had just gone off sailing, and was virtually incommunicado. For twenty-four hours, the report went undenied. Bill Leonard, the president of CBS News, was said to be looking for him desperately; such a story did nothing to enhance the network's image of objectivity. Finally, Cronkite reached shore and phoned in a reply. He had been misinterpreted, he said. The fact that the press had reported the story as something quite plausible, however, was a measure of how serious a candidate Anderson was then taken to be. Frankly, I thought Anderson should have reached Cronkite quickly before he could announce a denial. It reminded me, in reverse, of what Tom Eagleton was supposed to have said when George McGovern called him in 1972 to offer him second spot on the Democratic ticket: "Before you change your mind, I accept!"

Perhaps such an unusual ticket could inspire new interest in the campaign on the part of disgruntled fence-sitters and among the nation's great mass of nonvoters. Garth rejected such an approach, however, as too risky; he felt that Anderson, as an independent, was untraditional enough, and that an eminently conventional politician would be needed to balance his ticket.

In early August, the focus of politics in the country was turning to the upcoming Democratic National Convention. Carter had won enough delegates to be assured of the nomination if the delegates voted the way they had been elected to vote. But Ted Kennedy had steadfastly refused to concede victory, and other leaders in the party treated only grudgingly the prospect of Jimmy Carter once again marching center-stage as the Democratic standard-bearer. He was considered out of sync with many of the more liberal elements of the party, widely judged inadequate to the job, and, all in all, thought to be a weak candidate to field against an increasingly strong challenge presented by Ronald Reagan. The talk of the town became the possibility of an "open convention," in which the delegates would be freed from their pledges of the primaries, and asked only to vote their consciences. Even many non-Kennedy Democrats—including Pat Moynihan, Robert Byrd, Hugh Carey, Scoop Jackson, and Ed Muskie—were rumored to find the proposal attractive. Forty or fifty congressmen at one point banded together to promote the cause.

The open convention scenario had probably always been unrealistic, if only because it presupposed a consensus alternative to Carter. Kennedy was not such an alternative; many who would have liked to "dump" Carter were not any fonder of Kennedy. As for the other prominent figures who had been mentioned as prospective compromise choices, none of them seemed the type who would willingly challenge the incumbent president of their party unless he voluntarily stepped aside. But stepping aside seemed the last thing Carter would do; like Richard Nixon, he prided himself in not being a "quitter."

It had long been one of our campaign's guiding notions that Democrats unhappy with the nomination of Jimmy Carter would consider defecting to the banner of John Anderson. The time had come for Anderson to start sending stronger signals of his interest in welcoming these disaffected voters to his side. The success of Anderson's candidacy, many of us felt, depended on his passing Carter in the polls, and the race becoming perceived as a Reagan-Anderson contest. (Such a scenario may seem somewhat unrealistic and presumptuous looking back, but at the time many commentators regarded it as a serious possibility; Carter and Anderson at times did not seem unbridgeably far apart in the polls.) There would then be what Alton Frye called a "surge potential": some voters seemed to be supporting Carter only because they wanted to stop Reagan, and considered Carter the only realistic way to do it; were Anderson to surpass Carter in the polls, they would consider going to Anderson instead. And some people seemed to be supporting Reagan only because they disliked Carter so intensely; again, if Anderson suddenly looked credible in his poll standings, they would consider him instead.

The chances of Anderson's surpassing Carter in the polls, it seemed, would be improved the more that discord was evident among Democrats. Anderson might have contributed to this atmosphere by publicly meeting with prominent Democrats; their very act in meeting with him would be a visible sign of their dissatisfaction with Carter. To the extent the party looked disunited, Carter's political strength would appear diminished and his popularity would continue to sink. It seemed plausible that these Democrats would agree to such meetings as a way to show Carter they were not to be taken for granted. Many had large groups of constituents who supported Anderson, and themselves supported Carter only reluctantly or were holding out in stating a preference. When Anderson faded at the end of the campaign, barely a Democratic leader could be found admitting sympathy for his campaign; but in July and August, while he still seemed to many to have a chance, politicians proved adept at hedging their bets, and many could be heard to utter complimentary things about Anderson. Suggestions were made that Anderson meet with some of the well-known Democrats in the Senate: Pat Moynihan, Gary Hart, Birch Bayh, Robert Byrd, Ted Kennedy, Adlai Stevenson, Paul Tsongas, George McGovern, Scoop Jackson, and others; there were also several Democratic governors who seemed possibilities.

Garth agreed with this idea in theory, but for some reason delayed a long time in setting up meetings. Suddenly, with the Democratic convention closing in, and Anderson steadily sinking in poll standings and consequent press attention, Garth started searching for a quick fix of publicity which could be administered to the lagging campaign. A meeting with Kennedy seemed an obvious remedy. Unfortunately, it was the only meeting that ever ended up being arranged. As a result, the impression was left, erroneously, that Anderson had a special interest in dealing with Kennedy, rather than with dissatisfied Democrats in general.

The arrangements for the meeting were made hastily; late on the morning of July 31, Zev called me from New York to say that a meeting had just been set up. Anderson was to be at Kennedy's office at 2:00 P.M. Zev did not have time to tell me why that location had been decided on, or what the format was to be. No one else seemed to know anything, and so, as the appointed hour approached, I hurried across the Capitol to the Dirksen Senate Office Building. A huge crowd of press had begun to assemble in the corridor outside Kennedy's suite of offices. When Anderson arrived, he was ushered in alone to see Kennedy. I looked around for Keke, and found her in an anteroom immediately outside Kennedy's personal office. She seemed nervous. "This wasn't a good idea," she said. "What are they going to say?" I was forced to wonder myself. Wasn't there a prepared statement her husband would be making? "No, there's not," she said. "That's the problem."

She was absolutely right. Whenever we had envisaged a meeting with Kennedy or others, it had been assumed that they would simply allow themselves to be photographed, and let the picture speak for itself. No one had imagined that they would agree to hold a press conference, and that, if they did, they would not have before them a carefully deliberated and rehearsed script. Normally, I was all for spontaneity; but in this case, there were two people involved whose versions of what was discussed had to be coordinated. The subject was so delicate, so important, and so susceptible to misunderstanding, that there seemed no less reason for them to know exactly what they were going to say than there would have been for American and Russian arms negotiators issuing a diplomatic communiqué.

Yet after half an hour, Kennedy and Anderson emerged into the hallway to face the horde of screaming reporters. Each began with very kind words for the other. Kennedy said he had a "respect for Congressman Anderson's contributions to the whole campaign." Anderson, referring to Kennedy, said: "I admire a man who goes to the country, who is willing to debate with his opponent . . . [and takes positions which] represent a more positive response to the nation's problems than what we have seen coming out of the present Administration."

But then Anderson was pressed as to whether he had been asked by Kennedy to withdraw if someone other than President Carter gained the nomination. Anderson said that such a question had not been asked, and, moreover, that he had certainly not promised such a withdrawal. Unfortunately, Anderson did not stop at that. He went on: "Obviously, if a different decision from the one that has been so widely predicted should . . . emerge out of the Democratic convention in August, then it would only be prudent, for one like myself who believes very much in the two-party system, to perhaps

Ted Kennedy and John Anderson face reporters, outside Kennedy's Senate office, July 31, 1980. (Wide World Photos)

consider what my position then would be." The hearts of many of us sank. We could see the headlines the next day: "ANDERSON HINTS WITHDRAWAL IF KENNEDY NOMINATED." Such a headline would be a blow to our supporters, many of whom did not particularly admire Kennedy's positions or abilities. They would find it entirely mystifying as to why Anderson would go out of his way to puff Kennedy up, and wonder how someone who just a few months before had been a moderate Republican could now contemplate withdrawal in favor of the country's leading liberal Democrat. They would think a deal had been struck, and that Anderson was expecting something in return. Such an impression would do incalculable damage to Anderson's much-prized reputation for political integrity.

And yet we knew what Anderson had been saying. He was only trying to be candid, and stating the obvious. The premise for his independent effort, made explicitly and repeatedly, had been that a choice between Carter and Reagan was no choice at all, and unacceptable to large numbers of American voters. Anderson was always careful to say that he was not running against the two-party system, but only against the nominees it happened to produce this election year; that was the rationale for why he had refrained from establishing a third party and why he had made the decision to retain, at least technically, his affiliation as a Republican. In short, he was running on the expectation that Carter would be the nominee; if Carter turned out *not* to be the nominee, clearly a reassessment would be in order.

We tried to put the best face we could on the episode. At first glance, we acknowledged, it would look as though Kennedy got the better of the situation because Anderson had implied he might withdraw in Kennedy's favor. But after a few days, we argued, it would begin to dawn on people that Kennedy in fact had no chance of winning the Democratic nomination. At that point, his supporters—feeling kindly toward Anderson for having gone out on a limb and saying such generous things about Kennedy, and being so dismayed by the nomination of Carter—might well be disposed to joining forces with Anderson. Kennedy himself would be prevented from doing so out of lifelong identification as a Democrat, and out of concern about his own future in the party. But it did not seem unreasonable to hope that, in deference to Anderson, Kennedy might withhold his support of Carter, or offer it only at the last possible moment in the most reluctant sort of way. In any case, we rationalized, the thought might occur to people that Anderson could not be on such an ego trip after all, since he had seemed willing to take himself out of contention under the circumstances of a nominee other than Carter. This would reinforce the premise of his candidacy that it was Carter, not the Democratic party, that was unacceptable, and others who agreed might be further motivated to join him.

Keke, however, remained upset about the Kennedy meeting, especially after she saw the headlines the next day, which confirmed her worst fears. On August 7, a week after the Kennedy meeting, Anderson was in Philadelphia facing yet another barrage of questions from reporters as to the meaning of his exchange with Kennedy. He was tired of the incessant questioning; he was acutely mindful of Keke's views as well. He decided to say what he hoped would end speculation once and for all. Under no circumstances, he told the press, would he withdraw—irrespective of whether Carter, Kennedy, or anyone else became the nominee.

This statement produced large headlines across the country the next day. Anderson had reversed himself from just one week before! If the original Kennedy meeting had caused needless controversy, this latest statement compounded it a hundred times. Now Anderson had the worst of both worlds: the image still lingered that he had been willing to cut a deal with Kennedy, and now, in addition, he was being seen as fickle, unsure of himself, and perhaps opportunistic. People compared his reversal to George McGovern's statement in 1972 that he backed Tom Eagleton, his ill-fated running mate, "1,000 percent." Anderson would no longer be able to charge Jimmy Carter with making policy flip-flops without inviting comparisons to his own. Any Kennedy supporters we had picked up by means of the earlier meeting would now have second thoughts about Anderson. Kennedy himself, to put it mildly, was said to be "puzzled" by the sequence of events.

On the morning the headlines appeared, I called Zev to see if he knew why Anderson had said what he did. Zev was in a state of great agitation. "The campaign's finished," he said. "Now Anderson's done it. David," Zev continued, referring to Garth, "is going to quit. We were going to tear the Democratic convention apart, we were going to get an incredible v.p., but now it's over, done with." As usual, Zev did not mince his words. I knew that it was unlikely Garth would be leaving; he had made that threat too often in the past. It seemed to be a tactic designed to provoke reassurance from the Andersons that they would maintain or even bolster his authority, and also to let people know that he was not responsible for the disasters the campaign was suffering. In this case, one suspected, it also proved a convenient explanation for why Anderson might not be profiting as much as Garth had asserted he would from the state of affairs at the Democratic convention, and for why we might not succeed in obtaining the services of a towering vice-presidential running mate.

Later in the day, Anderson came back to Washington. I knew he was being bombarded with criticism from all directions and could use some consolation. "It's a bad development, obviously," I said, "but it will blow over in time." "Oh, I know that," Anderson replied. "I've been in politics twenty years. I know people don't have that much of an attention span." A little later, Garth and Zev, who had just flown down from New York, came into the office to let Anderson know their feelings about his performance in Philadelphia. The doors of Anderson's office were closed, and loud words flew about. Some time after the meeting was over, Anderson came out into the larger office adjoining his private one, and leaned over the partition at one side of my desk. He looked like the famous figure of Kilroy. "How did it go?" I asked. "Well," he said, with a little sigh, "there's a lot of flotsam and jetsam floating around the campaign, and I guess we'll just have to flow with the tide." He had accepted his tongue-lashing from Garth, exempted him from blame, and now wanted to forget about what had happened and simply forge on. It would have been worse to have Garth quit; the campaign would look as if it were falling apart. Anderson was resigned to a difficult road ahead.

On Saturday, August 9, highly critical articles about the campaign appeared in both the *New York Times* and the *Washington Post*. Adam Clymer wrote in the *Times* that, in the preceding few days, John Anderson had succeeded in angering and confusing both his and Kennedy's supporters by his comments and his reversals on the Kennedy meeting. Clymer quoted unnamed "campaign associates" as saying that Anderson had confided to them, "I've blown it." Then in the *Post*, Bill Peterson, who had been traveling with Anderson the previous week, said that the candidate who had at one time been known as "St. John the Righteous" had now turned into "John the Expedient." He was spending more and more time talking to special interest groups, Peterson wrote, delivering emotionless speeches, and changing his story about Ted Kennedy.

I came into the office in the morning and found Anderson. He was sitting quietly at his desk, with a look of melancholy in his eyes. "Did you see these?" he asked, pushing the papers across his desk toward me. I had. "Why would someone say that?" he asked. "Why?" He was referring to the comment by "campaign associates" that he had "blown it." He sat shaking his head. "It's not me they've hurt, you know. It's the campaign. But why?" The answer, I thought, was obvious: because there were now people close to Anderson who were not interested first and foremost in the campaign, but in saving their own skins; they wanted to absolve themselves from blame for the Kennedy fiasco and let the world know that Anderson admitted fault. But I said none of this; Anderson was in too glum a mood. He was capable of drawing his own conclusions.

The Democratic convention, held in mid-August, did not prove anywhere near the boon for the campaign's fortunes that we had long hoped. There were a few minor triumphs: long-time liberal leader Joe Rauh said, after the Carter nomination, that Anderson had just gained a million votes, and Rauh himself then announced his own support of the campaign; former Wisconsin governor Patrick Lucey resigned as a delegate in implicit protest against Carter's nomination and the media quickly began speculating as to whether he might announce his support of John Anderson; Walter Cronkite, Barbara Walters, and others sought out Anderson for interviews, helping to cast his long shadow on convention proceedings. But, for all the hopes and calculations, our illusions were shattered in an instant when Ted Kennedy did, in the end, walk up to the platform following Carter's nomination speech, and, however reluctantly, shake hands with his party's nominee. Subsequently, he campaigned conspicuously for Carter, and the mass of disaffected Democrats whom we had at one time hoped would walk away from a badly split party simply never materialized. Already, to them, Anderson was looking less and less like a realistic alternative.

At this point, much of the campaign's hope for recovery began to focus on the prospect of Anderson's being included in a series of nationally televised debates with Carter and Reagan. The League of Women Voters, which had sponsored several Ford-Carter debates in 1976, had won the agreement of both Carter and Reagan for a similar series in 1980. When John Anderson declared as an independent, however, and polls showed him attracting a sizable fraction of the electorate, the situation became clouded, and discussion ensued about whether to enlarge the scope of the debates to include three participants. Early on, Jimmy Carter announced that it was not fair, in his judgment, that he be required to debate both Reagan and Anderson since they were "just two Republicans." Jody Powell said his boss would simply refuse to debate Anderson. Carter expressed another rationale as well: that if the precedent were set for debating a third candidate, then every fourth, fifth, and sixth party in town would soon be demanding its rights. Carter would have to debate the Prohibition party before it was over, Powell said. We disagreed, of course, arguing that it would be perfectly practical to draw a line, depending on poll standings. Candidates like Anderson, if a large number of Americans supported them, surely were in a different category from those on the fringe. Carter received considerable publicity as he waxed and waned on the subject of a debate. Most of the publicity was negative, for his position was taken generally to reflect political calculation rather than principle. Anderson was the happy beneficiary of the controversy. It looked as though Carter were picking on the underdog, and the tide of sympathy turned to us. During an otherwise long and dry summer, this ongoing controversy inadvertently gave the Anderson campaign some of the few bursts of positive publicity it enjoyed.

If Anderson were included in the debates, it was our hope that this would appear to put him on the same level as the other candidates, and that the public would begin to think about him in terms of similar electoral credibility. Perhaps poll results would reflect this new perception accordingly. Moreover, Anderson had a reputation as a skilled debater, and it seemed likely he would do well against either or both of his opponents. More and more it looked as though Carter would simply not budge from his position of refusing to debate Anderson. Were a debate held with Reagan and Anderson as the only participants, it seemed to have a potential to establish Anderson as the real alternative to Reagan.

Given Anderson's high standing in early polls, the League had seemed inclined to include him in its debates. As he slipped in the polls during the summer, the campaign increasingly looked upon the debates as the event that would boost him once again in his standing. What an irony, then, that as the time approached for the League to make the formal selection of participants, there arose a serious question as to whether Anderson was still high enough in the polls to qualify. The League, seemingly as a gift to Anderson, whom many of its officials were known to admire, set a 15 percent average national poll ranking as the cutoff for qualification. At first, it seemed a level that Anderson would easily reach. But when the designated week approached during which the poll results were to be assessed, the latest standings were not encouraging. One day, the *Christian Science Monitor* editorialized:

> John Anderson is the only non-major party candidate likely to qualify for the debates, unless he fails to rally from the weekend's slip below 15% for the first time in months. What might hold him back is a public feeling after his remarks abroad, and his meeting with Senator Kennedy, that he may be playing the political game to the disadvantage of the higher ground impression conveyed earlier on. For him to return to a genuine stance of "I can do no other" independence could enhance his campaign standing as well as the level of the debates.

On Sunday, August 17, Anderson had still another appearance on "Meet the Press." He asked me to come out to his house early, as in the old days, to talk informally about questions which might come up. Knowing that in recent months his retinue had grown, and that other staff members might want to join him as well, I asked who else he would like me to call and invite over. "No one!" he snapped. "Why do all those people have to surround me? They all think they're useful, but I don't even know their names. All I want to do is sit down with some coffee and read the papers. Maybe an idea will pop into my head. I don't need to be programmed." I told him Garth wanted to come. "I wish he'd stay in New York and save the airfare," Anderson said, "That guy comes down at the drop of a hat. Our campaign's not rich, you know." By mid-morning, however, invited or not, a breathtaking assemblage of eight or nine campaign staffers had turned up at Anderson's house, much to his consternation. Everyone seemed to have a piece of advice to offer him on what he should say and how he should say it. Anderson's eyes betrayed a desire to take refuge in the next room. This was not his idea of the relaxing morning he liked to spend before a tension-producing television appearance.

Anderson seemed stiff and less comfortable than usual in his performance on the program. Moreover, some of his comments did not sound particularly natural. After the program, Anderson needed to go back home to pack a suitcase and then catch an afternoon plane out of town. He asked Margot and me to join him for the ride and, as a bonus, to stop for a hamburger on the way. We were glad to have the opportunity to talk to him; there was much we wanted to say.

I had decided in the previous few days that I needed to talk to Anderson about Garth one last time. The evidence of fundamental problems, it seemed to me, had accumulated beyond a point of reasonable doubt. Everything that could go wrong was going wrong, and it seemed to be both predictable and avoidable. This opinion was coming to be shared increasingly both among the Washington staff and by supporters who followed the decisions and the events of the campaign closely. (To more distant observers, the hand of Garth, and some of the cause-effect relationships, were not as evident.) It was hard, if not impossible, for most people to talk about such a matter with Anderson. Few people had the access to him that Margot and I did. Far fewer still had the relationship that permitted them to speak openly and frankly to him; he knew that we loved and admired him, and treated like family as we were, virtually felt obliged to deal with him honestly. Otherwise, there was great pressure in the nature of a campaign for people to avoid bearing bad news to the candidate. Anderson was so often tired and overworked, and doubts about his standing in the polls so often weighed him down, that it was tempting not to add to the unpleasantness. On the contrary, one wanted to speak optimistically, and to relieve him of his constant worries. Those who were directing the campaign tended always to be upbeat in their predictions and explanations, lest they cast doubt on their own methods and effectiveness. For them, prosperity was always around the corner; they did not wish to be replaced. I had the luxury of saying what I thought: Garth had already removed me from the center of action, and there was not much more he could do. Moreover, having gone through so much with John Anderson, having seen such a change in his style and his fortunes, I felt compelled to express myself bluntly. I did not feel as though I would have any value to him otherwise. As for Margot, she had never become involved in the campaign, and, as a longtime moderate Republican, was known to be unenamored of Anderson's independent status. She, too, had nothing to lose to speak her mind.

And yet, I had come to tell Anderson so many negative things over the months, since the advent of the independent campaign, that I began to long for an occasional positive thing to say. Whenever I thought the time had come again to express more criticism, I felt a knot in my stomach, and sometimes cringed from telling him things as strongly as I felt them. It took all my courage to walk in and talk with him under these circumstances, knowing that it might make him feel only worse than he was already feeling about the campaign. I could understand, at times like this, how it was so easy in the Nixon White House to avoid blowing the whistle on Watergate. No one wanted to be, as one of the Watergate conspirators later put it so memorably, the skunk at a garden party. This was an exquisite irony in our own campaign, however, because it had long been one of our themes that John Anderson was different precisely because he felt it was important sometimes to tell people things they did not want to hear.

As Margot and I drove in the car with Anderson to his home in Bethesda, we began by mentioning some impressions we had of his television appearance that morning. As politely as we could, we ventured that some of the answers he had given on the show were noticeably different from those he would have given in earlier days of the campaign. There were several examples. At one point, for instance, mention was made of President Carter's recently disclosed nuclear doctrine, "PD-59," embodying, in effect, a new official concept that nuclear war could be limited, and perhaps even fought and won. Anderson had long denounced such military strategies, arguing that the most effective deterrent to nuclear war would be a conviction that it was unwinnable and too horrible to contemplate. This, however, was before Garth had lectured Anderson as to how presidential candidates need to avoid specific commitments for or against most controversial policies. On the show, the question was asked of Anderson point-blank: "Do you support or oppose the President's new nuclear doctrine?" In the old days, Anderson would have said, "I oppose it." Now, however, rather than addressing himself to the substance of the issue, he evaded it by saying simply he was opposed to the way it had been handled, namely, that the president had not consulted his own secretary of state, Ed Muskie, before promulgating such an important doctrine. Who could disagree with this? At the same time, it constituted a good, partisan criticism. By Garth's standards, it was a perfect answer.

A second example we cited was the question Anderson had been asked as to whether he supported the plank in the Democratic platform calling for $12 billion in new spending on the creation of public service jobs. Kennedy supported it, and Carter, despite his ultimate acquiescence, was known very much to oppose it. Anderson's life-long record as a fiscal conservative clearly predisposed him also to oppose it. Throughout the entire campaign to date, he had strongly argued the need for private sector solutions to unemployment, and severely criticized massive public sector jobs programs as wasteful and unproductive. Now, however, visions danced in the campaign's head of attracting Kennedy supporters. By rights, Anderson should have answered, "No, I very much oppose Senator Kennedy's solution. I myself prefer. . . ." Instead, Anderson said, "I sympathize with the goals of this program and what Senator Kennedy is trying to accomplish. . . ." He never quite came out and said he opposed the program. To the contrary, he probably left the impression with most viewers that he supported it.

Finally, we noted, Anderson had been asked by one questioner whether he agreed with Jimmy Carter that there was a stark difference between Carter and Reagan. Anderson seemed to reach into a repertoire of answers he had rehearsed specially for the occasion. What he came up with was not at all germane to the question. He said, "Well, there are four candidates: myself, Governor Reagan, Jimmy Carter, and Candidate Carter." He then went on to explain how Carter's record as president, and his rhetoric as a candidate, were worlds apart. The answer was simply too cute, too unspontaneous. In the past, Anderson would have answered the question directly and naturally. That had been his charm, and that is what had made him tower above most other politicians: his directness, his honesty, his bluntness.

Anderson responded to these examples sharply. "Well, what else can you do with the press? They're just trying to put you in a box. Trying to trip you up. They're not interested in your answers. They just want to trick you." He sounded like he had been listening to Garth. This was not the attitude Anderson had had about the press in the past; to the contrary, he had liked the press, and, sensing it, they had very much liked him.

I had prepared a lengthy memorandum to Anderson, summarizing my feelings about the state of the campaign, and had wondered until this moment whether to give it to him. I had been reluctant to do so earlier, but now there was no doubt. I felt compelled to make my feelings as clear as possible. I handed him the memo, and for the next several minutes, as the motorcade sped through Rock Creek Park and then up Massachusetts Avenue to Bethesda, he read it in stony silence.

The memorandum represented a blunt appraisal of the campaign's accomplishments and prospects from the vantage point of the current moment, twelve weeks before the election, and it began:

> Why is it that on April 24, when you announced as an independent, some polls showed you at 25%, and today, four months later, you are barely sure you'll be able to meet the League of Women Voters' standard of 15% to qualify for the Presidential debates? Your name is better known than ever before, and yet your support, rather than going up, has gone drastically down. You should be at 30% or more today, not at 13% or 14%. You should not have to depend on being rescued by the debates, and you should not have to be under the pressure you are to come up with a larger-than-life running mate.

The memo went on to summarize the reasons Anderson's poll standings had declined: his statements on Jerusalem, his meeting with Kennedy, his avoidance over the summer of national publicity, his new soft-spokenness on issues, a perception that his campaign activities were being orchestrated for media effect, campaign spending practices which were leaving no money for paid advertising, a perceived self-righteousness on the part of the candidate, controversy over the Christian amendment, and the overshadowing effect of the Republican and Democratic conventions. Of these nine factors, the last three were ones over which he had no control: he could not change his personality; the Christian amendment had been introduced years ago, and there was no hiding it; the conventions were bound to distract attention from the Anderson campaign. But the first six problems had been avoidable. It was clear who was responsible for them, and hence my urging was the same as it had been for three months: either Garth should be replaced, or his responsibilities should be confined to producing TV ads, at which he was acknowledged to be expert.

The memo concluded:

> The whole summer phase of the campaign was supposed to be one in which we got ready for the fall. And yet, what have we done? We've declined almost a point a week in the polls. Rather than saving up a big nest-egg for advertising, we've practically gone bankrupt. You've been exhausted in the process, having to go to all of your fundraisers. The public has not been impressed by our grand-scale campaign— any more than they were impressed by John Connally's.

And finally:

> Before April 24, when we were a simpler campaign, and you spoke out freely, and followed your own instincts, we did much better than we're doing now. To the extent we have support, we are still coasting from your performance in the primaries. We are not going to win this way. And we are in danger of losing our self-respect.

Anderson finished reading, and looked pained. "Why is it, it's always so *negative?*" he said. "Here I am, concerned about money, polls, getting a running mate, putting out a platform, and all you want to discuss is problems." We sat silent. "Oh, I suppose there may be something in this. I'll talk to Keke about this, I promise, I'll think about it, and let you know." There was reason to be hopeful. Maybe something would give. Maybe the campaign could still be turned around.

9

September–November, 1980:
A Last Breath

Wednesday night, August 27, I was just sitting down to dinner as the phone rang. It was one of MacLeod's assistants at the campaign. Cryptically, he said, "Mark, you'd better get over here immediately. Things are happening." "Can't it wait until tomorrow?" I asked. "I'm just about to eat." "Get over here immediately," he repeated. "Garth wants to see you."

I had no idea what was coming, except that the invitation to see Garth sounded ominous, to say the least. Was the jig up, I wondered? Would Garth tell me that I had been such an interference to him that he had decided to remove me once and for all from the scene? Or had Anderson, after reflecting on my memo, decided to do something about Garth? My heart pounded. Why was I being summoned over to the campaign office at such an odd hour and with a message of such dramatic overtones?

I arrived at the headquarters a half-hour later, and proceeded to Garth's office. There seemed to be an unusual level of activity going on as I walked through the corridors. Typically, many dedicated campaign workers and volunteers toiled late into the night, but this evening they seemed to be working in a more somber and businesslike fashion than usual. Here and there, a hushed conversation was taking place. It was obvious that something had happened. Garth's office was much larger than any other, often doubled as a conference room, and had a big picture window on one side, facing a main hallway. As I walked past, I saw him inside, engaged in animated conversation with deputy campaign manager Ed Coyle. Garth saw me, and signaled he would be finished shortly.

In the meantime, I found other staffers and pieced together what had happened. Apparently, Anderson had arrived at the headquarters earlier in the evening, unannounced, and had called together everyone who was present. He had made only a brief statement, explaining that the campaign management would be changing to allow a shift into high gear for the critical last weeks before the election. Garth was to become full-time campaign manager, resident in the Washington office from here on out; to date, he had spent most of his time in New York, functioning as more of an overall campaign strategist than as a day-to-day manager of operations. MacLeod was to be relieved of his position as campaign manager and made treasurer instead. Given the precarious financial condition of the campaign, for which many felt his spending practices were partly responsible, such a position seemed a curious place in which to put him. Mike Rosenbaum was to be brought back to Washington on a permanent basis, there to supervise the daily routine of the press office. He would be replaced on the road by Tom Mathews, who had been only occasionally advising Anderson over the summer, but who was now prepared to take a higher-profile role. Finally, it appeared that Coyle as well as Fran Sheehan, the current campaign treasurer, might be resigning, rather than agree to diminished authority under a regime tightly controlled by Garth, someone with whom their relations had already turned cool. The loss of Coyle, I realized, would be a blow to the campaign. He was a cool-headed and experienced campaign hand. In the memo I had recently given Anderson about Garth, I had included the recommendation that MacLeod be replaced by Coyle. Obviously my influence at this point was even less than I knew.

In the context of these other changes, I had absolutely no inkling how Garth would decide my own fate. Waiting nervously, I braced either to be told to leave, or to resign if I did not like the conditions that Garth attached to my remaining.

When it came my turn to see him in his office, Garth was almost effusive in welcoming me. "Well, maybe you've heard, we've made some very good changes." I nodded, more in acknowledgment of his statement, than in assent. Then Garth turned his more accustomed acerbic self. "Now, listen," he began, pointing his cigar at me. "John and Keke have given me full power. Full power to hire and fire, and full power to decide how this campaign is run. Anything that happens around here, I'm in charge." I still did not know what he was leading to. "I've decided what to do with you," he said finally. "You're going to be my assistant, right here at my side, where I can keep an eye on you. That's your choice, here or nowhere." I nodded again, not sure of the appropriate response. It was too late to argue. On past occasions, I should have stood up to Garth directly, as I had expected Anderson, MacLeod, and others to stand up. I had not, thinking it would be useless. Instead, I had contented myself with writing memos to Anderson, and complaining to him behind Garth's back. Now I felt my efforts had been misdirected and, worse, cowardly. At this point, however, I had no more energy to fight back.

After I left his office, and for the next several days, I thought very seriously about resigning. Clearly I had lost the battle with Garth over the direction of the campaign, and the loss was of stunning proportions and obviously final. I sought advice from a number of people, but their counsel was unanimous: only two months remained in the campaign, and if I still supported Anderson for president, I should leave it to his judgment what was best, and should be willing to remain loyal to him until the end. I even had a talk with Bob Shrum, one of Ted Kennedy's chief aides. He had attained a certain celebrity several years before for having resigned a high position in the campaign of Jimmy Carter, after serving barely a week. Shrum urged me to stay. "But you resigned," I reminded him. "Yes, but that was because I didn't like the candidate. It had nothing to do with Hamilton Jordan or Jody Powell, or anyone else but Jimmy Carter," he said, referring to Carter's closest aides. "Your situation is the opposite. You like the candidate, but not some of the people around him. You owe it to him to stay."

And so I gritted my teeth, and agreed to stay. It even seemed possible that working for Garth could be educational. The working conditions were nothing to look forward to; Garth had announced, on being introduced by Anderson, that if people thought they had been working hard, they had seen nothing. Campaign staffers grimaced; many of them had been working much longer and much harder than they imagined Garth appreciated. One of the most frequent comments made about the somewhat bizarre events that took place that Wednesday night was that Anderson, in announcing the changes at the campaign, had neglected to use the opportunity to thank any of his workers for their efforts. And then when Garth got up, he seemed intent on displaying to Anderson what a stern taskmaster he was going to be, rather than expressing his own gratitude to the troops.

The next day, in the campaign office, a joke circulated that Anderson's poll standings had risen again to 15 percent—among his own workers. A few people seemed pleased by the latest turn of events; they assumed that Garth might bring discipline to a campaign which had suffered more than its share of organizational and financial problems. Many more, however, seemed mystified or upset by the change. Garth was not well liked; his personality was too strong for that, and his pragmatic approach rubbed many of the campaign's young idealists the wrong way. But more than that, few professed to see any evidence that his strategies had been paying off, all the more a disappointment in light of the extravagant hopes that had been built up as to what miracles he might accomplish.

And yet, as unpopular as Garth's new prominence in the campaign was to the workers he would be managing, the change relieved Anderson of many of his anxieties. At first I found it difficult to accept that Anderson, in the face of my strenuous criticism of Garth's management, which Anderson had not at all dismissed, could make such a decision. Far from reining Garth in, he was bolstering his authority to the hilt. Yet the more I thought about it, the more I understood. Anderson's back was to the wall. He had been told from all directions for some time that things were going wrong; he could tell that himself from his standing in the polls. Everyone agreed something had to be done. But it was a mistake on my part to think that Anderson had, at this point, any option other than Garth. Anderson repeatedly expressed the concern as to how it would look if Garth left and where, with so little time remaining in the campaign, he would find someone to replace him. Who could be sure that the new management would be any better; wasn't Garth supposed to be the best? The presumption was clearly against changing horses in midstream.

Moreover, Garth continued to be extremely persuasive. He assured Anderson that the situation could be salvaged if only he were given the proper authority: he would make the campaign a mean fighting machine, create stupendous television commercials, help Anderson exploit the opportunity of the presidential debates. At times, it was hard to believe that Garth could be wrong. He cultivated an air of extraordinary self-assurance, and had a ready explanation for every adverse event. Even as the polls seemed to be taking irretrievable nosedives, he would say, "Oh, no, it's all going according to plan. This is just what I expected. Stick with me, baby, and I'll deliver you to the front door of the White House." By late August, he was asserting categorically: "It'll be a Reagan-Anderson race by October 1. No doubt about it." Garth was the perfect stereotype of a Madison Avenue media whiz, and he inspired confidence almost on the strength of his style alone. Moreover, he had a larger-than-life reputation, based on a record of outstanding successes in previous campaigns.* The rest of us, by comparison, were rank amateurs. Even when his prophecies did not come to pass, he could offer compelling consolations: "You were bound to be eclipsed by the Democratic and Republican conventions." "Carter and the Democratic National Committee are doing what they can to deny your existence." "We don't have the money of the other campaigns for all the media we need." "The League of Women Voters is caving in to pressure from Carter." "We got too late a start." "People are too wedded to the two-party system." Come fall—whatever was to blame for the decline over the summer—there was a tendency to feel that the situation was so difficult that Garth was doing just about as well as anyone could be expected to do under the circumstances.

Perhaps Anderson should have been more critical. At times, he and Keke did take serious issue with various campaign practices, but they had so many other things on their minds that it was easy

---

*This reputation suffered a major setback in 1982, when Garth managed Ed Koch's campaign for governor of New York and Tom Bradley's campaign for governor of California. At the time he took over their efforts, both were favored easily to win; Koch in particular enjoyed an enormous margin of support and seemed almost unbeatable. Although there were many arguable reasons for the final election results, Garth's help manifestly did nothing to prevent them both from losing badly.

to accept the repeated representations of Garth and MacLeod that reforms would be made and breezy predictions that the poll standings would improve. Anderson would have been the first to admit that he himself was not an administrator. Indeed, he barely cared to know the broad outlines of management policy, let alone to decide the details. It was tempting to vest confidence in Garth, whom the outside world seemed to regard with such reverence, and trust that he would do whatever was in the best interests of winning. Once the decision had been made to hire him, Anderson wanted very much to avoid the problems and headaches associated with making a major change in campaign management. Disdain of administrative detail is not necessarily a fatal flaw in a leader. To the contrary, Winston Churchill, Franklin Roosevelt, Charles de Gaulle, and Anwar Sadat exemplify national leaders of broad vision who showed little patience for minutiae. But to compensate for this, one needs to choose capable lieutenants, and to be willing to change them or restrain them as necessary. It is noteworthy that Ronald Reagan faced a situation in 1980 strikingly parallel to Anderson's. His campaign manager, John Sears, successively forced out many of Reagan's long-time and closest aides: Mike Deaver, Lynn Nofziger, Martin Anderson, and, finally, Ed Meese. Reagan allowed Sears the leeway to do this only up to a point. When it became evident what turmoil Sears was causing the campaign, and how he was changing so drastically its original character, Reagan, who otherwise preferred to delegate considerable authority, stepped in and showed Sears the door.

Another reason for Anderson's relative complacency was that, apart from myself, the people who had the most influence on him were by and large supportive of Garth. MacLeod was concerned most of all about stability in the campaign and did not wish to undermine the regime that was in place; he placed high value on smooth relations with his superiors. The Andersons later expressed disappointment that, knowing what he did at the time, MacLeod had not stood up to certain of Garth's strategies, such as centralizing so much authority in the Washington office, to the detriment of grass-roots organization around the country. Clearly there were other strategies as well which he might have opposed, but did not. This did not prevent him from assuring the Andersons regularly that everything was under control. Cliff Brown had a limited role in overall campaign direction. Moreover, he was content to have his research department take the cautious approach Garth requested. He shared Garth's concern about the danger of controversy, not so much for political reasons as, it seemed, because an academic instinct told him that issues always needed to be discussed with great subtlety and circumspection. Mitch Rogovin seemed on occasion to entertain doubts, but apparently decided to work out a *modus vivendi* with Garth, so that each would let the other supervise his own turf. Tom Mathews did not become involved in day-to-day operations until a late stage in the campaign; he was helpful in reviving some of Anderson's original style of campaigning, but by then the effects of such changes were too late to make much difference. Ed Coyle and Fran Sheehan did question Garth's policies, but they resigned from the campaign in early September, and thereafter wielded no influence; moreover, they were never close enough to Anderson to have his ear.* As for Keke, once in late summer I had suggested to her the possibility of trading Garth for a new campaign strategist, and she had asked whom I had in mind. "Well," I said, "perhaps Bailey-Deardourff," referring to a well-known consulting firm for moderate Republican candidates. "After all," I reminded her, "Garth has never done a national campaign, other than John Lindsay's utterly abortive one years ago. Bailey-Deardourff, on the other hand, did Ford's campaign in 1976." "But they lost," she said. "Yes, but it was close," I said. "But they lost," she repeated. "Yes, but it was pretty miraculous that it came so close, considering that Ford was 30 points behind Carter at one point." "BUT THEY LOST," Keke said with finality. Perhaps Garth had never really run

---

*One particular objection they had was that Garth was slighting the needs of field organization in favor of an emphasis on future media advertising. Their own experience in grass-roots campaigning had convinced them that money and staff resources had to be made available to help organize an Anderson effort "from below," and to turn out supporters on election day. Telling evidence for their proposition came, interestingly enough, from Garth's recent experience in directing the campaign of senatorial candidate Bess Meyerson during the 1980 Democratic primary in New York. Meyerson, who had much going for her—including name recognition, glamour, endorsements, and money—lost out to Congresswoman Elizabeth Holtzman. Many commentators blamed the loss on Garth's strategy of stressing television advertising, in contrast to Holtzman's reliance on field organization.

a national presidential campaign. At least he had never lost one.

The upshot of this was the incongruous situation that much of the rank-and-file campaign staff, much of the traveling press, and an increasing number of our supporters were openly skeptical about Garth's influence and strategies; but the people who surrounded Anderson continued to reassure him in the face of doubts. All in all, it proved irresistible to Anderson to put his fate in Garth's hands and simply not worry about it anymore. If he lost, at least it would be with the help of someone regarded as perhaps the country's leading political strategist. Anderson could concentrate on being himself, and leave the details more than ever to others.

As Labor Day approached, the traditional time for kicking off the final phase of general election campaigns, the fates momentarily smiled again on the Anderson adventure. By dint of determined petition drives and hard-fought legal battles, the campaign at last managed to secure a place on every one of the fifty state election ballots. A ruling by the Federal Elections Commission decreed the campaign eligible for postelection reimbursements to cover a portion of its expenses, something that raised the possibility of taking out loans for the media advertising that Garth had long been waiting to begin. The campaign published a long-in-the-making 317-page platform, containing many of the specific, if not particularly bold, proposals that people had complained were missing from the self-advertised "campaign of ideas." Anderson found a congenial running-mate in former Wisconsin Governor Patrick Lucey. And finally, by the skin of his teeth, Anderson attained the 15 percent rating in the polls that qualified him for what was thought to be the all-important League of Women Voters debate.

Anderson was lucky to have netted Pat Lucey as a running mate. In late August, when the selection was made, virtually no major national figure seemed willing to run with Anderson. His standing in the polls was too precarious. The campaign floated many names, but not many were seriously considered. With great fanfare, Anderson paid a call in Boston on Kevin White, the city's veteran mayor. Later, Anderson admitted that the two had no interest in running with each other, but mainly wanted to tease the press for purposes of publicity each of them wanted. The name of Barbara Jordan, the black congresswoman from Texas, was rumored for a while to be under consideration, more because Garth wanted to flatter black and liberal constituencies than because either Anderson or Jordan was serious about it; in fact, Garth considered such a choice politically too risky. At one point, however, the options seemed so few that Anderson talked privately about the possibility of running with Shirley Chisolm, another black congresswoman, of considerably less renown than Jordan. Anderson met with her, did not hit it off particularly well, but by then, in any case, was beginning to be intrigued by the prospect of drawing someone else to the ticket who had come to his attention.

To the public at large, Patrick J. Lucey was as unknown as John Anderson had been not long before. He was better known to political afficionadoes. He had been a two-term governor of Wisconsin, who enjoyed a solid reputation for having conducted a progressive and effective administration. In 1972, he had been a top contender to serve as running-mate to Democratic presidential nominee George McGovern. Among Jimmy Carter's early foreign policy appointments, a prominent one was his selection of Pat Lucey as ambassador to Mexico. In the fall of 1979, when Ted Kennedy formally mounted his challenge to Carter, Lucey made news again by resigning his post in Mexico to take a leading role in the Kennedy effort. But he was most on John Anderson's mind in August of 1980 because of the recent splash he had made at the Democratic convention when he resigned as a delegate. Television cameras stalked Lucey's every move. Here was what the press had been waiting for: a veteran Democrat so disenchanted with the prospect of a Carter renomination that he was moved to defect from his party. Added to this air of excitement was the instant rumor that the Anderson forces, which had been following events in New York closely, were seeking aggressively to bring Lucey over to their side.

By August 21, the rumor that Anderson had chosen Lucey as his running mate was very much in circulation. Four days later, at a National Press Club news conference, the formal announcement was made. Anderson had steadfastly refused to acknowledge the constant reports from inside his own camp that he had settled on Lucey; one close advisor had been urging a last-minute approach to former Massachusetts Senator Ed Brooke, and Anderson, temporarily tantalized by the prospect, agreed to hold off. But nothing came of it. Reporters accused Anderson of being less than candid in his silence on the subject. He protested that no decision had been made. In a technical sense, this was true; the final details had not been locked up. Among other things, Jean Lucey, the Governor's wife, needed to be convinced that her husband was doing the right thing. Keke was delegated to fly out to the remote cabin in Wisconsin where Jean was vacationing to have a heart-to-heart, wife-to-wife talk with her. The fact that both women were of Greek ancestry, and proud of their reputations for a certain temperamental toughness, lent a compelling logic to the situation: Jean gave her nod.

Anderson told me Monday morning, as we departed for the press conference, that the past weekend had been one of the worst times of his life. He had been under terrible pressure to pick a running mate. He had delayed moving on the matter the entire summer, hoping, on Garth's encouragement, that someone of great stature would break loose in the aftermath of Carter's nomination at the Democratic convention. The one prospect who materialized—Pat Lucey—was not the dramatic figure for whom some Anderson supporters had hoped. True, he was intelligent, hard-working, extremely amiable, and a seasoned politician whose judgment could be very useful. But Anderson's main emotion, having made the choice, was simply to feel relieved that, whoever his running-mate, the long-anticipated and much-fretted-about vice-presidential hurdle had been overcome. He could move on to other things. He told me: "Maybe Pat Lucey is no Pat Moynihan. But in a few days, the press will forget who it is anyway. It's just a formality."

Yet the vice-presidential selection turned out to have importance, not so much for the intrinsic merit of the selection, as for what it signaled to people about the status and prospective success of the campaign. Had Pat Moynihan been the name announced, for example, the message would have gone forth that the Anderson campaign was indeed a formidable one which was still picking up steam. The announcement of a lesser figure, on the other hand, was taken in many quarters as an acknowledgment that the campaign was fading, that it was losing its drawing power, that it was as long a shot as ever.

The other symbolism that attended the selection of Lucey concerned the campaign's politics. As much as the explanation was

At last, a ticket: Patrick Lucey and John Anderson. (Wide World Photos)

given that a Democrat had been chosen precisely to complement Anderson's Republican background—this for the sake of a "national unity" campaign, which had become a guiding motto—it was hard to avoid the conclusion that the campaign was making a bald appeal for Kennedy Democrats unhappy with Carter. Lucey was not simply a Democrat, but a distinctly liberal one. (He made no secret that Ted Kennedy had been his first choice for president, and that in the past he had supported the campaigns of brothers John and Robert as well. One reporter who covered him for several days began to ask jokingly in advance of his speeches, "Will this be a 'three-K' or a 'four-K' speech?" He was referring to the number of times a Kennedy was quoted.) It was not clear, in short, how someone like Pat Lucey could be compatible with a candidate who not many months before had taken pride in his "fiscal conservatism," unless Anderson's campaign was henceforth to toe a much more liberal line.

And that was indeed the development. Under Garth's influence, Anderson began targeting his appeal to traditional Democratic constituencies and various cause-oriented liberals. His platform reflected their positions. Where Anderson had once strongly supported a "youth differential wage," for example—a program designed to encourage the hiring of unemployed teenagers by permitting employers to pay something less than the minimum wage—this position was quietly dropped over the summer in anticipation of the opposition of organized labor. Where Anderson had previously been an eloquent exponent of relatively free-market economic policy, suddenly he began to mention ideas for a contingency program of wage and price controls. As a result of such shifts in philosophy, Anderson may have made himself more attractive to would-be Democratic supporters, but over time he found himself simultaneously losing much of his original moderate Republican support.

Tuesday, September 2, the first day I was supposed to report to work for my new boss, David Garth, I arrived early at the campaign office, hoping to make a good impression. Garth was not there yet. Time went by. Finally Zev arrived on the scene with news that he would be late. But he had other news as well. "Pat Lucey needs a right-hand man," Zev said. "Someone to do speeches, give advice, keep him coordinated with Anderson." Would I be interested in it? I thought about it quickly. Given the obscurity in which we would be laboring, it seemed like a kind of exile within the campaign; perhaps that was Garth's design. Yet it sounded much better than staying in Washington and working directly under Garth's thumb. The Lucey entourage would be much smaller than Anderson's (though it still got, incredibly, the same size complement of Secret Service) and Lucey would not be surrounded by Garth surrogates, who took themselves so seriously. It even held the potential to be a back-to-the-womb *Doonesbury*-like experience, traveling around the country, saying what we wanted, doing what we wanted, even if the crowds were thin, and the press not particularly interested. I said yes. Zev said, "Good, your plane leaves for Detroit in one hour." By the early afternoon, I had arrived in Detroit and made my way to the vicinity of the Book Cadillac Hotel, where Anderson and Lucey were addressing a joint rally.

It was a sunny day, and a crowd of five hundred or so had gathered to hear them. Anderson had begun using some one-line jokes in his speeches, and, judging from this occasion, to good effect. "Let's give Carter credit," he said. "He did accomplish something the last four years." Pause. "He gave us a recession!" These were not exactly thigh-slappers, but such public humor was a rare commodity for Anderson, and was a measure of how he was finally loosening up. When he finished the rally, and got back to the hotel to have lunch in his suite, I stopped by to see him. He was alone, wrapped in a towel, and dining in the ornate Louise XIV-style surroundings of his suite. He explained to me his informal appearance. Apparently the Secret Service had received word of a potential threat, and had requested that he wear a bullet-proof vest throughout his speech. He said it had made him sweat profusely, and he was trying now to cool off. He wished me luck in my travels with Lucey; the two halves of the ticket would be going their separate ways.

I found Lucey in his own room, talked with him over lunch, and then joined him on the ride by car to Toledo, our first stop. He was very much concerned about a comment he had made earlier that day in an interview. Somehow the question had come up of what sort of car he drove himself. This was an important matter in the Motor City. "I should have said that the last ten years, I've always had jobs that furnished American-made limousines," he said, kicking himself that he had not said it. "Well, what did you say?" I asked him. He had been candid: "A Peugeot." I laughed. Had Anderson said this, Zev and Garth would have been beside themselves. Garth might even have threatened to quit. But who would care what the running-mate had said? "Oh, I think you were being refreshingly honest," I told him, reminding him that that was what the Anderson campaign was supposed to be known for, after all. "I wouldn't worry about it." And so we did not.

The next few days we spent visiting towns in Ohio and Pennsylvania. As a politician who had long been supported in his own state by organized labor, Lucey was expected to represent the ticket in visits to factory gates and assembly lines. This usually required rising at about 5:00 A.M., to make a six o'clock whistle. Often it was not even light when the motorcade pulled up to a gate, and, as November approached, it could sometimes be very cold. Lucey enjoyed it, however. Unlike Anderson, he loved many of the more mundane elements of politicking, like shaking hands, signing autographs, making conversation with strangers. He did not even mind his obscurity. Almost no one recognized him, certainly not by sight, and frequently not even by name. (It always struck me that the sight of Lucey being whisked through airports by a team of Secret Servicemen must have looked to the casual observer like a white-collar felon being transported to prison.) Outside the factory gates, someone in our party had to stand with him, announcing to each passerby, "Meet Governor Pat Lucey . . . JOHN ANDERSON'S RUNNING-MATE." The extra description seemed to impress people, and the fact that the title Governor could be attached to Lucey's name also seemed to add a nominal amount of stature. But these routines, after a while, even got to Lucey. He was reminded, he told me, of something John F. Kennedy had once said during the 1960 Wisconsin primary, when Lucey had run Kennedy's campaign in that important state. "Pat," Kennedy asked him one day, "do you think we've gone to a lot of factory gates?" "Yes, Senator," Lucey replied. "And do you think we've demonstrated our willingness to go out and meet the people?" "Yes, sir." "And do you think we've clearly demonstrated our concern for the unions, and for organized labor?" "Absolutely." "Well, then," Kennedy said, "do you think we can cut out all this shit!" I was sympathetic.

However unheralded, the Lucey campaign certainly proved a way to see the U.S.A. In the course of two months, we visited thirty-seven states, and innumerable cities. Perhaps our most memorable feat was the day we made appearances in six different states. We started out early one morning at a plant gate in Philadelphia, went from there to Hartford, then to Albany, then to Bennington, Vermont, then to Boston, then for the night to Portland, Maine. On other occasions, we went to county fairs in Seattle; hog farms in Sioux Falls, South Dakota; tenements in Newark; Hispanic rallies in East Los Angeles; coal mines in West Virginia; and universities from Oregon to Indiana to Connecticut. One day we toured Liberty City, the black ghetto in Miami; another day we visited residents of the chemical dump area of Love Canal outside of Buffalo, and then stopped by Niagara Falls for lunch; and one whole weekend we spent "campaigning" on Waikiki Beach in Honolulu. In a real sense, a running-mate was supposed to be seen and not heard: he was supposed to be seen traveling busily around the country, reminding people of John Anderson; but, on the other hand, he was also supposed to avoid saying anything that would put him at odds with his other half, or create undue controversy. No one covered us enough to permit any controversy to arise, and so, in our mission, we proved eminently successful.

At this same time, Anderson, for his part, was taking a more aggressive campaign posture, reasserting many of his original and outspoken positions. And Garth, far from discouraging him, was drawing him out. One day, our paths crossed and Garth told me he had been thinking: "What we need now," he said, "are some of those old against-the-grain speeches." He used the expression as if to refer to a particular type of media strategy, rather than a sincere effort to discuss controversial issues. But Garth now acknowledged that the strategy of soft-pedaling issues had gone awry. Besides, he had long planned to unleash Anderson in the fall. Subsequently, Anderson spoke out against the M-X missile program at the plant of a defense contractor in Southern California, against federal aid to Chrysler during a stop in Detroit, and proceeded to revive strong talk about a gas tax, stringent budget cuts, and, in general, the philosophy of sacrifice. Anderson even reverted to the style of the early Republican campaign. At the beginning of every press conference, for example, he began by making a strong statement about a timely national issue. This often turned out to be a natural addition to network news coverage of the issue later that night, and a means of getting the free and favorable media attention that had served the campaign so well months before. Garth had put a stop to this over the summer because he did not want Anderson to stumble into controversy, and because he generally wanted Anderson to take a low profile. But now even Garth wished Anderson to be his old self. When the practice was inaugurated again, some of the reporters who had not covered the campaign originally took it to be a very clever new trick, and wondered why Anderson had not thought of it before.

Unfortunately, at this point, as much as Anderson started coming to the attention of voters again, and stirring their admiration, they were concluding that he no longer had a chance to be elected. He had fallen too far, and the time remaining to catch up was too short. And yet it was notable that as the election approached, and Anderson received a number of newspaper endorsements, most of them seemed to be based not on the new, Independent Anderson—the one who took traditional liberal positions—but on the old Republican Anderson—the one who took candid and courageous "nonpartisan" positions. References were common in these editorial plaudits to the stands Anderson had made before the Gun Owners of New Hampshire, or in his advocacy of the gas tax, or in his support of the president's grain embargo.

As the polls continued to tell their discouraging news, the League of Women Voters' debates assumed a towering importance in Garth's strategy: it was the only chance to shake things up and make people take John Anderson seriously again. Carter had encountered such an adverse public reaction to his initial refusal to debate Anderson that he eventually relented in a qualified way: he said he had no objection to debating Anderson, either one-on-one or in a threesome with Reagan, but that the first debate must feature only himself and Reagan. These were the only two candidates, Carter insisted, who had any realistic chance to be elected. Clearly, his supposition was that the first debate would be the most significant, the most widely viewed, the one that would set the real terms of reference for voters. Reagan, on the other hand, while willing to engage Carter one-on-one, stipulated the condition that a three-way debate occur first. Reagan's strategy was equally clear: a three-way debate would enhance Anderson's stature as a candidate, something assumed to siphon off more support from Carter than from Reagan; and such a format would also permit some of Carter's potential attacks on Reagan to be deflected onto Anderson.

As it turned out, the League issued an invitation for its first debate to all three candidates. When Carter formally declined the invitation, it was not immediately clear that a debate would be held. The League decided that it should be, and even contemplated at one point leaving an extra chair on the stage to remind the audience of Carter's absence; that idea was later scotched as too rude. Reagan's advisors were at first divided as to the wisdom of his taking on only Anderson. Some thought, as Reagan's former campaign manager, John Sears, had written in a newspaper column, that a performance by Reagan inferior to that of "lesser candidate" Anderson would represent a serious embarrassment. Ultimately it was decided, however, that Reagan would look as though he were scared if he did not debate, and stood to look magnanimous—especially in comparison to Carter—if he did debate. Moreover, those who knew Reagan well recognized that, as an experienced performer, he might not do too badly, whereas Anderson might prove too "hot" for the "cool" medium of television. Anderson, of course, quickly accepted the League's invitation, happy to have the opportunity for exposure on national television, and thinking that an Anderson-Reagan debate might succeed in leaving the impression that they were the two principal candidates, and that Jimmy Carter was simply afraid to face them.

The debate was set for September 21 in Baltimore. Carter lost little opportunity during this period to vent his frustration about the Anderson candidacy. Sources in the White House were quoted as saying that he showed enormous irritation even at the mention of Anderson's name. (At one point, columnist James Reston joked that a coup in Turkey, which had just taken place, must have given some relief to the president, who otherwise seemed to be preoccupied with worrying only about John Anderson.) In mid-September, Carter displayed considerable pique in speaking to a group about his rival. He charged that Anderson had been, in fact, just a "creation of the press," that he had never won a primary, not even in his own state, that he had no party and was in effect (as Reagan, too, had once said) on nothing more than an ego trip. "He and his wife have picked his vice presidential nominee," he added gratuitously. (One newspaper editorial later remarked that the difference between Anderson's selection of his running-mate and Carter's selection of his running-mate, was that in the latter case, Carter had not only had the help of his wife, but of his mother, too.) The Carter forces did what they could to denigrate the significance of the debate. But the evening it was held, the Baltimore Civic Center was packed with partisans of both debaters and with hundreds of reporters. Police lines ringed the streets outside. Searchlights filled the air. Tickets were a prized possession. Network TV cameras prepared to beam the event live. All in all, the occasion had the aura of a full-scale presidential debate, not the half-a-debate that Carter claimed it to be.

The event lasted only an hour, but in that time Anderson and Reagan managed to convey very clear impressions of themselves to the audience, both in style and in substance. Anderson was, for the most part, stiff and formal. At times, he became so intense and long-winded that I squirmed in my seat wishing I could pass him a note to calm down. Reagan, on the other hand, despite an occasional look of nervousness, seemed generally relaxed, easygoing, and humorous. He referred to his opponent as "John," whereas Anderson addressed Reagan as "Governor" or "Sir." Anderson's answers no

John Anderson, an unidentified television technician, and David Garth (right, pointing) preparing for the Anderson-Reagan debate. (Wide World Photos)

doubt struck many as more direct, elaborate, and sophisticated, but Reagan came across in a folksier and perhaps more appealing way. Given that Reagan had been caricatured in the minds of many voters as not smart enough to be president, and Anderson was seen as the intellectual in the race, the fact that no one emerged as a clear winner reflected particularly well on Reagan. On the specific issues, Reagan seemed content to state his own positions, while Anderson made a point of drawing contrasts between his own and those of both Reagan and Carter. About the only position Anderson and Reagan had in common was their opposition to draft registration. On the topics of the economy, energy, abortion, urban problems, and national defense, the lines between the two debaters were vividly drawn. It was not surprising that in the aftermath of the debate surveys indicated that liberals thought Anderson had won, and conservatives thought Reagan had won. In a sense, this amounted to a loss for Anderson, since his lower standing in the polls required him to broaden his base and attract whole new groups of voters.

Overall, Anderson's performance was creditable, but ultimately disappointing. He had not shone as much as many had expected he

John Anderson shaking hands with Ronald Reagan, with (left to right) Senators Howard Baker (R-Tenn.) and John Tower (R-Tex.) looking on, before the Anderson-Reagan debate. (Wide World Photos)

would in a match-up with Reagan. He did not jolt many into thinking differently about his candidacy. He may even have turned some off by a passionate nature and seeming self-righteousness of style. In the ensuing days and weeks, it was common to run into people who said, "Oh, yeah, I saw the debate, and I thought Anderson was good. I agreed with most of what he said. I think I like him the best of the candidates. But vote for him? He doesn't have a chance." Anderson was not regarded any longer as a candidate with a real chance to win, worthy of a voter's ballot. For many Democrats, more attracted to Anderson than to Carter, voting for him seemed only a means of aiding Ronald Reagan; for moderate Republicans, he posed the threat of forcing an election in the House of Representatives, which might redound to the advantage of Carter. Had Anderson truly excited these voters, rather than simply impressing them as a somewhat more intelligent candidate than the others, they might have said, "What the heck: Anderson's so good, I don't care if I take a chance electing Reagan (or Carter); it's worth a try." His performance in the debate did not excite them. The *Milwaukee Journal* had summed up the challenge in an editorial a few days before the debate, entitled, "How Different is John Anderson?"

> In many respects, the Anderson platform overlaps that of the Democratic Party. . . . Both documents are centrist, designed to appeal to the broad midsection of the electorate. . . . What, then, is the touted "Anderson difference?" We have to conclude that it is mainly a difference of persona, not policy. Anderson offers his image and style of leadership as a replacement for Carter's version. The question for wobbly Democrats: Is that stylistic difference alluring enough to risk an electoral defection that could simply help Reagan win the White House?

As it became clear that the debate had failed to stem Anderson's continuing decline in the polls, the campaign was suddenly confronted by the virtual impossibility of winning. With a month left in the campaign, however, no one wanted to admit it; many clung to the hope that a multimillion dollar media splash, or some terrible gaffe committed by one of the other candidates, would miraculously push Anderson out front. But not every Anderson supporter had the patience or the optimism to wait. And so the polls kept sinking. One weekend in late September, several newspaper articles appeared quoting anonymous Anderson campaign sources as admitting privately that "It's all over." Everyone who cared about the campaign was aghast at these extraordinarily indiscreet and damaging statements. Soon thereafter, press analyses began appearing as to how Anderson's support stacked up on a state-by-state basis, and what electoral votes he stood to draw. The verdict: he led nowhere, and had a chance to win only in Massachusetts or Connecticut, and then only by a stroke of great luck.

Garth and others about this time were scrambling around for large sums of money to use for television commercials. They asserted that this could save the day, but one was hard put to believe it. In the first place, the other candidates were planning to spend a great deal more on advertising than we would be able to afford, even if we succeeded in raising up to the ten million dollars Garth contemplated, which was itself doubtful. Moreover, it was not at all

THE DEAR JOHN LETTER

Paul Conrad, © 1980, *Los Angeles Times*. Reprinted with
permission.

clear how any amount of money would be enough to raise a candidate's standing from 9 percent or so, at which we were hovering
now, to the 35 percent or more which would be required to win.
The idea that a campaign could rise out of the ashes on the basis of
a last minute advertising blitz represented, at best, the most extreme wishful thinking.

If any approach could still help at this stage, it needed to be far
more fundamental. Once again, I talked with Anderson about the
suggestion that he announce his withdrawal unless he climbed in
the polls within two or three weeks to a level of, say, 25 percent, or
to the point of surpassing one of the other candidates. This might
have convinced Democrats in particular, worried about tipping the
election to Reagan, to give Anderson a chance again. It might also
have countered the charge that Anderson was on an ego trip and
destined only to be a "spoiler" in the race. Finally, it might have
created new drama for the campaign, and brought Anderson back

into the center of the political picture. Anderson listened, but by now seemed inclined to go on to the end, whatever his prospects; having come this far, quitting seemed almost cowardly. Moreover, the crowds that he addressed remained large and enthusiastic. Whether he would win or lose, he still had an important forum.

It mattered little. Garth was dead-set against any strategy so risky. He continued to bank on raising money for television advertising. Some suspected that his determination to keep Anderson in the race at this point had to do with his own intention to be paid for his campaign work. Election law stipulated that if Anderson received over 5 percent of the vote on November 4, his campaign would be eligible for retroactive federal subsidies. If the campaign did not receive them, it stood to be greatly in debt and unable to afford its bills; Garth had agreed to defer his compensation until the end of the campaign. (Because of this deferral arrangement, he frequently stated that he was "doing the campaign for free." In fact, at the time of the election, he billed the campaign for hundreds of thousands of dollars in retainers, commissions, and personal expenses. MacLeod promptly paid these bills, even though the campaign had contracted enormous debts to others, including many small contributors of loans, which remained unpaid.) The suspicions raised about these matters may have been unfair, but that they existed was a measure of what some took to be the true motivations now driving the campaign.

By the beginning of October, Garth had pretty much disappeared from the Washington office. The word he left was that he was spending time in New York negotiating for loans, and reviewing ideas for television commercials. But the more commonly held belief among campaign staff was that he had given up. It was also supposed that he wanted the time to work on his other political races, ones in which his candidates had much better chances. Being able to claim victory in those races on election night might distract attention from an Anderson fiasco, and help salvage his reputation. That he did not formally leave the campaign was assumed by the staff to be in part because he did not want to be considered a quitter, and because he did not want to jeopardize his prospects of being paid. But his physical absence from the campaign office made it evident that he did not think the campaign any longer had a chance, an attitude which had a tremendously demoralizing effect on the campaign staff. Nonetheless, Garth continued to commit the campaign to whatever media purchases it could afford with money raised from loans, causing it to sink deeper and deeper into debt and ensuring that Anderson would remain in the race to the end so as to qualify for retroactive subsidies.

On October 6, Anderson happened to be in Washington for a few hours, and I went over to the congressional office to see him. I knew he would be feeling discouraged, and I thought he might be able to use some reassurance that, however the campaign fared, he would retain his original friends and admirers. It was an incongruous scene as I entered. Here was John Anderson, who at the time could still draw thousands of screaming and cheering students to a speech on college campuses, sitting alone and weary back at his old congressional desk. He looked up and welcomed me with a smile, but was absorbed in an article he was reading. "I'll tell you," he said, "I give two, three, four speeches a day, and then the *Washington Post* reporter here," he said, pointing at the article, "tells you your speeches are long and tedious. I'd like to see them get up and do it." He sighed. "And what are we going to do about money?" His voice turned soft. "I'm just afraid people are going to be disappointed if all we can announce is one or two million dollars for TV ads instead of eight or ten, like we've been talking about." Anderson went on. "Everywhere I go," he said, "those press people come up and they say, 'Well, I see you're sliding in the polls, you're dropping, what are you going to do about it?'" He was mimicking their voices. "And just what am I supposed to say? That I'm planning to win? Do they believe that?"

And so it was that by mid-October, Anderson was being asked by reporters incessantly, "Isn't a vote for Anderson a vote for Ronald Reagan?" At first, he answered with the rhetorical flourish, "A vote for Anderson is a vote for Anderson." Not everyone agreed. It seemed clear that Anderson's participation in the election would very likely distort its outcome. He needed a better answer. More convincing was the argument that by now it was too late: Anderson's name was on the fifty state ballots, and even if he dropped out, millions of people would still cast their votes for him if only as an opportunity to register a protest against the other candidates. Anderson also argued that dropping out of the race would be a betrayal of the two million people who had signed petitions to put him on the ballot, and of all those who had contributed money. Yet surely not all of them had meant to give Anderson their unconditional and perpetual support; many had been willing to help only insofar as they thought he had a chance, or hoped he would have a chance. Now that it was clear he did not, their attitudes could be different. This seemed obvious from the polls: in fading from 25 percent to 9 percent or less now, what other interpretation could there be but that Anderson had lost the vast majority of his original support? At times acknowledging this, Anderson contended that if people regarded him as nothing more than a spoiler, then they simply would not vote for him. His vote total in the end, he argued, would then prove insufficient to make a difference in the election. To those still worried about a Reagan victory, Anderson quipped, "Listen, Carter ain't no bargain."

Even as Anderson continued to fade, reality did not immediately change the ways of the campaign. It continued at times to take itself very seriously. At one point, on a swing through New Jersey, I was with other campaign workers, riding in a staff car. "You have a nice car," I told the driver, who seemed to be a middle-aged homemaker, the type who does charity work. "Oh, it's not mine, it's one the campaign rented," she said. "Well, that's nice," I replied, "that they did that for you, so you don't have to get your own car dirty." "No it's not," she said. "I wanted to use my own car. I've got a brand new Buick, and I don't mind using it at all. I would have loved to." "So why didn't they let you?" I asked. "Well, the advancemen said that the campaign headquarters requires that all staff cars have four doors, and my Buick only has two doors."

On another occasion, when we were back in Washington, Margot gave me a ride in her car to a speech Lucey was delivering at American University. We fell into the motorcade, several cars back from Lucey's limousine. An advanceman ran up to us. "Don't you go in that motorcade," he snapped. "Why not?" I asked. "Because you've got a foreign car. We can't have the press see foreign cars in our motorcade." Of course we disregarded the advice. No press were covering Lucey; we would have been only too happy to attract much-needed publicity for him. Indeed, we imagined to ourselves what the headline the next day would read: "FIANCÉE OF ADVISOR TO RUNNING-MATE OF INDEPENDENT CANDIDATE SEEN DRIVING JAPANESE IMPORT." Somehow we doubted that Anderson would have lost the election on that account.

As money became scarce, and the campaign belatedly became zealous in trimming its budget, word circulated that a large number of advancemen were going to be laid off. "A disaster!" many exclaimed. Others wondered about the essential importance of much of the advance work performed in the campaign. Even after the budget-cutting, twenty-nine advancemen remained, approximately 2,800 percent more than the campaign had employed during its Republican phase, the time when it had enjoyed its greatest successes. Advance work had been costing the campaign as much as $50,000 to $75,000 a week; squads of advancemen arrived several days in advance of each event (often crisscrossing the country to get there), stayed one to a room in expensive hotels, charged overpriced hotel meals to their rooms, rented fleets of cars for transportation. They worked hard, generally did an excellent job, and no doubt deserved much more compensation than they received, yet such a grand style was being supported not by a Wall Street law firm, which could bill its corporate clients for expenses, but by a campaign on a shoestring budget which had to plead with supporters for each small contribution, and which needed desperately to save money for more important things. In such circumstances, the appropriate question was not whether the services of so many advancemen were useful; it was whether they were actually *necessary*. Much of the work, for example, consisted of building crowds for Anderson's college speeches, something which had been done successfully in days past by campus volunteers; or arranging local press interviews, something that could be done by telephone from Washington. Some felt the campaign would have fared just as well with skeletal advance crews; others, perhaps accustomed to working with wealthier campaigns, treated such skepticism as radical dissent.

Now that the pressure was off Anderson, and he was resigned to his rapidly declining status in the polls, he seemed to relax and begin enjoying himself more. Suddenly he showed the playful, humorous side that had usually been kept so well hidden from the public. On a TV interview one Sunday, a questioner mentioned his criticism of the other candidates for their sharp attacks on him, and then asked whether Anderson himself was not waging a personal attack when he had recently charged Reagan and Carter with being "Twee-dle-Ron and Tweedle-Jimmy." Anderson, with a twinkle in his eye, did not hesitate in answering, "I hardly think that calling someone Tweedle-Ron or Tweedle-Jimmy qualifies as something for which one must have one's mouth washed out with soap." When another questioner noted that Anderson was still one of the major candi-dates, certainly "compared to Commoner or Clark," Anderson in-terjected, "Well, thanks at least for that." And when someone char-acterized certain of Carter's activities as "hardball politics," An-derson replied that such a term was an insult to the baseball players who were at this time battling each other in the World Series. They were playing hardball, too, Anderson said, but they were playing by the rules! As the program ended, Anderson saw someone in the studio wearing a button that read "ANDERSON—WHO ELSE?" He smiled, and said, "Well, at least the button people have made some money off this campaign."

As if the campaign needed any more nails driven into its coffin, it began to look as though the League of Women Voters might relent and invite Reagan and Carter to a one-on-one debate which exclud-ed Anderson. Heretofore, the League had refused to consider such a debate unless and until Carter had first agreed, as had Reagan, to meeting Anderson in a three-way forum. The League had seemed very principled in doing so, and in holding out despite criticism from the president and the prestige that would attach to sponsoring a Carter-Reagan debate. But now that Anderson was slipping badly in the polls, the League was said to be having second thoughts.

At the time of the Anderson-Reagan debate, an interesting sug-gestion had been put to Garth. Carter's position was that he would be willing to participate in a three-way debate so long as he were assured first of a two-man debate with Reagan. Reagan's position was that he would not consent to such a two-man debate until Carter first participated in a three-man debate; otherwise, Reagan said, it would be unfair to John Anderson. Given Carter's intransi-gence on the score, and the seeming unwillingness of the League as well to budge, it looked as though there would be no more debates during the campaign. One had the intuition, however, that all was not as it seemed. If Anderson continued to decline in the polls, surely the League would come under enormous pressure to stage a Carter-Reagan debate after all, and Reagan would very likely feel forced to accept. This would be disastrous for the Anderson campaign, because the debate would probably come in the final days and make it look as though Anderson were totally out of the race.

In these circumstances, it had been suggested, why not have Anderson take the initiative to break the logjam? He could announce that, in the interest of having more debates, it was all right with him if Governor Reagan went ahead and debated Carter first; no one should worry that Anderson would feel offended. In return for this, Reagan and Carter would have to agree to participate in a three-way debate sometime afterward. At one point, both Carter and the League had expressed their approval of such a plan. The only thing that stymied it was Reagan's refusal, based, he said, on his feeling of fairness about Anderson. This objection would evaporate if Anderson himself made the proposal.

Garth rejected the idea. He argued that if Carter and Reagan held any debate at all, even if it were followed by a three-way debate, it would destroy the Anderson campaign. He dismissed the possibility that the League would change its mind and end up allowing Carter and Reagan to have a debate without Anderson's approval. The Anderson campaign thus lost an opportunity. A Carter-Reagan debate might have been held in late September or early October, and a Carter-Reagan-Anderson debate in mid- or late October. This would have provided the Anderson campaign with a burst of new publicity in a critical period, and perhaps significantly increased its credibility and support. Instead, Carter and Reagan held their own debate in late October, and John Anderson was not to be seen on stage again.

On October 17, when the League extended its invitation to Carter and Reagan, and implicitly "disinvited" Anderson, the Anderson campaign was quick to react. Rogovin accused the League of "appeasing" President Carter. MacLeod issued still another stinging statement. When pressed on the issue at news conferences, Anderson himself responded in like fashion. Such criticism did little to elevate the tone of the campaign. The League had been generous in setting its original standard at 15 percent, and including Anderson in a first debate; it was not unreasonable that it had now reassessed its position in light of Anderson's lesser status in the polls. It was hard to see what absolute right Anderson had to be included.

News of the debate situation was enough to bring the campaign to the edge of despair. Anderson gave a press conference one day which was reported in the papers as having been almost melancholy in tone; at one point, he acknowledged that he "might have been a better candidate." I talked to him on the phone about it the next day. He was in San Francisco; I was in Boston. "I don't care what you hear about it on the other side of the country," he volunteered, "I haven't given up, and I'm not going to." He went on, "I guess I just won't say those things anymore in press conferences, because they read so much into it. They think you're admitting failure." Far from feeling he had failed, he said, he had a notion that perhaps his effort was only just beginning. "I haven't said this to anyone else," he confided, "but there's something out there that's going to endure beyond 1980. There's a movement waiting to be formed. There's just no reason the two parties should have a monopolistic hold on politics in this country." And so began Anderson's thinking about a formal third party, though he was not to begin discussing it publicly until months after the election.

It was not clear what the premise would be for a separate new party. Anderson had staked out a difference during the Republican primaries largely by virtue of his personal style: a willingness to tackle issues honestly and directly; an intellectual, rather than a political, approach to national problems; a combination of fiscal conservatism and progressive social views. Dennis Farney of the *Wall Street Journal* had noticed this early on: "What [Anderson] is trying to do . . . is to challenge the lock that the Republican and Democratic Parties have on presidential politics. Yet, unlike George Wallace, the last man to seriously do so, John Anderson is building a campaign around no central issue, no regional protest. What he offers, essentially, is himself." Yet now his positions, and his style, had come to resemble those of a traditional and mainstream politician. For the first time, political cartoonists began to lump Anderson in with the other candidates in spoofing their pretensions and foibles; in the past, Anderson had been almost universally portrayed in a noble or heroic light. At the University of Washington, once a stronghold of Anderson support, a campus poll reported that Barry Commoner and Ed Clark, minor third party candidates though they were, now drew more support from students than did John Anderson. One day, when I introduced myself during a plane ride to a small-businessman from the Midwest, he told me that he had originally been an Anderson supporter, but had become turned off after having heard Anderson take so many "me-too" positions. Now this fellow was leaning toward Libertarian candidate Ed Clark. "I don't agree with all his positions," he said, reminding me of what so many people had once said about John Anderson, "But he sure has guts taking 'em."

On October 20, "CBS Evening News" announced that it was going to inaugurate a new segment, to last through election day, which would highlight and compare the positions of the candidates on the major issues. Fantastic, we thought: Anderson will be getting a big chunk of free prime time in the critical last days. Our illusion was not long-lived. The "candidates" who were discussed, it turned out, consisted only of Carter and Reagan.

On October 23, Doug Fraser, president of the United Auto Workers, Patsy Mink, president of the liberal Americans for Democratic Action, and seventy-three other prominent Democrats announced their opposition to the Anderson candidacy—labeling Anderson a conservative—and their support of Jimmy Carter. Something in this incident reminded one of the experience Ted Kennedy had had with many of his more prominent supporters. At first, Kennedy was said to have been approached by as many as thirty of his fellow United States senators, making the argument that they needed him at the head of their ticket in 1980, given Carter's weakness as the party's standard-bearer. By the time Kennedy became a full-fledged candidate, his campaign had suffered setbacks and Carter had regained strength. Suddenly, many of his original boosters had scattered to the four winds. This seemed true in the Anderson experience as well. Countless were the numbers of well-known Democrats who at one time expressed to us their chagrin at the prospect of a Carter—or a Kennedy—nomination, and broadly hinted at, or privately admitted, their support of an Anderson candidacy. When his fortunes faded, however, so did they—right back into the political underbrush.

And the Anderson campaign was fading fast. Only about $1.5 million in loans had been secured in the last several weeks for use in putting television commercials on the air. Commercial banks had been unwilling to lend the money. Although MacLeod and Rogovin called a press conference to level the charge that the banks were fearful of regulatory retribution from the Carter administration, in fact it did not seem unreasonable that the banks were more concerned with the possibility that Anderson would not reach the 5 percent threshold on November 4 which would qualify him for federal subsidies and allow his loans to be repaid. A supporter in Boston proposed a novel scheme to raise the needed money, which the campaign adopted. Loans would be solicited from individuals, up to the legal maximum of $1,000. These loans would be repaid at 8 percent interest, assuming Anderson's vote totals qualified him for sufficient federal reimbursement. A great number of Anderson supporters proved willing to take the risk: $1.5 million was an impressive amount, coming from small contributors, though nowhere near the amount Garth had originally estimated to be needed for media purposes.

It was remarkable that this turned out to be all that was applied to advertising, for the independent campaign of John Anderson succeeded overall in spending $18.5 million, and it had always been thought that advertising would be a key objective and a major expense. The Carter and Reagan campaigns each received $29 million from the federal government (the amount to which major party nominees were entitled under provisions for public financing of presidential elections), and each budgeted $15 million for advertising. So while the Anderson campaign spent only a very small fraction of what the other campaigns spent for media, it did, interestingly enough, spend about the same on nonmedia, administrative functions. In spending so freely in this latter category, apparently the supposition was that contributions would keep flowing into the campaign at the robust rate at which they flowed in at the beginning, and that since advertising was not going to be begun until the fall anyway, it could be financed from contributions received at a later stage of the campaign. By the time it was recognized that money was drying up, early contributions had already been spent or committed. Thus the great irony of the campaign was that though Garth had been hired because of his reputation for media wizardry, ultimately he had no money available to perform it.

The commercials that finally aired were not bad, but neither were they sensational. Anderson was at this time fighting for his political life, and it was assumed that he needed something dramatic to rescue him. The commercials had the look of low-budget ones: they zeroed-in on Anderson's "talking head," and highlighted his rather too intellectual and didactic demeanor. Mechanically, even, they had their problems. The camera's picture of Anderson actually seemed out of focus; there also seemed to be abrupt changes in the tape, as if the camera had been starting and stopping while Anderson studied his next lines. Anderson did come off as the "thinking man's candidate," and also as someone who was not hesitant in stating his specific positions on major issues. But his message was the same as it had been for some time, and he gave no new or compelling reason for people to choose him, a candidate whose poll ratings were dropping by the day and who seemed to lack any serious chance of being elected.

The day before the election, the Anderson and Lucey campaigns converged for a political rally at the University of Minnesota. This would be the grand finale of the campaign. The Twin Cities were chosen as the site because they seemed an All-American location in the middle of the country, a symbolic last place to campaign. Of course the huge student body which attended the university was an important drawing card as well, thought to provide the raw material for a dramatic crowd scene which could be pictured stomping and cheering that night on the network news.

When the candidates and their staffs had arrived in Minneapolis, the atmosphere in the corridors of the hotel was one of almost disbelieving relief at the prospect of a wearying campaign about to end, mixed with an inescapable sadness and frustration about the fate the campaign had suffered and the disappointing final outcome likely to unfold the next day. Still, everyone clung to what hope one could. Frequently, staff members would be asked what they were planning to do after the election. Such questions reminded me of movies about the war, in which American spies behind German lines would be discovered when Germans said to them, "Good morning, how are you?" If a spy, without thinking, answered in English, his identity was revealed. Similarly, I was sure that if someone asked me what I was planning to do, and I said, "Oh, I don't know yet, perhaps look for another job," my questioner would leap to his feet, point an accusing finger, and shout, "Aha! So you admit Anderson's going to lose!" (Incredibly enough, John Anderson was still holding publicly to the proposition that he was going to win. This was because of his conviction, he explained, that people would have a new appreciation of the gravity of their vote when they stepped into the polling booth, drew the curtain, and were faced with deciding the future of the country.) And so, in keeping with such official optimism, I would put on my best poker face and reply instead, "Oh, work in the White House, I suppose." Once in a while, someone quick on the draw would call my bluff. "Why do you think Reagan would hire you?" they asked.

In the morning, Anderson presented himself at a last press conference. He asked for suggestions beforehand on what he might say that would explain in a nutshell why people should still wish to vote for him. I suggested trying a variation on a line from Woody Allen: "We have come to a fork in the road. One path leads to total oblivion. The other, to utter hopelessness and despair." Then, quickly, Anderson could add, "Ah, but there is a third way out. . . ." Anderson was not sure that such whimsy befit the occasion, and so he made a more conventional opening statement, saying he was looking forward to the election, and thought he had waged a good fight. It was a measure of what the large group of assembled reporters thought about his chances that their questions focused in large part on what his plans were for 1984, or for a permanent third party. (Answer: "That will involve the sort of post mortem I have firmly resolved not to indulge in for some time.")

The campaign's last rally was held in an expansive plaza surrounded by large and ornate school buildings. Five or six thousand students jammed into the area, craning their necks for the best view. The sky was perfectly blue, and the weather mild and pleasant. In introducing Anderson, Pat Lucey tried to explain what had captured the public imagination about him during the early primaries: "John Anderson did not go around asking what people wanted to hear. He did not spend his time putting his finger to the wind. He did not waste his energies playing to special interests. . . . He said the tough things that needed to be said. . . . His only weapon was the strength of his convictions and the power of his own courage and honesty." Anderson strode to the podium to wild applause. This was his last day in the sun, and he was being treated as an authentic hero. He gave an excellent stump speech, and urged his audience to help him the next day in defying the odds. The crowd loved every moment, and so did Anderson. The reality of the election results was still twenty-four hours away.

It was remarkable the next night at the Hyatt Regency Hotel in Washington what jubilation there was among those watching the returns in the Anderson suite when Anderson's tally at last inched above 5 percent— the threshold for matching funds—and then even 6 percent, in the national totals. Not many weeks before, such an outcome would have been regarded as a humiliation. It was the same with returns from certain states—Massachusetts and Connecticut, in particular—where not long before one had heard optimistic talk about Anderson's actually winning; now his supporters were delighted to see him registering in the 10 to 12 percent range.

It became evident early on that Reagan had won. Many Anderson supporters breathed easier that his margin was bigger than Anderson's total, lest Democrats level the charge during the next four years that Anderson had cost Carter the election. Carter conceded early, and so, by about 10:00 P.M., Anderson was more than ready to emerge from his suite, make his way down to the ballroom of the hotel, and address the thousand or so supporters waiting to hear him. There was no great sense of disappointment in the room: it was not as though Anderson's loss had been unexpected. Instead, he was saluted with the warmth and enthusiasm accorded a victor.

Pat Lucey began to make a speech of introduction. It was to be about a five minute speech. Lucey had just spent two months of his life trooping across the country in behalf of the campaign, and this would be his last public appearance. It seemed fitting that he be permitted a nominal valedictory. About two minutes into the speech, however, Garth came running up to me. "He's got to cut it," Garth said. "We just heard that Reagan's going to give his acceptance speech in three minutes. If Anderson doesn't go on now, he's going to lose national TV." Garth's concern struck me as odd, and also as about six months late. "Well, " I said, "it's silly for Lucey to stop, because Anderson will take much more than three minutes to speak." "Oh, no," Garth said, "he'll speak only three minutes, that's how long the speech is we prepared for him." "If you think John Anderson can speak for three minutes," I said, "then you don't know John Anderson." Undeterred, Garth sent someone to the podium with a note. Lucey was puzzled, and stopped abruptly. To the crowd, it must have seemed peculiar. As Anderson was suddenly introduced—he had been waiting in the wings—and advanced to the podium, the crowd erupted into sustained applause. The applause itself consumed the two minutes that was supposedly left until the TV networks were going to switch to Reagan. As it turned out, Reagan did not give his speech for another two hours.

After the applause subsided, Anderson took another ten minutes to introduce his wife and children. Then he launched into the theme

Last night: the returns are in. John and Keke Anderson, with daughters Diane (left) and Susie (asleep at podium). (Wide World Photos)

of his speech, that the point of the campaign had been to "Wake Up, America." This meant, presumably, waking it up to the unpleasant realities of the energy crisis, the need for fiscal discipline, and the like. It struck me as something that would have made a good theme during the campaign.

Anderson said it has been one of the most exciting nights of his life. "I hope the totals hold at 6 percent or more . . . or it may be one of the most expensive!" Clearly, Anderson had resigned himself to a glorious defeat, and was determined to enjoy life again; only a couple of times did he look somber as the results of the evening appeared to sink in. "History will record," he went on, "that at 8:35 this evening, I called Governor Reagan to offer my congratulations, when I realized I was not going to win." He paused. "Actually, the thought that I might not win may have crossed by mind a little earlier than 8:35 P.M." Great laughter ensued, and then Anderson held up his hand to continue his sentence: ". . . but that," he said, evidently referring to the electorate's unwillingness to elect him this time around, "is a decision deferred." At this point, the crowd broke into chants of "EIGHTY FOUR! EIGHTY FOUR!" Anderson and Keke, standing next to him, basked in several minutes of audience pandemonium, until Anderson held his hand up again, and in his wriest voice added, "Now, you have chosen to put your own interpretation on my enigmatic statement." On the podium behind Anderson stood a number of people most closely associated with the independent campaign: David Garth, Mike MacLeod, and others they had brought on. These were the people who had helped change the course and the character of the campaign, and who ultimately has been so influential in its fate. Anderson stood with them proudly. Somehow, I could not bring myself to join in the cheering.

Weeks later, in December, as I was continuing to work for Anderson in his remaining months as a congressman, we drove across town one evening to a seminar we had decided to attend on foreign policy. He had been shorn of his Secret Service protection immediately after the election, and only a handful of campaign staff members were still on the job, just enough to take care of necessary auditing and accounting as the campaign books were closed and his records and mementos were removed from his congressional office. I walked with Anderson to his car in the congressional garage. "I'll drive," I volunteered. "Oh, no, don't be silly," he said. "I've got to get back down to earth." When we arrived at our meeting, it happened a pollster was speaking about American attitudes on foreign policy. A questioner in the audience, unaware that Anderson had just walked in, was making the comment, "We don't need polls—all you have to do is read *Doonesbury* to see which way people are thinking. It's very revealing the way that comic strip treated John Anderson so sympathetically. That's the way people thought about him." Anderson turned to me and said, "Too bad more people don't read the funny papers."

Later in December, Anderson was considering an offer from Stanford University to teach a course on the Congress. With typical dedication, he began preparing a course outline to submit for the university's review. I got him on the phone with an academic expert in the subject area. Anderson explained his purpose, and the type of material he was interested in. The expert said he had a number of papers that might be of interest. "That's great," Anderson said, "would you mind sending them to me?" The expert asked what address to use. Anderson recited his congressional office number and zip code. For a moment, he found himself slipping back into days long past. By pure habit, he continued, "Be sure you have the right Anderson—it's Congressman John B. Anderson of Illinois." We were back down to earth.

Index

Adams, Brock, 235
Alaska lands bill, 80
Amherst College speech, 128
Anderson, Diane, 183, 320
Anderson, John, Jr., 24–25
Anderson, Keke, 2, 6, 10, 13, 14, 18,
   31–32, 56, 71–72, 89, 94, 95, 96,
   100, 101, 104, 112, 121, 122,
   123–24, 128–29, 136, 144, 146–48,
   149, 150, 151, 172, 174, 187, 192,
   195, 199, 202, 217–19, 238, 241,
   242, 248, 249, 255, 286, 320, 321;
   announcement of independent candidacy, 203; on budget cuts, 155; as
   campaigner, 244, 247; campaigning
   in New Hampshire, 85; on campaign's image as unprofessional,
   247; on Carter Doctrine, 125; on
   Garth, 293; general description of,
   85–86; on George Ball, 114; at Iowa
   debate, 110; involvement in
   vice-presidential selection, 296, 304;
   on Kennedy meeting, 274–77; in
   Los Angeles, 180–82; in *Newsweek*
   story, 234–35; on press coverage,
   194; and "Saturday Night Live," 119
Anderson, Martin, 292
Anderson, Susan, 320
Anderson as administrator, 14, 290
Announcement of candidacy: for Republican nomination, 53–56; as independent, 201–3
Antibusing amendment, 87

Armour, John, 184
Arms sales to China, 210–11
Arnold and Porter (law firm), 268–69
Ashbrook, John, 22
Ashley, Ted, 117
Asner, Ed, 266
"Asterisk" (in the polls), 88, 206

Bailey-Deardourff (political consulting
   firm), 293
Baker, Howard, 84, 182; announce-
   ment of candidacy, 93; campaign of-
   fice, 191–92; in Des Moines debate,
   105, 106
Bali, Indonesia: Anderson's visit to, 7
Ball, George, 113–15, 224–27
Balz, Dan, 95, 196
Barre, Raymond, 263
Barrett, Larry, 198
Bartlett, Charles, 52
Bayh, Birch, 273
Begin, Menachem, 258–59
Bell, Alphonso, 81
Bell, Daniel, 53
Bennett, Dick, 83–84
Bentsen, Lloyd, 22
Bisnow, Oscar and Jean, 100, 180
Borman, Frank, 235
Bradford, Bill, 50–51, 78, 192
Bradley, Thomas, 208
Bradner, Jeanne, 85
Briefing book: for Des Moines debate,
   102–3

Broder, David, 7–8, 28

Brooke, Ed, 115, 235; advice on independent candidacy, 185; as possible vice-presidential candidate, 295

Brown, Clifford, 172, 210, 293; with briefing book, 102; organizing task forces, 237–38; vetoing meeting with George Ball, 225

Brown, Edmund G., Jr. (Jerry), 37, 251; in Wisconsin primary, 177

Buckley, John, 143

Budget cuts suggested by Anderson, 155

Bundy, William, 225

Burns, James McGregor, 53

Bush, George, 182; announcement of candidacy, 47; campaign finances and organization, 44, 82–83; caricature on "Saturday Night Live," 120; characterized by Dole, 107; in Chicago debate, 158–59; concentration on politics, 152; in Des Moines debate, 106, 111; image of, 77; in Maine straw vote, 94; "momentum" of, 163; in Nashua debate, 134–37; perception of as moderate, 66, 133; in Wisconsin primary, 175

Busing: Anderson speech on, 64–65. *See also* Antibusing amendment

Byrd, Robert, 23, 272, 273

Byrne, Brendan, 208

Byrne, Jane, 166

California primary, 188–91

Cambodia famine, 89, 213

Campaign finances: Anderson's, 20, 27, 43, 47, 80–83, 264, 266–67, 310–11, 316

Campaign office: Anderson's, 77–79, 192, 267. *See also* Field office

Campaign organization: early, 44

Carey, Hugh, 208, 272

Carrington, Peter, 264

Carstens, Karl, 261

Carter, Amy, 217

Carter, Jimmy: Anderson's opinion of, 284–85; Ball's opinion of, 113; on Cambodian famine, 89; characterized by Dole, 107; on debate with Anderson, 280; on energy, 75; image of, 77; inevitability of nomination, 202; "new foundations" speech, 34–35; on nuclear conflict, 283; opinion of Anderson, 304; poll predictions for, 180; on press, 59; unpopularity of, 210; withdrawal from Des Moines debate, 99

Carter administration: shortcomings of, 202

"Carter doctrine," 125

Carter grain embargo, 100

Chaban-Delmas, Jacques, 263

Chancellor, John, 90, 149

Chapman, Steve, 52

Childs, Marquis, 52

Chirac, Jacques, 263

Chisolm, Shirley, 22, 295

Christian amendment, 222, 251

Chrysler: federal aid to, 302

Clark, Ed, 315

Cleveland: motorcade in, 241

Clymer, Adam, 57, 278

Cohen, William, 94

Columbia University speech, 48

Commager, Henry Steele, 128

Commoner, Barry, 87, 246

Conable, Barber, 18, 47

Concord, NH, 58

Congressional office: Anderson's, 11–12

Connally, John, 90; announcement of candidacy, 47; caricature on "Saturday Night Live," 120; in Des Moines, 106–7; image of, 77; Keke Anderson's comment on, 21

Connecticut primary, 167

Connelly, Maureen, 205

Constitutional amendment proposed by Anderson, 222, 251

Cooper, John Sherman, 246

Cousins, Norman, 126

Cover story. See *Newsweek; Time*

Cox, Archibald, 271

Coyle, Ed, 248, 288, 293

Crane, Philip, 20–22, 44, 160; in Chicago debate, 158–59; in Des Moines debate, 106; Keke Anderson's comment on, 21

Craver, Roger, 172

Crisp, Mary Dent, 244–45

Cronkite, Walter, 115, 279; Anderson's interview with, 90; as possible running mate, 270–71
Curb, Michael, 191
Curtin, Jane, 115, 119

Dayan, Moshe, 256
Deaver, Michael, 292
Debate: Baltimore, 280–81, 294, 303–6, 312–14; Chicago, 158–60; Des Moines, 98–103; Nashua, 134–37
Dellums, Ronald, 65
DePaul University, 154
Dewey, Thomas: poll predictions for, 180
Dole, Robert, 134; in Des Moines debate, 107
Doonesbury (comic strip), 121, 124, 200, 322
Drew, Elizabeth, 52
Drinan, Robert, Father, 19
Dukakis, Michael, 235

Eagleton, Thomas, 271, 277
Egypt: Anderson's visit to, 259–61
Eisenhower, Milton, 96–97
Election night speech, 320–21
Emerson, Ralph Waldo, 148
Emery, David, 94
Energy. *See* Gasoline tax
England: Anderson's visit to, 264
Equal Rights Amendment, 19
European trip: Anderson's, 251–65
Evans, Michael, 53

"Face the Nation" (TV show), 61–62
Farkas, Robin, 81–83
Farney, Dennis, 314
Fernandez, Benjamin, 81
Field, Mervin, 240
Field office: Anderson's first, 84–85. *See also* Campaign office
50–50 Plan. *See* Gasoline tax
Foley, Thomas, 52
Ford, Gerald R., 16, 182, 202; moderacy of, 63; offer of judgeship to Anderson by, 145
Foster, June, 19
Fowler, Jane, 85

France: Anderson's visit to, 262–64
François-Poincet, Jean, 263
Fraser, Douglas, 315
Fritchey, Clayton, 52
Frye, Alton, 269–70, 273
Fund-raising. *See* Campaign finances
Furst, Zev, 219–23, 232, 242–43, 255; and Anderson's visit to Israel, 251–55, 258; on Kennedy meeting, 277–78; on vice-presidential choice, 235

Gallup, George, 240
Gannon, James, 33
Garth, David, 172–74, 196–201, 207–321; advice on independent candidacy, 185; first contact with, 91–93
Gasoline tax, 68–77, 87, 88–89, 107, 126, 302
Gay rights, 49
Genscher, Hans-Dietrich, 261
George Washington University speech, 180
Germany: Anderson's visit to, 261–62
Gettysburg Address: parody of, 27
Giscard d'Estaing, Valéry, 253, 262–63
Glew, Bill, 130
Grain embargo. *See* Carter grain embargo
Grasso, Ella, 208
Greenfield, Meg, 52, 58
Gulf of Tonkin resolution, 107
Gun Owners Association: appearance of Anderson before, 131–33

Hager, Elizabeth, 85
Harris, Fred, 22
Harris, Lou, 171–72, 240
Hart, Gary, 273
Harvard Club speech, 27
Healy, Timothy, Father, 115
Heinz, John, 208
Heiskell, Andrew, 81
Henry, Paul, 18
Herblock cartoon, 75–76, 108–9, 140
Herman, George, 166
Herrera, Luis, 208
Hill, Luther, 101, 104
Holtzman, Elizabeth, 293

House Rules Committee, 8–9
Humphrey, Gordon, 136
Hyland, William, 53

Illinois primary, 154–67
Independent candidacy, 161–63, 170–206; distinction from third party, 174
Iowa caucuses, 113
Iran: Anderson statement on, 232–33
Iran rescue mission, 203
Israel: Anderson's speech on, 221–24; Anderson's visit to, 255–59
"Issues and Answers" (TV show), 29–30, 91

Jackson, Henry (Scoop), 41, 272, 273
Javits, Jacob, 50
Jeffords, James, 123
Jerusalem: Anderson's visit to, 255; as capital of Israel, 221–24
Johnson, Lyndon, 107
Jordan, Barbara, 294

Katzenbach, Nicholas, 225
Keene, David, 133
Kemp, Jack, 17
Kemp-Roth tax bill, 17
Kendall, Donald, 240
Kennan, George, 126, 225
Kennedy, Edward, 19; Ball's opinion of, 113; on Cambodian famine, 89; caricature on "Saturday Night Live," 120; image of, 77; on jobs bill, 284; meeting with Anderson, 273–79; at National Governors' Conference, 25; and "open convention," 272; poll predictions for, 180; retinue of, 127; statement on Iran, 233
Kidder, Margot, 266
Killian, Michael, 74
Kissinger, Henry, 16–17
Koch, Edward, 208
Kohl, Helmut, 261
Kondracke, Morton, 198
Kotek, David, 81
Kraft, Joseph, 52, 236

Lang, Jennings, 188
Langdon, Dolley, 2
LaRouche, Lyndon, 81
Leach, James, 32
Lear, Norman, 117–18, 266; advice on independent candidacy, 171–75; Garth's reaction to, 197
Leonard, William, 271
Lesotho: Anderson's visit to, 5–6
Lewis, Samuel, 255
Limits to Growth of Government Act, 80
Lindsay, John, 208
Linowitz, Sol, 254
Lipset, Seymour Martin, 53
Loans: to Anderson campaign, 316
Lodal, Jan, 53
Lodge, Henry Cabot, 66
Logan, Polly, 27
Lucey, Jean, 296
Lucey, Patrick J., 294–302, 304, 317–19; resignation as delegate to Democratic convention, 279; selection as Anderson's running mate, 294
Lyon, Don, 16–17

McCarthy, Colman, 52
McCarthy, Eugene, 185, 208
McCloskey, Paul, 66
McGovern, George, 271n, 273, 277; characterized by Dole, 107; glad of Anderson's candidacy, 247
McGrory, Mary, 110, 200
Machakos, John and Mary, 122
Machol, Margot (fiancée of Mark Bisnow), 85, 95, 96, 100, 111, 124, 130, 195, 217, 282, 283
Machol, Robert and Florence, 89
MacLeod, Michael, 91, 93, 172, 199; as advisor in 1978, 18; as campaign manager, 192–93; on campaign spending, 250; and Pennsylvania primary, 179; reaction to Mott, 226–27; reassignment as treasurer, 288; relationship to Garth, 229, 292, 308
McNamara, Bob, 257
Madison, WI, speech: Anderson's, 68

Maine convention speech: Anderson's, 95

Maine straw ballot, 94

Maiorana, Ron, 248

Manchester Rotary Club speech: Anderson's, 126

Mathews, Tom, 171–72, 185, 270, 288, 293

Massachusetts Institute of Technology (MIT) speech, 121

Massachusetts primary, 139–53

Massachusetts primary speeches: election eve, 143–44; election night, 147–48

Meese, Ed, 292

Meyerson, Bess, 293

Michael, Lorne, 119

Milliken, William, 185

Mills, Wilbur, 22

Mink, Patsy, 315

Mitchell, Parren, 65

Moline, IL, speech, 164

Mondale, Walter F., 45, 67

Moos, Malcolm, 53

Mott, Stewart, 185, 226–28

Moyers, Bill, 61

Moynihan, Pat, 270, 272, 273, 296

Mudd, Roger, 118

Mugabe, Robert, 152

Muskie, Edmund, 41, 252, 272, 284

MX missile, 302

Name identification: Anderson's, 83–84

National Governors' Conference speech, 24–26

Navon, Yitzhak, 256

Nelson, Jack, 52

New Hampshire primary, 123–38

Newsweek: cover story on Anderson, 199, 203–4, 233

Nixon, Richard, 102

Nofziger, Lynn, 292

Nolan, Martin, 52

Nowlan, James, 42–45, 50–51

O'Donnell, Bill, 124, 125, 128

Office. *See* Campaign office; Congressional office; Field office

Ogilvie, Richard, 43

"Open convention," 272

Open housing legislation, 15

Peckham, Ann, 85

Penner, Rudolph, 53

Pennsylvania primary, 178–79

Peoria, IL, speech, 165

Percy, Charles, 29–30, 42

Peretz, Marty, 115

Peterson, Bill, 279

Polls: Anderson's decline in, 214

Polsby, Nelson, 53

Pottinger, Stan, 95

Pouliot, Herman, 134

Powell, Jody, 112, 217, 280

Primary: 1978 congressional, 16–17. *See also* California primary; Connecticut primary; Illinois primary; Massachusetts primary; New Hampshire primary; Pennsylvania primary; Vermont primary; Wisconsin primary

Quie, Albert, 185

Quinn, Sally, 2–4

Rabin, Yitzhak, 256

Rangel, Charles, 4

Raspberry, William, 52

Rauh, Joe, 279

Ray, Robert, 185

Reagan, Ronald: acceptance speech, 264; caricature on "Saturday Night Live," 120; change of campaign manager, 292; at Chicago debate, 158–59; criticism by Anderson, 165; Eisenhower's opinion of, 97; friendliness of, 131; image of, 77; inevitability of nomination, 202; poll predictions for, 180; unpopularity of, 210; in Wisconsin primary, 175

Regulatory Reform Act, 80

Reston, James, 52, 304

Rhinelander, WI, speech, 169–70

Rockefeller, Jay, 235

Rockefeller, Larry, 82

Rockefeller, Nelson, 41, 64

Rockford, IL, 16, 18; speech in, 160

Rogovin, Mitchell, 268–69, 293, 313; advice on independent candidacy, 185
Romney, George, 41
Ronstadt, Linda, 251
Rosemont, IL, speech, 65
Rosenbaum, Michael, 208–10, 244, 288
Rowan, Carl, 52
Running mate: selection of, 235, 270–72. *See also* Lucey, Patrick J.

Sadat, Anwar, 260–61
Salinger, Pierre, 264
SALT treaty, 130
Sandburg, Carl, 176
Sann, Robert, 112, 171, 217
"Saturday Night Live" (TV show), 115, 119–21
Saudi Arabia, sale of F-15s to, 242
Sawhill, John, 81
Sawyer, Kathy, 194
Scales, James, 124, 210
Scharansky, Anatoly, 19
Scheer, Robert, 115
Schmidt, Helmut, 253, 261–62
Sears, John, 135, 292, 303
Secret Service, 156–58, 168; conspicuousness of, 181, 183; in Israel, 256; use of armored car, 186
Seidman, Larry, 126
Shafie, Ghazali bin, 7
Shapp, Milton, 22
Sheehan, Fran, 288, 293
Sheinbaum, Stanley, 116–19, 174
Shephard, Charles, 181
Shields, Eileen, 198
Shriver, Eunice, 191
Shrum, Robert, 289
Sidey, Hugh, 52, 96
"Sixty Minutes" (TV show), 128
Smith, Howard K., 158
"Snow White and the Seven Dwarfs," 112
Snyder, Gene, 17
Solarz, Stephen, 89
Somalia: Anderson urges economic aid for, 49
South Africa, 6
Spaulding, Josiah (Si), 143–45

Spending, campaign. *See* Campaign finances
Sperling, Godfrey, 116
Spoiler: Anderson as, 217, 242, 307
Stanford University: Anderson's offer to teach at, 322; speech at, 190
Stanley, Max, 81
Steinem, Gloria, 95–96
Stevenson, Adlai, III, 67, 165, 273; consideration as Anderson's running mate, 235; possibility of Anderson's running for seat vacated by, 40
Strauss, Franz Josef, 261
Strauss, Robert, 222
Streisand, Barbra, 266
Students: Anderson's support among, 48–50, 121–22, 127–28, 139, 141, 154
Swillinger, Daniel, 86

Taggart, Peter, 82
Thatcher, Margaret: Anderson's meeting with, 253, 264
Thimmesch, Nick, 52
Third party, 314, 318. *See also* Independent candidacy
Thompson, James, 185
Thornburgh, Richard, 185
Thorne, David, 184
Time: cover story, 198–99, 203–4
Tinker, Grant, 117
Trettick, Stan, 2
Truman, Harry: poll predictions for, 180
Tsongas, Paul, 273
Tunney, John, 208
Turkey, 49

Udall, Morris, 22; as possible running mate for Anderson, 235
Udall, Stewart, 235
Uganda: Anderson urges economic aid for, 49
University of California at Los Angeles (UCLA) speech, 188
University of California at Santa Barbara speech, 49

Vader, Darth, 233
Valenti, Jack, 90

Vermont primary, 139–53
Vice-presidency: Anderson's lack of
  desire for, 67
Vice-president: choice of, 235, 270–72
Volpe, John, 27

Walker, Bob, 72, 222
Wallace, Irving, 117
Walters, Barbara, 279
Weshsler, James, 57
White, Kevin, 294
White House correspondents' dinner,
  217
Wicker, Tom, 52
Wieghart, James, 52
Wiesner, Jerome, 121

Wildavsky, Aaron, 53
Will, George, 31
Wisconsin primary, 167–76

Yadin, Yigal, 255
Yale University speech, 154
Yankelovich, Daniel, 240
Yorkin, Bud, 180
Yorty, Samuel, 23
Youth differential wage: Anderson's
  position on, 299

Zev. *See* Furst, Zev
Zimbabwe: Anderson's comments on,
  152

Mark Bisnow worked on Capitol Hill eight years for a number of congressmen, senators, and congressional committees. Between 1978 and 1980, he was press secretary and speech writer for Congressman (and presidential candidate) John Anderson, and was considered his closest aide. In July of 1980, the *Wall Street Journal* said, "Mr. Bisnow is the symbol of the Anderson campaign, celebrated as a disheveled young aide in the panels of the popular 'Doonesbury' comic strip." A 1973 Phi Beta Kappa graduate of Stanford, Mr. Bisnow also earned a master's degree there in history, studied international relations at Princeton, and has now returned to school as a law student at Harvard.

Tom Wicker, popular columnist of the *New York Times* and also associate editor of that newspaper, was chief Washington correspondent and head of the Washington bureau of the *Times* from 1964 through 1968. Mr. Wicker has covered politics closely for several decades and is the author of numerous critically acclaimed works of both nonfiction and fiction.